By the same authors
All the President's Men

Bob Woodward
Carl Bernstein THE

FINAL DAYS

SIMON AND SCHUSTER : NEW YORK

Copyright © 1976 by Bob Woodward and Carl Bernstein
All rights reserved
including the right of reproduction
in whole or in part in any form
Published by Simon and Schuster
A Gulf+Western Company
Rockefeller Center, 630 Fifth Avenue
New York, New York 10020

Designed by Irving Perkins
Manufactured in the United States of America
Typography by Dix Typesetting Company Inc.
Printed by The Murray Printing Company
Bound by The Book Press

1   2   3   4   5   6   7   8   9   10

Library of Congress Cataloging in Publication Data

Woodward, Bob.
    The final days.
    Includes index.
    1. Nixon, Richard Milhous, 1913–   —Impeachment.
2. Nixon, Richard Milhous, 1913–   —Resignation.
I. Bernstein, Carl, 1944– joint author.   II. Title.
E861.B47   973.924'092'4   75–43719
ISBN 0-671-22298-8

ACKNOWLEDGMENTS

The *Washington Post* gave us a leave of absence, twice extended, to write this book. Our special thanks to Katharine Graham, Ben Bradlee, Howard Simons, Harry Rosenfeld and Len Downie.

Several friends took time to read and criticize the manuscript at various stages. Our gratitude to Nora Ephron, Richard Cohen and Robert Kaiser. We would also like to thank David Obst and Arthur Klein for their help and counsel. And Laura Quirk, for keeping everything straight.

Richard Snyder and the staff of Simon and Schuster have been a source of constant encouragement; their dedication to the project has been extraordinary. We are especially grateful to Gypsy da Silva, Joni Evans, Dan Green, Frank Metz, Harriet Ripinsky, Sophie Sorkin and Ed Schneider. Vera Schneider's work in copyreading the manuscript was of enormous assistance.

Finally, with affection and esteem, we thank Alice Mayhew, our editor, for the hundreds of hours she spent with us and with this manuscript.

B. W.
C. B.

AUTHORS' NOTE

The Final Days is the work of four people. Scott Armstrong, a former Senate Watergate Committee investigator, and Al Kamen, a free-lance writer/researcher, assisted us full time in the reporting, research and some of the writing. Their contributions were immeasurable. We are the beneficiaries of their intelligence, imagination, sense of organization and diligence. We will never be able to thank them enough.

FOREWORD

As reporters for the *Washington Post,* we began covering the Watergate story a few hours after five men were arrested at the Democratic National headquarters on June 17, 1972. Our work for the *Post* on that story lasted more than two years—until Richard M. Nixon resigned the presidency on August 9, 1974.

After the resignation, some of our most reliable sources said that the real story of those final days of the Nixon presidency had not been adequately told; to report that story and sort through the contradictions would require a concentrated effort of perhaps a year or more. Our editors at the *Post* agreed. We took a leave of absence from the paper and set up an office on the sixth floor of the *Post* building. Scott Armstrong, a former Senate Watergate Committee investigator, and Al Kamen, a free-lance writer–researcher, were hired to assist us.

We divided the project into twenty-two areas of inquiry:

> President Nixon
> the Nixon family
> key White House aides
> the White House lawyers
> other senior members of the White House staff
> the presidential speech-writing staff
> the White House press office
> former Nixon aides

the President's personal staff
the medical staff
the congressional liaison staff
the anti-impeachment lobby
the office of Secretary of State Kissinger
the other Cabinet members
the office of Vice-President Ford
the unofficial transition team
the House and Senate leadership
the House Judiciary Committee
the Office of the Watergate Special Prosecutor
the Senate Watergate Committee
others who visited or talked with the President
the public record—newspaper stories, books, public
   statements, testimony and documents

From these areas of inquiry, we drew up a preliminary list of several hundred persons to be interviewed. We spent six months at the task. *The Final Days* is based on interviews with 394 people. Some persons spent dozens of hours with us and volunteered information freely; one person was interviewed seventeen times. Many supplied us with contemporaneous notes, memoranda, correspondence, logs, calendars and diaries. Others granted interviews simply to give their version of events or to respond to information we had obtained elsewhere. A few, including President Nixon, declined to be interviewed.

All interviews were conducted "on background"; that is, they were on the record—we could use the information—but only upon our assurance that the identity of the source would remain confidential. With this guarantee, those we talked to were willing to give us information we would never otherwise have been able to obtain.

In general, we tried to interview the principals described in *The Final Days* only after extensive details had already been gathered from members of their staffs. We made clear to each person that we would attempt to check every detail.

The notes from each interview were typed and each significant detail was indexed under the appropriate area of inquiry. The subject areas were further divided chronologically into each of the final 100 days of the Nixon Administration—the period we initially planned to describe in the narrative. In the course of interviewing we realized that to explain the last 100 days we would have to deal extensively with earlier periods, particularly the six months after April 30, 1973, when President Nixon's chief aides resigned.

We have attempted to check every detail in the course of reconstructing events. In reporting meetings, for example, we were able in almost all instances to talk to one or more of the participants. If we obtained two versions, we resolved disagreements through re-interviewing. If this proved impossible, we left out any material we could not confirm. In a few instances, there were meetings between two participants where we were unable to obtain a direct account from either; in those cases, we interviewed people the participants talked to immediately afterward. Nothing in this book has been reconstructed without accounts from at least two people. We were fortunate: in those last days in the White House, the principals compared notes among themselves and with their assistants.

We did not accord equal weight to all sources. In the course of over three years of reporting on the Nixon Administration, we had learned to place extraordinary trust in the accuracy and candor of some sources. We had also talked regularly over the same period of time with a small number of people who consistently sought to give versions of events that were slanted, self-serving, or otherwise untrustworthy; we used information from them only when we were convinced by more reliable sources of its accuracy.

Bob Woodward
Carl Bernstein

December, 1975

CAST OF CHARACTERS

ROBERT ABPLANALP — Friend of the President

CARL ALBERT — Speaker of the House

OLLIE ATKINS — Official White House photographer

RICHARD BEN-VENISTE — Assistant Watergate Special Prosecutor

LT. COL. JACK BRENNAN — Military aide to the President

PATRICK J. BUCHANAN — Assistant to the President; speech writer

PHILIP BUCHEN — Friend of the Vice-President; coordinator, transition team

STEPHEN BULL — Personal aide to the President

DEAN BURCH — Political counselor to the President

WARREN BURGER — Chief Justice of the United States

ARTHUR F. BURNS — Chairman of the Federal Reserve Board; former counselor to the President

GEORGE BUSH — Chairman, Republican National Committee

CALDWELL M. BUTLER — Congressman, Republican of Virginia; member, House Judiciary Committee

ALEXANDER P. BUTTERFIELD — Former assistant to H. R. Haldeman

J. FRED BUZHARDT — Special White House counsel for Watergate; former counsel, Department of Defense

JOSEPH CALIFANO — Washington attorney

KEN W. CLAWSON — Director of Communications, the White House

15

CHARLES W. COLSON	Former special counsel to the President
BARBER B. CONABLE, JR.	Congressman, Republican of New York; fourth-ranking member of the Minority
LT. CMDR. ANDREW COOMBS	Skipper of the presidential yacht *Sequoia*
ARCHIBALD COX	Watergate Special Prosecutor
EDWARD COX	Son-in-law of the President
TRICIA NIXON COX	Daughter of the President
JOHN W. DEAN III	Former counsel to the President
TOM DE CAIR	Press aide, the White House
JOHN DOAR	Counsel, House Judiciary Committee
JAMES DOYLE	Press chief, Watergate Special Prosecution Force
LAWRENCE EAGLEBURGER	Assistant to Secretary of State Kissinger
JOHN D. EHRLICHMAN	Former Assistant to the President for Domestic Affairs
DAVID EISENHOWER	Son-in-law of the President
JULIE NIXON EISENHOWER	Daughter of the President
SENATOR SAM ERVIN	Chairman, Senate Watergate Committee
MARGARET FOOTE	Secretary to Raymond K. Price, Jr.
GERALD R. FORD	Vice-President of the United States
FRANK GANNON	Deputy to Ronald L. Ziegler
LEONARD GARMENT	Counsel to the President
DAVID GERGEN	White House speech writer
CONNIE GERRARD	Secretary, White House press office
BARRY GOLDWATER	Senator, Republican of Arizona
L. PATRICK GRAY III	Former Acting Director, the Federal Bureau of Investigation
ANNE GRIER	Secretary, White House press office
ROBERT P. GRIFFIN	Senator, Republican of Michigan; Minority Whip
GEN. ALEXANDER M. HAIG, JR.	Chief of staff, the White House
H. R. (BOB) HALDEMAN	Former chief of staff, the White House
BRYCE HARLOW	Political counsel to the President
BROOKS HARRINGTON	Friend of David Eisenhower
MURIEL HARTLEY	Secretary to Gen. Alexander M. Haig, Jr.
ROBERT HARTMANN	Chief of staff, Office of the Vice-President
WILLIAM HENKEL	Chief of White House advance team
BRUCE HERSCHENSOHN	Public-relations aide, the White House
LAWRENCE HIGBY	Former assistant to H. R. Haldeman; aide in Office of Management and Budget
LEON JAWORSKI	Watergate Special Prosecutor

JERRY JONES	Staff secretary of the White House
MAJ. GEORGE JOULWAN	Aide to Gen. Alexander M. Haig, Jr.
RICHARD KEISER	Secret Service agent in charge of presidential detail
KENNETH KHACHIGIAN	Aide to Patrick Buchanan
HENRY A. KISSINGER	Assistant to the President for National Security Affairs; Secretary of State
RABBI BARUCH KORFF	Chairman, Citizens Committee for Fairness to the Presidency
TOM KOROLOGOS	Aide to William Timmons for liaison to the Senate
PHILLIP A. LACOVARA	Counsel, Watergate Special Prosecution Force
CHARLES LICHENSTEIN	Assistant to Dean Burch
LT. CMDR. WILLIAM LUKASH	Physician to the President
LAWRENCE LYNN	Member, transition team; former aide to Henry A. Kissinger
MIKE MANSFIELD	Senate Majority Leader
JACK MCCAHILL	Deputy to James St. Clair
FATHER JOHN MCLAUGHLIN	Public-relations aide, the White House
JOHN N. MITCHELL	Former Attorney General of the United States; manager of the 1972 Nixon re-election campaign
PAT NIXON	Wife of the President
RICHARD M. NIXON	President of the United States
SAM POWERS	Assistant special counsel to the President for Watergate
RAYMOND K. PRICE, JR.	Assistant to the President; speech writer
THOMAS F. RAILSBACK	Congressman, Republican of Illinois; member, House Judiciary Committee
CHARLES G. (BEBE) REBOZO	Friend of the President
JOHN J. RHODES	House Minority Leader
ELLIOT L. RICHARDSON	Attorney General of the United States; former Secretary of Defense
PETER W. RODINO, JR.	Chairman, House Judiciary Committee; Congressman, Democrat of New Jersey
WILLIAM P. ROGERS	Secretary of State
JAMES D. ST. CLAIR	Special Counsel to the President for Watergate
MANOLO SANCHEZ	Valet to the President
DIANE SAWYER	Deputy to Ronald L. Ziegler
HUGH SCOTT	Senate Minority Leader

LT. GEN. BRENT SCOWCROFT	Deputy Assistant to the President for National Security Affairs; aide to Henry A. Kissinger
JOHN J. SIRICA	Judge, United States District Court for the District of Columbia
HELEN SMITH	Press secretary to Mrs. Nixon
LARRY SPEAKES	Press secretary to James D. St. Clair
BENJAMIN J. STEIN	White House speech writer
JOHN C. STENNIS	Senator, Democrat of Mississippi
WILLIAM E. TIMMONS	Chief of White House liaison to the Congress
MAJ. GEN. WALTER TKACH	Physician to the President
LT. GEN. VERNON WALTERS	Deputy Director, Central Intelligence Agency
GERALD WARREN	Deputy press secretary to the President
CLAY T. WHITEHEAD	Director, White House Office of Telecommunications Policy; coordinator, transition team
CHARLES WIGGINS	Congressman, Republican of California; member, House Judiciary Committee
ROSE MARY WOODS	Personal secretary to the President
CHARLES ALAN WRIGHT	Special counsel to the President for Watergate
RONALD L. ZIEGLER	Press secretary to the President

A Chronology of the major developments of Watergate, the cover-up, and the subsequent investigations begins on page 457.

PART I

PART I

CHAPTER ONE

THIS was an extraordinary mission. No presidential aides had ever done what they were about to do. J. Fred Buzhardt and Leonard Garment settled into their first-class seats on Eastern flight 177 from Washington, D.C., to Miami. They had reached an inescapable conclusion, and had reviewed the reasons over and over. Garment had a list on a yellow legal pad—now twenty-two or twenty-three items. It was a bleak and very unpleasant business.

The two men left behind a cool Saturday in Washington. It was November 3, 1973. The only good news for the White House that day was an unexpected strike at the *Washington Post*. The newspaper that morning had been only a real-estate section.

For most of the travelers, the flight was an occasion for relaxation, the beginning of a vacation. But Buzhardt and Garment were grim and tense as they rehearsed their presentation.

They were both lawyers. For the past six months they had handled President Richard Nixon's Watergate defense. They had become close friends. Because the two men, seemingly so different, had agreed about this mission, their advice might carry some weight. They knew they would not be facing a receptive audience, but together they might be persuasive: Garment, the liberal, intellectual New Yorker, and Buzhardt, the conservative, practical Southerner. They sometimes thought of themselves as reflecting two sides of the Nixon personality—good and bad, some would say, or hard and soft. It was not that simple.

Buzhardt nervously tapped his hand on the armrest. His West Point class ring struck the metal. The "1946" was nearly worn from the setting. A slightly hunched figure with thick glasses and a slow, deliberate manner, Buzhardt came out of the political stable of Senator Strom Thurmond, the archconservative South Carolina Republican. Thurmond's preoccupation was the military, and as an aide to the Senator in the 1960s, Buzhardt had developed an extensive network of informants among the Pentagon's officer corps, meeting them at times in all-night drugstores. Later, as general counsel to the Defense Department, he had been in charge of making the best out of the military horror stories of the early 1970s—the Mylai massacre, the Pentagon Papers, Army spying, unauthorized bombing raids in Southeast Asia, multimillion-dollar cost overruns by defense contractors.

He had come to the White House to make the best of Watergate for Nixon, and since then Buzhardt had spent a lot of time with the President. "Now, you're a Baptist," Nixon would say to him before arriving at one decision or another, "this is right, isn't it?" And Buzhardt, balking, would say he didn't think it was his job to give moral advice—he was a lawyer.

Garment had been one of Nixon's law partners in New York. He was distinctly the odd man out in the Nixon White House: a Democrat among Republicans, a liberal among conservatives, a theatergoer among football fans, a Jew among fundamentalists. His relationship with Nixon was personal, not political. He was the philosopher in the court.

Some six months before, Garment had been alone with Nixon when the President had decided he had no choice but to ask for the resignations of his two top aides, H. R. (Bob) Haldeman and John D. Ehrlichman. Nixon had seemed crushed by the weight of the decision, and Garment had found the President's torment strangely reassuring. Nixon would never cut his two top men loose if he was hiding the truth, Garment had reasoned. It showed the President's innocence in a simple human way.

Just before the President had gone to tell Haldeman and Ehrlichman that they must resign, he had said to Garment, "Last night I went to sleep and hoped I'd never wake up."

Now Garment and Buzhardt were on their way to Key Biscayne to recommend that the President resign.

FROM THE Miami Airport, a White House car took them across Biscayne Bay to the Key Biscayne Hotel. They checked into the villa next to the one occupied by the President's principal deputies, General Alexander M. Haig, Jr., the White House chief of staff, and Ronald L. Ziegler, the press secretary.

Haig, forty-eight years old, a career Army officer, had risen from colonel to four-star rank in the four years that he served as chief assistant to the President's foreign-affairs adviser, Henry A. Kissinger. Ziegler, thirty-four, the chief holdover from the Haldeman-Ehrlichman regime, was a former Disneyland guide and assistant to Haldeman at an advertising agency. The Nixon Administration's purest creation.

The lawyers knew they would have to first make their case to Haig—maybe Ziegler too. Then, perhaps, they would see the President, who was in his quarters at 500 Bay Lane, across the narrow peninsula.

Buzhardt and Garment had dinner together and reviewed the situation once again. Hardened in their conviction, they met afterward with Haig and Ziegler in one of the villas.

They couldn't function as lawyers anymore, Garment and Buzhardt said. Their work consisted of pooling ignorance. They couldn't get the evidence to defend their client, even if it existed. The President wouldn't give them access to it. Instead, he gave them excuses.

In defending himself, the President had planted time bombs, Garment said. Nixon had concealed, he had hedged, he had lied. Some of the bombs had already gone off, and the rest lay ticking. Individually the problems might be manageable, but taken together they were insurmountable. They all interlocked, and the single thread that linked the problems together was the President's tapes. The lawyers represented a President who had bugged himself, who had blurted his secrets into hidden microphones. They had not yet heard the tapes, nor seen any transcripts of them. The President would not permit it. They were told to mount a defense, but were not given the information to do so. They could no longer assume their client's innocence, not unless they had evidence to the contrary.

Garment took the yellow legal pad from his briefcase and looked at the roster of allegations against the President: that International Telephone & Telegraph had virtually bribed him with a donation to his 1972 reelection campaign; that he had cheated on his income taxes; that he had used government funds to vastly improve his estates in Key Biscayne and at San Clemente, California; that he had backdated the deed to his vice-presidential papers in order to claim a half-million-dollar tax deduction ("the Presidential Papers Caper," Garment called it).

There was more: that the President had raised the price of milk supports in exchange for campaign contributions from the dairy industry; that his two principal campaign officials—former Attorney General John N. Mitchell and former Secretary of Commerce Maurice H. Stans—had sought improperly to influence the Securities and Exchange Commission as quid pro quo for a $200,000 contribution from a swashbuckling international swindler named Robert Vesco. Then there was the so-called "brother problem"—allegations that the President's two brothers and a nephew were also involved in the Vesco transaction and in other questionable business deals. The President's closest friend, Charles G. "Bebe" Rebozo, was also under investigation, for accepting an unreported $100,000 contribution from billionaire Howard Hughes.

Perhaps some of the allegations were unsupportable, Garment said, and some of them were obviously guilt by association. "But they're all sharks in the water."

And Nixon still had to account for what had been done in the White House: the Huston plan expanding covert domestic intelligence activities—wiretapping, breaking and entering, mail opening; the 1971 break-in at the office of Daniel Ellsberg's psychiatrist; the "Plumbers" unit which investigated news leaks; the seventeen wiretaps on reporters and Administration officials; orders to the Central Intelligence Agency to have the Federal Bureau of Investigation limit the initial investigation into the break-in at the Watergate headquarters of the Democratic National Committee; payments to the burglars to buy their silence.*

There would be at least another year of government investigations into the conduct of the President and his men, Garment said. The Senate Watergate Committee, headed by Senator Sam Ervin of North Carolina, was still in business. One special prosecutor, Archibald Cox, had been fired—just two weeks ago—and another, Leon Jaworski, had been hired. In the aftermath of the so-called Saturday Night Massacre, when Cox had been fired and Attorney General Elliot L. Richardson and his deputy resigned, the House of Representatives appeared ready to authorize a deadly serious impeachment investigation. That inquiry would not be directed at the President's aides, or his campaign advisers, or his friends, but at Nixon himself. And the President had abandoned his legal defense to the tapes. With nothing more than the President's word to go on, Haig himself had gone to the Hill on Wednesday and told Republican Senators that the tape of a crucial meeting on March 21 between Nixon and his former counsel, John Dean, was exculpatory. Did he really believe that? If it was exculpatory, why hadn't Nixon let Haig or the lawyers listen to it? Or to any of the other tapes, for that matter?

---

* Those arrested in the break-in were James W. McCord, Jr., security coordinator for the President's re-election committee, a former FBI agent and CIA employee; Bernard L. Barker, a Miami realtor and former CIA employee who was involved in the 1962 Bay of Pigs invasion of Cuba; Frank A. Sturgis, also of Miami, a soldier of fortune with CIA connections; Eugenio R. Martinez, another anti-Castro Cuban and part-time informant for the CIA; and Virgilio R. Gonzalez, also Cuban-born, a locksmith.

Finally, there were the various court actions. Criminal indictments of Haldeman, Ehrlichman and Mitchell were assured in the cover-up. The trial, or trials, would be a spectacle. The tapes would be played. Richard Nixon would be in the courtroom—on the tapes for sure, maybe as a witness and possibly as a defendant.

"A lot of sharks in the water," Garment said again.

"Typical in today's sick atmosphere," Haig responded. Pursuing Nixon had become a national mania. Watergate was crippling the Administration. There seemed to be a momentum which was beyond control.

Ziegler was puzzled. He had heard much of the same before, though usually from the press, not from members of the White House staff. The President himself had heard it all and seemed confident that he would win in the end. Why were the lawyers so panicked? Why was their tone so ominous?

Buzhardt answered in his slow South Carolina drawl. The President had hidden evidence, first from his lawyers and then from the courts. Then he had proposed to manufacture evidence to take the place of what was missing. He might even have destroyed material that was under subpoena. He had proposed to obstruct justice and had tried to entangle his lawyers in the attempt. The cover-up was continuing and the President was dragging them all into it. Buzhardt himself had now been called to testify publicly in the courtroom of United States District Court Judge John J. Sirica. If the right questions were asked, his testimony would be devastating to the President, Buzhardt warned.

Ziegler was clearly angry. Haig lit one of his Marlboro Light cigarettes and, primarily for Ziegler's benefit, asked Buzhardt to review the ugly details. Haig already knew most of them.

The chronology would make everything apparent, Buzhardt said. Several days before the Haldeman-Ehrlichman resignations, the President met with Assistant Attorney General Henry E. Petersen, the man in charge of the Justice Department's initial investigation into Watergate. In the course of defending himself against accusations that John Dean had made to federal prosecutors, Nixon told Petersen that he had a "tape" of his meeting with Dean on April 15; it would prove that he was not involved in the cover-up, Nixon said.

Archibald Cox, shortly after his appointment as special prosecutor, consulted with Petersen, who quoted the President as saying, "I have Dean on tape." On June 11, Cox sent a letter to the White House asking for the April 15 "tape."

Buzhardt, who had not yet learned of the existence of the President's secret automatic taping system, took Cox's letter to the President. "There is a Dictabelt, that is what I was talking about with Petersen," Nixon told him. He said it was his normal practice to dictate his recollections at the end of each day.

Buzhardt was confused. Why had Petersen quoted the President as saying, "I have Dean on tape"? He asked Nixon if there was also a tape of his meeting that day with Dean.

The President insisted there was not. Petersen had misunderstood, he had misquoted him. There was only the Dictabelt.

Buzhardt then called Petersen, who stuck by his story.

Meanwhile, the President said he would not surrender the Dictabelt to the special prosecutor; he had an "executive privilege" to insure the confidentiality of his papers and other materials. Accordingly, Buzhardt dispatched a letter to Special Prosecutor Cox on June 16, explaining that although there was a Dictabelt of the President's recollections of April 15, it would be inappropriate to provide it. Buzhardt took care not to specifically deny the existence of a tape-recording of the President's meeting with Dean. He was suspicious. A few weeks later, Buzhardt learned from Haig that all the President's meetings and phone calls were recorded by an automatic taping system.

The existence of the system was disclosed publicly in July, and Cox subpoenaed the recordings of nine Nixon meetings and conversations, including the one of April 15. Once again citing executive privilege, Nixon refused to provide any tapes. Cox took the matter to court and was upheld in the Court of Appeals. On October 20 Cox was fired. A storm of protest followed. Nixon reversed ground and agreed on October 23 to turn over the nine tapes.

But then the problems mounted. Buzhardt started a search for the tapes. Two either were missing or had not been recorded on the automatic system. One of the two was of the April 15 meeting. The lawyers tried to find the exact explanation. The handling and accounting of the tapes, they discovered, was atrocious—records had been kept on scraps of brown paper bags. Nixon, Haldeman and Rose Mary Woods, the President's secretary, had all checked out recordings at various times, but it was impossible to determine who had taken what and when.

Buzhardt went to Nixon and said that the April 15 Dictabelt would have to be supplied. Technically it was called for in the subpoena just as the missing April 15 tape was. If they could supply at least the Dictabelt, Sirica's suspicions—and the public's—might be diminished somewhat.

But, incredibly, Nixon sent word through Haig that he couldn't find the Dictabelt. "Come on," Buzhardt had said to the general, "the President assured me there was a Dictabelt. I didn't write that June 16 letter without checking with him very carefully."

The search for the missing Dictabelt had consumed the lawyers during the past few days. The President found what he said were his handwritten notes of the meeting. But there was still no Dictabelt. Buzhardt warned the President how bad it would look if the court was told that both the tape and the Dictabelt for the same April 15 meeting were missing.

The President's reply was chilling: *"Why can't we make a new Dictabelt?"* Nixon was suggesting that the problem be solved by dictating a new recording from the handwritten notes. They would submit it to the court and attest that it was the original. By even suggesting that evidence be manufactured, the President had attempted to obstruct justice, Buzhardt said. Judge Sirica had already been informed of the two missing tapes and was conducting an inquiry in open court. Buzhardt would probably be the next witness called. Did Haig and Ziegler understand what he might have to testify to?

The problem was fundamental, added Garment. The President's willingness to manufacture evidence showed how desperate he had become. It demonstrated that the President had neither respect for the law nor an understanding of it. Buzhardt's testimony could establish what the President had denied for months: that it had been his intent all along to cover up, to conceal, to fabricate.

To make matters worse, Buzhardt said, the President was still insisting there was a Dictabelt of that April 15 meeting. Nixon was personally continuing the search for it. Suppose he produced a Dictabelt? There would be no assurance that he had not undertaken to dictate a new recording on his own. Admittedly, it was a terrible suspicion to entertain, but the President's actions had created it. Crucial evidence was missing, perhaps even destroyed. The lawyers couldn't trust their client. He had lied too many times before—witness his telling Buzhardt that there was no automatic taping system. Maybe there had never been a Dictabelt at all and the President had been afraid of what Buzhardt might hear in an actual recording of his meeting with Dean on the 15th.

Garment defined the immediate difficulty in legal terms. All of them—the President, Haig, Ziegler, the lawyers—could be cited for obstruction of justice if they didn't handle this carefully. Nothing could be concealed from a legitimate inquiry. The lawyers had done all they could to defend the President. Now they had to protect themselves.

"What's the bottom line?" Ziegler asked.

Buzhardt and Garment drew it. They were recommending that the President resign his office.

Haig and Ziegler were stunned. Moments passed.

"How can you come to such a conclusion?" Ziegler said finally. The President had merely been thinking out loud when he suggested that a new Dictabelt be made. It had not been done. They had all heard the President propose ideas which were ridiculous, outrageous. That was the way he made decisions, by dealing with all the alternatives.

Resignation was absolutely out of the question, Ziegler declared.

Haig's composure slipped. His face tightened.

"We don't even have a Vice-President," he said. Spiro T. Agnew had resigned the month before. House Minority Leader Gerald R. Ford had been nominated to succeed Agnew, but he had not yet been confirmed by Congress.

Several disparaging comments followed about the prospect of House Speaker Carl Albert succeeding to the presidency. He was next in line until the vice-presidency was filled, and he was a Democrat with a history of heavy drinking.

Buzhardt and Garment explained that they were hardly recommending that the President resign immediately. He could step down after Ford was confirmed and sworn in.

Haig still balked. What would be the impact in the country if the President resigned so soon after the Vice-President had been forced to resign? The two questions needed to be "decoupled." Time was needed. But even time might not be enough. If the President resigned in a criminal haze as Agnew had done, the effects on foreign policy would be disastrous. The loss of faith in the United States would be incalculable. There was the Middle East crisis to contend with. Another outbreak of war there could come at any moment. A President unschooled in foreign affairs . . . The thought went unfinished.

Haig and Buzhardt were caught in a trap of their own making. They had pushed hard for Ford's nomination over Nixon's first choice, ex-Governor John B. Connally of Texas. Connally, they had told the President, was too much a wheeler-dealer, unloved in both the Democratic Party he had quit and the Republican Party he had just joined. His confirmation hearing would be a free-for-all—divisive and embarrassing.

They had been persuasive, and Nixon had sent Ford's name to the Hill. The President could not resist one final jab, however. He had sent Buzhardt one of the two pens he had used to sign the Ford nomination. It arrived with the message, "Here's the damn pen I signed Jerry Ford's nomination with."

Now they were saddled with him. Ford was not good enough to be President of the United States, Haig said.

No one disagreed.

Haig continued his recitation of the foreign-policy disasters that would befall the nation under President Ford. "Do you know what could happen in the Middle East?" he asked again.

Buzhardt and Garment turned the argument against Haig. The Middle East crisis was just another reason for the President to resign. Watergate had crippled his capacity to lead, Haig himself had admitted. The Middle East was yet another "shark," they said.

Haig paced the room, saying nothing for a while. There was no immediate solution, he concluded.

Buzhardt persisted. One way or another the President could not make it through his second term. In his best military jargon, the lawyer put it to the general in terms he could understand: "Everything after this is a damage-limiting operation."

"We'll be happy to present the recommendation to the President ourselves," Garment said.

Haig would have none of that. If anyone was going to see the President it would be Haig. He knew that Nixon would reject the suggestion out of hand. He reminded them of the President's repeated statements that he would not resign. Nixon had said it as an oath, a solemn pledge. Haig had no stomach for scenes. No, it was out of the question. He would merely tell the President why the lawyers had come to Florida and why they wanted to see him.

Was it really that bad? he asked Buzhardt and Garment. Perhaps they were tired. It had been a dreadful time for all of them.

Fatigue was not the problem. "We are not saying that the President should go out and hang himself," Buzhardt said. They were merely attempting to show Nixon the reality of his situation.

Haig continued to resist. In Key Biscayne he didn't have the same access to the President as in Washington, he said. The President was not down the hall, he was half a mile away in his compound. He had flown down suddenly on Thursday to get some rest, and to get away from his problems. The President wasn't ready to deal with this. There was the question of emotional health. There was the question of timing. It was premature.

Garment became angry. Buzhardt and he had been out on the front lines —taking calls from reporters, enduring the snide comments in the halls of the Executive Office Building, being humiliated almost daily in Judge Sirica's courtroom. The President's position was absurd. His explanations were not being bought by the judge, the special prosecutor, the public, or even the traditional Nixon supporters on the Hill. Not to mention his lawyers. Someone had to appreciate how perilous the situation had become. Someone had to deliver the bad news and get through to the President.

Ziegler became combative. The President was ill-served by such comments and conclusions, he said. The lawyers were turning against the President. It wasn't their job to judge these matters.

Garment let it pass. He could never get a fix on how much Ziegler knew about Watergate. Buzhardt was sure that everything Garment and he said would be dutifully reported to the President by Ziegler—in his own way. He was counting on Haig to find out the President's reaction to what Ziegler would secretly report to Nixon, and to correct any false impression.

The debate in the Key Biscayne villa continued into the next day.

Finally, on Sunday, Haig carried the dismal message to the President. But Nixon was firm. He would not resign, nor would he see the lawyers. It was an awkward moment for Haig. He did not wish his own position to be misunderstood. He was merely conveying *their* judgment. He reassured the President that the lawyers were not doubting his innocence—only his chances to survive.

The President said he was not sure of the future—what "they" might do to him; but he wasn't resigning, in spite of the pressure that was coming from all sides. Things were closing in on him. Strangers would soon be listening to his private conversations, his telephone calls. The bureaucrats, whom he loathed, were studying his tax returns with an eye to finding something bad. They would. They always could. Bebe was being harassed, and so were his brothers. Garment, an old friend, had joined Buzhardt, a stranger to whom he had entrusted the future of his presidency, to tell him to quit. All this depressed him terribly, but he would never resign.

Haig returned to the villa and delivered an abbreviated report. "The President doesn't want to see you."

CHAPTER TWO

THE lawyers were not surprised at the President's refusal to see them. Nor was Haig. The previous spring, when Haldeman resigned, he had warned Haig about Nixon's tendency to isolate himself, to refuse to see advisers with bad news or unpalatable recommendations.

Haldeman knew that, in spite of the accepted wisdom, it was not he who cordoned Nixon off. He had not erected the so-called "Berlin Wall" around the Chief Executive. He did not insist on an inflexible palace guard. It was the will of the President.

Haldeman was so concerned about this predilection of Nixon's to retreat into himself that he spent the days immediately before and after his resignation as chief of staff trying to find his own successor. The new White House chief of staff had to be someone who would oppose Nixon's preference for dealing with paper rather than people. He had to be capable of presenting to the President a full range of options for each decision, of knowing how and when to ignore Nixon's intemperate orders.

Haldeman had watched admiringly as Colonel Alexander Haig maneuvered his way through Henry Kissinger's National Security Council staff system in 1969–70, rising from a military aide to become Kissinger's chief deputy. Haig had taught himself how to structure and schedule Kissinger in very much the same way that Haldeman had kept Nixon on the track. Haig grasped the nature of bureaucracy, and he was tough besides. Most important, he knew how to harness Kissinger's personality, which, Haldeman believed, was astonishingly like Nixon's. Haig's long working hours were legend in the White House, and he already had a working relationship with Nixon.

Haldeman quickly concluded that Haig was the only man for the job, the perfect faceless "staff man," a presence that could balance off Ron Ziegler's influence with the President. Ziegler was too young, too pliable and disorganized, Haldeman thought.

THE PRESIDENT had gone into a deep depression after Haldeman and Ehrlichman resigned on April 30, 1973. On Thursday, May 3, he flew to Key Biscayne for a rest. Haggard and sleepless, Nixon skulked desolately in his quarters, scarcely using the pool between his office and the residence. It was not unusual for Nixon to avoid his wife; he had slept alone for years, and when he was in Key Biscayne he used a bedroom in the converted office two lots away from the residence. Nor was it out of character for him to remain aloof from his staff, sometimes sitting silently with his friend Bebe Rebozo for hours on end.

Ziegler, the only senior member of the old team who had come to Florida, was accustomed to Nixon's depressions, but even he had never seen the President so despondent, so uncommunicative. Ziegler felt that everything was falling on his shoulders—dealing with the press, keeping the Washington staff going, serving as Nixon's valet, trying to help him as Haldeman and Ehrlichman once had. He attempted to get the President to think about building a new staff, but Nixon had recoiled from the whole question of "What next?" and instead had simply poured out his grief to Ziegler. He could not envision a White House without Haldeman and Ehrlichman.

Finally, on Haldeman's recommendation, the President agreed to ask Haig to take over the day-to-day management of the White House. Haig, who had left Kissinger's staff the previous January to become the Army Vice-Chief of Staff, was summoned to Florida. In offering him the job, Nixon informed him that it would be temporary, probably for only a month or so, just until they found someone permanent. Haig said he preferred to stay at the Pentagon. He worried that if he went to the White House it would wreck his career. He would be stamped indelibly as a "Nixon general." But the President insisted, and Haig could not refuse his Commander in Chief.

Kissinger's immediate reaction was to oppose the choice. If the appointment went through, he would quit, he told Rose Mary Woods.

"For once, Henry, behave like a man," Woods said.

Kissinger's opposition had to do with the close, often competitive, usually touchy relationship he had had with Haig for four years. Yes, Haig had been an effective deputy, but making him White House chief of staff would give him too much power. Now when Kissinger was at last rid of Haldeman and Ehrlichman—"the Fanatics," he had called them—he would once again have a rival in the White House. Also, Kissinger believed that Nixon's propensity to issue irrational orders had to be watched and dealt with. Haig was much too inclined to say "Yes, sir."

When Kissinger expressed his dissatisfaction, the President asked him whom he would propose. The Secretary, unable to think of anyone else, dropped his opposition.

On May 4, Haig, still wearing his Army uniform, moved into Haldeman's old office in the West Wing. He needed help immediately, and he turned to J. Fred Buzhardt, the Pentagon's general counsel. Buzhardt had steered Haig's confirmation as Army Vice-Chief of Staff through the congressional Armed Services Committees with ease. Haig telephoned Buzhardt. "The President would like you to come over tomorrow," he said.

When Buzhardt reported to Haig's office, the general asked him to come to work in the White House. He promised Buzhardt that the assignment would be temporary, just as his own was. Then he took him to see the President.

Nixon and Buzhardt scarcely knew each other, but there were few formalities. Nixon started in at once about "the Dean problem." The President's former counsel had been fired on April 30 and was now busily leaking stories all over Washington about the Watergate scandal. Some of them hinted that the President was involved in the cover-up.

It was clear to Haig that the President felt himself almost powerless to deal with Dean's campaign. He was, in fact, frantic. Dean seemed to have some record of White House misdeeds; he had told Judge John Sirica that he had removed certain documents from the White House to protect them from "illegitimate destruction." Dean had put them in a safe-deposit box and given the keys to the judge.

What could be in those papers? the President asked. They had to find out. Dean had said publicly only that there were nine classified documents. "What's in the Dean papers?" the President demanded once more.

Buzhardt said he didn't know.

"Find out."

"Yes, sir."

Haig reassured the President that Buzhardt was accustomed to working under enormous pressure and that he would find out. More important, Haig said, Buzhardt was capable of developing legal justifications for almost anything. He could be trusted.

The President hoped Dean didn't have any tape recordings.

Knowing that the Dean documents were classified, Buzhardt turned immediately to his contacts in the intelligence community; he was looking for something incriminating. And, backed by the full authority of the President, he soon found out what Dean had secreted away.

The safe-deposit boxes contained copies of a top-secret plan for the unlawful expansion of domestic-intelligence-gathering activities by the FBI, the CIA and military intelligence units. The President had authorized government agencies to conduct break-ins ("surreptitious entries"), illegal wiretaps, mail surveillance and a program of spying and infiltration directed at the anti–Vietnam War movement in the cities and on the campuses. The author of the plan, former White House aide Tom Charles Huston, had warned that elements of the program were "clearly illegal." Still, the President had approved it in writing in 1970; then he had canceled it, also in writing, four or five days later. Buzhardt guessed correctly that some agencies had disregarded instructions to return their copies of the plan after it was canceled. He found two copies and took one to the President. Instead of being upset, Nixon was relieved. The press had been speculating that Dean's documents linked Haldeman and Ehrlichman to the cover-up, and that Dean might even have something that involved the President. Now at least he knew what he had to face, Nixon said.

Buzhardt soon learned of another peril facing the President. A Senate appropriations subcommittee, riding herd on the Central Intelligence Agency's budget, wanted Lieutenant General Vernon Walters, deputy director of the CIA, to supply highly classified memoranda he had drafted after his conversations with Haldeman and Ehrlichman concerning the Watergate investigation.

Walters asked Buzhardt whether the memos could be withheld on grounds of executive privilege. Send them over, Buzhardt said, and he'd check. One memo was a summary of a conversation at the White House on June 23, 1972, among Haldeman, Ehrlichman, Walters and CIA Director Richard M. Helms—just six days after the Watergate burglary.

Buzhardt read:

Haldeman said the bugging affair at the Democratic National headquarters at the Watergate apartments had made a lot of noise and that the Democrats were trying to maximize it. The investigation was leading to a lot of important people and this could get worse. He asked what the connection with the

Agency was, and the Director repeated that there was none. Haldeman said the whole affair was getting embarrassing and it was the President's wish that Walters call on F.B.I. Acting Director L. Patrick Gray and suggest to him that since the five suspects had been arrested, this should be sufficient and that it was not advantageous to have the inquiry pushed—especially in Mexico, etc.

Buzhardt understood the reference to Mexico. Eighty-nine thousand dollars in Nixon campaign money had been laundered through Mexico before it landed in the bank account of one of the Watergate burglars. On June 23, 1972, this Mexican connection was still unknown to the FBI. If, as it did later, the bureau made the connection, the Nixon campaign committee could be tied to the financing of Watergate.

It was the President's wish. The phrase troubled Buzhardt. It tied the President to an order that seemed intended to throw the FBI off the track. Buzhardt was worried. General Walters was no John Dean, he knew. Walters had neither an ax to grind nor an ass to save. As a young Army colonel, Walters had been Vice-President Richard Nixon's translator on foreign trips. Nixon had appointed him as deputy director of the CIA to make sure that he had a friend high in the agency.

Buzhardt read the memo again. It was clear enough. He asked to see the President. He expected that Nixon would tell him that Walters was mistaken, or that Haldeman was so accustomed to doing things in the President's name that he had acted on his own authority.

"National security," Nixon told Buzhardt straightaway. That was the basis of the directive. He freely acknowledged that he himself had issued it. He said that he had done so to insure that no CIA operations would be compromised. It had nothing to do with political consequences of the Mexican connection, the President insisted. He intimated that something about the Bay of Pigs operation may have figured in his decision.

Buzhardt was skeptical, but he didn't press the point with the President. The memo stated explicitly that political considerations were the basis of the order. Besides, not one of the other Walters mem-cons (as the memos of conversations were called) mentioned national security. Should the memos be given to the Senate subcommittee? Buzhardt asked.

"Take them up and give them to the committee," the President replied. He seemed confident that there was a national-security justification for the order, though it escaped Buzhardt.

Buzhardt had been the President's special counsel on Watergate for less than a week, and he was trying to coordinate a response to challenges that were flying at them from all sides. He found it hard to share the President's confidence. The President consistently underestimated the dangers posed by a small army of government investigators and reporters who were bent on prying into the innermost secrets of his White House. For example, the FBI's acting director, William D. Ruckelshaus, had ordered a thorough inquiry into reports that had been appearing in the press—and denied for months by his predecessor, L. Patrick Gray III, and Ron Ziegler—that the Administration had wiretapped reporters and White House aides to track down news leaks. On May 14, Ruckelshaus announced that his agents had discovered records of seventeen such taps in John Ehrlichman's White House safe.

Increasingly worried, Buzhardt and Haig sought each other's counsel. Charges were escalating. Too much was out of control. Neither man knew whether the President was innocent or guilty. "I'll help the guy," Buzhardt told Haig, "but I'm not about to go to jail for him."

Haig concurred. They could protect themselves if they trusted each other totally. But no one else. Haig had known the President for four years. He had spent hundreds of hours in conversation with Kissinger that turned, directly or indirectly, on the Nixon personality. Kissinger was intimately familiar with what he considered the vulgar strands of the Nixon psyche. The President was a man consumed by memories of past failures, a man who let his enemies dictate to him, whose actions were often reactions, Kissinger said. Nixon tried to fool even those closest to him, even Kissinger. He kept things from him. He was isolated, secretive, paranoid, Kissinger had always told Haig.

Haig was never sure whether Kissinger was describing himself or Nixon. The general had disliked living in Kissinger's shadow, and Nixon had noticed that and made use of it. The President had reached over Kissinger to Haig many times during his first administration. He had sent him to Vietnam as his personal emissary about a dozen times to see what was really going on there, had made him his principal adviser on troop withdrawal, on strategic alternatives—all this somewhat independent of Kissinger.

Nixon liked Haig's tough talk about "pinkos" and "peaceniks" and those queer, soft, left-leaning eggheads who went to Harvard and couldn't be counted on to storm the trenches in Asia. The President made derogatory comments about Kissinger to Haig, complaining about "The Professor's" paranoia and his excessive concern with his own image. Privately he had requested that Haig report on Kissinger's work, and the general had complied. It had been a confusing, often untenable position.

But now Haig was not required to balance off his loyalties between two superiors. He was the President's principal deputy. Nixon had appealed to him on clear and precise grounds: patriotism, respect for the presidency, trust, the conviction that the President of the United States needed him. Only Haig could help him lead the nation out of this nightmare, the President implied. Haig was committed. He would serve, and he would do his best.

Much of Buzhardt's knowledge of Nixon came from his ex-boss at the Pentagon, former Defense Secretary Melvin R. Laird. Laird saw Nixon as a stage manager. The President would not deal directly with people or events. He preferred papers: memos didn't talk back, didn't push him. Laird had told Buzhardt that he always had the feeling that the President didn't want any one person to have the full picture. No one was ever to be given the entire story. With matters thus arranged, the President could counter any argument by hinting that only he had the necessary facts and background. Nixon's strange methodology made timid ministers, Laird had said. Who would confront a President in the full awareness that he had been dealt out of essential information?

But Buzhardt too was committed now. He would serve and do his best.

"The biggest problem here is credibility," Haig told him. The President's new team would meet matters head on. They would launch a counter-offensive.

Buzhardt was pleased. Throughout Watergate, he firmly believed, Nixon's mistake had been a failure to move off the defensive, to seize the issues and shake them to death. Buzhardt and Haig wanted finally to get ahead of the problem, meet the current charges, anticipate future ones, answer them all. Right now. The barrage of half-truths and speculation was devastating. The general and the lawyer went to the President.

Haig did the talking. A final and definitive statement that dealt with the major allegations, both direct and implied, should be drafted, he said. It would have to stand for all time. It was essential that the statement be consistent with *anything* that might surface.

The President said he was willing to let them give it a try. This would be the new team's first major effort, but they couldn't do it alone. They needed the members of the old White House team, who might have some information and some influence with the President. That would include Garment— it would be good to have the house liberal in on this—and Nixon's two principal speech writers, Raymond K. Price, Jr., and Patrick J. Buchanan, who were regarded by the President as respectively the heart and the soul of his Administration. Price, a forty-three-year-old Yale graduate who had worked for *Collier's* magazine, *Life,* and the *New York Herald Tribune,* was the idealist and gentle theoretician. Buchanan, thirty-five, a conservative former editorial writer for the *St. Louis Globe-Democrat* who had signed up with Nixon in 1966, was the hard political realist, the gut fighter, the resident expert in media manipulation.

Time was short, Buzhardt knew. The Senate Watergate Committee's hearings were scheduled to begin on May 17. Four separate matters had to be met head on—and reasons found to explain the President's actions. A rationale had to be offered for (1) the approval of the Huston plan authorizing illegal intelligence-gathering; (2) the wiretapping of Administration aides and of reporters; (3) the directive to the CIA to keep the FBI from investigating the Mexican money connection as stated in the Walters memcon; (4) the presence of the Plumbers unit in the White House. E. Howard Hunt, Jr., a former CIA agent, and G. Gordon Liddy, a former FBI agent, both convicted in the Watergate case, had been Plumbers. Their role in the Ellsberg break-in had also to be explained.

The President was not very cooperative, Buzhardt and the others discovered very quickly. He did not wish to sit down with Haig or Buzhardt or anybody else and offer his version of events. He told Buzhardt to draft the best defense he could and bring it back for review. The process was excruciating. Slowly, Buzhardt started piecing something together. Though the President always seemed ready, even eager, to review his lawyer's work, he never volunteered anything to Buzhardt, never offered to tell him what had actually happened. Buzhardt would bring a set of postulates to him, and the President would respond, "That's wrong, try it again." Hide-and-seek. Buzhardt wanted to wrap up the wiretaps, the Plumbers and the Walters mem-cons in a national-security blanket. Approval of the Huston plan would be acknowledged and would be cast as a response to a wave of violence, arson and bombing in the cities and on the campuses in 1970.

Buzhardt and Garment were reasonably certain that the President had authorized the Ellsberg break-in, even though he still denied it. Buzhardt thought they might yet dredge up legitimate national-security grounds. But the others resisted the idea of even suggesting that the President had approved the break-in. If they dared take such a suggestion to Nixon, he would certainly fly into a rage.

Buzhardt persisted, though, and wrote it into a draft which admitted that Nixon had authorized the break-in—for national-security reasons, justified by the dangers that release of the Pentagon Papers posed to the President's efforts to bring peace in Vietnam with honor. The admission had a bold and confessional quality. It recalled to Buzhardt the way President Kennedy had absorbed the responsibility for the Bay of Pigs invasion.

Everyone else was sure Buzhardt wouldn't dare take the draft to the President. But he did.

The President read it. "I like the theory," he said calmly, "but the thing is that I didn't do it."

Buzhardt cut out that part of the draft.

Now the group turned to Walters' mem-cons about the June 23 conversation and about other discussions that had taken place at the White House in the week following the Watergate break-in.

Buchanan searched the memos for any hint, any veiled reference, about national security. He couldn't find one. Buchanan had never maintained in private that the President was nearly so ignorant of the cover-up as he claimed. But it was the job of the prosecutors to prove otherwise, not his own, Buchanan reasoned. Still, this matter was especially troubling. The Walters mem-cons were not the kind of thing to trifle with. "Walters is a goddam memory expert, for Christ's sake," Buchanan exploded. "He can listen to a guy talk for ten minutes and then give it back word for word in French."

Price was also skeptical. He could see how Nixon might have thought, then and now, that national security was at stake when in fact it wasn't, strictly speaking. The President had always discussed the Watergate revelations with Price in the context of his own national-security responsibilities.

Buzhardt was disturbed. He went back to the President.

National security, Nixon reiterated.

Where? How? What?

The President didn't respond directly. National security was sufficient; it had to do. He instructed Buzhardt to make the statement broad. Buzhardt and Buchanan drafted another paragraph, which Nixon finally accepted:

> It seemed to me possible that, because of the involvement of former CIA personnel [in the Watergate break-in], and because of some of their apparent associations, this investigation could lead to the uncovering of covert CIA operations totally unrelated to the Watergate break-in.

Buzhardt then asked the President for some particulars.

The President wouldn't deal with the question, but he insisted on one point: with the exception of the Ellsberg break-in, Howard Hunt and Gordon Liddy's work for the Plumbers had been undertaken for legitimate purposes of national security.

Slowly, Buzhardt and Buchanan elicited what they felt had been Nixon's state of mind at the time. With the aid of Garment and Price, they fashioned another paragraph in the President's name:

> I wanted justice done with regard to Watergate; but in the scale of national priorities with which I had to deal—and not at that time having any idea of

the extent of political abuse which Watergate reflected—I also had to be deeply concerned with ensuring that neither the covert operations of the CIA nor the operations of the Special Investigations Unit [Plumbers] should be compromised. Therefore, I instructed Mr. Haldeman and Mr. Ehrlichman . . . to see that this was personally coordinated between General Walters, the deputy director of the CIA, and Mr. Gray of the FBI. It was certainly not my intent, nor my wish, that the investigation of the Watergate break-in or of related acts be impeded in any way.

Buchanan was not convinced and insisted that Buzhardt ask the President once more whether there had been any political considerations. It was the sixth time he had gone back.

National security! There could be no mistake! the President said.

Okay.

Buzhardt returned to Buchanan. "That's what the man says, Pat."

ON MAY 22, a four-thousand-word presidential statement was released to the press. Garment and Buzhardt were assigned to appear to answer reporters' questions.

The press corps became abusive and incessantly interrupted the two lawyers as they tried to answer. Garment was offended by the scene; it affronted his sense of refinement, of what was civilized, courteous behavior. Even so, the reporters' questions were not very different from those that Buzhardt had continually carried back to the President: When, why, how? What reasons were there to believe that this statement would not be rendered as inoperative as all the others?

Garment could only reply that neither the President nor the President's lawyers could know precisely what he had been told, and precisely when he had been told it. The President had searched his mind and his notes. "There is no fundamental difference between the situation of the President and any other individual who has to deal with problems of recollection of events and transactions many months removed," Garment explained.

Garment left the briefing convinced that the four-thousand-word statement was a disaster—not because anything was held back, but because the President had admitted to so much: questionable wiretapping; a domestic intelligence plan that, to Garment's mind, was Hitlerian; the Plumbers—a term and concept that should have come from a Broadway comedy, not the White House; and an obstruction of the early Watergate FBI probe for reasons steeped in mystery and in unconvincing claims of national security.

A week passed during which Garment was surprised that there was no call for impeachment. He could not comprehend the mildness of the reaction. Was the country so unaccustomed to candor from the White House that a reckless assertion of the truth, no matter how squalid, was welcomed for its openness rather than condemned for its content?

Buchanan, for one, was now certain that the President could get away with almost anything. It was important now to dispose of the matter, to get Watergate behind them, to move on, he said. Buzhardt was content. *This* statement would never have to be declared inoperative. Now it seemed that Watergate might soon be over, and Buzhardt could get back to the Defense Department, where he retained his title as general counsel.

"GODDAM THE *Washington Post!*" Ziegler shouted when the newspaper's Sunday edition of June 3 was dropped on his desk.

The lead story was headlined "Dean Alleges Nixon Knew of Cover-up Plan." It stated that Dean planned to "testify under oath at the Senate's Watergate hearings, regardless of whether he is granted full immunity from prosecution, and he will allege that President Nixon was deeply involved in the cover-up."

Dean intended to swear that he was present or received telephone calls "on at least 35 occasions between January and April [1973] in which the cover-up was discussed with the President," the story said. All this was attributed, as usual, to "reliable sources." Ziegler was sure that meant Dean and his lawyers.

Dean's testimony, the article stated, would claim that the President had advance knowledge of the executive-clemency offers and of payments of "hush money" to the Watergate conspirators.

"Impossible, absolutely impossible!" Ziegler shouted at Judy Johnson and Diane Sawyer, two of his principal assistants. "All right, go back and see why the President was meeting with Dean."

It was a tedious assignment. An enormous number of lists of meetings and phone calls had to be retrieved from the White House Archives office. No detailed records of the subjects of conversations between the President and his aides had been kept, so the meetings had to be approximately reconstructed through newspaper clippings, from copies of the White House news summaries that Buchanan's office prepared daily, and from handwritten notes that the President sometimes passed on to Haldeman or Ziegler. The record, pitifully incomplete, was assembled in a three-ring binder for Ziegler. It was Dean versus the President.

At Camp David, Maryland, the presidential retreat that Dwight Eisenhower had named after his grandson, Nixon read the newspapers that Sunday and found much to distress him. The *Post* was reporting:

> One of the strongest charges against Mr. Nixon that Dean has made to investigators refers to a meeting Dean said he had with Mr. Nixon shortly before the sentencing of the seven Watergate defendants March 23.
> Dean said that Mr. Nixon asked him how much the defendants would have to be paid to insure their continued silence.
> Dean, the sources reported, maintains that he told Mr. Nixon the additional cost would be about $1 million, and Dean also claims that the President replied there would be no problem in paying that amount.

The *New York Times,* also citing anonymous informants, said that one of its sources "suggested that Mr. Dean may have tape-recorded some of his White House conversations during the January–April period in the White House. 'Everybody taped everybody else then,' the source said. 'Dean did it himself.' "

Before he left Camp David that afternoon, the President called Haldeman three times. At 4:18 P.M. his former chief of staff arrived at the White House to meet him. Haldeman stayed for nearly two hours. It was the thirty-second time that the President and Haldeman had talked in the five weeks since Haldeman had resigned.

CHAPTER THREE

STEVE Bull looked and sounded like many other young men who joined the new Nixon Administration in 1969. His trim, athletic physique and his conservative business suits gave him the confident appearance of the man sure of his purpose, exuding the "can do" attitude of the Nixon team player. Bull was responsible for keeping the President on schedule, and he also served as his personal aide-de-camp. His friendly and easy manner with presidential visitors tempered the President's brusque and graceless style.

Without the visibly fierce ambition of the other young men who had attached their fortunes to Richard Nixon, Bull was easy to trust, even for the suspicious Haldeman. When Haldeman's principal deputy, Alexander P. Butterfield, left the White House in February 1973 to become head of the Federal Aviation Agency, Bull had inherited many of his responsibilities for organizing the flow of papers to and from the President. At the same time, he took over responsibility for overseeing an incidental and minor White House routine—the presidential taping system.

The existence of the taping system was perhaps the best- and longest-kept secret in the Nixon White House, known only to the President, Haldeman, Haldeman's aide Lawrence Higby, Butterfield, Bull, Ziegler, Butterfield's secretary and the handful of Secret Service technicians who maintained it.

Bull was aware of only one instance in which tapes had been taken from the vault in the Executive Office Building. On April 25, 1973, Haldeman had asked him to retrieve several reels that contained conversations between John Dean and the President. The President wanted Haldeman to review them. Haldeman seemed certain that the tapes would undermine Dean's statements to the Watergate prosecutors—that they would be Richard Nixon's salvation.

Now, six weeks later, on June 4, there came a second request—from Nixon.

On that morning, Bull had to come up with tapes of Dean's conversations with the President during February, March and April. Working from logs of the President's meetings and phone calls, he called Secret Service supervisor Ray Zumwalt and asked for the appropriate reels. Then he cued and marked each tape. Though he was familiar with the voices, Bull had difficulty finding the required conversations, buried as they were in hours of tape on the large reels. At 10:05 A.M. he took the first tape in to the President and explained to him how to operate the recorder: "Push the play button when you are ready to listen, sir. Depress the stop button when you are done or want to stop the machine, sir. And if you want to rewind the tape or replay a portion of it, push the stop button and then the rewind button. Okay? Got that, sir?"

The President was almost totally lacking in mechanical ability and was not well coordinated physically. After four years of handing out souvenir presidential favors of cufflinks, tie clasps, pens and golf balls, Nixon still required assistance to open the cardboard boxes. Bull was accustomed to providing such help. Once, the President had called him in to open an allergy-pill bottle, which Nixon had been struggling with for some time—the childproof type of bottle, with instructions saying "Press down while turning." The cap had teeth marks on it where Nixon had apparently tried to gnaw it open.

At 10:16 on this Monday morning, the President turned to the tapes. He was pleased with what he heard, as Haldeman had predicted he would be. This was his ace in the hole. He had exact accounts, whereas Dean had primarily his recollection. Nixon the lawyer realized the potency of this weapon, especially if it was used to arm those who were to cross-examine Dean.

Haig arrived at 11:58. As exhausting as the chore was for Nixon to listen to the tapes, it was necessary, Haig told him. Now they could "take the son of a bitch on." They might even catch Dean in perjury.

The President agreed. But, "We do know we have one problem," he reminded Haig. "It's that damn conversation of March twenty-first." Dean and the President had discussed the blackmail demands of the Watergate burglars and the question of whether Nixon should grant them executive clemency. "But I think we can handle that," Nixon said. Haldeman would refute Dean's version in his testimony, and that would take care of that. He didn't even need to listen to that conversation; Haldeman had reviewed it and briefed him.

Haig said it was good that the President had spent the morning listening to the record, good for his own peace of mind.

The President worried, however. "As you know, we're up against ruthless people," he sighed.

"Well, we're going to be in great shape now," Haig said, "'cause we're going to prepare." Perhaps, he suggested, there might come a time when they would want to release their version of events through Buzhardt.

But Buzhardt didn't know about the taping system, the President said.

Haig reminded Nixon that Buzhardt had learned that there was a taping capability—at least on the phones.

Nixon was disturbed that Buzhardt might know. "All right," he said. "No further. He shouldn't tell anyone. . . . Let's just assume we goofed. If you get back to Buzhardt you tell him you had national-security stuff." When the time came to issue the material through Buzhardt, they could camouflage the source of information. "Al, we can put out the story to the effect that he [Buzhardt] has mem-cons, chronologies, telephone recordings, and all that sort of thing."

Haig agreed. They were safe. They could put out a more complete version of the meetings and discredit Dean without revealing the taping system. Moreover, Haig suggested, Dean's threat was not all that great. "He's an unstructured guy."

Nixon went back to listen to some more tapes. He sighed again. "This is hard work. But I've got to do it. Got to do it. And it's best for *me* to do it, too."

Haig certainly didn't want to hear them himself. "Only you," he told Nixon. "Only you."

The President listened all through the afternoon. At 6:04 P.M. Ziegler joined him, and they gloated about how much better prepared they were than Dean. He had no documentation. ". . . For whatever it's worth, Buzhardt has been through Dean's files, and there isn't a goddam thing in it," Nixon said.

Ziegler had not expected anything. Dean had not seemed the disciplined sort who kept good records, he told the President.

The President gave Ziegler a rundown on what he had heard on the tapes, from notes he had taken. They agreed that Dean had told the President very little about the Watergate cover-up until March 21, "when he came in with the cancer-in-the-heart-of-the-presidency thing," Nixon remarked.

The President and his press secretary exchanged reassurances. Everything that Dean had told the President was related to limiting the *political* damage that the Senate Watergate Committee might cause, not to obstructing the Watergate prosecution and trial.

"There's no cover-up in this, uh—to this point, period," said the President. "Not one talk of cover-up."

"That's right," Ziegler parroted.

But, as he reviewed his notes from a conversation on March 13, the President seemed concerned. "There's a little, there's a feeling of it through here," he said. It was when Dean had told him that Haldeman's political aide, Gordon Strachan, knew about the Watergate wiretap. Still, the President gave himself the benefit of the doubt and dismissed the problem. "What the hell is that?" he asked rhetorically.

Nixon read aloud from his notes what, in essence, Dean had told him on March 17. He paused at the point where Dean said that he, the President's own counsel, was probably vulnerable to prosecution. " 'Because I was over this like a blanket,' " Nixon quoted Dean.

"But, I said, 'John, you didn't know about it.' He said, 'That's right, I have no knowledge. No prior knowledge.' "

The President seemed to ask Ziegler for reassurance: "How does it strike you? He was telling me that there was a cover-up?"

"Not at all," Ziegler assured him.

There was more, and it was worse. The President continued reading from his notes. "I said, 'We've, we've got to cut that off. We can't have that go to Haldeman!' But we just stopped right there. There was no— I suppose he could say there that I was telling him to cover up, wouldn't you say, for Haldeman?"

"I suppose he could say that in the context at the time that . . ." Ziegler paused to clear his throat. "Still, there's nothing, nothing, Mr. President."

It went on. As Nixon looked to Ziegler to confirm his innocence, Ziegler put the conversations with Dean in the best possible light. "And you were talking about political problems, not illegal problems," Ziegler told his boss. "Political problems as they related to the Ervin Committee hearings and what could come out in the course of those hearings . . . dammit, I know that's the case. And those notes are proof," he said, referring to the lined sheets of yellow paper from which the President had just read. Ziegler was pushing. "After a full ten months of a thorough investigation by the Justice Department and putting trust in the people around you, that this was being handled while you were in the process of everything else that happened in 1972. Goddammit, in March, when this started coming to you, you can tell by your reactions that you were saying, 'What in the hell is this going on?' And—"

The President interrupted him. "I should have reacted before the twenty-first of March, actually," he said. "Dean shouldn't have had to come in to me with the 'cancer in the heart of the presidency,' which, to his credit, he did."

"Yes, that's right," Ziegler replied.

"He did. Haldeman didn't tell me that; Ehrlichman didn't tell me that." Why had Dean come to him on March 21?

Ziegler assured the President that it was because Dean knew the President was not aware of the problem and of Haldeman and Ehrlichman's involvement in the cover-up.

Nixon was exhausted from all those hours of listening to the tapes. They were difficult to hear. "I mean, God, maybe we were talking about a cover-up—Watergate," he said. "I really didn't. I didn't know what the hell—I honestly didn't know."

The President asked Ziegler for options, ways to handle "the whole Dean problem."

"I think we let, let Dean run his string a little bit," Ziegler answered. "At least that's what I'd do at this point, and not respond . . ."

"We can't let it run to the point that it hurts us too much," the President said. "Not till the twenty-first of March did he come in and talk about a cover-up."

Ziegler tried to guide him to safer ground. "And he did not in any way suggest that he was involved directly. Yet—"

"On the twenty-first he did," the President corrected Ziegler.

"Did he?"

"He said, 'Even Dean.' "

But now the President recalled that he had asked Dean if he knew of the cover-up, and that Dean had denied knowing about it. Nixon and Ziegler were relieved: Ziegler's interpretation would stand. They stumbled on.

"I didn't want to burn Mitchell."

"That's right," Ziegler agreed.

"The key to this thing, Ron, is Mitchell. Always been the key. You haven't had a cover-up, Dean did it—shit, he didn't do it for Haldeman and Ehrlichman. . . . He did it for John Mitchell. So did Magruder* do it for Mitchell. Magruder lied for Mitchell. You know that."

"Sure."

"That's the tragedy of the whole thing. Mitchell would never step up to this. Well, I suppose, would you? No. No. Former Attorney General step

---

* Jeb Stuart Magruder, formerly Haldeman's assistant at the White House, who at the time of the Watergate break-in was deputy director of the Committee for the Re-election of the President.

up and say you bugged? Shit, I wouldn't. What I would step up and say—'Look, I haven't approved a goddam thing and so forth, but I take responsibility for it—bah, bah, bah, bah, you know—and I'm going to take, uh, take, you know, a suspended sentence or misdemeanor slapped in the face or whatever the hell it's going to be.' But once denied—under oath—he was stuck. See? God damn."

"The perjury's the thing, that is the problem," Ziegler agreed.

And they continued to attribute the basic cover-up to Dean and his efforts to protect himself and Mitchell.

"Dean knew," Ziegler said, firming up their line.

"Of course he knew it. He knew all of this."

"Sure he did."

"He knew all of it. He didn't tell me. You hear any of that in here?"

"No, sir. I can't," said Ziegler.

"But, but you see—" Nixon made another start—"in fairness to Dean, when he mentioned the fact that Strachan was involved, he mentioned the fact that, that, uh, that it was not well to let it all hang out, that Ehrlichman might have a problem and so forth, he might well have drawn the conclusion, Ron, that the President wanted him to keep the lid on."

Ziegler was quick to show his boss how to turn the point to his advantage. "Yeah, the political lid in the Ervin Committee hearings, not the legal lid in terms of the trial."

"That's the difference. I see," said the President.

"That's the difference." Ziegler took the point further. "That's the conclusion I had during the whole period. Yeah."

"We were talking about the Ervin Committee," the President realized.

"That's right."

"We weren't talking about the trial," said the President. "The trial was over."*

"We were, we were concerned about the Ervin Committee," said Ziegler. "And what they would press for in terms not of illegality, but in terms of political embarrassment. Uh, you know, of, of, uh, of, uh, uh, some of the, some . . ."

At last the President seemed satisfied that he was innocent of the cover-up. "Don't you think it's interesting, though, to run through this?" he asked. "Really, the goddam record is not bad, is it?"

"Makes me feel very good," Ziegler answered.

---

* At the first Watergate trial in January, 1973, Hunt, Liddy and the five burglars all either pleaded guilty or were convicted. All remained silent and declined to take the witness stand in their own defense.

To the President, that was overstating it a bit. "It's not comfortable for me, because I was sitting there like a dumb turkey."

Ziegler had an answer. "It's a *Rashomon* theory," he offered.

"Hm?" the President asked.

"It's a *Rashomon* theory," Ziegler tried again. "Five men sit in a room, and what occurs in that room or what is said in that room means something different to each man, based upon his perception of the events that preceded it. And that is exactly what this is. Exactly what it is."

The President grasped the point: Dean perceived that the President was involved in the cover-up based on his own, not Nixon's, special knowledge of what had gone before. It seemed to the President to be a pretty good theory. Perhaps it would hold up. But what about the problem of Dean being a loose cannon? "Suppose Dean goes out and says something?" the President asked.

"Well, that's why I think we should let, let Dean run his string," Ziegler suggested, "because he's saying so much, or so much is being said for him, that all is becoming so confused and distorted."

They agreed it would be a mistake to respond to each of Dean's statements. Dean was too poised. They would wait him out.

"And then he will have to be cracked," Ziegler said, "or dealt with in some way which we should determine down the line, you know."

The President appreciated the point. "Let Ehrlichman and Haldeman and the rest of them take him on," he said.

"Yes, sir," Ziegler agreed.

"We've got him dead to rights on that, Ron, haven't we?" the President asked.

They discussed Dean's work habits and once again concluded that he was not the type to keep detailed records. Buzhardt had plundered Dean's files on matters other than Watergate and had found no memoranda of conversations. He hadn't taken them with him; he had never made any.

They had their case. They had a complete record of the President's meetings with Dean. Let him commit himself to his own recollection. Haldeman, Ehrlichman and the rest would destroy him with a more precise version.

"We'll survive it all," Ziegler concluded.

ZIEGLER LEFT and the President went back to his listening. Later he summoned Buzhardt to his office and explained that he had developed his version of twenty of the key meetings and phone conversations with Dean about Watergate. In much the same exercise he had gone through with Ziegler, Nixon read from his notes, departing from them to make a point, punctuating his reading to reinforce his interpretation.

These notes clearly supported him and refuted Dean, Nixon said. Right?

Buzhardt nodded his agreement and wrote down the subjects that the President said were discussed during each conversation. He was beginning to feel waves of uneasiness. As Nixon read aloud, Buzhardt saw the intrinsic contradictions. A great deal didn't make sense. In one meeting Nixon had been told of Strachan's knowledge of the Watergate operation, and only one week later he heard and appeared to accept that there was "not a scintilla of evidence" as to any White House involvement.

Buzhardt kept quiet. The President was about to offer his version of the celebrated March 21 meeting—the meeting in which Dean claimed Nixon said that paying another million dollars to the Watergate conspirators would be no problem. Haldeman, who had heard the tape, and Nixon, who hadn't, were agreed on the details.

The President read softly and carefully, his eyes riveted on the yellow legal pad: "Dean gave the President his theory of what had happened. He still said no prior June 17 White House knowledge, that Magruder probably knew, that Mitchell possibly knew, that Strachan probably knew, that Haldeman had possibly seen the fruits of the wiretaps through Strachan, that Ehrlichman was vulnerable . . . , [that] Colson* had made a call to Magruder."

Buzhardt got the message: In other words, almost all the President's key advisers and aides could be implicated.

Buzhardt jotted furiously on his own legal pad as Nixon read from his notes: "Hunt was trying to blackmail Ehrlichman about Hunt's prior Plumber activities unless he was paid what ultimately might amount to one million dollars. The President said, how could it possibly be paid? 'What makes you think he would be satisfied with that?' "

Again, that last phrase in quotes, the President pointed out. Then, continuing: "The President stated it was blackmail, *that it was wrong,* that it would not work, that the truth would come out anyway. . . . Dean said Colson had talked to Hunt about executive clemency."

The more Nixon read, the more Buzhardt realized that John Dean had a case. Nixon saw it differently and wanted everything given to the Republican minority of the Senate Watergate Committee to aid them when they cross-examined Dean.

---

* Charles W. Colson, special counsel to the President.

Buzhardt passed the information to Fred Thompson, the minority's counsel. *That it was wrong.* The phrase stuck in Buzhardt's mind.

THE PRESIDENT gave Buzhardt little peace, often summoning him to his office on the "Bellboy" the lawyer wore everywhere except in church. The two men were spending a good deal of time together. Refuting Dean on the specifics was not enough, Nixon said; there was a more general problem. The Administration's legitimate national-security operations were being deliberately entangled by his enemies in Watergate. Those activities had to be separated from the scandal. Nixon said he knew that surreptitious entries and wiretaps—after all, that was what Watergate was all about, wasn't it?—were a way of life in the Kennedy and Johnson administrations. "I know this has been going on for twenty years. It is the worst kind of hypocrisy for the Democrats to make so much of it."

Thinking about stories he had heard on the Hill, Buzhardt agreed with the President. But the problem was to document the abuses of the Kennedy and Johnson administrations, in the same way that the Ervin Committee was presently calling the Nixon Administration to account.

Nixon pointed out that he had asked John Dean, "of all people," to come up with a list of his predecessors' abuses. But Dean, usually so thorough, hadn't really come up with much.

The FBI didn't have records on the blatantly political work done for the Democratic administrations, Buzhardt said, and certainly it did not keep records of illegal break-ins. However, he had heard from good FBI sources that Congressmen had been tapped during the 1960s.

Was there any way to prove it? Nixon wanted to know.

Buzhardt was sure there was not. But the FBI did have records of national-security taps, and there must have been some abuses.

There had to be a way to make the other side pay the price, Nixon said. This was a partisan battle. Dean was going to tell the world about *his* White House; what he said should be measured against the record of prior administrations. Get a comprehensive list of all the national-security wiretaps conducted by the Kennedy and Johnson administrations, Nixon ordered. Call the Attorney General and get the Justice Department started on it now.

Buzhardt found that Elliot Richardson was reluctant to cooperate. Buzhardt therefore took the heat from the President, for a while, but eventually he passed it back to Richardson. After the fourth call to the Attorney General, a list came back. It was impressive, as Nixon had predicted.

Though incomplete, it was political dynamite. The same kind of taps that had caused Nixon grief. The President might be right, Buzhardt concluded.

Nixon was elated. There had been hardly a hint in the press. Fascinated by the fact that many of the taps had been authorized by former Attorney General Robert F. Kennedy, the President read the list with delight:

—Lloyd Norman, Pentagon and military-affairs correspondent for *Newsweek*. (Supposedly ordered by President John F. Kennedy himself because Norman had obtained classified information.)

—Hanson W. Baldwin, military-affairs specialist for the *New York Times*.

—Robert Amory, Jr., the former number-three man in the CIA and a close personal friend of President Kennedy. He had reportedly been a close friend of a Yugoslavian Embassy official who was an undercover intelligence officer.

—The law firm of Surrey and Karasik, which had lobbied for Dominican Republic sugar interests and was under investigation for trying to raise the United States sugar quotas.

—Bernard Fall, the late French historian and author of seven books on Vietnam, who had interviewed and maintained contact with North Vietnam's President Ho Chi Minh over a period of years.

—The chief clerk to the House Agriculture Committee, who had worked for Representative Harold D. Cooley (D., N.C.), after the committee had handled sugar-quota legislation.

Buzhardt was sure there were more taps on the Hill, but they could at least document these.

Nixon continued his reading.

—The Reverend Dr. Martin Luther King, Jr. That had been extensively reported.

—Frank A. Capell, the right-wing author of *The Secret Story of Marilyn Monroe,* a book published in 1964 which alleged a relationship between Robert Kennedy and the late movie actress.

The President chortled. The Capell tap surely didn't sound like a national-security matter to him. It confirmed everything he had always suspected about the Kennedys.

He could stand on his record. He had taken the extreme action of wiretapping staff and reporters only in cases where secret negotiations were in jeopardy. He was not the sort of man who would tap a writer who had written about his private life. Kennedys, not Nixons, did that sort of thing. Could Buzhardt get a list of all the illegal break-ins conducted during the Kennedy and Johnson administrations?

Buzhardt explained again that the agencies were very unlikely to have kept records of blatantly illegal activities. There was just no way he could get a list.

All right, Nixon said. Leak the Kennedy wiretaps.

BUZHARDT WENT to Haig. They both thought that leaking the information was too obvious a strategy. Instead, they released, without any names, a statistical summary of national-security wiretaps that had been conducted under the Kennedy, Johnson and Nixon administrations. It indicated that there had been fewer under Nixon than under his Democratic predecessors.

The President was not satisfied. He pushed Buzhardt again and again to leak the names of those tapped during the two preceding administrations. It was not a very good idea, Buzhardt insisted. It could backfire; it might well appear to be one more use of the FBI files for political advantage.

Nixon said he wanted it done. He would not tolerate defiance. He had not asked for Buzhardt's opinion.

Buzhardt and Haig stalled. The President called from California. Dean was going before the Senate Watergate Committee in a few days. Nixon was screaming, "I want that out. I haven't read it in the newspaper. I don't want excuses. Do it."

Buzhardt and Haig conferred. There was also pressure from other senior White House staff members. "Anything that happened in this Administration happened in spades in others," Haig told selected reporters. He knew very well that there had been a consistent pattern of executive abuse under the Kennedy and Johnson regimes, but he couldn't figure out how to get the message out more specifically. If they leaked the details, they would be pulled ever deeper into a partisan cross fire. There was no way to make the public focus on past administrations, not while the current one was being attacked daily in the press or in some congressional investigation or another. Nevertheless, Haig told Buzhardt, he was not sure he or anyone else could control the President on this particular matter. All they could do was stall.

When the President got back from California, it was Buzhardt who reopened the subject. He laid out his reasoning patiently. It wouldn't do any good. They would be doing exactly what they had accused the Watergate Committee and others of doing. It just wouldn't fly.

At last the President capitulated. But he knew, the staff knew and the other side knew that what *his* people had done was nothing—literally nothing—compared to what had gone on before. They were all innocent.

FINALLY, ON June 25, John Dean appeared in public before the Senate Watergate Committee. He read a 245-page statement that described the Watergate cover-up in elaborate detail. Over the next four days, Dean fielded questions adeptly, contradicting the President's versions of events with impressive consistency. His story, basically unshakable, held up as an extended accusation against the Nixon White House: wiretapping, burglary, secret funds, money-laundering, enemies' lists, dirty tricks, Plumbers, physical surveillance, choreographed character assassination, cover-up, obstruction of the federal agencies. But Nixon had been right: Dean's account of the President's participation in the Watergate cover-up rested only on his own recollection of the events. It sounded authentic, but it was legally inconclusive. There was no documentation.

Almost in desperation, the Watergate Committee's investigative staff began a series of interviews with so-called satellite witnesses—assistants, secretaries, clerks and aides who had worked at the White House and for the Committee for the Re-election of the President. These were people who might have seen a memo, overheard a conversation or kept records that could document Dean's allegations. Each was questioned closely for some small confirmation or denial of the charges against the President. Dean's testimony about pre-Watergate intelligence-gathering and political retribution was repeatedly confirmed. But the President had, at least by inference, admitted and justified most of the activities in his statement of May 22. The crux of Dean's assertions, the President's direct participation in the cover-up, could not be corroborated. Only six relatively minor witnesses remained to be heard before Haldeman and Ehrlichman were to testify. Time was running out for the Watergate Committee.

At the White House, things were running according to plan. The President authorized his former chief of staff, Haldeman, to listen to more tapes of White House conversations. Haldeman would be well prepared to undercut Dean's testimony. The threat would soon pass.

THE TEMPERATURE was in the nineties in Washington on Friday, July 13, the day witness Alexander Butterfield was to be interviewed by the Watergate Committee's staff. Room G-334 in the New Senate Office Building had only one small air-conditioning vent, and it was oppressively hot. A haze of tobacco smoke obscured the pale-yellow walls. The chairs were stained with grease from fast-food meals. Wastebaskets spilled over with cigarette butts and packages and sandwich wrappings. The faded green carpet was filthy. No janitors had been allowed in for fear that someone might plant an eavesdropping device.

Both Butterfield's manner and his memory impressed the committee's junior staff. With his hands folded in front of him, he considered carefully each question that was posed to him. He looked directly at his interrogator; he spoke in calm and even tones. He had resigned his commission as an Air Force colonel to work for Haldeman in the White House. He described, precisely and laboriously, every aspect of his job as deputy assistant to the President. He seemed to enjoy this rare opportunity to talk about the responsibilities he had been charged with. But his candor and memory were not much help in determining whether it was John Dean or Richard Nixon who was lying. Butterfield's job and his access to the President were matters of routine. He kept the keys and the files.

"Did you see or hear anything which indicated to you that the President was involved in the alleged effort to keep the facts from the public?" Butterfield was asked.

"No, but the way the White House operated it could have happened certainly." The witness paused to reflect. ". . . The series of meetings in question [with Dean] didn't begin until February 1973. I was phasing out of my job and getting ready to leave for the FAA. I can't document anything or prove anything. I don't remember Watergate being anything."

The staff, trying to make the most of the situation, turned back to Butterfield's expertise on the President's office routine. The minute detail of material submitted to the committee from Buzhardt was puzzling: one memorandum listed the times, dates, locations and participants for all the Dean-Nixon conversations; another described the substance of Dean's calls and meetings with the President.

"We received a listing from the White House of the conversations between the President and Dean, which we understand are from the President's diaries," a member of the committee's staff said.

"We have three types of back-up materials from which these listings could be constructed," Butterfield carefully explained. "The switchboard operators kept track of all phone calls to and from the President. Secret Service personnel, ushers and secretaries record who comes and goes from the President's office. Staff members prepare memos for the President before each formal meeting with outsiders, outline the purpose and points to be covered and then prepare another memo after each meeting, summarizing the tone of the meetings and any commitments made." All this was put together into a daily log for the President—where, when and with whom he had met.

"Would there be a file on the substance of each meeting with staff members?"

"If the staff member was in alone or only with other White House staff members, there would probably be no memo written. If there was a highly significant meeting, the President might say, 'Write this up.' "

Pulling out a typed transcript of the summary that Buzhardt had dictated to the Republican minority counsel—the President's version of his conversations with Dean—an investigator asked Butterfield where such an account might have originated. Could it have been from someone's notes of the meetings?

Butterfield glanced over the document. He paused several times to remark on how detailed the account was. He appeared to be fascinated by that. He lingered over it. "Somebody probably got the information from the chron-file and put it down," he said finally.

As he continued to read, he was asked whether the summary described the kinds of meetings the President would ask someone to write up.

No. Resuming his reading, Butterfield arrived at the account of the March 21, 1973, meeting and stopped. He noted aloud that the summary stated that Dean had told the President that Hunt was trying to blackmail Ehrlichman. Butterfield was surprised. It was he who pointed out to his questioners that the next sentence included an actual quote: "The President said how could it possibly be paid, 'What makes you think he would be satisfied with that?' "

"Where did you get this?" Butterfield inquired.

"Mr. Buzhardt provided it to the committee. Could it have come from someone's notes of a meeting?" he was asked.

"No, it seems too detailed," Butterfield replied.

"Was the President's recollection of meetings good?"

"Yes, when I came I was impressed," Butterfield replied. "He is a great and fast learner. He does recall things very well. He tends to overexplain things."

"Was he as precise as the summary?"

"Well, no, but he would sometimes dictate his thoughts after a meeting."

"How often did he do so?"

"Very rarely."

"Were his memos this detailed?"

"I don't think so."

"Where else could this have come from?"

Butterfield stared down at the document. Slowly, he lifted it an inch off the table. "I don't know. Well, let me think about that awhile." He pushed the document toward the center of the green-felt-covered table.

The questioning moved into other areas.

"Did the President ever note an article in a news summary and write in the margin?"

"Yes."

"Did he ever write 'Get this guy'?"

"Yes. Not necessarily in those words. He is profane, but in a nice sort of way."

"Do you recall when he said 'Get this guy'? Do you remember the phrase he used?"

"He said several times, 'I remember him—he's no good'—oftentimes referring to news people," Butterfield said. "Sometimes he'd write something like 'Ziegler should get wise to this guy.' "

The questioners went back to Dean's testimony.

Don Sanders, the deputy counsel to the Republican minority, thought there might be some way to document the President's innocence. He led to his question cautiously. "Dean indicated that there might be some facility for taping. He said that on April 15 in the President's EOB office he had the impression he was being taped, and that at the end of the meeting the President walked to a corner of the room and lowered his voice as if he was trying to stay off the tape himself while he discussed his earlier conversation with Colson about executive clemency. Is it possible Dean knew what he was talking about?"

Butterfield thought for a moment, trying to frame a response to the complicated question. Then he leaned over to the center of the table and picked up the Buzhardt account of the Dean-Nixon meetings. "No, Dean didn't know about it," he said at last. "But that is where this must have come from. There is tape in each of the President's offices. It is kept by the Secret Service, and only four other men know about it. Dean had no way of knowing about it. He was just guessing."

Then, for forty-five minutes, Butterfield described the taping system in detail. When the interview ended, the Democratic staff members raced to brief the Democratic majority's chief counsel, Sam Dash. Dash told them to move cautiously to verify the system's existence before the White House heard about Butterfield's revelation.

Meanwhile, a minority staff representative located his boss, Fred Thompson, at a bar in the Carroll Arms Hotel, talking to two reporters. Thompson called Buzhardt.

The next Monday, Butterfield testified publicly. He concluded his televised testimony by noting, "This matter which we have discussed here today, I think, is precisely the substance on which the President plans to present his defense. I believe, of course, that the President is innocent of any crime or wrongdoing, that he is innocent likewise of any complicity."

Gathered around their television sets, members of the White House staff were mesmerized by Butterfield's revelation. Surely this disclosure had been carefully engineered, some thought. There were expressions of relief. At last there was something definitive. The tapes had been deliberately exposed. They would prove that John Dean was lying.

THE PRESIDENT was in Bethesda Naval Hospital in Maryland with pneumonia. Buzhardt, Garment and University of Texas Professor Charles Alan Wright, a constitutional scholar and the newest member of the White House legal team, visited him. They wanted Nixon's permission to review the tapes.

Nixon appeared offended. "No. Never." He cut off the discussion. "No, no, no," he said, his voice rising.

Two days later the President was back at the White House. Buzhardt went to see him. Cox would want the tapes, and Buzhardt was not at all confident that the President would prevail in a claim of privilege. The special prosecutor had a powerful argument: the tapes were evidence in a criminal prosecution of the President's aides.

Nixon was adamant. The indiscretion of installing the tape system should not forever burden the office of the presidency, he told Buzhardt. No outsider could comprehend the breadth of the intimate material on those tapes. Those tapes were the *essence* of the presidency. They contained the private thoughts and comments not only of the President but of foreign leaders, Congressmen, his aides, even his family. Buzhardt must understand. *If the President broke the confidence of those who unburdened themselves in his office, it would shatter the presidency*—not only his own but also his successors'. What about those Democrats who had come to him to say they supported his reelection—Senators James O. Eastland of Mississippi, Russell Long of Louisiana and John L. McClellan of Arkansas? Nixon was becoming emotional. Buzhardt could see he wanted desperately to be believed, that it was crucial that Buzhardt understand that this decision was a matter of the highest principle.

A President's conversations must be protected, Buzhardt answered. The only solution seemed to be a claim of executive privilege.

The problem was no longer academic. On July 23, Cox subpoenaed nine of the President's recorded conversations.

Pat Buchanan had a blunter solution: destroy the tapes. He sat at his typewriter in his EOB office and described the advantages of his "bonfire" approach: there would be a firestorm afterward, but it would blow itself out; the President and the presidency were strong enough to withstand the assault.

Buchanan's memo was delivered to the President on the twenty-fifth. Nixon read it and summoned Buzhardt and Haig. They disagreed with Buchanan. It was too late now to destroy them. With the receipt of Cox's subpoena, the tapes had become potential evidence and destroying them might constitute obstruction of justice, Buzhardt counseled. Worse, said Haig; destroying the tapes would look like an admission of guilt.

There was nothing on the tapes that would hurt him in Watergate, Nixon assured them. At most, there were a few ambiguous statements that might be misconstrued if they were taken out of context. Nothing more.

Still, the option occupied the President's thoughts. He sought Garment's counsel.

Garment told him it was too late.

Chapter Four

AT the end of April, when he'd had to jettison Haldeman and Ehrlich-man, the President had also appointed a new Attorney General to replace Richard G. Kleindienst, who had presided over the first, discredited investigation into Watergate.* Secretary of State William P. Rogers declined the job, and Nixon had settled on his Secretary of Defense, Elliot L. Richardson.

The two men met at Camp David on Sunday, April 29, 1973, the day before the Haldeman and Ehrlichman resignations were announced.

Richardson's chilly, formal manner evoked images of the Eastern, academic establishment which Nixon despised. The slow, winding rhetoric that weighed down Richardson's conversation drove the President to distraction ordinarily. Still, he needed Richardson's impeccable reputation to redeem his Justice Department.

Richardson was to take charge of the Watergate investigation. There might be some areas of national security that would have to be left alone, Nixon said, but the investigation must be thorough and complete.

Richardson responded that there could be no other way.

"You must pursue this investigation even if it leads to the President,"

* Kleindienst, on May 16, 1974, pleaded guilty to a misdemeanor charge—failing to provide full information to a Senate committee—in the ITT case. On June 7, 1974, he was given a one-month suspended sentence and a suspended fine of one hundred dollars.

Nixon said, and his eyes met Richardson's. "I'm innocent. You've got to believe I'm innocent. If you don't, don't take the job."

Vastly relieved, Richardson nodded his acceptance. That seemed to clinch it—Nixon would never set such an investigation in motion unless he was innocent.

"The important thing is the presidency," Nixon continued. "If need be, save the presidency from the President."

Richardson, writing on a legal pad, paraphrased the thought: "If the monster is me, save the country."

Almost immediately he appointed his old Harvard law professor, Archibald Cox, as special prosecutor to handle Watergate, promising him full independence.

By July, Richardson's faith in the President's innocence was severely shaken. Haig was trying to make him limit Cox's work, telling him that the President might fire Cox if he were not reined in. "If we have to have a confrontation, we will have it," Haig warned Richardson on July 23, the day Cox subpoenaed nine of the President's tapes.

Elliot Richardson did not want a confrontation. A few days later, he went to see Haig at the White House.

Haig told him that he had recommended to the President that he turn over the subpoenaed tapes. Nixon had refused. He would resign first.

Why?

Haig said he didn't know whether the President was hiding something or whether he was merely concerned with the principle of confidentiality, but he had never seen Nixon so worked up. "It makes you wonder what must be on those tapes," Haig said.

Richardson also had to wonder, but he would assume the better interpretation. There was a more immediate problem, he informed Haig. Federal prosecutors in Baltimore had gathered evidence that Vice-President Spiro Agnew had been accepting illegal cash payoffs for years.

Haig was aghast.

By August, the details of the Agnew investigation were all over the newspapers. In September, Richardson began plea-bargaining with the Vice-President's attorneys.

It wasn't until October that Richardson finally met with the President on the Agnew situation. As Richardson was leaving the Oval Office, the President called after him, "Now that we have disposed of that matter, we can go ahead and get rid of Cox."

Richardson didn't know Nixon very well, and he didn't know how to take the remark. In any case, he was absorbed by the Agnew problem until October 10, when the Vice-President resigned.

Five days later, Richardson was summoned to the White House. The Cox "situation" was closing fast. The Court of Appeals had just upheld Judge Sirica's order and ruled that the President must turn over the nine subpoenaed tapes—unless the White House could reach "some agreement with the Special Prosecutor" out of court. Nixon had only until midnight Friday, October 19, to comply, to appeal to the Supreme Court, or to reach a compromise with Cox. It was Monday now. Richardson was doubtful that the White House and Cox could agree on much of anything.

When the Attorney General arrived at the White House, he was escorted to Haig's office. Buzhardt was there. They presented a plan to Richardson: The President would personally listen to the subpoenaed recordings and supervise the preparation of transcripts that would be turned over to the court as a substitute for the tapes. The special prosecutor, long a bone in Nixon's throat and a bad idea in the first place, would be fired. That would eliminate the question of any litigation for still more of the President's tapes.

Richardson, outwardly calm, raised an objection. The plan was contrary to the agreement he had made with the Senate Judiciary Committee during his confirmation hearings. He had promised that the special prosecutor could be removed only for "extraordinary improprieties." If he were ordered to fire Cox, he might instead have to resign himself.

Haig and Buzhardt held their ground. Cox would have to go.

Richardson left the White House bewildered and uncertain of what would happen next. He was unaware that a plan to submit transcripts instead of tapes had been under consideration for three weeks and that, in late September, Rose Mary Woods had begun transcribing the subpoenaed conversations.

Haig called Richardson forty minutes later to suggest a compromise: Senator John C. Stennis, the seventy-two-year-old Mississippi Democrat who chaired the Senate Armed Services Committee, would be asked to make a comparison between the transcripts and the tapes. His authenticated version would be submitted to the court.

Haig said he would present the idea to the President. Within an hour he was back on the phone with good news for Richardson. The President had resisted the notion, but he had conceded, Haig said. He assured Richardson that Cox would not have to be fired, provided that "this was it" in regard to his demands for tapes. The phrase was not defined. The President, Haig added, would expect Richardson's support if it came to a showdown with Cox.

Richardson was relieved. Over lunch he reviewed the morning's developments with members of his staff. Some of them were concerned that their boss was being set up to get Cox. They convinced Richardson to call Haig back and make it clear that he was committed only to the Stennis authentication of the nine subpoenaed tapes. "This was it" would have to wait.

HAIG AND Buzhardt visited Senator Stennis on Capitol Hill the same day. They left him with the impression that his authenticated version was intended only for the Senate Watergate Committee, which also had issued a subpoena for the President's tapes. Stennis, a former judge, was not told that the transcripts were also to be used to meet the special prosecutor's subpoena.

Now Richardson had only to sell Cox the Stennis compromise. At 6 P.M., and again the next morning at ten, the Attorney General met with the special prosecutor. Cox wanted to see the terms of the compromise in writing. Richardson gathered his assistants at the Justice Department, and an initial draft was made: "A Proposal—ELR #1." A section entitled "Other Tapes and Documents" stated: "The proposed arrangement would undertake to cover only the tapes heretofore subpoenaed by the Watergate grand jury at the request of the Special Prosecutor."

Wednesday morning Richardson submitted the draft to Buzhardt, who was troubled by the section "Other Tapes and Documents." Buzhardt said that section was redundant. The compromise clearly dealt only with the tapes now under subpoena. Why state the obvious?

He redrafted Richardson's proposal eliminating the section. The President, Buzhardt knew, wanted a permanent solution to the question of future access to his tapes; by avoiding the question, he reasoned, perhaps a confrontation could be averted.

Richardson acquiesced.

On Thursday afternoon Cox sent Richardson his written comments on the abbreviated proposal.* He too wanted to avoid a confrontation with the President, he wrote. But, "The public cannot fairly be asked to confide so difficult and responsible a task to any one man operating in secrecy, consulting only with the White House." The court might want the actual tapes,

---

* The White House also proposed to empower Stennis to "paraphrase language whose use in its original form would in his judgment be embarrassing to the President." No mention was made of the fact that the Senator was partially deaf and that the tapes were difficult to hear under the best of circumstances.

the best evidence, for any trial. Cox wanted an agreement that would "serve the function of a court decision in establishing the Special Prosecutor's entitlement to other evidence."

Richardson took Cox's memo to a 6 P.M. meeting with Haig, Buzhardt, Wright and Garment in Haig's White House office. Cox had in fact rejected the proposal, Haig observed coldly. The White House was seeking a compromise, but the special prosecutor's response differed in spirit so completely that agreement was out of the question. If Cox refused, he should be fired, Haig said, and the President's three lawyers agreed. They were confident that the President could persuade the public of the reasonableness of such an action.

Richardson did not think so. He made it clear that he could live with Cox's voluntary resignation, but that he could not fire him for refusing the Stennis plan. He urged Wright, who had been the most vigorous proponent of the Stennis compromise, to approach Cox directly and try to persuade him.

Later that night, Richardson sat in his study in McLean, Virginia. The rush of the Potomac River was barely audible in the distance. He wrote at the top of a yellow legal pad: "Why I Must Resign."

He was sure Cox could not be persuaded to acquiesce, and he also knew that the President wanted Cox out.

Richardson's first "reason" was his own promise to the Senate to guarantee the independence of the special prosecutor. Second, he wrote down that Cox was being required to accept less than he had won in two court decisions. "While Cox has rejected a proposal I consider reasonable, his rejection of it cannot be regarded" as grounds for his removal. "I am in fact loyal to the President," he wrote slowly. "And I am by temperament a team player." But it was dawning on Richardson that he wasn't going to be able to play much longer. Writing it down helped him make it clear to himself. The next morning he planned to make it clear to the President.

Haig and Buzhardt talked to the President late that night. They were sure Cox would resign rather than accept, they said. Richardson was on their side. Nixon again bore down on the question of access to other tapes. The line had to be clearly drawn. The matter had to be settled. Now.

Buzhardt suggested that the White House remain silent on the issue. Putting forward the Stennis compromise was sufficient for the present. Its acceptance would be a giant step toward the end of Watergate.

But Nixon wanted the larger problem of access to his tapes settled forever. When he couldn't get the message across to Buzhardt, he blew up.

"Leave it open," Buzhardt recommended again.

"No," the President said. "No, period!"

Now THE whole problem was magnified immensely; a showdown was inevitable. Buzhardt had been sure he could maneuver Cox into a position where the special prosecutor would have to resign, since the White House *and* Richardson would be lined up against him, but to do it he needed some negotiating room. The President had just denied him exactly that. By asserting that the special prosecutor could not subpoena additional evidence, they were playing into Cox's hands, laying credible grounds for his defiance—instead of for his resignation. And they were probably throwing Richardson into Cox's arms.

Meanwhile, Charles Alan Wright called Cox. It was a nasty conversation. Wright announced that the President was willing to permit an unprecedented intrusion into his privacy, but that Cox's response had departed from the intent of the Stennis compromise. Unless Cox was willing to reconsider his position, further discussions would be a waste of time.

Cox was offended at Wright's tone, still more at the implied threat. He was willing to talk, but he could only conclude that Wright had called to slam the door.

The next morning, Friday, Cox dispatched to Wright a "Dear Charlie" letter which kept the door open slightly. But, Cox said, he could not, and would not, break his promise to run a thorough investigation. To relinquish his right to additional evidence, he said, would be to break that promise. "I cannot break my promise now."

By return letter, Wright said, "The differences between us remain so great that no purpose would be served by further discussion. We will be forced to take the actions that the President deems appropriate in these circumstances."

Early that Friday morning, Richardson had "Why I Must Resign" typed and put it in his pocket. He called Haig and asked to see the President. But when Richardson arrived at Haig's office at about 10 A.M., Haig had a new deal. "Maybe," he said, "we don't have to go down the road we talked about last night. Suppose we go ahead with the Stennis plan without firing Cox."

Buzhardt, Garment and Wright came in. How might Judge Sirica be convinced to accept the Stennis transcripts rather than the tapes themselves? They would forget Cox and concentrate on persuading Sirica. Perhaps the Senate Watergate Committee would also accept transcripts.

Richardson was taken aback. That would be fine, he said, thinking to himself that he wouldn't have to resign, either. Haig said he would try to persuade the President.

Richardson was in for another surprise when he was given a copy of Cox's letter to Wright, which referred to the fact that the special prosecutor had been asked categorically "not to subpoena any other White House tape, paper or document." Obviously, Cox could not accept that. Richardson pointed out that this had not been part of the proposal he had submitted to Cox.

Buzhardt said that it had been added Thursday night at the direction of the President. They had had no choice.

Haig left his office and came back soon to announce that the President had agreed to keep Cox. It had been "bloody, bloody," Haig said. "I pushed so hard that my usefulness to the President may be over."

Richardson tried to add things up in his own mind. The Stennis compromise had a new element—no future access; he was willing to accept it. Barely. Cox could resign or keep his job, as he chose—Richardson would not have to fire him. That was crucial. Richardson wouldn't have to resign. Negotiations could continue. His reasons for resigning, neatly typed, stayed folded in his pocket.

For his part, Haig thought he had Richardson on board. Now, Buzhardt said, the problem was to find a way to contain Cox. Might it not be simply done? Just order him not to go to court again for tapes.

Cox would likely resign, Richardson said. But neither he nor the others appeared particularly concerned by that prospect.

When Richardson left the meeting he was sure there would be further discussion before any such orders were issued to Cox.

BACK AT his office, Richardson reviewed the White House meeting with his aides. They had expected him to resign, and they were less persuaded than Richardson was that he could permit a restriction on Cox's future access without violating his agreement with the Senate.

Richardson called back Haig and then Buzhardt, insisting to each that the question of future access must not be linked to the Stennis plan. He hung up convinced he had gained ground with both men. They had promised to take up the question with the President again. Richardson relaxed, sure that he had avoided the immediate bind.

But the President was immovable. Whatever solution was arrived at, it had to solve the problem of the tapes once and for all, he told Buzhardt and Haig.

They continued to cast about for other pliant customers who would buy the Stennis compromise. Since the Senate Watergate Committee had lost its own suit for the tapes two days earlier, it might be receptive. They tracked down the chairman and the vice-chairman, Senators Sam Ervin and Howard J. Baker, Jr., in New Orleans and Chicago. They were flown back to the White House to meet the President late in the afternoon. The Stennis plan would be fine with them, both agreed. It was better than nothing.

Now the compromise had the stamp of reasonableness—Richardson, Stennis, Ervin and Baker.

At 7 P.M., Haig called Richardson to read him a letter from the President that, he said, was on its way to him: " 'I am instructing you to direct Special Prosecutor Archibald Cox of the Watergate Special Prosecution Force that he is to make no further attempts by judicial process to obtain tapes, notes or memoranda of Presidential conversations.' "

Richardson was distressed that he had not been consulted.

Haig said he had done his best. He had twice tried to make Richardson's position clear to the President. He had failed.

Richardson took care to avoid saying whether or not he would issue the order.

Haig figured that Richardson was balking on the order to Cox, but that he was still with them in supporting the Stennis compromise in principle. He hung up. They had to act fast. It was decided to announce the order through a White House press release, thus eliminating Richardson as intermediary. The order, in the President's name, was made directly to Cox, "as an employee of the executive branch."

Haig called the senior staff to the Roosevelt Room. Bryce Harlow, a presidential counselor of the first Nixon administration, who had been recalled to White House service after the Haldeman-Ehrlichman resignations, was cranky because he hadn't been included in the negotiations. He was also due at Jean Pierre, a popular Washington restaurant, for dinner. But he drew the assignment of notifying the Cabinet members of the Stennis compromise and of the order to Cox to cease and desist. Harlow thought he had reached all of them when the White House operator called him to say that Attorney General Richardson was on the line.

"Elliot," Harlow said, "I didn't mean to call you. There is no point in my talking to you about this compromise. You already know about it. I've been calling all your damn peers around the country and telling them—"

"Well, Bryce," Richardson interrupted, "I'm sitting here preparing a press statement.* I'm not at all sure I can do what is requested of me. I will not do what the White House asks of me."

"What are you talking about, Elliot?" Harlow was amazed at the contrast between Richardson's tone and Haig's earlier enthusiastic presentation.

"I've never been so shabbily treated in my life," Richardson said.

---

* It said that the Stennis compromise was "reasonable and constructive," but took issue with the restriction on future access to the President's tapes. "I plan to seek an early opportunity to discuss this with the President," it ended lamely. Because the President never released his letter to Richardson, the Attorney General did not issue his response.

"Elliot, there is no sense in your telling me. I don't know, and I don't want to know. Just don't do anything irretrievable or irrevocable."

Harlow hung up. Surely Haig was aware of how Richardson felt. Why hadn't Haig told him that Richardson was so out of sorts about the whole thing? He went over to the restaurant and had a good solid martini. Haig called him there, wanting to know how the Cabinet members had reacted.

"I didn't bother to call you," Harlow replied, "because they all liked it. Except Elliot, of course."

"What do you mean, 'except Elliot, of course'?"

There was a pause, and then Harlow said, "Al, don't tell me. It can't be that you don't know what Elliot is about to do?"

"What do you mean?"

"He's drawing up a press statement. He feels put upon and shabbily treated."

"That's absolutely dumbfounding," Haig said. "On what grounds does he feel put upon?"

Harlow said he had no idea.

Haig called Richardson and angrily led him back through the events of the week, reminding him that he had been party to each phase of the compromise. He had gone along with everything that had happened, even the restrictions on future access. And on that, Haig reminded him, the President was inflexible. Haig had, after all, taken Richardson off the hook by having the order issued through the White House, rather than forcing Richardson to issue it himself. So why was Richardson so upset?

"You're probably right," Richardson replied. "I'm home now. I don't feel so bad about it now that I've had a drink. Things look a little better and we'll see where we go from here."

Haig began to discuss initial reactions to the compromise. Prominent members of both parties were favorably disposed toward it.

Richardson let one more opportunity for confrontation pass. He did not like bloodletting. He thanked Haig for his call. Richardson had negotiated the Agnew resignation, and he felt he could once again avert a national trauma.

Cox was now faced with an order from the President to abstain from seeking more tapes. In fact, Cox was getting no tapes. The Stennis compromise—no compromise, in his mind—was being railroaded through. Cox reasoned that he had the court, the law and the Attorney General on his side. He announced that he would have a press conference early the next afternoon, Saturday, October 20.

When Buzhardt heard about Cox's conference, he thought: Cox is going to resign; that will be tough, but the President can weather it.

Richardson reached Cox just as the special prosecutor was about to appear before the television cameras. Richardson said he was sending the President a letter stating his disagreement with the restriction on future access. He made no attempt to dissuade Cox from having the press conference. Wary that Cox no longer trusted him, he did not ask the prosecutor what he was going to say.

Cox stepped before the cameras. ". . . Now, eventually a President can always work his will," he said. "You remember when Andrew Jackson wanted to take the deposits from the Bank of the United States and his Secretary of the Treasury wouldn't do it. He fired him and then he appointed a new Secretary of the Treasury, and *he* wouldn't do it, and he fired him. And finally he got a third who would. That's one way of proceeding."

Cox was not going to resign, he told the country. He would press in court for the tapes. He might be compelled to ask that the President be held in contempt if he refused to turn over the tapes.

To Nixon this was the ultimate defiance. He had issued a clear order to Cox, who was an employee of the executive branch. Everyone in the government was going off on his own tack. The Defense Department had refused to voluntarily provide technical advice on the tapes to the White House, and a presidential order had been necessary to get them to do so. Kissinger and the new Secretary of Defense, James R. Schlesinger, were openly fighting. Treasury Secretary George P. Shultz and Budget Director Roy L. Ash were going at each other in public. There was no way the President could hold the government together in the face of Cox's grandstand challenge on national television. There was a war on in the Middle East. He needed to show he was in control. He told Haig to have Cox fired.

Haig called Richardson and ordered him to fire Cox. He was pretty sure Richardson wouldn't do it. As expected, Richardson replied that he wanted to see the President, to submit his resignation. In the midafternoon Richardson went to the White House, and Haig started working him over. He must not resign now. Fire Cox, wait a week, and then resign.

"What do you want me to do," Richardson asked sarcastically, "write a letter of resignation, get it notarized to prove I wrote it today, and let it surface in a week?"

"That's not a bad idea," Haig replied matter-of-factly.

"I want to see the President," Richardson said.

THIRTY MINUTES earlier, speech writer Pat Buchanan had gone into the Oval Office to talk to Nixon. Cox had to go, Buchanan told him. The presidency could not endure insubordination. The President said that the Cox situation and the Middle East were symbiotic. He had to show strength. If he was weak on Cox, he would have no credibility with the Russians or the belligerents in the Middle East. A Harvard professor must not be allowed to undermine his power.

Buchanan concurred, though they both knew that firing Cox would invite a move to impeach. The President was willing to face the consequences. Buchanan admired the Old Man. He had guts.

Richardson came in at 4:30 P.M.

"Elliot," the President pleaded with him as the Attorney General entered, "Brezhnev wouldn't understand if I didn't fire Cox after all this." Nixon urged Richardson to delay.

Richardson said he could not. He was thinking to himself this was the worst moment in all his years of service in government. He was standing there, refusing an urgent demand of the President of the United States. Richardson the team player.

"I'm sorry you feel that you have to act on your commitment to Cox and his independence," the President said, "and not the larger public interest."

There was a flash of anger. "Maybe," Richardson replied hotly, "your perception and my perception of the public interest differ."

That was the end.

Deputy Attorney General William D. Ruckelshaus was now the Acting Attorney General. Haig phoned him, pounding away on the Middle East situation. He painted a picture of cataclysm if Ruckelshaus did not fire Cox. "As you probably know," he said, "Elliot Richardson feels he cannot execute the orders of the President."

"That is right, I know that."

"Are you prepared to do so?"

"No."

"Well, you know what it means when an order comes down from the Commander in Chief and a member of his team cannot execute it."

"That is right."

Haig thought Ruckelshaus was fired. Ruckelshaus presumed he had resigned.

AT ABOUT 6 P.M., Solicitor General Robert H. Bork, the third in command at the Justice Department, accepted the order and signed the White House draft of a two-paragraph letter firing Cox. At 8:22 P.M., Ziegler appeared in the press briefing room at the White House to announce that Cox had been discharged. Though Richardson had never delivered the order to Cox, Ziegler announced that "the President took this action because of Mr. Cox's refusal to comply with the instructions given Friday night, through Attorney General Richardson. . . ." Further, "the office of the Watergate Special Prosecution Force has been abolished as of approximately 8 P.M."

Some of Ziegler's aides counted in split seconds the interval between Ziegler's return to his office and the moment when the television correspondents, having sprinted to the White House lawn, began talking, panting, live on the air.

The firestorm, as Haig referred to it, had begun.

After 9 P.M., Haig sent FBI officers to seal off the offices of Richardson, Ruckelshaus and Cox to prevent any files from being removed.

The television networks offered hour-long specials. The newspapers carried banner headlines. Within two days, 150,000 telegrams had arrived in the capital, the largest concentrated volume in the history of Western Union. Deans of the most prestigious law schools in the country demanded that Congress commence an impeachment inquiry.

By the following Tuesday, forty-four separate Watergate-related bills had been introduced in the House. Twenty-two called for an impeachment investigation.

To THE President and Haig, Richardson had failed them. He had accepted the Stennis compromise. He had been willing to let Cox resign. He had voiced no objection to bypassing Cox and taking the compromise directly to Sirica. They had accommodated Richardson and made it possible for him to avoid personally ordering Cox to seek no more evidence.

It was only when Cox publicly defied the President that he had to be fired. It was that damned Saturday press conference that had done the most damage, Haig concluded. And Richardson had let Cox have that press conference; in fact, it seemed he had even encouraged it. If Richardson had held a tighter rein on Cox, the press and the public would have perceived the issue differently. It would have been Cox who seemed unreasonable, who was unwilling to compromise.

Cox, Richardson, and Ruckelshaus had become overnight folk heroes. Haig's resentment of Richardson was deep. Haig had to deal with a President who had been irrational on the subject of Cox, calling him a "fanatic" and worse, railing at the fact that some of the Kennedys had attended his swearing-in. It had been difficult to contain the President, and Haig had depended on Richardson for support. When the going had gotten rough, Richardson had folded. It amounted to desertion under fire.

Haig and Richardson had often commiserated on how difficult it was to deal with the President. They had shared their deep-seated concern about Nixon's stability. Now Richardson had dumped it all on Haig, and Richardson was being praised for insubordination. Loyalty, working for the good of the country, staying on the team, were being called into question.

Haig warned the White House staff, and a few reporters, about Richardson: "Beware of holding Richardson up as a hero." Haig said he would not go into specifics, he did not want to get into a shouting match with Richardson, but . . . "Elliot has a drinking problem . . . he has been less than honest."

IN THE aftermath of the Saturday Night Massacre, the options for the White House were not attractive. Haig and the lawyers reasoned that the credibility of the Stennis compromise had vanished.

In their determination to push the Stennis plan through, they had decided not to submit the Supreme Court appeal which Wright had drafted. The deadline for compliance with the Court of Appeals' order had passed at midnight Friday. Though appeal to the Supreme Court was still technically possible, another appeal would strain White House credibility even further and prolong the public focus on the tapes. And it would risk the possibility of losing in the Supreme Court, thus setting a dangerous precedent. Buzhardt guessed that they would have no better than a 50–50 chance in the Supreme Court.

Sirica had called a hearing for the afternoon of Tuesday, October 23, at which the White House was to formally respond to his order to begin giving up the tapes. Over the weekend, the lawyers had submitted a copy of the Stennis plan and a supporting brief to the judge.

At noon that Tuesday, Buzhardt asked urgently to see the President. He was told to wait. The President was busy. Wright was waiting for Buzhardt. They were due in court by 2 P.M. By the time Buzhardt entered the Oval Office, there was less than an hour left. Options, Buzhardt informed the President, were scarce. They could defy the order to turn over the tapes or they could comply.

The President asked whether there were other alternatives.

Buzhardt said that Judge Sirica was not likely to grant an extension for an appeal to be made to the Supreme Court. Such extensions were normally requested before the expiration of the first deadline. In the present climate, such a request would be absurd. If the tapes were not produced, Sirica would order a show-cause hearing. The President's attorneys would have to appear in court to argue why the President should not be held in contempt. That would be ugly. Outright defiance would end in impeachment.

The President just sat there. He had established this elaborate staff system, with option papers, with sufficient lead time, to prevent this sort of panic. Cox was gone. That was the central issue. Nixon tapped his fingers on the desk.

Buzhardt repeated himself. There was really no choice, he said. Turning over the tapes would have tremendous shock value. It would show everyone that Cox had not been fired because of damaging information on the tapes— as most of the President's critics claimed. Turning them over was precisely what no one expected.

"Okay, comply," the President said finally.

BUZHARDT LEFT the Oval Office and went down the hall to Haig's office. Haig and Wright were there. Wright had been preparing to argue on behalf of the Stennis compromise, and he was relieved to hear of the President's decision to relinquish. He began to formulate his response to Sirica. At one-thirty, as he was getting ready to leave for court, the President summoned him to the Oval Office, along with Buzhardt and Garment.

For nearly a half hour, the President wondered out loud if he was making the right decision. Wright was concerned that he would be late to court. "Mr. President," he said, "we've got to go."

The President sought one last reassurance. "Do you really think this is the right thing to do, Charlie? We've fought for this principle so long—should we give up now?"

Wright reassured the President that the principle was not lost. No precedents were being set. It was the right course.

The President simply nodded as he dismissed them, and Wright rushed off for court. It was just after 2 P.M. when Wright, wearing a brown suit and a lime-green shirt, arrived at the crowded courtroom. He paused nervously to drink several cups of water.

Sirica entered. He didn't like dramatic courtroom confrontations, and he expected one this afternoon. His nerves were getting to him. Without mentioning the Stennis compromise, he read for ten minutes from the Court of Appeals decision. The reading had a calming effect. Sirica expected the White House to offer the Stennis compromise formally. He didn't agree with it, primarily for the reasons Cox had rejected it. Besides, he knew Senator

Stennis, and he doubted whether the Senator was capable of spending the dozens of hours it would take to review the tapes. The White House would appeal his ruling rejecting the Stennis compromise, Sirica presumed, or else they would ask for more time to appeal the Court of Appeals decision. Either way, the matter, it seemed, was going to the Supreme Court. Sirica welcomed it.

But Charles Alan Wright rose to announce that the President would comply in full. "This President does not defy the law."

The courtroom was silent for a few seconds.

Flabbergasted, Sirica broke into a grin. "The court is very happy the President has reached this decision," he said.

Reporters almost fell over themselves racing to the telephones.

Sirica retired to his chambers. As he often did after a tense hearing, he lay down to wait for the pounding of his heart to slow. Finally he was going to hear some tapes.

THE ABOLITION of the special prosecutor's office had been largely an afterthought, a last-minute attempt by the President to get the investigation back on a more manageable track, within the Justice Department. But the furious reaction to the Saturday Night Massacre persisted; Nixon agreed to the appointment of another special prosecutor. The main problem had been that "fucking Harvard professor," not the office.

Haig began the search for Cox's successor with his political consciousness raised. The new man would be examined under a microscope by the Congress and the public. He would have to be universally respected, a man with a reputation for integrity and toughness, a Democrat but not a partisan, a man known for his independence. But obviously Haig needed a man sensitive to the special problems of the White House, who would recognize the need to protect national security, and who would be flexible in balancing the necessity of prosecuting the accused and the need to protect the presidency: a reasonable man, who would avoid the stridency of a Cox and keep the channels to the White House open.

Haig called Morris Leibman, an old friend from his days in the Johnson Administration. Leibman, a senior partner in the prestigious Chicago law firm of Sidley and Austin and an unpaid adviser to the White House on defense matters, had been urging Haig for months to bring in an eminent legal panel to advise the President on Watergate. Leibman had pulled together an all-purpose list of candidates: past presidents of the American Bar Association, prominent trial attorneys from the nation's top law firms, deans of law schools, former Justice Department lawyers. Haig and Leibman had been over the list before: James D. St. Clair, a Boston trial lawyer; Albert Jenner, a Chicago trial attorney; John Doar, a former Assistant General in the Kennedy Justice Department; dozens more.

Haig pared the list down. He wasn't interested in anyone who wanted to write his role into history, or any law professors. One had been enough. Haig asked Leibman about one person on his list, Houston trial lawyer Leon Jaworski.

Leibman said Jaworski was well known and had a good track record. He would pass muster with the Senate. Jaworski, sixty-eight, had served as a special prosecutor before, in 1962, when Attorney General Robert Kennedy appointed him to represent the United States against Mississippi Governor Ross Barnett's attempt to prevent the registration of James H. Meredith as the first black student at the University of Mississippi. Jaworski had prosecuted war criminals at Nuremberg. The son of a rural Baptist minister, he had made a fortune in private practice in booming postwar Houston. He was a Rotarian and a director of the Red Cross. He had been president of the American Bar Association in 1971–72. And he was a Democrat.

On October 30, Jaworski received a call from Haig in his green-carpeted office on the eighth floor of the Bank of the Southwest in downtown Houston. The plaques and autographed pictures on all four walls testified to Jaworski's energetic service to the bar, the community, the state, the nation, and the well-connected friends he had made in the process, among them Lyndon Johnson, John Connally and Chief Justice Warren Burger.

Jaworski's energy matched an ego of equal proportion. He was not surprised by the call. It was his impression that he had already turned down the job of special prosecutor once, in May, when Cox got the job. In fact Jaworski's name had been one of several under consideration, and one of Elliot Richardson's assistants had called to sound him out. He was not interested under the circumstances. "There's not enough independence," he said. The Department of Justice would control the special prosecutor.

Now, one special prosecutor later, things had changed. "We have this problem," Haig told Jaworski. "We have been conducting an investigation. Both Acting Attorney General Bork and I have been calling around, and we're convinced that you are the person to succeed Cox."

"General Haig," Jaworski replied, "are you aware of the fact that I, in effect, turned down the job once because it lacked the necessary independence?"

Haig said it was going to be different this time, but Jaworski acted dubious.

"We're ready to meet your terms," Haig said. "If you'll at least come up here to discuss it . . ."

Jaworski was still disinclined, but they talked for an hour.

"Will you at least come up in the morning? We'll send a plane to pick you up," Haig said.

The next morning, October 31, Jaworski boarded a government jet at Ellington Air Force Base, and he was in Haig's office by noon. He found Haig's friendliness almost overbearing. Haig had a penetrating stare, and his eyes appeared to change colors according to his mood, from cold steel gray to a warm, twinkling sky blue. His face was remarkably mobile, at one moment taut and pained, at the next relaxed and genial, then stern, sober, soldierly.

The country was in a state of virtual revolution after the Cox firing, Haig said. Watergate might wreck the nation. The Middle East, arms limitation, the economy, were all hanging in the balance. Really, only Jaworski would do.

Haig was persuasive, and flattering: Only Jaworski had the personal and professional stature; he was tough, independent-minded and not politically ambitious; he knew and understood the presidency, and he understood what national security and state secrets were. Haig appealed to his patriotism. Did Jaworski want to see the President?

"I prefer not to," Jaworski answered. If he could get the White House to accept his terms, he wanted to be able to say he had had no contact with the President. And his terms were stiff. The President could not fire him except for extraordinary improprieties; he must be guaranteed the right to sue the President in the courts for tapes or other evidence.

"You will have the freedom," Haig told him.

Haig asked again if Jaworski wanted to see the President.

No.

Would he take the job?

Yes.

Haig was exultant, and as for Leon Jaworski, he had the most secure job in the government. Jaworski had to go to the Baylor University homecoming parade to be grand marshal. He would be back on Monday.

Jaworski's appointment, announced on Sunday by the White House, was viewed skeptically by the shaken Cox loyalists on the prosecutor's staff. But when two of them picked him up at the airport on Monday, Jaworski stepped off the plane alone. To underline his commitment to the staff, he had not even brought his secretary. The special prosecutor moved into an apartment in the old Jefferson Hotel, five blocks from the White House.

CHAPTER FIVE

THE relief that the White House lawyers felt when Nixon finally decided to turn over the tapes died quickly. On Saturday, November 3,
Buzhardt and Garment were on that Eastern flight 177 to Florida,
with their recommendation to the President that he resign.

Nixon's refusal to see them was only symptomatic of a situation that had
become nearly impossible. By Monday, back in Washington, a kind of group
acquiescence had evolved among the lawyers. Had their client been anyone
other than the President of the United States, they would have resigned
from the case. But their problem was more complicated—a mixture of fact
and law, law and public policy, responsibility to the bar, to the presidency,
to Richard Nixon, to their own consciences. They agreed for the moment to
accept the rules of engagement, rules which were bound by presidential
service. They would stay for the next act.

Buzhardt had the immediate problem: he was due to testify in Sirica's
courtroom that week. He and Haig, sometimes joined by Garment, began
meeting regularly in the general's office to debate the ethics of the situation
and to calculate their next moves. The sessions were long, interrupted only
by tense three- or four-minute meetings between Haig and Nixon. The
atmosphere was charged; the lawyers felt themselves in an almost adversary
relationship with their client. Nixon informed them, through Haig, that he
would forbid Buzhardt to testify; he would invoke the attorney-client
privilege.

The lawyers went to Sirica and, in chambers, gloomily made known the President's intention. The judge served notice that he would rule against any such claim of privilege.

Haig, Buzhardt and Garment discussed the matter with Nixon. If he claimed the privilege, the lawyers warned him, it would further an appearance of cover-up. Haig concurred. He knew that Buzhardt had reluctantly decided that he must testify, even if Nixon were to order him not to. The lawyer couldn't be part of a privilege invoked because the President feared disclosure of his proposal to manufacture a Dictabelt. Buzhardt hardly wanted to be the instrument of Nixon's destruction, but he had to protect himself now.

At last the President relented. He was counting on Buzhardt to help him.

Haig and the lawyers sat down at the big work table in the general's office to discuss what Buzhardt should say on the witness stand. They agreed on an evasive approach: Buzhardt would volunteer no information and he would try to avoid the whole subject of the April 15 Dictabelt. But he would answer questions truthfully.

On Friday, November 9, Assistant Special Prosecutor Richard Ben-Veniste began his questioning. Buzhardt was represented by Sam Powers, a Florida attorney who had been retained by the White House to assist in the tape proceedings. It was late in the afternoon when Ben-Veniste finally got to the subject of the Dictabelt. Sirica wanted to adjourn until Monday.

"Your honor, I have one question," Ben-Veniste said.

Sirica told him to proceed.

"Mr. Buzhardt, did you have personal knowledge of the existence of a tape recording made by the President, dictated by him, following the meeting with John Dean on the fifteenth of April?"

Buzhardt squinted at his interrogator. "Would you ask that again, Mr. Ben-Veniste?"

"Did you have personal knowledge as of June sixteenth, 1973, of the existence of a recording made by the President on a Dictabelt or other machine, a one-sided recording, where the President dictated a recollection of a meeting which he had with John Dean on the fifteenth of April, 1973?"

"I will answer it this way, Mr. Ben-Veniste. My letter indicated the state of my knowledge at that time, so I don't know how to answer your question as to personal knowledge. I had never seen such."

"You had never seen such?"

"I had never seen such," Buzhardt repeated.

"Had you ever seen such a recording?" Ben-Veniste tried again.

"No."

"Have you ever asked to see such a recording?"

Sam Powers was on his feet. "If your honor please, I submit we are going beyond—counsel said he had one question, and I think that matters are being entered into—"

Sirica interrupted him. "Well, we will have to probably decide this Monday morning. So let us adjourn now until Monday morning."

On November 12, Ben-Veniste resumed his questioning.

"Now as a matter of fact there is no Dictabelt conversation of the President's recollections of his meeting with Mr. Dean, isn't that so?" he asked.

"Yes, that is correct," Buzhardt responded. "We have not been able to locate one. Later on that day, he [the President] found contemporaneous notes he made from the meetings."

"When did it come to your attention for the first time there was no Dictabelt of the President's recollection, Mr. Buzhardt?"

"I believe that was on November fifth, last Monday, a week ago," Buzhardt said. That was the day of the final search. He did not mention the discussions of the week before that—first with Nixon at the White House, then with Haig and Ziegler in Florida.

". . . Did you personally make any effort to find this Dictabelt?"

Buzhardt described the search in vague terms. Ben-Veniste turned to the question of the other missing tapes. Buzhardt was off the hook.

THAT AFTERNOON, the White House released a long detailed presidential statement about the two missing tapes and the Dictabelt.* There were more headlines and more ugly questions, but the outpouring of protest abated somewhat.

The larger question now was the contents of tapes, not their accounting or the absence of some. When finally, on November 14, Buzhardt sat down to listen to the President's recordings, he felt that it was only because he had outlasted Nixon's intransigence.

Haig had insisted to him, "The President decides who listens to what, and he is not delegating his responsibility to lawyers." But now the tapes were going to Judge Sirica, and someone had to make a damage assessment.

---

* In his statement the President said: "Over the weekend of November 4 and 5, 1973, upon checking my personal diary file for April 15, 1973, . . . I found that my file for that day consists of personal notes of the conversation held with John Dean on the evening of April 15, 1973, but not a dictation belt. . . . I believed in June that I had dictated my recollections of April 15, 1973, of conversations which occurred on that day. The response to the Special Prosecutor made on June 16, 1973, referred to such a dictation belt. At that time, however, I did not review my file to confirm that it contained the belt."

The other seven subpoenaed tapes had been copied the day before, and the originals placed under court seal. Buzhardt was holed up in an anteroom next to the Oval Office with Sam Powers at his side. They were to analyze the contents of each conversation and prepare an index to the sections for which executive privilege was to be claimed. Under Sirica's order, the judge was to rule on each claim of privilege before submitting the tapes to the special prosecutor.

Buzhardt had grown accustomed to the long hours and the constant pressure. He accepted the fact that this day and night would be particularly long and tiring.

He flipped through the white cardboard boxes of 3M tape on the round mahogany table, reading the handwriting on the bindings as he searched for the earliest reel: "EOB Office," "Start 6-12-72," "End 6-20-72" . . .

Powers and he turned to the special prosecutor's subpoena to determine which conversations were required. The first listing read: "(a) Meeting of June 20, 1972, in the President's Executive Office Building (EOB) office involving Richard Nixon, John Ehrlichman and H. R. Haldeman from 10:30 A.M. to noon (time approximate)."

This was the conversation that, six weeks earlier, Rose Mary Woods had told him she'd had trouble finding, Buzhardt explained to Powers. There had been no single meeting with all three participants on June 20, 1972, according to the President's daily log. The log indicated two meetings. The President had met Ehrlichman from 10:25 to 11:20, and Haldeman from 11:26 to 12:45.

Buzhardt had advised Woods that the subpoena applied only to the Ehrlichman meeting; she was not to concern herself about the Haldeman meeting. Haig and the President had told Buzhardt a few days later that there was a problem: As Woods was transcribing the first meeting and searching ahead to find when Ehrlichman had left the room (and thus where the meeting ended), she had accidentally erased four or five minutes of the second conversation.

Well, Buzhardt told Powers, that explained why the technicians' meter readings indicated that segments of the tapes were blank. They could expect to find such a place on the tape just after the subpoenaed discussion. Double-checking what was called for by the subpoena, he asked if Powers agreed that the Haldeman conversation, now partially obliterated, was not among the items called for. Powers pointed out that a memorandum submitted to the court by Cox in support of his subpoena had a clarifying clause. After listing the Ehrlichman conversation, the memo added: ". . . then Haldeman went to see the President." Though the subpoena's reference to a single meeting involving all three men might be ambiguous, the supporting memo was clear. It contained an additional distinction: "From 10:30 A.M. until 12:45 P.M." Powers was sure both meetings had to be provided.

Buzhardt unhappily agreed. Why hadn't he read the prosecutor's memo carefully when it arrived in August? he wondered aloud. The erased portion of the tape was under subpoena.

With Powers' assistance, he began plowing back and forth through the Ehrlichman meeting on the Sony 800B. First Buzhardt listened alone, then he rewound the machine and turned one of the earphones toward Powers. The two men listened, their heads pressed together like Siamese twins. They timed each segment with a stopwatch, marking the indices to privileged material. They struggled to hear the words. Voices rose and fell and sometimes faded completely. China cups met saucers in a clamor, feet crashed onto desks. Straining, they listened to the voices through the background noises. What they heard had nothing even remotely to do with Watergate. The conversation would be covered by executive privilege.

They listened on beyond the point that Woods had been told was the end of the subpoenaed conversation, waiting for the four- or five-minute segment she said she had erased.

They heard the buzz and waited for it to end. They waited longer than five minutes, longer than ten, longer than fifteen. At last it ended.

They rewound the tape and listened again, this time using the stopwatch. Four and a half minutes into the buzz, the pitch changed. It sounded like a separate erasure to Buzhardt. The total gap was eighteen minutes and fifteen seconds long.

Buzhardt hurried to tell Haig, leaving Powers to guard the tapes. Even in the security of the White House, they were afraid of leaving the tapes alone for a few minutes in a locked room. Buzhardt poked his head into Haig's office, and the general walked over to the door.

"I've got yet another problem," Buzhardt said.

"Fine—I'll be with you when I finish," said Haig, and he went to resume his discussion of the Middle East with William E. Timmons, head of the congressional-relations staff, and General Brent Scowcroft, Haig's successor as deputy to Henry Kissinger. Buzhardt, effectively dismissed, went back to the tapes.

It was almost 9 P.M. when Haig walked down the hall and into the office where Buzhardt and Powers sat fretfully preparing the index.

Buzhardt's normally soft voice was now nearly inaudible. "Do you recall the accident that Rose described to the President?"

Of course Haig recalled.

"We have just put a timer on the gap, and instead of four and a half to five minutes it runs eighteen-plus minutes," Buzhardt said.

Haig looked surprised.

"But that is not all," Buzhardt continued. "I have reassessed and re-checked the subpoena, and both Sam and I have concluded that this in fact is a subpoenaed conversation."

Haig exploded. "Well, dammit, Fred, this is a pretty late date to be telling me something like that."

He demanded to see the subpoena. His eyebrows pulled together as he read. "This is pretty goddam ambiguous, Fred. How can you tell what this means, anyway? It could be interpreted either way, couldn't it?"

"Yes," said Buzhardt, "but there is an additional exposition describing the subpoenaed items." He passed him the Cox memorandum.

"I must share your judgment," Haig said finally. "How the hell could we have been confused on this, Fred?"

Buzhardt had no satisfactory answer. He simply hadn't focused on the clarifying memorandum when it came in, he said. It was a small portion of the special prosecutor's brief in the earlier litigation.

Haig was too practical to waste time arguing. What sort of gap was it?

Buzhardt didn't know. There were two distinct parts to the buzz.

What could they do now? Haig asked. Perhaps the conversation could be recovered.

Buzhardt's four years in the Army Air Force as a communications officer and electronics and radar repair specialist made him skeptical. Perhaps, but it was doubtful.

Haig was faced with informing the President. The timing was absolutely awful. The President was in the midst of a very, very difficult week. In addition to the Middle East and energy crises, Nixon was conducting a public-relations campaign to assert his innocence and reestablish his credibility. Over the next two days he was scheduled to meet with five different congressional groups. By the next day, he would have met with all 234 Republican members of Congress. At that very moment he was seeing some Senators. The next morning he was to address the National Association of Realtors. There would be heavy press and photo coverage.

Haig worried about the effect of the news on the Old Man. The constant public exposure throughout the week would be a strain. This news, coming so soon after the disclosure that two of the subpoenaed conversations were not on tape, would be devastating to the President's position. The additional pressure would take its toll. Haig wanted to wait.

THE NEXT morning, while Haig kept his silence, the President met with seventy-eight Republican Congressmen, who applauded as Nixon said emotionally, "I'm not going to walk away from my job." Even the President's critics in the room were impressed by his determination to stay and fight. Haig thought the session had gone well, and he still kept quiet.

Later in the morning, the President was given a standing ovation by three thousand members of the National Association of Realtors. Blaming Watergate and other campaign abuses on "overzealous" associates, Nixon said they had made "mistakes that I never approved of, mistakes that I would never have tolerated, but mistakes for which I will have to take the responsibility."

Haig waited another fifty minutes while the President sat for pictures with members of the American Legion and met with Cambodia's ambassador and Minister of Foreign Affairs. Then, at 12:36 P.M., he went into the Oval Office to break the news.

The President blew up. He was so enraged that such a mistake had been committed that Haig didn't know for a while which mistake Nixon was referring to. Then it was clear. The President was outraged not at the gap but at Buzhardt's error. What the hell were they supposed to do now? he wanted to know. It was incredible that Buzhardt could have made such a blunder. Did they have to turn the tape over? How would they explain the gap? What was wrong with his lawyers?

Haig adroitly stepped aside. Perhaps, he suggested, it would be best if the President talked directly to his counsel about it. Reluctantly the President agreed. He would see Buzhardt at his first opportunity, that afternoon. Haig walked his very disturbed boss out of the Oval Office. The President went to his EOB office for lunch and a quick nap.

By three o'clock, Haig was checking on why the President was taking so long to see Buzhardt. Ziegler, Rose Woods and Steve Bull had been in and out of the President's EOB office all afternoon. Aside from Nixon, Haldeman and the Secret Service, Woods and Bull were the only ones who had handled tapes.

A few minutes before 4 P.M., the President walked back to the White House and upstairs to the residence. Half an hour later he finally returned to the Oval Office, where he rang Haig's aide, Major George Joulwan, and said he was ready to meet with Buzhardt and Haig.

They found the President sitting with Ziegler; his ire had subsided, at least visibly. Haig knew very well that the President rarely allowed his anger to show. Predictably, Nixon did not confront Buzhardt.

Buzhardt, in his mild way, reported what he had found the previous evening. The President appeared concerned but calm as Buzhardt described the sounds of the two tones.

What did he think might have happened? the President asked.

Buzhardt said he had no answers.

What had been on the tape?

Buzhardt didn't know that either.

Nixon said he could not recall what had occurred in the conversation. He had tried, but . . .

Buzhardt probed discreetly. Did the President have any explanation for what might have happened?

Well, he had spoken to Rose Mary earlier in the afternoon, Nixon said, and she was very upset and confused. Could there be some explanation other than an erasure? Nixon asked. Some technical fault with the equipment? Something which would account for the discrepancy between the length of the gap as Rose recalled it and the fact that it was now more than eighteen minutes long? Could it have been caused by a foot pedal, by some combination of two controls activated at once, anything like that?

Buzhardt was not sure, but he would check. He discerned that the President was extremely concerned about the gap, but there was something evasive in Nixon's approach, something disturbing about his reaction. To Buzhardt, he seemed to be suggesting alternative explanations for the lawyer's benefit, speculating on various excuses as if to say, "Well, couldn't we go with one of those versions?"

Buzhardt prided himself on being able to tell when the President was lying. Usually it wasn't difficult. Nixon was perhaps the most transparent liar he had ever met. Almost invariably when the President lied, he would repeat himself, sometimes as often as three times—as if he were trying to convince himself. But this time Buzhardt couldn't tell. One moment he thought Nixon was responsible, at another he suspected Woods. Maybe both of them had done it. One thing seemed fairly certain: it was no accident. On balance, Buzhardt was more inclined to think it was Woods. If the President had erased it, he would have told someone: A client willing to suggest manufacturing evidence would be as recklessly candid about destroying it.

Buzhardt tried again. Perhaps Woods had mentioned something else, or perhaps she knew more than she had told.

No, the President said. Buzhardt knew as much about it as he did.

There would be serious trouble ahead, Buzhardt warned him.

Nixon exploded. "What the hell do you expect me to do about it?" he shouted at Buzhardt.

Buzhardt recoiled.

Calming down, Nixon turned to the possibility of recovering the conversation through some electronic means. Buzhardt doubted that it could be done, but he agreed to pursue it.

"We should try to get hold of any notes that Bob may have made during the meeting," Buzhardt suggested. "They might shed some light."

The President agreed. Then Haig sent Buzhardt off to get the notes from Haldeman's files, which were secured in a file room in the EOB and guarded by the Secret Service. Within minutes Buzhardt was back in Haig's office. He did not have the combination to Haldeman's file cabinet.

Haig remembered that when he had taken over from Haldeman in May the departing chief of staff had told him he had ordered the combination changed. Fine, Haig had said, but be sure to leave the combination with the President.

While Buzhardt waited, Haig went to Woods. Had Haldeman given the President the combination? She checked her files. He had not.

Haig was angry. Apparently Haldeman's arrogance knew no bounds; he still thought of the White House as his private preserve. Haig called him at his home in California and explained the problem. "Bob, I want that combination held at the White House," Haig said, "and nowhere else." Haldeman responded that the quickest way to get the material would be to have his former administrative assistant, Larry Higby, retrieve it. There were more than forty drawers of notes and papers stored in the file room. He would call Higby with the combination and direct him to locate the file.

Passively, Haig accepted Haldeman's arrangements.

Higby was in the White House gym when Haldeman called from California at 5:45 P.M. He was trying to get a quick shave before going out for the evening with his wife.

Higby had worked for Haldeman for five years, carrying out his orders in such efficient style that administrative assistants in the executive branch were called "Higbys" by the White House staff. Higby had an aide who was known as "Higby's Higby." Now banished to the office of another former Haldeman aide, Fred Malek, deputy director of the Office of Management and Budget, Higby loyally ran Haldeman's Washington errands.

Haldeman was typically precise and direct. Describing the problem briefly, he gave Higby the combination to his file cabinet and specific instructions: "Go to Haig's office; tell him you will get the notes; go to the file room; open the safe; pull out the second drawer; remove the brown cardboard pouch for April to June 1972 and the pouch for April 1973; in one of the two you will find a yellow pad of notes for the meeting in question; remove it from the pouch and call me back; read me the notes; and do not under any circumstances give the document to anybody until you have called me and gotten my approval. Do not under any circumstances deviate from this procedure. If there is any deviation from my instructions, call me before proceeding."

Higby understood. He went to Haig's office and said he would retrieve the files. Stopping by Buzhardt's office to get a more precise description of the required material, Higby went to the file room on the fifth floor of the EOB. Buzhardt followed him inside and waited.

As directed, Higby removed the pouches. Going through their contents at a corner table, he told Buzhardt he had found the right notes. Then he called Haldeman and read them over the phone while Buzhardt waited for him across the room, out of earshot.

"Hm," Haldeman said. "That's no problem. Go ahead, turn over the notes."

"Buzhardt wants the originals of the notes, Bob," Higby said.

Haldeman was troubled by that, but agreed, provided that Higby place a photocopy in his file.

CHAPTER SIX

AFTER the meeting with Haig and Buzhardt, the President walked through the Rose Garden portico to the residence. Inside, uniformed members of the Executive Protection Service straightened to attention. Nixon followed the ground-floor passageway, past the portraits of former First Ladies, to the arched entrance of the residence elevator. At the third floor he stepped out, and as he walked up the ramp he straightened from his stooped posture just before he reached the solarium.

The nine Republican Senators who were waiting for him there had been the core of the President's support within his own party. They represented both the right and the moderate wings. Their constituents wanted to know why Nixon deserved such unquestioning loyalty. The Senators were concerned about the party and their careers. They could not take any more of the revelations that had been filling the newspapers. They had to know if they could stand behind their President. They wanted his personal assurance.

He gave it. He was innocent. He would prove it. The nation needed a strong President. He needed their support to be strong. They pledged it.

The President's top political aides—Timmons, Bryce Harlow and Tom Korologos—were there to see that nothing in the way of White House hospitality was lacking. The Senators stayed for cocktails. Nixon left with Haig, who had stopped by to mingle. As they walked, the President wondered aloud what Buzhardt had found in Haldeman's files. Haig needed no further hint. He rushed dutifully to the file room. Buzhardt had just gotten the originals from Higby. Haig grabbed the notes and turned to run back. Buzhardt stopped him in midstride and directed Haig's attention to page two of Haldeman's notes.

Haig read: "What is our counter-attack? PR offensive to top this, hit the opposition w/their activities. pt out libertarians have created public clamor (?), do they justify this less than stealing Pentagon papers, Anderson file, etc. We should be on the attack—for diversion—"

Haig was really upset now. There might be some question as to exactly what was said during the meeting. There might be some question as to who or what had obliterated the stretch of tape. But there was no question about one thing: the gap wiped out a discussion of Watergate.

Haig went to tell the President.

BUZHARDT AND Powers returned to the task of listening to the subpoenaed conversations, wondering whether more tapes had gaps. The next taped discussion, of June 30, 1972, encouraged them. The material was intact and most of it was privileged—unrelated to Watergate. They reached September 15, 1972: a discussion about Watergate, involving Haldeman, Dean and the President. Dean had testified that the President had told him in this conversation, "Bob tells me what a good job you've been doing, John." Would the tape support Nixon's contention that he didn't know much about the cover-up when the original indictments* were returned that day?

The lawyers heard the President praise Dean's work: ". . . the way you, you've handled it . . . has been very skillful, because you . . . putting your fingers in the dikes every time that leaks have sprung here and sprung there." But it was impossible to know exactly what Nixon was referring to. The conversation was troublesomely ambiguous.

Buzhardt and Powers were more disturbed by another part. The President was discussing the *Washington Post* and its lawyer, Edward Bennett Williams, with Dean. "I wouldn't want to be in Edward Bennett Williams' position after this election," the President said. "We are going to fix the son of a bitch, believe me. We are going to. We've got to, because he is a bad man."

Another of the President's remarks was equally damaging. "The main thing is, the *Post* is going to have damnable, damnable problems out of this

---

* Against Hunt, Liddy, and the five men arrested inside the Watergate on June 17, 1972.

one—they have a television station and they are going to have to get it renewed," the President said.

Dean mentioned how common the practice of filing challenges to license renewals had become. "It is going to be goddam active here," the President shot back.

The President's remarks worried Buzhardt and Powers, but they decided that this portion of the conversation did not technically relate to Watergate. They would claim it as privileged and see if Sirica would uphold them.

A third segment was more disturbing: Dean complained that the IRS was not cooperating with him in his efforts to uncover damaging information about one of the contributors to the campaign of Democratic presidential candidate George McGovern. The President was outraged. "Well, goddam, they ought to give it to you," he told Dean. Nixon went on to plan how after the election he would make sure that the IRS became more cooperative. He would fire IRS Commissioner Johnnie Walters for his failure to cooperate. Then he threatened to fire his Secretary of the Treasury, the cabinet officer responsible for the IRS. "I don't want George Shultz to ever raise the question, because it would put me in the position of having to throw him out of office," the President had said. "He didn't get to be Secretary of the Treasury because he has nice blue eyes. It was a goddam favor to him to get the job."

This was exactly the kind of presidential abuse of power which the impeachment clause of the Constitution was intended to remedy, Buzhardt observed. The President was planning to use a federal agency for blatantly political purposes. But, strictly speaking, it too had nothing to do with Watergate. They would claim it as privileged, on the off chance that Sirica would see it their way.

Buzhardt expectantly threaded the March 21, 1973, tape onto the recorder. Nixon rested almost the whole of his case on this date, claiming that Dean had first informed him then of the details of the cover-up. For all its importance, the President had never listened to this tape. He had relied instead on Haldeman's reading, which matched his own recollection—that when he was told that day that the Watergate burglars were demanding a million dollars as the price of their continued silence, Nixon rejected the blackmail decisively: "It would be wrong, it would not work, the truth would come out anyway."

John Dean was claiming differently. Nixon and Dean also disagreed as to whether the President had rejected the notion of granting the burglars executive clemency.

Buzhardt listened as Dean led the President through a relatively inoffensive discussion of Patrick Gray's confirmation hearings as chief of the FBI, and of how to keep the Senate Judiciary Committee from getting FBI files. The conversation led Nixon to a favorite subject—telephone tapping by Democrats. When, he asked, was Bill Sullivan of the FBI going to bring over the list of offenses committed by previous administrations? "As soon as you get that, I'll be available to talk to you this afternoon," he told Dean. Buzhardt could hear the enthusiasm in the President's voice as he contemplated what Sullivan might have.

Dean solemnly changed the subject. "The reason I thought we ought to talk this morning is because in, in our conversations, I have, I have the impression that you don't know everything I know."

"That's right," the President said, his voice returning to normal.

Buzhardt relaxed. Dean and the President were going to corroborate what the President had been insisting on all along—that Dean had been off on his own.

Dean alerted Nixon to the "cancer," and then summed up how the cover-up had progressed through the summer of 1972 and the following winter. The problem was growing daily, geometrically, compounding itself. "That'll be clear as I explain some of the details," Dean said. "It is basically because (1) we're being blackmailed [and] (2) people are going to start perjuring themselves very quickly that have not had to perjure themselves to protect other people and the like."

Buzhardt could not have been more pleased. It was as the President had said. Dean was explaining Watergate to the President for the first time. He played it back for Powers, and then let the tape run. He could hear Dean clearly. He strained to hear the President's voice.

"How much money do you need?" Nixon asked.

"I would say these people are going to cost a million dollars over the next two years."

"We could get that," Nixon said. ". . . I mean, you could get the money . . . you could get a million dollars. And you could get it in cash. I, I know where it could be gotten. I mean it's not easy, but it could be done."

Buzhardt waited to hear the President say, "It would be wrong."

"But, uh, the question is who the hell would handle it?" Nixon droned on instead. "Any ideas on that?"

The President and his young aide discussed who could be relied on to raise the money. The payments to the burglars might be made under the cover of a Cuban defense committee. It could be concealed from a grand jury.

Buzhardt's brief optimism faded as he listened to Nixon and Dean conspire. Four times the President discussed ways to accommodate the black-mail demands, never once implying that it would be wrong. Hunt was demanding $120,000 immediately.

"Well, your, your major, your major guy to keep under control is Hunt," the President suggested. "Don't you, just looking at the immediate problem, don't you have to have—handle Hunt's financial situation damn soon?" Nixon answered his own question. It was necessary "to keep the cap on the bottle that much in order to have any options."

Powers noticed a sour expression on Buzhardt's face.

Dean told Nixon that the situation was so dangerous that aides would soon begin toppling like dominoes until finally they collapsed backward on the President. Dean was worried about being charged with obstruction of justice. He had been the conduit for paying the defendants.

The President seemed to be getting the point. "Oh, you mean like the uh, oh—the blackmail."

"The blackmail. Right."

"Well," said the President, "I wonder if that part of it can't be—I wonder if that doesn't— Let me put it frankly. I wonder if that doesn't have to be continued?"

Buzhardt shook his head and turned one earphone toward Powers.

"Let me put it this way," the President went on. "Let us suppose that you get, you, you get the million bucks, and you get the proper way to handle it, and you could hold that side. It would seem to me that would be worthwhile."

Clearing his throat, Dean started to respond. But the President inter-rupted. "Now we have one problem. You have the problem of Hunt and, uh, his, uh, his clemency."

Buzhardt and Powers exchanged glances. It was not, after all, Dean who had raised the subject of clemency.

"That's right," Dean agreed. Nixon had defined the problem. "And you're going to have the clemency problem for the others," Dean said. "They all would expect to be out and that may put you in a position that's just un-tenable at some point. . . . I am not sure that you will ever be able to deliver on the clemency. It may just be too hot."

It was not the President who had suggested that clemency was out of the question, but Dean. By now, Buzhardt was expecting still worse. Nixon delivered.

"You can't do it till after the '74 elections, that's for sure," said the President. "But even then your point is that even then you couldn't do it." He sounded disappointed.

"That's right," said Dean. "It may further involve you in a way you shouldn't be involved in this."

The President agreed. "No, it's wrong; that's for sure."

At last. That was what the President considered his decisive rejection of meeting the burglars' blackmail demands. It was about the clemency, not the blackmail. Even on that count, the President seemed to have gone along for practical political reasons, and not until Dean had told him it probably wouldn't work.

Buzhardt listened to Nixon as he kept looking for a solution. Dean estimated that Ehrlichman was probably vulnerable to indictment by the grand jury for soliciting the money that had been going out for months to the burglars. "But what I am coming to you today with is: I don't have a plan of how to solve it right now, but I think it's at the juncture that we should begin to think in terms of, of how to cut the losses, how to minimize the further growth of this thing, rather than further compound it by, you know, ultimately paying these guys forever. I think we've got to look—"

The President interrupted impatiently. "But at the moment, don't you agree that you'd better get the Hunt thing? I mean, that's worth it, at the moment."

The President wanted Hunt paid off. He didn't want to be told that it wouldn't work.

Buzhardt heard Haldeman enter. Mercifully, the tape was approaching its end as Nixon led the search for ways "to take care of the jackasses who are in jail." Six more times the President returned to the subject of the blackmail, and then he restated his conclusion: "For your immediate thing, you've got no choice with Hunt but the hundred and twenty [thousand dollars] or whatever it is. Right?"

"That's right," Dean agreed.

"Would you agree that that's a buy-time thing [and that] you'd better damn well get that done, but fast?" the President asked.

"I think he ought to be given some signal, anyway—" Dean said.

"Well, for Christ's sakes," Nixon continued, "get it in a way that, uh— Who's, who's going to talk to him? Colson? He's the one who's supposed to know him."

"Well, Colson doesn't have any money, though," Dean noted. "That's the thing. That's been our, one of the real problems." They were broke.

Someone remembered a secret $350,000 stash in the White House. The press had already learned about it. "We are so goddam square that we'd get caught on everything," Haldeman laughed.

It was a moment of singular truth amidst the squalor, Buzhardt reflected.

He marveled at their resourcefulness. In the course of the discussion the President had considered almost every conceivable alternative: granting Hunt parole instead of clemency, using priests to help hide payments to the burglars, "washing" money through Las Vegas or New York book-makers, convening a new grand jury before which the President's men would plead the Fifth Amendment or experience memory failure, co-opting the Assistant Attorney General by having him appointed as a special Water-gate prosecutor—everything but telling the truth.

Finally they agreed to send John Mitchell out on an emergency fund-raising mission. Haldeman, Dean and the President were discussing the logistics. Then Buzhardt heard the worst part of all. It was what he had dreaded. The President was addressing Dean: *". . . You had the right plan, let me say. I have no doubts about the right plan before the election. And you handled it just right. You contained it.* Now, after the election we've got to have another plan. . . ."

Buzhardt sat for a few minutes after the machine had stopped, consider-ing what to do. He and Powers finished the analysis and indexing, and then Buzhardt went to see Leonard Garment.

Maybe Garment would have an idea. . . .

ON THE evening of November 17, the President faced an audience of sev-eral hundred newspaper editors in a question-and-answer session scheduled as part of his campaign to regain credibility.

The session began badly. The President, agitated and combative, confused his syntax several times. Reporters, he observed, "answered" tough ques-tions. He referred to himself as "he." When asked whether he still consid-ered Haldeman and Ehrlichman two of the finest public servants he had known, he responded: "I hold that both men and others who have been charged *are guilty* until we have evidence that they *are not guilty.*"

He was asked about his low tax payments, reported at $792 in 1970 and $878 in 1971. Bobbing on his feet and gripping the podium with both hands, he gave a rambling account of his finances—not of the period in question, but of more than a decade earlier. In 1960, after fourteen years as a Con-gressman, Senator and Vice-President, his net worth was $47,000 "and a 1958 Oldsmobile that needed an overhaul," he said.

Watching the performance on television, Buzhardt and Garment pon-dered the President's strange demeanor. As he completed his answer, they felt Nixon was addressing them:

"In all of my years of public life, I have never obstructed justice. And I think, too, that I could say that in my years of public life, that I welcome this kind of examination, because people have got to know whether or not their President is a crook.

"Well, I am not a crook," said Richard Nixon.

BUZHARDT AND Garment knew they were already treading perilously close to the cover-up line. The 18½-minute gap was not something about which they could wait and see if the prosecutors asked the right questions. This was not about a proposal to manufacture evidence; this was destruction of evidence. The lawyers were certain there was no innocent explanation, and they wanted the gap disclosed at once to the special prosecutor. If Jaworski were to learn about it secondhand—after the subpoenaed tape was turned over to Sirica—he might draw the inference that the President's lawyers had conspired to hide the destruction from investigators.

The lawyers did not ask Nixon for permission to inform the special prosecutor; they simply told the President of their intention. They met with Jaworski on the morning of Wednesday, November 21, at his office. Buzhardt proposed that a joint investigation be undertaken by the special prosecutor and the White House to determine the cause of the gap.

Not unexpectedly, Jaworski insisted that Sirica be informed of the gap at once. That afternoon, the day before Thanksgiving, Buzhardt, Garment and Jaworski met in chambers with Sirica for a secret conference.

"Your honor . . ." Buzhardt began. He tried to soften the blow. While listening to one of the seven remaining tapes, he had encountered a new problem. "The intelligence is not available for approximately eighteen minutes. There is an obliteration of the intelligence for approximately eighteen minutes. You can't hear the voices." Buzhardt paused. "It doesn't appear from what we know at this point that it could have been accidental."

"Does not appear?" Sirica was puzzled.

"At its worst it looks like a very serious thing, your honor. If there is an explanation, quite frankly I don't know what it is at the moment." The missing portion was part of the conversation of June 20, 1972, three days after the arrests inside the Watergate. "Between the President and Mr. Haldeman."

"It would indicate Mr. Haldeman was there talking to the President?" Sirica asked.

"Yes."

"Then there is a lapse?"

"Yes. Then the circumstance is even a little worse than that, your honor."

"I don't know how it could get much worse."

"Just wait," interjected Garment.

"We found Mr. Haldeman's notes of this meeting," said Buzhardt. "They consist of two legal pads of paper . . . The notes reflect that the discussion was about Watergate."

Later that afternoon, Sirica made the matter public and ordered an immediate inquiry, to be conducted in open court. For the next two weeks, news of the gap filled the nation's front pages. Buzhardt, Haig, Woods, Bull, Secret Service personnel and other White House aides were called to the witness stand to explain. Woods was a star witness. She steadfastly maintained that she had accidentally erased about five minutes of the conversation, no more, while talking on the telephone. The photograph released by the White House to support her testimony was cruel. It pictured the President's secretary, contorted at her desk, one arm flung back to a phone, a foot on the transcribing pedal.

The statements were inconsistent. Witnesses could not agree on dates, or whether recording machines were examined for malfunction, or when tapes had been checked out. Woods had kept certain tapes locked in her desk, others had been taken to Key Biscayne, others had been given to Haldeman to take home. Sirica referred the matter to the panel of technical experts he had appointed to determine why the two tapes were missing.

In the White House, the President was angry about how the whole episode had been handled. He spent hours talking to Woods and Rebozo about how all of Watergate, this problem and the ones before, seemed somehow to derive from the incompetence of his lawyers. He was growing increasingly furious. On November 29 he instructed Ziegler to announce that the legal team had made "some mistakes" and, accordingly, was being reorganized. It was a clear statement of no confidence. Haig expressed his private distress to the lawyers. The President was cutting them off at the knees. "If we're going to do this, I'll quit," Haig told Buzhardt.

Buzhardt and Garment went to see Nixon.

Now subdued, Nixon asserted that Ziegler had issued the statement without consulting him. He looked away from Buzhardt as he spoke. He would order Ziegler to issue a clarifying statement. The exchange bolstered Buzhardt's belief that Nixon was the most transparent liar he had ever met. Ziegler approached Buzhardt later, very upset. Mrs. Buzhardt was with her husband. Ziegler insisted that he had acted on the President's specific orders, and asked Mrs. Buzhardt if she would ever speak to him again.

"Yes," she said. Sure. Of course. She was used to government.

Afterward, meeting with Haig, Buzhardt was succinct. He would adopt, he said, "the dilatory approach" in defending the President. If there was a reasonable way to explain the President's conduct, he would try. But he could no longer pretend, even to himself, that his client was a helpless victim of Watergate. The tapes, what was left of them, made that clear. At best, Buzhardt and the other lawyers could try to establish the President's technical innocence. "We are officers of the court," he warned Haig. "If in a file or tape search we come across a smoking pistol, we've got to disclose it."

Still, he would proceed slowly, Buzhardt assured Haig. He would not search for the weapon.

Nor would Haig. On December 6, from the witness stand in Sirica's courtroom, the general speculated that "some sinister force" had been responsible for the tape gap.

"Has anyone ever suggested who that sinister force might be?" the Judge asked.

"No, your honor," Haig replied.

At the White House, Jan Barbieri, a secretary in the speech-writing shop, pasted a picture of Bela Lugosi on a lampshade. Beneath the picture she typed: "Sinister Force."

GARMENT REFLECTED on the situation: missing tapes, gaps, sinister forces, suggestions to manufacture evidence, lawyers on the witness stand, a client and old friend who would not hear his advice. But he was not really surprised. He had seen Richard Nixon lock himself into unreality and depression before. Garment went to see Haig. "I want out," he said. Technical innocence was not enough. He could not function as a lawyer under these circumstances. It was a charade.

Haig was sympathetic.

"Given the peril of the situation, I can't accept the fact that all the information is derivative," Garment said. Everything came to the lawyers indirectly, almost never from the client they were supposed to be defending.

Haig was impressed by Garment's refined language, his precise mind, his sense of humor. But Garment was a panicker, in his view, not a man to hang in for the tough battle. In war, one had to risk his own ass. Haig was willing. Garment wasn't.

Garment elaborated on his position. He did not wish to do anything that would suggest disloyalty or defeatism. He would stay on at the White House, but he would drop out of sight. He could deal with cultural affairs, American Indians. There would be no noise, he would not resign.

More in sadness than in anger, Garment recounted how he had hoped there would be some tapes or some evidence to prove the President's innocence. They didn't seem to exist. Garment wasn't blaming anyone. The real meaning of Watergate, he told Haig, was to be found in the passive acceptance of hiring two men, Howard Hunt and Gordon Liddy, and then standing by, letting it all happen. And after that, still more passive acceptance about how to handle Hunt and Liddy's exposure in an election year. The tapes that Buzhardt had described to him were so unclear, so ambiguous, he observed. "Like every conversation in the Oval Office."

Haig was in perfect accord.

Garment began to reminisce about conversations in the Oval Office. "Someone would say, 'Let's bomb Tel Aviv.' Now, that's not policy, but the tape would sound bad. While you're kicking around policy decisions, things come up. So the President told Dean, 'Good job, John.' The President said it, but he always says, 'Good job.' "

Haig agreed.

"He'll say, 'Good job, Len,' on this or that. He says it when it has been a bad job. Or no job at all. Often it has been no job, but it becomes 'Good job, Len.' The President is guilty of misdemeanors. It is inherent in the office."

Garment thought back to the weekend when the President had dismissed Haldeman and Ehrlichman, calling them "two of the finest public servants it has been my privilege to know." That dissonant phrase should have rung several million alarm bells across the country, he realized. If Haldeman and Ehrlichman were such fine public servants, why had the President gotten rid of them? The day after their departure, Nixon arrived at a Cabinet meeting trembling with anger: passing the offices of his former aides, he had found FBI agents stationed outside—to secure their papers and files. It was an outrage, an insult to the integrity of two great and good men, Nixon said. Who had ordered the FBI agents posted? he demanded. Who was it? He wanted them out of the government immediately, fired. He would see that somebody paid the price. (In fact, Garment was responsible; he had raised the matter with Richardson and Ruckelshaus, and they had agreed that agents should be posted immediately. All three kept quiet on the matter during the Cabinet meeting.) The President calmed down only when he seemed to perceive that his own Cabinet appeared concerned about his behavior.

In the following weeks and months, Nixon repeatedly urged Haig to set up a mechanism to raise funds—either in secret or through public channels —for Haldeman and Ehrlichman's legal defense. Garment had advised Haig that it was out of the question, but Nixon pressed. If the Berrigans could have a defense fund, why not Haldeman and Ehrlichman? Eventually, however, Nixon seemed reconciled to the idea that no one on the White House staff would undertake the mission.

The decision to fire Haldeman and Ehrlichman must have consumed the President with guilt, Garment thought. He felt tremendous compassion for Nixon.

An act of both conscience and cowardice, Garment thought of his own decision to abandon the President's defense.

Chapter Seven

H
UGH Morrow was puzzled by the call from Robert Abplanalp. Aside from Bebe Rebozo, Abplanalp was the President's closest personal friend. Morrow was aware of the suspicion, the distrust and jealousy, with which the President regarded Morrow's boss, Nelson A. Rockefeller. Morrow, who was press secretary to the New York governor, had heard Henry Kissinger and Rockefeller talk about Nixon's concern that the Secretary of State maintained too close an association with his old patron. Now Nixon's friend was calling Morrow to insist that he come to Key Biscayne immediately. Abplanalp was sending his private jet to pick up Morrow in Albany.

Morrow was escorted into the five-house presidential compound. The warm Florida breezes were a pleasant relief from the bitter December chill of Albany and Pocantico Hills. The men who were gathered in the converted office were all familiar to Morrow: Rebozo, quiet and polite, of Cuban descent, a self-made millionaire, the President's closest friend for nearly twenty years; Abplanalp, outspoken and brash, fabulously wealthy from his invention of the aerosol valve; Haig, Kissinger's former chief deputy, with whom Morrow had spoken frequently before the general had become White House chief of staff.

Haig came right to the point. "Hugh, we want you to be the President's new communications director, with Cabinet status. The President wants you to take it. Bob wants you to take it. I want you to take it."

Morrow told the three men that he was very flattered, but he would consider the offer only if two conditions were met. First, Ziegler would have to leave the White House. It was not a question of whether Ziegler was good or bad, said Morrow; the fact was, he had become a symbol of public mistrust. Second, the President would have to start answering hard questions about Watergate and, if necessary, allow himself to be questioned by the Senate Watergate Committee. Nixon had never really answered John Dean's charges, Morrow said. The White House had to stop this Chinese water torture in which every new fact, every new admission, had to be wrung out of the President.

Haig didn't like that. He doubted that he could persuade the President to dump Ziegler. Not that he wouldn't like to see it happen, he said, but he was sure that the boss could never bring himself to banish Ron. Haig proposed instead that Morrow be given absolute jurisdiction over all aspects of press affairs while Ziegler continued as assistant to the President.

Rebozo and Abplanalp were more interested in getting Morrow on board than in haggling over Ziegler's future. If Ziegler had to go as a condition of Morrow's acceptance, then perhaps it could be arranged for him to move to the United States Information Agency or some other remote corner of the government bureaucracy, they suggested. They were less sure than Haig that the President would be intransigent on the point. They knew that Nixon recognized Ziegler's shortcomings in dealing with people. And they were convinced that Ziegler often presented the President and Watergate in the worst possible light, needlessly antagonizing both the press and the public. A new approach to media relations was essential. Everyone agreed on that. It was imperative that it begin at once.

Knowing how heavily the President had lately come to lean on Ziegler, Haig was pessimistic. Ziegler might move out of the press area but would have to stay on with the President.

Morrow saw that Haig did not want to press the point with Nixon, and he recognized that the general's analysis was probably correct. Politely declining, he returned to New York.

Ned Sullivan, whose wife and Mrs. Nixon were cousins, called Morrow several days later. "Pat and Julie asked me to call, and they want you to take the job," Sullivan explained.

Morrow held to his original position.

Sullivan pushed harder, urging Morrow to reconsider once more, for the sake of the President's family.

Morrow was firm. No, he said, he could not accept if Ziegler remained at the White House.

IN A White House where evangelist Billy Graham served as spiritual adviser to the president, the arrival of a rabbi from Providence, Rhode Island, might have seemed incongruous. But Rabbi Baruch Korff and the faithful who accompanied him into the Oval Office on December 19 were not there about religion. Rabbi Korff had begun a citizens' campaign to support the President six months earlier. The President had written Korff several letters thanking him. A five-minute meeting had been arranged.

The President gave members of the delegation the standard mementos— pins with the presidential seal for the women, tie clasps and cufflinks for the men.

"How did you get started?" the President asked Korff.

"I was offended by the Ervin Committee hearings," said the clergyman. "It was theater. Someone would implicate others and then he would be asked what legislation he would recommend to prevent things like this. It just didn't sit well. Senator Ervin pontificated. He is a good actor. Clergymen have to be good actors, too. He quoted from the Bible. I was incensed. I couldn't find some of the quotations. They weren't in the Bible."

The President dismissed the complaint with a wave of his hand. "He's a nice man," he said. "He was just doing his job."

Korff told the President that he had been wrong not to destroy the tapes. Nixon seemed startled.

"The day Mr. Butterfield appeared before the Ervin Committee," Korff said, "you should have. I found it morally and ethically offensive that the people didn't know they were taped. You had an obligation to make a big bonfire on the south lawn."

"Where were you eight months ago?" the President laughed. The five minutes were long up. Nixon wanted more details about The Movement, as Korff called it, and its founder.

"I'm just a small-town rabbi," Korff said. "I did not find The Movement. The Movement found me." Korff's organization was carefully named the National Citizens' Committee for Fairness to the Presidency. The issue was a strong presidency, not Richard Nixon, Korff explained.

The President agreed with that.

Korff said that he hadn't voted for Nixon in 1960 or 1968. But he had in 1972.

"Why?" the President asked.

Korff's reasons were the issues Nixon thought were important and was sure had reelected him—law and order in the streets, a strong national defense, détente with Russia and China. The President smiled.

Korff spoke passionately about how the group had gotten started, and how he had used his own vacation money to finance part of a $5,000 ad in the *New York Times*. The ad had netted more than twice that in contributions. A similar ad in the *Washington Post* brought in three times the cost.

The meeting lasted forty minutes, and the President asked Korff to come back and visit again.

THE NEXT evening, Nixon appeared at the staff Christmas party in the East Room. He seemed happy, and his appearance was a boost to everyone's morale. The spiked punch flowed freely.

"Six days before Christmas," the President said to a large group gathered around him, "and all through the house not a creature was stirring, not even the President."

There was awkward laughter.

"It might be kind of hard to do," the President continued, "but if you can't get enough here, come on upstairs. We've got plenty. If you drink too much, you might go in the wrong door and surprise some girl. But if you say you were at the White House, she'll say come on in."

It didn't make any sense, but they laughed anyway.

IN THE clear light of the next day, the President could see he faced grave difficulties on two fronts. His legal strategy had collapsed with the Saturday Night Massacre, the tapes that never existed, and the eighteen-and-a-half-minute gap. In the process, his public-relations strategy had been made a mockery. Begun in early November and dubbed Operation Candor by the press, it had been based largely on Nixon's repeated assurances that there would be no more bombshells. But each time that the President announced that Watergate was behind him once and for all, another disaster had hit. Nixon cursed the times, the unfairness of it all.

The impeachment investigation was beginning. There was speculation about resignation. His staff was restless. Bryce Harlow had written a letter saying he wanted to leave. Garment had signed off the legal team. Ray Price had been prevailed upon to stay beyond his planned departure date in December, but he was not happy. The Republicans on the Hill were unhappy. Senator Barry Goldwater, a key to his support in the Senate, had given an interview to the *Christian Science Monitor*. His words stung:

> "He [Nixon] chose to dibble and dabble, and argue on very nebulous grounds like executive privilege and confidentiality when all the American people wanted to know was the truth. . . . I hate to think of the adage 'Would you

buy a used car from Dick Nixon?' But that's what people are asking around the country. General Haig doesn't know anything about political matters. . . . I just can't believe that [Nixon] would listen to Ziegler. That, in my opinion, would be something disastrous. Again, there is nothing personal but Ziegler doesn't understand politics."

Worried and miserably unhappy, the President asked a small group to join him and his family for dinner on December 21: Bryce Harlow and his wife; Barry Goldwater and Mary Brooks, the director of the Mint; Pat Buchanan and his wife; Ray Price and Rose Mary Woods. None of the lawyers was asked, nor was Haig or Ziegler.

The President, waiting for all the guests to arrive, downed a quick Scotch in the Yellow Oval Room, the formal living room in the family quarters. At the dinner table, he sniffed the cork from the wine and pronounced the choice inadequate. A bottle more to his satisfaction arrived. During dinner he was jovial at first, bantering with those seated closest to him, but by the end of the main course he had begun to ramble. He told his guests he wanted to spend the holidays in Key Biscayne, but that the energy crisis made a plane trip for a vacation inadvisable. A train trip was conceivable, but it would be unsafe, and expensive as well.

Turning to Price, the President referred to the State of the Union address that Price was working on. What ideas should they focus on? Then, before Price or anyone else could respond, he shifted rapidly to another subject. Kissinger's name came up. Mrs. Nixon complained bitterly that Kissinger was getting credit for all the good things her husband had done.

The group left the table for after-dinner drinks and more conversation. Nixon seemed to be trying to reach out to each person—as if to convince himself that this was his team, Harlow thought. But the President was having trouble getting his words out. "Bryce, explain what I'm saying to Barry," he said several times, after having given up himself.

Harlow would start to explain, but then the President would interrupt him. Watergate was mentioned. The President, observing that he was beset from all sides, offered a rapid-fire catalogue of the ways he might recoup his fortunes. But Republican support on the Hill was limp, he said. Impeachment was a partisan issue, but his side didn't seem willing to do what was necessary to defend him. He was a victim of circumstance, of uncontrollable forces. It was the timing, the particular point in history. The Democrats and the press were now working together to get him. He had inherited a much abused office, flagrantly misused by Kennedy and Johnson. But the liberals and the press hated him, and so the rules were being changed and he was going to be made to pay.

The President was, in some way, only trying to thank his family and the others for their support, Price was thinking. But he certainly wasn't handling it well.

Buchanan thought, The Old Man is tired and can't hold his liquor well, especially when he's exhausted.

The next day Goldwater called Harlow. "Is the President off his rocker?"

"No. He was drunk."

Goldwater was half convinced.

The President had felt trusting enough about those at the table to let down his guard, Harlow told him. "Barry, it's the highest compliment that can be conveyed by the President of the United States." It was very healthy that Nixon had been able to do it, he added.

Haig disagreed. The President was drinking more than usual and telephoning Haig, and others, late in the night. The President was overexcited, filled with anxieties, carrying on.

Nixon's inability to handle more than one drink was well known to his intimates. During campaigns he had wisely chosen not to touch alcohol. But now, on too many afternoons, he started sipping in his office with Rebozo. On the mornings after, the President arrived in his office late, sometimes not until noon. Haig was worried that the press would learn about it, and he ordered that the time the President left his residence to go to work no longer be recorded.

Undersecretary of the Treasury William E. Simon, who met frequently with Nixon in December, often found the President dazed. Simon was reminded of a wind-up doll, mechanically making gestures with no thought as to their meaning.

Nixon was increasingly moody, exuberant at one moment, depressed the next, alternately optimistic and pessimistic, especially in his nocturnal phone calls. He wondered aloud to Haig whether it was worth it to stick things out and fight and then vowed he would never be driven from office. Back and forth, up and down. His motives were suspect, the President said; his words went unbelieved by all sorts of people. Maybe he should resign. What did Haig *really* think? Should he resign?

No, Haig recommended each time.

Nixon raised the possibility with his family as well. If it came down to surrendering any more tapes, he said, he would burn the remaining recordings and quit. It was the only protest left him. The powers of the presidency were being stripped away, at his expense and also his successors'.

Daughter Julie's husband, David Eisenhower, wasn't sure whether the President was serious or whether he was simply letting off steam, provoking his family to urge him to fight. This sort of talk reminded David of the President's remarks about the peace marches around the White House in 1969 and 1970. Then Nixon had told his family that he just might order the police to clear the Ellipse behind the White House of the thousands of demonstrators, every goddam one of them.

But he had never done it.

Chapter Eight

T HE seven tapes were already in Sirica's hands, and it was only a matter of time before they would become public at a trial. Haig wanted to blunt the impact of their disclosure in any way he could, to seize the issue on the President's terms. The preferable course was for Nixon to make a speech of contrition—accept responsibility for past mistakes, acknowledge the abuses documented in the tapes, pledge a bright future. But Nixon could never undertake an act of public confession. He was too proud, it would break him. Haig knew Kissinger had already suggested something like that. Ziegler had rejected the notion, saying "Contrition is bullshit."

In mid-December Pat Buchanan began reviewing the transcripts for Haig. In their raw state, the transcripts were devastating. But Buchanan believed there must be a way they could be used to support the notion of Nixon's technical innocence and to discredit John Dean. Buchanan managed to find two pluses for the President's case. The September 15, 1972, tape lent little explicit support to Dean's contention that the President was actively involved in the cover-up at that point. Also, the tapes established that Dean did not make his major disclosures to the President on March 13, as Dean had claimed, but instead on March 21, as Nixon asserted. Buchanan found plenty of minuses: the tone of the conversations, the language and, worst of all, the substance of the March 21 discussion. Reading it for the first time, Buchanan had winced. Nixon was suggesting ways to keep the conspiracy from coming unstuck, proposing methods of meeting the burglars' blackmail demands.

But Buchanan looked at the tapes essentially as a public-relations problem. He believed there was a way to live with anything—witness the success of the May 22 statement. If the media were properly handled, the damage could be minimized.

He proposed to Haig that the White House take the initiative in releasing the transcripts, claim credit for candor, float them out in the most favorable context before they were forced out under the worst circumstances.

The key, Buchanan argued, was preparation and packaging, briefing the right members of Congress first, carefully timing the release of each individual transcript, accompanying their disclosure with detailed legal analyses written to the President's advantage.

He laid out his scheme in detail.

First, release all the pre–March 21 transcripts on a single day, force-feeding the reporters and columnists with a glut of printed matter that would seem to undercut Dean. If the transcripts were accompanied by the right speeches, explanations and legal briefs, all of them stressing Dean's confusion as to the dates, Dean's credibility would be severely damaged.

The next day, Buchanan explained, they would release those tapes most harmful to the President's case, including the March 21 conversation. A day later, they would put out the tapes of April 1973, the ones most advantageous to the President. Some of those conversations with Dean were obvious setups, Buchanan believed. Nixon had known the tapes were rolling, and Dean had not. But the only people who would recognize that the President was playing to the microphones would be those few who were intimately aware of how the President worked and talked. To the uninitiated, the transcripts would show the President making exculpatory statements and telling Dean to testify truthfully. With the March 21 conversation thus sandwiched between more palatable material, the situation could be "neutralized," Buchanan said.

Haig endorsed the scheme and moved quickly to implement it. Selected members of the Republican leadership would be invited to come to the White House on December 22, the last Saturday before the Christmas recess, to be briefed and shown the material. The lawyers began to construct analyses and drafts for the speech writers. Buchanan arranged the material neatly in folders. The plan was to test the material on the leadership before deciding whether to release it publicly.

The day before the meeting, Bryce Harlow walked into Haig's office. He had just learned of the plan. "Al, I've got news for you," he announced. "You're going to be fired tomorrow."

Haig looked up. "Not that I wouldn't welcome it, but why do you say that?" He leaned back in his chair, anticipating one of Harlow's congenial lectures.

"You haven't read the transcripts," said Harlow, who hadn't read them, either, "and you're preparing to recommend to the great man that he dump all these. And if he is as astute as I think he is, he'll say, 'You're incompetent, you're fired.' And I'll actively support that action. It would be irresponsible to do what you're about to do. You're just taking the word of the lawyers, and Pat. You haven't read a line of them."

"What do you think I should do?" asked Haig. "You're right—I haven't seen them." He lowered his voice. "And I don't want to see them."

"You better read them tonight."

"I will and you will, too," Haig directed. "We're both going to read them."

Harlow stayed up until 3 A.M. reading and returned bleary-eyed to Haig's office in the morning. "Al, those tapes will destroy the President," he said. "They'll kill him."

Haig considered Harlow's words.

Harlow assured him passionately that the amorality of the transcripts would not wash, even in the political world of Washington, that Christmas season or any other season for that matter. Certain sections would reduce the impeachment process to a one-hour House debate. " 'Vote! Vote!' they'll scream." Harlow knew the House of Representatives. Once the members got agitated, there would be no stopping them, he said. Granted, those people on the Hill were a bunch of hypocrites. The tapes reflected the real political world, the real White House, he and Haig knew that. But those transcripts would force the politicians on the Hill to react, to tell their constituents and themselves that the real world wasn't that way.

Haig felt chastised, and he was now less than elated at the prospect of releasing the material to anyone, much less the leaders of the President's own party. He called Ziegler, Buchanan, Price, Garment, Buzhardt and Harlow to a meeting. Haig knew when to keep his own counsel and when to drag others into a no-win decision. The question, he announced, was whether a decision on releasing the transcripts should be put off until the next Watergate trial, which was expected to begin sometime in April.

Harlow said that release flew in the face of political wisdom. The March 21 conversation could finish the President, no matter how much candy it was coated with.

THE FINAL DAYS : 109

Buchanan dissented. The President had to get the problem behind him. The argument of technical innocence could be made compelling if it were made forthwith. Nixon hadn't paid off the burglars himself. Clemency had not been granted. "It's not like the Catholic Church, where it's a sin just to think about it," Buchanan said.

Positions shifted, but the fact of what was actually on the tapes was more persuasive than Buchanan's oratory. After a while Buchanan was the only one left in the room who favored release. Copies of the transcripts were collected and put back into the vault. The larger the meeting, Buchanan decided, the more cautious and less courageous the decision.

That afternoon, Haig telephoned Senate Minority Leader Hugh Scott at home and asked if he could visit him. Scott had lately been agitating for full disclosure of the tapes and other Watergate evidence in the President's possession. Haig wanted to shut him up. He arrived at Scott's home with a folder of partial transcripts from the March 13 and March 21 meetings and handed them to the Senator. "This is the story," he said. But under no circumstances could Scott say he had seen the transcripts.

Scott read about a dozen pages of the March 13 conversation, and then about twenty pages of the one from March 21. He didn't like the talk about blackmail, about meeting Hunt's demands.

But the President had indicated that blackmail was wrong, Haig said. The transcript, taken in its entirety, showed that Nixon was not actively involved in the scheme.

Scott had about seven or eight pages left to read when Haig looked at his watch and said he had to go to Camp David with the President.

Scott wanted to finish reading.

Haig said he had to go.

Scott handed the folders back and Haig left.

BEFORE GOING home to Texas for the Christmas holidays, Leon Jaworski heard the March 21 conversation. Judge Sirica had just delivered the tapes to the special prosecutor. Sitting in an assistant's office, the blinds drawn, a pad and pencil on the bare table, Jaworski listened for two hours. He was offended and dismayed by the tawdry discussion of paying off blackmailers, but even more at hearing Nixon, a lawyer, block out the scenario for lying to a grand jury (". . . You can say I don't remember. You can say I can't recall"). This tape—and Jaworski had already heard others—confirmed Dean's version of events. The prosecutor marveled at the precision of Dean's memory, his correctness of detail.

Now, only six weeks into his job, Jaworski concluded that the country had a criminal for a President. He tried to broach it obliquely with Haig—the two spoke frequently—but the general did not seem to understand. Even if the President had discussed unseemly matters, Haig was still asserting, Nixon had not engaged in any overtly illegal acts and had no criminal liability.

"What makes you think that?" Jaworski asked.

Haig replied that the lawyers had told him so.

Jaworski cited the provisions of the federal conspiracy statute. A person could be charged as a member of the conspiracy even if he did nothing more than participate in discussions leading to the criminal acts of others.

"Alec," Jaworski advised, "you better get yourself a good criminal lawyer. Get the best criminal lawyer available and let him pass judgment on whether the President has committed a crime."

Haig decided that there was wisdom in Jaworski's counsel, especially now that Garment had removed himself and since the President was still fuming at Buzhardt. The general consulted Leibman's list of attorneys for information about a Boston trial lawyer, James D. St. Clair, who had already been recommended to the President by Charles Colson. St. Clair's credentials seemed impeccable. Twenty years earlier he had been the chief assistant to Joseph N. Welch when Welch defended the U.S. Army before Senator Joseph R. McCarthy's Special Investigations Subcommittee. Haig liked defenders of the Army.

St. Clair was fifty-three, a Midwesterner, educated at the University of Illinois and Harvard Law School. Though he had limited experience in Washington, he was reputed to be a courtroom wizard. It was said that he compiled voluminous books of information before trying a case and that no one entered a courtroom better prepared. That kind of lawyering, Haig was convinced, was exactly what the President required. The work of the White House attorneys had been sloppy.

The general had St. Clair tracked down at the Innsbrook Golf Resort in Tarpon Springs, Florida, where he was vacationing with his family. Within hours, St. Clair was in Haig's office in the corner of the West Wing.

Haig enjoyed recruiting, pouring on the charm, smiling, cajoling, flattering and then landing big talent. St. Clair, a short, heavyset man whose smile revealed a gap between two front teeth, sat in a comfortable green chair as Haig recited his standard text. The good of the country was at stake. A state of sickness and distrust had arisen, he said, and there was an innocent man in the Oval Office down the hall. That man was working for peace, and Watergate was eating at the foundation of his office. Men like St. Clair had to be willing to abandon their lucrative law practices to come to Washington and take the President's case. "Things are in a shambles," he said. The President's legal defense was out of control. The lawyers weren't the only ones at fault. He, Haig, hadn't had time to devote enough attention to the case himself. They had all been flooded with more work than they could handle.

St. Clair thought that this moment was perhaps what his legal career had been building toward. Few lawyers were ever approached to represent the President of the United States. It was inconceivable to say no. He was not formally offered the job, but the Boston lawyer indicated he would accept if he were asked. Haig said he would be in touch.

On the last day of 1973, St. Clair flew to California. At San Clemente, he was ushered into the President's office for a one-hour meeting. "I want you to represent the office of the presidency exclusively," the President said, provided that St. Clair got the job, of course. It was the presidency that needed to be defended, Nixon stressed, not any one man.

St. Clair was impressed. He left to see Haig again. The general had already checked with the President, who had approved St. Clair's selection, and now Haig offered the job formally to St. Clair and it was formally accepted. The salary was $42,500 a year. St. Clair was struck by Haig's power. It was Haig, not the President, who had offered him the job. St. Clair was also impressed by Haig's directness, his get-up-and-go attitude.

Haig had neglected to tell St. Clair that eight weeks earlier his predecessors, Buzhardt and Garment, had recommended to their client, the President, that he resign his office. Nor did he mention that Nixon had proposed to manufacture evidence.

An Army sergeant drove St. Clair from the presidential compound to the Los Angeles airport that evening. As the car maneuvered through the maze of California freeways, St. Clair exchanged pleasantries with the sergeant, who complained about not being with his wife on New Year's Eve. Settling into the soft upholstery of the rear passenger compartment, St. Clair felt anxiety, curiosity, excitement. But more, a sense of great achievement.

St. Clair was due in Washington within the week. That meant he would have to quickly put his affairs in order at the Boston firm of Hale and Dorr and reassign his pending cases to his partners. The President's lawyer could not afford even the appearance of a conflict of interest. He wondered about the White House, the staff, the administrative problems. He did not know the case, he would have to get acquainted with Buzhardt and Garment. For him, Watergate had been a faint and seemingly endless sequence of news stories that often dominated the *Boston Globe* and the evening television news. He had thought about it as a political issue, never as a legal case. He had to focus on that. His task was to defend the President against impeachment, in perhaps the biggest case of the twentieth century. It was certainly bigger than the Army–McCarthy hearings, when St. Clair had sat next to Joe Welch and when Welch had found *his* moment as he crushed McCarthy, on television, in front of millions.

St. Clair would save Richard Nixon and the presidency, and he would follow the President into the history books. His appointment was announced on January 4. In Washington, he checked into a drab room at the Fairfax Hotel, a mile northwest of the White House. An office had been readied for him in Room 188½ of the Executive Office Building, furnished haphazardly with rejects from other rooms. St. Clair did not object when delivery of the *Boston Globe* to his office was canceled on grounds of economy.

Almost immediately, he called a meeting of the staff of ten young lawyers, some on leave from the Justice Department. "As far as I'm concerned this is another lawsuit," St. Clair told them confidently. "We have a client. We're lawyers and we are going to be professional—one hundred per cent. We're going to give the client the best defense. If he's innocent, he's innocent. If he's guilty, then he is." The case, he implied, was no longer going to receive political treatment. He warned them not to talk to the press. "If others have credibility problems around town, it is a result of talking too much." He hoped they could all work together as a team. He promised to hold weekly meetings of the entire legal staff.

One night during the first week, St. Clair asked two of his staff to join him for dinner and then wondered aloud how they would get to the restaurant. They informed him that he had sufficient seniority to call the White House transportation office and order a car. Somewhat amazed, St. Clair said, "Let's see if it works." It did, and they were driven to Anna Maria's on Connecticut Avenue. St. Clair reminisced about the Army–McCarthy hearings. It was a very exciting time for a young man then, he said. There were exciting issues a lawyer could sink his teeth into.

CHAPTER NINE

ETER Wallace Rodino, Jr., of Grafton Avenue, Newark, New Jersey. Age sixty-four. In World War II, one of the first enlisted men to be commissioned while overseas. A man proud of his awards. In the 1971 *Congressional Directory* he included the Cavaliere di Gran Croce of the Order of Al Merito della Republica, and the Bloomfield College Upward Bound Certificate of Appreciation for Outstanding Service, Personal Interest and Concern.

After the Saturday Night Massacre, twenty-two resolutions of impeachment had been introduced in the House of Representatives, and Speaker Carl Albert decided they would go to the Judiciary Committee, which was headed by Rodino. The committee had handled the confirmation hearings of Vice-President Ford and done a thorough, fair job, Albert thought.

Rodino searched for the right person to head the staff of the committee's impeachment investigation. All the men who were interviewed for the job were asked how they would conduct an inquiry. By Christmas, Rodino had found the perfect candidate: John Doar, fifty-two, a Wisconsin Republican, former head of the Justice Department's Civil Rights Division under Presidents Kennedy and Johnson. Doar's answers corresponded with Rodino's thoughts on an impeachment inquiry: keep it nonpartisan, objective, thorough; saturate the members with the evidence. Doar, skeptical, stone-faced, nearly humorless in demeanor, was not the type to repeat the mistakes of the Senate Watergate Committee. The White House had likened that inquiry

113

to a witch-hunt—secret testimony had been routinely leaked and witnesses had been compelled to testify under grants of limited immunity from prosecution. Rodino and Doar were determined to reestablish public confidence in the integrity of congressional investigation.

Doar set up shop in seedy quarters in the old Congressional Hotel, where the staff's work was carried out in small rooms with the blinds pulled as security guards patrolled the halls. Doar's solution to the possibility of leaks was to compartmentalize the inquiry and, therefore, the developing information. Only he and a few others had full access to material. Doar announced three absolute rules to his staff of 101: Be punctual to all meetings; learn to understand and respect the filing system; make sure your desk is clean every night.

When he learned that a member of the staff, William Dixon, had taken some campaign-financing files from the office—some were in his car, others at home and still more in his briefcase—Doar dressed him down. What would happen if Dixon were killed on the way home from work? he asked.

Dixon tried a joke, "I have some life insurance—"

Doar interrupted. "The greatest tribute to a man would be that if he died someone could come into his office the next day and pick up where he left off."

EVEN WITH James St. Clair on the scene, Haig thought he ought to maintain the personal relationship he had so carefully nurtured with Jaworski. He informed St. Clair that he would continue to act as the pipeline to the special prosecutor's office. That would allow St. Clair to focus totally on the impeachment inquiry.

At all costs, Haig wanted to avoid a court battle with Jaworski over additional tapes, the very question of future access which had figured in Cox's firing. Stepping away from confrontation in December, Haig had persuaded the President to let Jaworski come to the White House and listen to some tapes which were not under subpoena, and to look at some files. Though the flow of information was a trickle, it was useful to Jaworski. He too wished to avoid a protracted court struggle. But in late December the President ordered Haig to reject any further requests.

Jaworski contacted Haig in early January. He had another request: he wanted to hear one more tape. If he could listen, he told Haig, he might be able to judge which additional tapes—if any—were essential to his investigation. Deliberately, he let Haig form the impression that the requests for more evidence would soon cease if this single tape were made available.

Jaworski's plan was to proceed one step at a time. He wanted to hear the tape of June 4, 1973, the so-called "tape of tapes," a recording of presidential conversations on the day when Nixon had spent almost twelve hours listening to his conversations with Dean.

Haig went to ask the President, indicating that this would probably be the last request from Jaworski. Nixon asked Buzhardt to listen to the tape. Buzhardt strongly recommended that Jaworski not be allowed to hear it. The tape clearly showed the President, Haig and Ziegler plotting to ambush Dean, and, as well, the President acknowledging that he might be involved in the cover-up. Buzhardt told Haig that the tape would provide Jaworski with a list of other conversations the President deemed sufficiently important to have listened to that day himself. In a court battle for possession, such information might provide Jaworski with proof of relevancy. But Haig saw a possibility of bringing Watergate, at least the special prosecutor's investigation of it, to an end if Jaworski could be convinced that the White House had nothing to hide. He persuaded Nixon.

And so, on January 8, Jaworski came to the White House and listened for half a day. The quality of the tape was not good; much of it sounded like jibberish. Jaworski asked for a copy to take back to his office.

Buzhardt said it was out of the question. The President and Haig were in San Clemente. Buzhardt called Haig, and the general told him to let Jaworski have the copy.

Buzhardt replied that Haig must not realize what was on the tape.

Haig said Buzhardt was being too cautious. He ordered Buzhardt to turn the copy over.

The next day Buzhardt received a letter from Jaworski requesting twenty-five more White House tapes. Buzhardt phoned Haig once again.

Haig felt that he had been double-crossed. With trepidation, he informed the President.

Nixon ridiculed Haig for his trust in Jaworski. Never again, said the President, would he give up any more tapes. Not under any circumstances.

JAWORSKI'S DEPUTY, Henry Ruth, always found Garment ready to listen to reasonable argument. In early February they met for lunch, at Ruth's invitation, at a restaurant on the Potomac waterfront in Southwest Washington.

Could Garment possibly persuade the President to resign? Ruth asked. He was certain that Nixon was headed for impeachment and conviction. Resignation, he argued, would spare the country a terrible convulsion.

Garment listened impassively, offering no hint that he had already tried, and failed, to make the same argument to Nixon. Ruth was virtually certain that the President would never resign since resignation would leave him vulnerable to prosecution. Still, Ruth wanted to try.

Later, Garment briefed Haig on the conversation, and the general took notes. Haig shook his head. No. This wasn't the time to take such a message to the President.

IN THE days that followed, Jaworski spent long hours in his small, dark office on K Street in downtown Washington, days and nights given over to thinking and debating with his key assistants.

In the forty-eight years since he had made his courtroom debut—defending a man accused of moonshining in dry, Prohibition-era Texas—Jaworski had never imagined he would have to face a decision such as the one he confronted now. With the tapes and Dean's testimony, there was sufficient evidence to indict the President for conspiracy to obstruct justice in the Watergate investigation. The unresolved question was pervasive, hanging over the prosecutor's office: a frightening possibility on the one hand, and on the other an incomparable opportunity to prove that no person, not even the President, was above the law.

The handful of lawyers who were familiar with the evidence and who knew the decision Jaworski had to make debated the point heatedly in their cramped offices. Every legal, constitutional, moral and practical ramification they could think of was hashed over. "President Indicted"—that would be the screaming headline if Jaworski decided to go forward.

Jaworski's instincts were against it.

Perhaps he had already decided not to, and further talk was superfluous, his aides thought. But the debates continued and Jaworski took them seriously. The legal complications of indicting a sitting President were almost argument enough not to. The Constitution said clearly that if a President were impeached and removed from office, he was subject to criminal prosecution. But it was silent on the question of whether an indictment could be brought while he remained in office. If the President were indicted, his lawyers would challenge the indictment. A legal and public-relations offensive would be launched against the special prosecutor's office. The White House arguments would be strong. Ziegler and St. Clair would pound away at the ghastly spectacle of a President on trial in a courtroom. There seemed to be some reasonableness to the position they would probably take. What would the President do if someone started a nuclear war—ask for a recess?

Also the question of indictment would doubtless go to the Supreme

Court. This would delay the trial of the other defendants charged in the conspiracy. With impeachment proceedings under way, a good argument might be made that indictment represented a form of double jeopardy against the President.

There was the awful thought of an arraignment. How would Jaworski get a sitting President into court if, as seemed likely, he refused to come voluntarily? Would the special prosecutor send the marshals to pick him up at the White House and drag him to court? A ridiculous notion—but if it got down to raw power, the President had the armed forces at his disposal.

Jaworski calculated that the Supreme Court would have good reason, probably a duty, to rule the indictment unconstitutional. In addition, Jaworski was persuaded that he had an obligation to look beyond his prosecutorial role. Could a President, or the presidency, function while the Chief Executive was under indictment? On trial? What would the President's indictment do to the country's position abroad? The action would taint, if not demolish, every act of the Chief Executive. Jaworski firmly believed that. Even routine appointments and nominations would appear suspect.

Jaworski was doubtful of his right to take such a monumental step, and he also pondered what the personal consequences might be. It could go down as one of the great blunders of history. He was not about to accept such a burden, and he questioned the wisdom of anyone who would choose to do so. That, Jaworski reflected, must be why impeachment and removal had been assigned by the Constitution to the elected representatives of the people, the House and the Senate. The presidency was too much for one prosecutor and a grand jury of twenty-three citizens to take on.

Still, the debate in Jaworski's office continued full scale, tedious, often bitter. Some of the attorneys did not feel that the House Judiciary Committee could be relied on. The President's participation in the cover-up was a criminal matter, while impeachment was political. The committee could find many ways to evade its responsibility. Anything could happen.

But Jaworski had faith in the committee, and particularly in John Doar. And the prosecutor was searching for some way to give the committee some help.

DOAR WAS doing his best to prevent the inquiry from becoming politicized. When he discovered the Judiciary Committee members could attend interviews of witnesses who had been placed under oath, he switched to informal, unsworn interrogations for purposes of preliminary investigation. Some committee members, particularly Jack Brooks, a feisty Texas Democrat, were infuriated. Brooks started referring to Doar as "The Chairman."

On February 14, John Doar met with James St. Clair for the first time. St. Clair wanted to know how the committee was going to define an impeachable offense. He wanted it narrowed to a clear violation of criminal law—commission of a felony. The lawyers sparred. St. Clair asserted that it was necessary to define the alleged offense if he was to know how to proceed. He made clear that he had no authority to consent to anything without the President's approval, especially if the committee did not agree to such a basic ground rule.

Doar didn't wish to concede anything. He knew he was in trouble. The Constitution granted the House of Representatives the sole power to impeach, but Doar well knew that the President held most of the cards. The committee could ask for material from the White House, could even subpoena it, but the President could say no. Rodino and Doar were both convinced that the committee must never go to court to get documents or tapes, as the special prosecutor had done. If they went outside the Congress, it would be a concession that the House's "sole" power to impeach was subject to interpretation by the judicial branch.

Accordingly, Doar and Rodino decided that they would have to rely on the willingness of the President to turn material over, or they would have to summon the power of public opinion to force his hand.

Almost from the outset, Doar had proceeded on the assumption that, with such limitations, the committee was unlikely to find a single tape, a single other piece of evidence—the smoking pistol—which would connect the President conclusively to a clear criminal offense.

Doar's skills were those of a scholar rather than an investigator. He pored over the record with his aides—material from the Senate Watergate Committee, the grand-jury testimony, and the White House statements. Doar's staff did little primary investigating. As they sifted through the evidence, they would go hot and cold—convinced at one moment that they could make a case for impeachment, and at the next that the White House could "stonewall" them to the end. There was a pattern of flagrant abuse—wiretapping, concealment, half-truths, outright lies, consistent misuse of the executive power—but there was very little to tie specific criminal activities directly to the President.

Though Doar expounded the theory that a President was responsible for the actions of his subordinates, both he and Rodino knew that an effective impeachment case could not be made without direct evidence. Impeachment based merely on the strength of the witnesses was inconceivable. The case would then rest almost wholly on John Dean's uncorroborated accusations.

Doar was in much the same position as Archibald Cox had been in the fall: he needed the tapes. Doar and minority counsel Albert Jenner had several meetings with Jaworski. Doar explained their dilemma: There was little to catch hold of beyond the broad pattern of presidential misconduct. He doubted that it would be sufficient to move the politically sensitive committee. He needed more evidence.

Jaworski explained *his* position. *He* had the evidence, but he lacked the mandate to proceed.

Doar wanted the tapes.

Jaworski wanted him to have them.

But the special prosecutor's position was delicate. He was still negotiating with the White House for more tapes and documents, even though Haig and St. Clair had indicated that his chances were slight. If he passed on to Doar what he had now, it would wreck whatever chance he had to get additional evidence without a court battle.

Jaworski was intent on quieting the debate that raged in his office. He admired the zeal of the assistants who were pressing for the President's indictment, but he also acknowledged to himself that the White House had a point. Some of the young lawyers were partisan. There were a few Kennedy Democrats who sometimes allowed their ideology to lead them, who would, indeed, be gleeful if a panel of twenty-three citizens dragged President Nixon into the dock.

Jaworski saw his job as arbiter between extremes. He thought of himself as different from Cox. Cox was wedded to scholarship, to procedure and, Jaworski believed, to a pristine vision of the law as a monument to man's goodness. Jaworski was more a realist; he was not a professor but a decision-maker. Practical. The man who talked both to Al Haig and to the young Kennedy Democrats on his staff, and to everybody in between. The task was to find a middle ground—not to indict Nixon, but certainly not to walk away from the evidence. He wanted to throw the ball to the House committee, but only in the shape of well-organized and complete evidence. He wanted to give Doar a road map that included the tapes. Then it would be up to the Judiciary Committee.

Jaworski outlined the principles that must govern such a transaction between the prosecutor and the committee. First, the evidence itself could not be made public by his office. But the White House should be told that a transaction was taking place, so that the President would have an opportunity to raise objections. Second, the evidence would have to be transmitted from the prosecutor to the committee through the judicial process. Jaworski was not going to send his deputy down at midnight with a U-Haul truck. There would have to be an intermediary. Someone or some group had to receive the material and hold it while the White House had time and opportunity to seek a judicial remedy. Finally, the evidence could not be presented in an accusatory manner, nor could it be accompanied by any conclusions. It must be basic—raw, uninterpreted documents, testimony and tapes.

It would have to come to the committee from the grand jury. By the grand jury's vote. Not from Jaworski. There it was.

IN THE last week of February, Jaworski met with the grand jury. The panel had been investigating Watergate for nineteen months. He knew from those of his assistants who usually met with the jury that the jurors were determined to indict the President. They had voted unanimously in a straw poll to charge the President with a crime. When the vote was taken, some of them had raised both hands.

Solemnly, Jaworski outlined the enormous problems that were posed by indicting a President. Though he agreed that there was sufficient evidence to charge the President with a crime, there were other ways to proceed. In unusual circumstances, grand juries had sometimes issued reports. He suggested that a report be drawn up and given to Judge Sirica to be transmitted to the House committee.

The members of the grand jury had many questions. Some of them were so incensed at Nixon that Jaworski was afraid he might have a runaway grand jury. With slow and reasoned argument, the special prosecutor told them that he understood their feelings and shared their frustrations. But he insisted that such a report represented their best way of holding Richard Nixon accountable. In the end, the jury agreed. It then voted, in secrecy, to indict Haldeman, Ehrlichman, Mitchell, Strachan, Colson, Robert C. Mardian and Kenneth Wells Parkinson.*

Following Jaworski's advice, the jury named Richard M. Nixon, President of the United States, as an unindicted co-conspirator in the plot to

---

* Mardian, formerly Assistant Attorney General in charge of the Justice Department's Internal Security Division, was one of Mitchell's assistants at the Committee for the Re-election of the President. Parkinson, a Washington attorney, defended the re-election committee in an invasion of privacy suit filed by the Democratic Party after the Watergate break-in. He was later acquitted.

obstruct justice. That information, Jaworski had informed the panel, would go only to the judge for the time being. The vote was unanimous.

Jaworski went to see Judge Sirica. "You can expect a report from the grand jury," he said. "The grand jury wants the report to be sent to the House Judiciary Committee. It pertains to the President."

CHAPTER TEN

A LINE of spectators stretched down the block-long corridor outside Sirica's courtroom on the morning of March 1, 1974. Only a handful were allowed into the room, which was already packed with reporters and lawyers. The clerk called for order, and Jaworski stepped to the lectern.

"May it please your honor, the grand jury has an indictment to return," he said. "It also has a sealed report to be delivered to your honor."

After the roll was called, the jury foreman, Vladimir N. Pregelj, came forward and handed a large brownish-yellow envelope to Sirica. The judge slit it open, took the report out, and read it silently. Assistant Special Prosecutor Richard Ben-Veniste hoisted a heavy briefcase with a combination lock onto the judge's bench. It contained material that was referred to in the grand jury's report, he said.

"The court will at the conclusion of these proceedings this morning reseal the envelope that I opened," Sirica said. "It will be held in the custody of this court in a safe place until further order of this court."

Then the indictment against the President's former aides was made public.

The next morning, St. Clair read in his newspaper that the secret report of the grand jury contained evidence against the President and its recommendation that the material in the briefcase—tapes, testimony and documents—be forwarded to the House Judiciary Committee.

St. Clair was disturbed. He studied the indictment. It outlined, in the vaguest terms, the case compiled by the grand jury. It did not mention the President, but said the conspiracy was still continuing. It listed a series of overt acts, including attempts to obstruct the FBI and the CIA, which culminated in the payment of $75,000 on the evening of March 21 to Howard Hunt's lawyer.*

Going over the list of the forty-five overt acts, St. Clair focused on items 40 to 43. They pertained to the March 21 conversation. Haldeman had committed perjury when he testified that Nixon had said "it would be wrong" to pay the blackmail, the indictment charged. That must be what was in the black briefcase, that was the only case against the President, St. Clair concluded. If he could disentangle his client from what was in that briefcase, he could beat impeachment.

He went to Haig and the President. It was useless to try to prevent the grand jury's report from reaching the House Judiciary Committee, he told them. They agreed. Since the committee would eventually have possession of the evidence, he continued, the White House should give the appearance of cooperation.

Accordingly, on March 6, the White House announced that it was voluntarily supplying the committee with all information it had turned over to the special prosecutor. That included seven hundred pages of documents, seven subpoenaed tapes and twelve other recordings voluntarily submitted.

John Doar was finally in business. After several long sessions with the March 21 tape, he was convinced that he had a case for impeachment. But to make the case airtight he needed more tapes. So did Jaworski.

Both men asked the White House for them, and the negotiations went

---

* The indictment charged that the seven associates of the President and his re-election committee, "and other persons to the Grand Jury known and unknown, unlawfully, willfully, and knowingly did combine, conspire, confederate, and agree together and with each other to commit offenses against the United States." The first count alleged that the conspiracy began on or about June 17, 1972, the date of the Watergate break-in, and continued "up to and including the date of the filing of this indictment." According to the indictment, the seven men and others "known and unknown" conspired "to obstruct justice . . . , to make false statements to a government agency . . . , to make false declarations . . . and to defraud the United States and Agencies and Departments thereof, to wit, the Central Intelligence Agency (CIA), the Federal Bureau of Investigation (FBI) and the Department of Justice, of the Government's right to have the officials of these Departments and Agencies transact their official business honestly and impartially, free from corruption, fraud, improper and undue influence, dishonesty, unlawful impairment and obstruction." The conspirators, said the indictment, did, "by deceit, craft, trickery and dishonest means, defraud the United States by interfering with and obstructing the lawful functions of the CIA." Among the acts of the conspiracy, it charged, were "offers of leniency, executive clemency and other benefits" to the Watergate burglary team, and "covertly" raising cash to buy their silence.

on for weeks. But Nixon had drawn the line: he would never give up another tape, he repeated.

On April 11, the House committee voted, thirty-three to three, to issue a subpoena for forty-two additional tape recordings.

On April 18, Jaworski issued a subpoena for sixty-four additional recordings.

THE PRESIDENT wanted to tell the committee to go to hell, to give them nothing and put an end to their demands once and for all. But St. Clair was alarmed. "We can't stand the charge of concealment," he warned. To defy the committee outright would almost certainly end in a citation for contempt of Congress, and impeachment. Buzhardt was of the same mind. They had to make a conciliatory move. Some legitimate evidence from the tapes had to be provided.

Grudgingly, the President agreed that there would have to be some kind of accommodation. The special prosecutor could be held off in the courts for a while longer, but not the Judiciary Committee. Nixon searched for half-measures, something less than actually surrendering the tapes. Perhaps an abridged transcript or summaries of the pertinent parts would do.

Either would do, Haig said. The lawyers disagreed. Neither alternative would hold water with an already suspicious committee.

If he dropped his guard now and gave up the forty-two tapes, Nixon argued back, he would leave himself open to unending demands for new evidence.

Buzhardt did not entirely disagree. They had to surrender enough information from the tapes to create the impression of reasonable behavior. The diehard Nixon haters on the committee could not be satisfied anyhow. What was needed was a way to give the appearance of compliance without conceding the President's prerogative. Nixon's point was correct: they could not abandon the principle of executive privilege. "We have to put out something," Buzhardt concluded. "We have to take the mystery out of those tapes." Suppose they were to offer full, verbatim transcripts of the relevant material from the subpoenaed tapes.

Ziegler was violently opposed. There was rough language on the tapes, candid discussions; the President's frankness was sometimes brutal, he said. Once in the hands of the committee, the material would leak. Eventually it would, in any case, be made public as part of the record. Its disclosure would undermine the President's position with the core of his constituency— it would offend Middle America, destroy his mandate, undercut his strength with the committee's Republicans.

Nixon found Ziegler's arguments compelling. He had spent five years projecting the careful image of a dignified statesman. The candor of his private moments could not be allowed to tarnish that.

Perhaps that would not be necessary, Buzhardt suggested. They would delete the offensive language. They would turn over edited transcripts and satisfy the committee without technically complying with the subpoena. No principle of privilege would be abandoned, no precedent set.

The President reluctantly authorized the lawyers to begin listening to the tapes and transcribing. Maybe they had finally found the right approach, he said. It would be a voluntary submission. He would tell the committee that, in spite of the unreasonableness of its demands, he was willing to meet it more than halfway. He would grant an unprecedented glimpse of a President's private thoughts and conversations to prove that he had not been part of the cover-up. But his decision was tentative, Nixon told his lawyers. He might change his mind.

Buzhardt ordered the tapes delivered from the vault. Once before, in March, he remembered, the President had relented briefly and told his attorneys they could listen to the additional tapes sought by the special prosecutor and the Judiciary Committee, to hear what they might have to contend with. But before they had gotten started Nixon had changed his mind, and the tapes had gone back to the vault. Now Buzhardt and two assistants, Dick Hauser and Jeff Shepard, began reading the rough transcripts that had been made months earlier by Woods and her secretaries. Each script had to be compared with the tape it had been transcribed from. It was a crash project. Secretaries were drafted from the counsel's office to correct erroneous passages and typographical errors and to type smooth copies. Most of the tapes they had to deal with had never been transcribed.

Nixon spent hours reviewing the transcripts, often working late into the night. Almost immediately he began making deletions. Long passages were cut by bold slash marks from his pen.

Buzhardt was distressed. The editing, which he himself had suggested, was intended to excise rough language and expurgate the personal characterizations. But relevant portions of conversations relating to Watergate were being cut—long and relevant sections. He talked to Haig but was told to take his complaints to the President. Buzhardt went to Nixon. The lawyers were being put in an impossible position, he explained. He recited the familiar litany: Lawyers could not cooperate in concealing relevant material; they were obliged to vouch that everything relevant was submitted; the committee's request was constitutionally authoritative; their position, as lawyers, was being compromised. The President was asking too much.

Nixon responded tersely that *he* would make the decisions, *he* would take the responsibility.

With St. Clair as support, Buzhardt pressed Haig, and then, once again, the President.

Nixon was adamant. They were *his* tapes. He, and he alone, would decide what went to the committee. His actions were justified. Impeachment, especially this impeachment inquiry, controlled as it was by the Democratic majority, was essentially a political matter. And he didn't want his lawyers to lose sight of that. A narrow, legalistic approach to his defense would not serve the office.

Buzhardt was worried that the President might be driven to a position of absolute defiance if they persisted in arguing the issue with him. Nixon might tell the committee to go to hell after all. Buzhardt and St. Clair continued to dispute individual deletions with him, however, one by one. They won some points and lost others. The arguments were protracted and draining. The mass of the material was staggering—there were hundreds upon hundreds of pages of typewritten sheets. Secretaries worked through the night. As the April 25 deadline for compliance with the committee's subpoena closed in, Nixon was hacking out passages, even whole pages, with a purposeful boldness—altering the basic meaning of some conversations, retaining passages which supported his version of events and deleting those which didn't.

"This is where I draw the line," Buzhardt told Haig. The general acted as if he were not involved. Maybe Buzhardt should take his objections to the President.

Buzhardt tried once again to tell Nixon that he was going too far. "We've got to be consistent," the lawyer explained. The only conceivable justification for major deletions could be that certain subjects were not relevant to the committee's investigation. There might be some leeway there. But once a topic of discussion was included in a transcript, related passages could not be cut. It had to be all or nothing, Buzhardt insisted.

The President seemed to accept the point, but with considerable reluctance. He would try to be consistent, he told his lawyer. Provided, of course, that he decided to give anything at all to the committee. He had not yet made his final decision.

Buzhardt left the President's office unsure as to what might happen next. The President went to Camp David to study more transcripts and his options as well.

Awaiting his return, Haig, Buzhardt and St. Clair discussed whether the lawyers should drop their objections to some of the less blatant deletions the President had made. Some retreat seemed advisable. Clearly, Nixon was having second thoughts about letting the transcripts go at all. They were risking the possibility that he would scrap the whole project.

One of the deleted passages was troubling them particularly, though little serious thought was being given to providing it to the committee. On March 22, the day after his discussion with Dean of ways to pay off Hunt, the President had met with Mitchell, Dean and Haldeman. "I don't give a shit what happens," Nixon had said. "I want you all to stonewall it, let them plead the Fifth Amendment, cover up or anything else, if it'll save it —save the plan. That's the whole point. . . . We're going to protect our people if we can." Neither the lawyers nor Haig doubted the devastating effect the President's words would have on the Judiciary Committee, or on the rest of Congress. Clearly, Nixon had ordered his aides to cover up, though St. Clair argued that a distinction might be made that Nixon had directed that the facts be hidden from the Senate Watergate Committee rather than the grand jury. The claim seemed dubious.

The subpoena called for the tape of Nixon's meeting that day with both Dean and Mitchell. Listening to the tape, St. Clair thought he heard a door close. Perhaps Dean had left the room when the President gave the cover-up order. (It seemed likely, since Dean had never testified about Nixon's statement.) Maybe the deletion could be justified on grounds that the subpoena applied only to that part of the meeting in which all three participants were present, St. Clair suggested.

Whatever the excuse, neither the lawyers nor Haig were ready to challenge the President's deletion. If they were to do so, and if they prevailed, it would probably assure his impeachment.

WITHIN AN hour after he arrived back at the White House from Camp David, Nixon summoned Buzhardt to his office. The President said that he had given the matter careful thought and that he now had a solution. It was based on the House Judiciary Committee's refusal to define an impeachable offense. The President noted that St. Clair had already laid the necessary groundwork—he had argued that the committee's lack of willingness to specify what was an impeachable offense made it impossible for the President's attorneys to determine what evidence was, in fact, relevant.

Certainly, Nixon said, he had no obligation to turn over every piece of paper or tape that might relate to some committee member's vague notion of what constituted impeachable conduct. Some of the members wanted to impeach him for bombing Cambodia or impounding federal funds. The whole process was outrageous, the President said. In a court proceeding, a jury would get no evidence at all if the prosecutor were to conduct an investigation without limits, or if he failed to define the charges. St. Clair had observed that the committee's position had left some room to maneuver.

The President explained how he proposed to take advantage of the crawl space, however narrow. The tests of his conduct in Watergate were his actions, not the discussions leading up to them, nor the alternatives he had considered before acting.

Buzhardt nodded his agreement, and Nixon continued. A President confronted with allegations that his top aides were involved in obstruction of justice had no choice but to examine every option. Some of them might sound bad. What mattered, however, was the final decision. And his final decision had been always to let the investigations go forward. That was, after all, what St. Clair was resting the greater part of his case on. The deleted material was irrelevant to his *actions*—he had merely been thinking aloud, feeling out the situation, testing his aides, examining the options. Nothing related to his own actions had been deleted from the transcripts of the tapes. The President's solution was simple: he would simply insert an appropriate phrase where he had made cuts—"Materials unrelated to *presidential actions* deleted." The burden was off the lawyers and on his shoulders, he told Buzhardt.

Buzhardt wasn't exactly sure what the phrase meant, but he understood the concept. It was certainly grasping at straws, he thought, but it might work. It was unethical for a lawyer to represent material as not relevant when in fact it was. Still, Buzhardt told himself, the client could claim what he wished.

Buzhardt, St. Clair and Haig talked it over again. The President clearly wanted to delete material that was relevant. Still, they decided, they had an obligation to look at the larger picture. Something had to be turned over to the committee if the President were to stand a chance. Something was better than nothing.

The President continued his work. Buzhardt and Haig began to look for a lever to get him to agree to fewer cuts. Once the committee saw all those "materials unrelated . . . deleteds," they realized, the effect might be almost as bad as if they had submitted nothing. Once again they went to the President. Some process of verification would have to be proposed by the White House to make the transcripts believable. That had almost worked with the Stennis compromise the previous fall. Why not allow Rodino and Representative Edward Hutchinson, the ranking minority member of the committee, to come to the White House and listen to the tapes?

The President seemed worried. "Will they come right away?" he asked.

Buzhardt assured him that the process would take months, if indeed they ever came at all. It was likely that they would refuse on the grounds that only their staff counsel had the necessary expertise to make a careful review of the material.

But the threat gave Haig and Buzhardt a lever to use on the President. If you cut this, they started saying, and if Rodino and Hutchinson come down and find it, it will be three times as bad. Still the President wanted to cut more. He refused to provide any transcripts from before March 21, 1973, the date he claimed he had first learned of the cover-up from Dean.

Buzhardt reminded him that Doar, Rodino and minority counsel Jenner had been insistent about getting the March 17 conversation with Dean. Moreover, the President had an incentive to provide them with a portion of that conversation. He had asserted that March 17 was when he had first learned of the break-in into the office of Daniel Ellsberg's psychiatrist. The tape supported his claim, probably proved it.

The President decided to supply the committee with a four-page segment of the forty-five-minute conversation—the part in which he said of the Ellsberg burglary, "This is the first I ever heard of this." He refused to provide the portion of the conversation that dealt with the Watergate cover-up: Dean had told him that the federal investigation was leading to Haldeman, and the President had replied, "We've got to cut that off. We can't have that go to Haldeman."

The lawyers and Haig accepted his decision. The President also wanted to eliminate the transcript of the conversation he had had with Haldeman and Ehrlichman on the morning of April 14.

Buzhardt said the conversation was clearly about Watergate. There were lengthy discussions of Haldeman and Ehrlichman's culpability and of how they were to go about sacrificing Jeb Magruder, John Mitchell and maybe Dean, to save Haldeman and Ehrlichman.

Disclosure of the conversation would do heavy damage to Haldeman and Ehrlichman, and the President tried to hold out, but his lawyers insisted. Finally he agreed to include it, but with several sections deleted—including one in which he seemed to imply that he had given his personal thanks to a Republican fund raiser for coming up with cash that was used to pay the Watergate burglars for their silence.

Buzhardt and St. Clair were able to accept some of the additional cuts. They rationalized that many of the deletions were largely repetitive of material that had been left in. Also, they all were wary of rubbing Haldeman and Ehrlichman's noses further into the Watergate grime. They didn't want to jeopardize unnecessarily the defense at the cover-up trial. It could harm the President if his two loyal former aides became angered.

Haig conferred with the lawyers again to consider their double-edged strategy—how to satisfy the committee and keep Nixon from scrapping the transcripts altogether. He could see that the President was getting tired of the debate. Perhaps it would not make too much difference if a few more ambiguous references were deleted, even if they did appear to be relevant. The heavily expurgated product would have to suffice. They could live with it unless some piece of definitive evidence against the President surfaced.

They also discussed a related problem which had been deferred since December. The special prosecutor, and now the Judiciary Committee too, had copies of seven of the tapes, including the March 21 conversation between Nixon and Dean. They were going to become public, either in the cover-up trial or at some point during the committee hearings. Buzhardt thought it remarkable that details had not leaked already. When a leak did occur, or when the facts were disclosed in a trial or a hearing, they would become public in the most unfavorable context. So Buzhardt argued that the edited transcripts should be released now, by the White House. And St. Clair agreed. If the material were put out in a single, huge block consisting of hundreds of pages, many of the damaging parts would be submerged. The most damning parts, which could not stay submerged, would draw less attention as part of a huge package than if they were to trickle out, line by line, over the weeks and months. It was the same argument Pat Buchanan had advanced in December.

The lawyers took the proposal to the President. "We've got to make this all public," Buzhardt said. Public release would give the President the edge. It would be *his* act of disclosure.

Nixon liked the idea. It was an act which he saw as fitting his style—dramatic and bold. The public would see once and for all that he had nothing to hide. He would show the worst, and it would prove him innocent.

ST. CLAIR WAS beginning to feel enthusiastic about the idea. Now he was starting to understand why people stuck with Richard Nixon through tribulation. As difficult as the President had made his life over the past few months, there were certain things about the man he had come to admire. Nixon was willing to spread out all of this material before the committee, and now he had agreed to let the public listen in on his most private discussions. That took real courage, St. Clair thought. It was clear that the President's image would suffer. But that was exactly what would lend the transcripts their stamp of authenticity.

St. Clair read through the ones that were ready. He would have to face up to the shabby language. There were so many ambiguous references, so many overtones of conspiracy. A large part of the public had already made up its mind that the President was guilty. The odds seemed to be shifting heavily against Nixon. But St. Clair thought he knew how to reverse them.

He had focused his case on a single pivot. The President claimed to have learned of the cover-up on March 21, 1973. The indictment charged that the last payment of hush money to Hunt had been made on March 21. If St. Clair could convince the House Judiciary Committee that the President had not in fact learned of the cover-up until that day, then the President could not have been involved in obstructing justice. The President was the devil's advocate on March 21, probing Dean, thinking out loud, perhaps leading Dean on. The President's actions after March 21 were all designed to bring out the facts. Some of the transcripts contained the support for the chronology St. Clair needed. He started to piece it together.

But one problem remained: the conversation of September 15, 1972, in which the President threatened to fire the chief of the IRS and George Shultz. ("He didn't get to be Secretary of the Treasury because he has nice blue eyes.")

Buzhardt had maneuvered successfully in November to claim that the passage was unrelated to Watergate. Oddly enough, the sleight of hand had worked. Sirica had withheld the conversation from the prosecutor.

Buzhardt and Haig had been lucky once; they were doubtful that they could get away with it again. The risks were higher this time. There was no way they could claim that that conversation was unrelated to the committee's inquiry. It was clearly more pertinent to the committee's impeachment investigation than to Jaworski's criminal inquiry. It was definitive evidence of misuse of power—which was exactly what the impeachment process was constitutionally intended to remedy.

Haig and the lawyers weighed the alternatives. To include that part of the conversation was to court impeachment, and to withhold it was perhaps even more dangerous. If Hutchinson or Rodino eventually obtained it, the injury would probably be fatal. To avoid the issue by withholding all transcripts prior to March 21 would leave the President vulnerable on the Ellsberg charge and support the notion that the cover-up was continuing even now. The committee already had a copy of the September 15 tape, sanitized cooperatively by Sirica. Withholding the pre–March 21 transcripts—with nonoffensive portions of the September 15 tape already in the committee's possession—would make it clear to all that the President had something to hide. Haig and the lawyers saw only one acceptable choice: they would try the same ploy, release only the segment that related specifically to Watergate.

But when they took their recommendation to the President, he came down on every side of the issue, moving back and forth, vacillating between unpleasant alternatives, wondering again whether he should tell the committee to go to hell or whether he should give them only the transcripts from March 21 on. Finally he decided that the lawyers and Haig were right. They had to try the same trick that had fooled Sirica before. Still, Nixon emphasized to them, he might yet change his mind and choose to release nothing. He was under heavy pressure from Ziegler to do just that. Even with all the deletions, Ziegler was fearful that the transcripts would bring them down. He was still arguing that the President had been merely thinking aloud, and that the transcripts would unfairly make it seem as if he had been participating in a crime. The committee and the public would form a dangerous and incorrect impression of the President's role.

Haig and Buzhardt were afraid that Ziegler would prevail with the President—that Nixon either would throw out much of the material they had persuaded him to include or would decide to provide nothing. They needed to get Ziegler off their backs. The general and the counsel decided to stage a piece of theater for his benefit.

The scenario was played out in Haig's office. As Ziegler watched approvingly, Haig blasted Buzhardt and St. Clair. He accused them of interfering too goddam much in the President's business. "The President will make these decisions about what to release and not some damn lawyers," he shouted. Ziegler nodded his encouragement.

That was Buzhardt's cue. Neither St. Clair nor he, nor any lawyer in fact, could stand for these deletions, he said. Though they worked for the White House, they were bound by legal ethics. Those ethics required that they certify that the President was making full disclosure consistent with the national interest. They must insist that the President's decisions be made on the basis of law, not public relations. The transcripts, as they now stood, demonstrated the President's innocence. The lawyers had already done everything that could be expected of them. Rather more, in fact. They had compromised themselves, and what was done was done, but no more. Buzhardt allowed Ziegler to form the impression that the President might find himself without lawyers unless he relented.

Haig feigned exasperation. Buzhardt's position gave him no choice, he said. There would be no more deletions.

Ziegler backed off for the moment; clearly Haig was doing all he could.

CHAPTER ELEVEN

O N Monday, April 22, St. Clair called John Doar and asked for a five-day extension of the April 25 deadline set in the committee's subpoena.

Doar asked why the White House could not at least hand over what was ready. It would demonstrate the President's good faith.

St. Clair gave no hint that the White House was preparing to turn over transcripts rather than tapes. The President wished to finish his review of all the material before anything was turned over, he explained.

Doar talked to Rodino and called St. Clair back. He would recommend the extension to the committee, Doar said, but the committee would not be able to meet until the twenty-fifth to consider his request.

ON THE evening of April 24, Haig was nervous about what the committee would do the next day. But he was even more concerned about another of the President's troubles, one that was rapidly becoming his own personal problem. Haig called his old friend from Pentagon days in the Johnson Administration, Joseph Califano, a prominent Washington attorney. Could they get together for dinner?

Though Califano had been counsel to the Democratic National Committee at the time of the break-in and, with Edward Bennett Williams, represented the *Washington Post,* Haig had stayed in close touch with him.

Over dinner at Jean Pierre, Haig explained his problem. The Senate Watergate Committee was calling him in to answer questions about Bebe Rebozo's receipt of $100,000 from Howard Hughes. Haig needed independent legal advice. Should he answer their questions or should he invoke executive privilege, as the President and his lawyers were urging him to do? Haig knew that the President had previously waived executive privilege for any testimony involving alleged criminal conduct.

Califano cut Haig's question short. Only the President, not his aides, could invoke executive privilege. He suggested that Haig position himself between the Watergate Committee and Nixon. If the President wanted executive privilege for Haig, make him ask for it by writing a letter to the committee.

Haig also told Califano that the President would probably release edited transcripts to the House Judiciary Committee. Haig was sure they would vindicate the President, though the initial reaction might be negative.

Califano asked his friend why he seemed so unusually troubled.

Haig said he was concerned about the world situation, the "unraveling" in Vietnam, the Middle East. "I'm concerned about the President's ability to lead in a crisis. The transcripts should help. The President is having difficulty dealing with these problems. He's distracted, spending so much time on Watergate, it's destroying his ability to lead. He's preoccupied."

Califano believed his friend was holding something back. Clearly, Califano thought, Haig didn't believe Nixon was guilty of anything serious, but his manner indicated that he thought things were worse than he was willing to admit.

"We've got to get rid of the Watergate problem," Haig said.

THE NEXT day, the twenty-fifth, the Judiciary Committee granted the President an extension until April 30.

In the White House, preparation of the transcripts continued frantically. Nixon's constant editing was making it doubtful that the deadline could be met. There wasn't time to retype all the pages, so many of them were only half filled and others were cut-and-paste jobs—all of which called attention to the number and length of deletions. To prevent leaks, and to keep the whole enterprise secret, the size of the group of people involved in the editing, transcribing, correcting and photocopying had been kept small.

Many of the secretaries were shocked at what the tapes revealed, and even more were shocked at the way the transcripts were being manhandled. Linda Zier was particularly upset. "Why so many deletions?" she asked

Pamela Dallas as they left the office, exhausted, late one night. Tears were streaming down Zier's face. What would happen if the originals were revealed?

Ziegler too was upset and was again wondering aloud whether anything should be released. He thought the lawyers were still leaving in too much, and he assigned his two personal assistants, Diane Sawyer and Frank Gannon, to review the editing and report back to him.

Poring over the hundreds of transcript pages, Gannon and Sawyer were dismayed at the sloppy presentation. Lines spoken by the President were mistakenly divided and attributed in part to Ehrlichman. The same expletives were sometimes left in, sometimes deleted. Harmless characterizations were eliminated and damaging ones retained. Certain passages referred back to matters that had been excised. Such references stuck out like sore thumbs; they could not fail to convey the impression that the really damaging parts had been eliminated. As Sawyer and Gannon worked late the night of Friday the twenty-sixth, they pleaded for more time. A document that was to be used to defend a President against impeachment could not be released in this condition.

The President was at Camp David, making still more deletions. Ziegler took the request to Haig. The general explained that the lawyers were firm: they had already gotten one extension from the committee, another was out of the question. No matter how sloppy the transcripts were, or how serious the inconsistencies and inaccuracies, the transcripts would have to reach the committee on the thirtieth.

Tensions were growing. The lawyers resented what they regarded as interference from Sawyer and Gannon. More public-relations veneer. Ziegler's aides resented the lawyers' objections. More legalisms.

Gannon and Sawyer returned to their proofreading and editing. It was difficult to cast the transcripts into uniform presentation. The people who had prepared them had operated under vague instructions to delete impolite or tasteless phrases, and they had had varying standards.

Gannon was further troubled that such a complex series of conversations was to be released without any attempt to explain the context of the discussions or the significance of the references. There had to be some kind of concordance. Some of the references were subtle; the reader might be overwhelmed by the tone and ignore the substantive support for the President's version. The transcripts left no doubt that the President had explored almost every conceivable avenue to prevent disclosure of the truth; but it made a big difference, Gannon thought, whether that fact was understood in the context of the Senate Watergate Committee and other congressional hearings, with their political overtones, or in the context of a grand jury. Without an explanatory text, every such reference would appear unfairly in the worst context.

Gannon, a Ph.D., was something of an expert on James Joyce. Parts of the transcripts, with their convoluted rhetoric and almost surrealistic thoughts, reminded him of Joyce's *Ulysses*—streams of presidential consciousness. Gannon feared that the President's words would be as misunderstood and as misconstrued as Joyce's. He wanted to write a commentary, a key that might unlock the meaning of the President's dialogues.

Ziegler prevailed on St. Clair to let Gannon review the draft of the legal brief he was preparing and contribute suggestions. Gannon borrowed a desk in the counsel's office and read each page as St. Clair completed it. The lawyer's developing brief seemed to be a fair representation of the President's case, Gannon thought, but it was an advocate's case. Intended for experts, it built on details. There was not much attempt to explain confusing and obscure references. Yet, painfully inadequate as it was, Gannon thought, the brief demonstrated that the President had ultimately chosen the right courses of action, if sometimes rather late. The transcripts might be a public-relations disaster. They might be embarrassing and humiliating. But they would show the President technically innocent of violating the law. St. Clair and Gannon agreed about that.

THE PRESIDENT wanted to announce his decision in a prime-time televised address from the Oval Office, a format he was comfortable with. Since 1969 he had delivered thirty-five speeches from the Oval Office on live television. The medium enabled him to appeal directly to his constituency, over the heads of a biased press.

Haig thought the approach had been overused on Vietnam and its usefulness almost totally exhausted in Watergate. In front of the cameras Nixon exuded self-righteousness, self-justification, self-pity. Nixon on television didn't sell anymore, Haig thought. He directed Ray Price, who was going to write the speech, to get copies of the transcripts from the lawyers. Price would have to find a way to put the tapes in some acceptable context.

Price did not think the conversations, in their edited form, established conclusively whether or not the President had broken the law. They seemed ambiguous, but that was only part of the problem. He worried about the emotional impact the transcripts were certain to elicit. They shattered the accepted mythology of the presidency, and certainly of this President.

He was not shocked, however. As he read, Price jotted down some thoughts. These were tactical discussions among people who were caught in a situation each one was convinced was not of his own making. Particularly the President, Price reasoned. He doubted that anyone involved in those discussions knew the whole truth, then or now. Watergate was like a hot potato, he thought; when the President realized it was in his hands, he had looked desperately for a way to get rid of it without creating a governmental crisis and bringing down his whole Administration.

Yes, the President was wrong at some critical junctures, Price thought, but the conversations had to be understood in the context of the presidency, of Nixon's enemies, of Nixon's aspirations for the country. Nothing was black or white ethically. The President had always weighed the effect of his actions in Watergate against the larger interests of national security—ending the war, winning the peace, keeping the government strong and functioning. Those might not be the concerns of the House Judiciary Committee or the special prosecutor's office, but Price was certain they had guided the President.

On Saturday, April 27, Price flew to Camp David to work with Nixon on the speech. He had already circulated a third draft to the inner circle— Haig, Ziegler and the lawyers. They were pleased, but they still did not know if there would be a speech. The President was continuing to examine all his options, Haig said.

Price met with the President that afternoon. Nixon was editing transcripts. He seemed to be leaning toward a final decision to release them. At least that would enable him to lay it all out from his perspective, he said, before other people laid it out from theirs. He wanted to stamp his interpretation on it. He was hopeful, Nixon said. There was little else he could do under the circumstances. But he had no illusions that releasing the transcripts would sweep everything away.

Price went to his office in Sycamore Cabin and began incorporating some of the President's handwritten additions into the text. He worked late into the night, breaking only once for an hour's nap, and missing that evening's movie in Laurel Lodge, *Magnum Force*.

On Sunday he conferred by phone several more times with the President on final revisions. Finally he walked over to Aspen Cabin to sit and talk with Nixon in his den. It was a good speech, they agreed.

Price struggled for words that did not come easily. "Mr. President, I've never admired you more than for the way you've held up under the pressure this past year."

The President seemed embarrassed and uncomfortable. He acknowledged that there had been pressure. It had been immense, he said. But he could take the pressure personally. A lot of it came from the same old crowd, those who had been out to get him for twenty-five years. But the pressure was keeping him from doing what he wanted to do, from doing things that were really important for the country.

Price was struck by the thought of how much more important it was to have this man around than to worry about who had bugged the Democratic chairman's phone. He knew it sounded simplistic. But wasn't it really more important to prevent World War III, and maybe a depression, than to destroy this man for something so silly, so insignificant, as Watergate?

"We've got to put Watergate behind us," Nixon said.

Price had heard him say the same thing many times before, but this time the words were conveyed with more emotion than perhaps anything he had ever heard the President say.

THAT AFTERNOON, two hundred miles to the north of Camp David, Sybil Kucharski, a young bank teller, completed her obligations as foreman of a jury in the United States Courthouse in Foley Square, New York City. At 12:57 P.M. she stood in front of the bench in an old and dark courtroom and proceeded to pronounce "Not guilty" eighteen times. Former Attorney General John N. Mitchell and former Commerce Secretary Maurice H. Stans, the principal officials of the President's 1972 campaign, were acquitted on all counts in the Vesco case.

"We got to the jury system and that always works," Mitchell said.

Nine minutes later the news reached Joulwan at the White House, and he called Camp David. The President was elated. It was surely the best news in more than a year. Haig and Ziegler had been briefing him daily on the case, and he had been looking for acquittals. He called Mitchell and Stans to congratulate them. Later he talked with David Eisenhower. The agony of his subordinates was the most painful part of Watergate, he said. It was a relief that these men weren't going to jail because of their association with him. They were close friends; it felt good to be able to communicate with them again. "They are good men," the President said.

The acquittals appeared to end the President's indecision about whether the transcripts should be released. He had fretted too long. It was time to act. He gave Haig the go-ahead, but not before he had solved some of his last-minute editing problems by literally throwing several pages away.

As the sheer mechanics of preparing the transcripts for public consumption intensified, David Hoopes, an aide in the office of the staff secretary, summoned the State Department silk-screener from a baseball game. Hoopes shared the general White House concern for packaging, and he had designed a cover for the master sets of transcripts. He ordered the silk-screener to prepare black vinyl binders, two for each conversation. Each binder was to be stamped with a gold presidential seal and, just above it, a gold-embossed legend: "Submission of Recorded Presidential Conversations to the Committee on the Judiciary of the House of Representatives by President Richard Nixon." They would look great on television, Hoopes thought.

That afternoon Pat Buchanan got a set of the transcripts—still unbound and without the President's final expurgations—from special presidential counsel Richard Moore. Buchanan had seen much of the material before, so the content did not much surprise him. But he was startled at the idea that the transcripts were to be just dumped on the press and the public without any explanatory text. The scenario he had devised last December for the release of certain transcripts had been ignored. A public-relations disaster was in the making, he told Moore.

Leonard Garment asked for a copy of the transcripts. His request was denied.

LATER IN the afternoon, a dozen members of the speech-writing and communications staffs gathered in the office of Ken W. Clawson, White House director of communications. Buzhardt and St. Clair, who had arranged the meeting, were delayed, so Clawson passed out copies of the forty-page brief that St. Clair had prepared for submission to the Judiciary Committee. The document quoted extensively from portions of the transcripts which tended to support the President's version of events. The brief was essentially a savage attack on John Dean, taking what advantage it could of his rare memory lapses before the Watergate Committee.

Clawson was buoyant—partly because of the Mitchell-Stans verdict and partly as a result of what the President's lawyers had told him. The end of Watergate was finally at hand, he assured his colleagues. The transcripts would win the day. He referred to the President's speech. "Watergate is going to go away tomorrow," he assured them.

Speech writer Ben Stein, a Yale Law School graduate and the son of Nixon's chief economic adviser, Herbert Stein, was dubious. "You don't really believe that, Ken, do you?" His tone was contemptuous. Stein had worked too long on the defense to take the lawyers or Clawson seriously.

Clawson ignored him. "I want you to go back to your offices and write speeches for our Congressmen based on St. Clair's brief. Say the President is innocent and it's finally been proven." The speech writers would get transcripts later; all they needed at present was the brief.

Stein exchanged skeptical looks with David Gergen, a tall Harvard Law graduate who ran the White House speech-writing office. "Knowing the lawyers, I sure hate to rely on this kind of summary for that kind of statement," Stein said. Gergen agreed.

Buzhardt and St. Clair had not yet arrived. They waited a few more minutes, and then Clawson recessed the meeting. "Write your little speeches and then we'll regroup later," he said.

At about 6 P.M. the group filed into Clawson's office again to watch televised accounts of the Mitchell-Stans acquittal. The verdict seemed to support the White House claim that Watergate was an obsession limited to Washington and the news media. The people, the real people, didn't much care about Watergate, they didn't find it so serious. Even in sophisticated New York City, the headquarters of the Eastern liberal Establishment, a jury of twelve men and women had voted not guilty on all charges.

But, beyond temporary morale boosting and not a little gloating, the news had even more serious, and more encouraging, implications. John Dean had been a key prosecution witness, and apparently the jury had not believed him.

"Now we should have the Attorney General ask the special prosecutor why perjury charges aren't being brought against John Dean," suggested Kenneth Khachigian, an aide to Buchanan.

Clawson announced that St. Clair and Buzhardt would arrive at any moment. Stein was struck by Clawson's tone: it approached reverence. "You would think we were waiting for the Wizard of Oz," he said to Gergen.

The lawyers at last joined the group around the large round conference table. In contrast to the informality of the staffers' Sunday sports clothes, they wore dark business suits. St. Clair took off his coat and began talking about "the light at the end of the tunnel." His enthusiasm was boundless as he reiterated Clawson's theme. "You can write something saying that the end of Watergate is near." The tapes would prove John Dean a liar.

Clawson hung on every word. He nodded encouragement. Then Buzhardt spoke briefly but no less optimistically.

Stein and Gergen were dumbstruck. Neither Clawson nor Buzhardt nor St. Clair had offered anything specific. How was this miraculous turn of events to come to pass? It was a pep rally—clichés, cheers, exhortations.

Stein rose. "Do you really think that this is the end?" He was facing St. Clair, his voice dripping sarcasm.

Clawson glared at Stein as if he were crazy to ask the question.

Stein thought the meeting had taken on a lunatic quality.

"There will be several rough days," St. Clair said. "But a careful examination of the transcripts will convince people we're right. We're definitely out of the woods."

Gergen shook his head. He was wondering why the tapes had been with-held for almost a year if they were finally going to end Watergate.

HAIG CALLED a Cabinet meeting for Monday evening, April 29. As the Cabinet members arrived, they passed the Oval Office furniture, which had been moved into the hallway to make room for the television crew that was setting up for the President's speech an hour later. They took their places in the high-backed brown leather chairs around the twenty-foot oval table. The President had bought the table and had said he would leave it to the White House when he left office.

The President's chair was empty. Vice-President Ford was the ranking official in the room. Finally the President's chief of staff marched in. This was Haig's meeting. The room was quiet.

Haig, deadly serious, began. There were 1,254 pages of transcripts that were going to be released the next day. They would make for a rough several days. The President's language was often coarse. "It's the kind of language you probably used in your office this morning," Haig told them. Then, finished with the bad news, he turned to the good news: the transcripts would put Watergate behind them. He turned the meeting over to St. Clair, who outlined the basic points of his brief.

To the junior staff aides seated on the side of the room, the Cabinet meeting sounded like the same pep rally they had attended in Clawson's office the evening before. Haig described how difficult the transcribing process had been, a tedious, almost impossible assignment because of the poor quality of the recordings. "I have purposely not listened to the tapes, because I take the President personally at his word," Haig continued. But he wanted them to understand the immense technical problems the transcribers and lawyers had been confronted with.

Buzhardt, sitting at the side of the room beside a tape recorder, got his cue from Haig. They were going to play a portion of one of the clearer tapes, Haig announced—though this was not true. It was not one of the clearer tapes.

Some of the Cabinet members could distinguish the President's voice, but the words were almost unintelligible. Buzhardt let the tape run for a minute or so to dramatize the problem. Buzhardt and Haig wanted a whole Cabinet of witnesses who could attest to the bad quality of the tapes. It might help them get by all the questions they were certain to be asked about the short-comings of the transcripts.

Now Haig raised a troublesome point. Some Cabinet members were de-fending the President vigorously—Earl L. Butz of Agriculture, Rogers C. B.

Morton of Interior and Frederick B. Dent of Commerce were doing a splendid job—but others were oddly quiet. Haig hoped that now, with evidence from the tapes to support them, they all would go out and proclaim the President's innocence.

A FEW minutes before 9 P.M., the President walked into the Oval Office and went to a side table on which the gold-embossed transcript binders were stacked side by side for the cameras. Some of them contained only a single page of transcript. Nixon picked up one binder, opened it for a second and, with a look of disbelief and a slight shake of his head, threw it back. Then he sat down behind the big desk and waited for the television technicians to check their lighting and camera positions.

As the President waited to deliver his speech, Buzhardt called the lawyers for Haldeman, Ehrlichman and Mitchell to tell them what was coming.

"Is it going to do my client any damage?" asked John J. Wilson, Haldeman's attorney.

"Yes," Buzhardt answered.

"What the hell is the President going to do that for? Did you recommend it?"

Buzhardt did not reply.

Wilson grunted. He didn't like it, but he understood.

At forty-five seconds past 9 P.M., the President began. ". . . In these transcripts, portions not relevant to my knowledge or actions with regard to Watergate are not included, but everything that is relevant is included—the rough as well as the smooth," he said. Holding the pages of the fourteenth draft of his speech, he referred to "the strategy sessions, the explorations of alternatives, the weighing of human and political costs" laid out in the transcripts. "These materials—together with those already made available—will tell it all." By providing transcripts instead of the tapes, he was at once protecting the principle of presidential confidentiality and enabling the Congress to meet its constitutional responsibilities.

The impeachment of a President was "a remedy of last resort [which] would put the nation through a wrenching ordeal . . . The impact of such an ordeal would be felt throughout the world, and it would have its effect on the lives of all Americans for many years to come. Because this is an issue that profoundly affects all the American people, in addition to turning over these transcripts to the House Judiciary Committee, I have directed that they should all be made public."

The camera panned across the room to the two stacks. "All of these that you see here."

They "will at last once and for all show that what I knew and what I did with regard to the Watergate break-in and cover-up were just as I have described them to you from the beginning. . . . In giving you these— blemishes and all—I am placing my trust in the basic fairness of the American people."

The President did not provide the transcripts that evening. He wanted the speech to be considered in its own context. Even Nixon's most severe critics thought the speech a very good one, at the least artfully constructed. The admissions he had made in the address ("I several times suggested that meeting Hunt's demands might be necessary") seemed to make his broader claim of innocence more believable. The speech was less strident than usual, and less self-serving.

The White House gathered an eight-page summary of favorable reaction to the speech. The most encouraging signs came from key Republicans on the Hill. Senate Minority Leader Hugh Scott welcomed as evidence of "good faith" the "wealth of material" which the President was forwarding to the House committee. Senator Robert P. Griffin, Republican whip, said, "It was an effective presentation by a confident President." Senator Barry Goldwater said the offer of the transcripts was "both fair and reasonable" and should be sufficient unless the House committee was "engaged in a fishing expedition." House Minority Leader John J. Rhodes said the plan "sounds logical to me." Vice-President Ford said, "The President is giving the Judiciary Committee more than enough information with which to carry out its investigation . . . I think the President is being more than cooperative."

Such statements were exactly what the White House had hoped for—the kind of reaction which would undercut protests from the House Judiciary Committee. Any further demands from the committee would seem like harassment.

ON THE next morning, April 30, a White House station wagon carried unbound copies of the transcripts to Capitol Hill—one set for each of the members of the House Judiciary Committee and the leaders of both parties. At the Government Printing Office, sets of the transcripts were being bound in bulky three-inch-thick volumes with blue covers.

As the first copies were being bound, Ziegler and Clawson put their plan into action. They canceled the morning press briefing and arranged for the reporters to receive St. Clair's brief, but not the transcripts, in the early afternoon. Thus the afternoon papers would have only the White House interpretation of the transcripts. The press office announced that the transcripts would be arriving as soon as they left the GPO presses.

But several unbound copies were already circulating among the staff. Gergen had gotten hold of one the night before and had stayed up reading in his office until 3 A.M. The next morning he approached Ben Stein, who was working on a housing statement. "The moral authority of the President is collapsing," Gergen said. "How can you be thinking about housing?"

When the bound transcripts arrived from the GPO, Buzhardt and St. Clair autographed copies for the secretaries. Buzhardt got 250 copies and sent them to his friends and former colleagues at the Pentagon.

The 200,000 words of edited transcripts were finally given to the press about two hours before the networks' evening newscasts. Ziegler had hoped that the reporters wouldn't have enough time to locate the material that would undermine St. Clair's brief. But they lost no time in getting to the March 21 transcript: "You have no choice but to come up with the $120,000"; "keep the cap on the bottle"; "buy time"; "tough it through." The evening newscasts were filled with these remarks and, as well, with the coarser side of President Nixon: "I want the most comprehensive notes on all those who tried to do us in. . . . They are asking for it and they are going to get it." "Have you kicked a few butts around?"

The transcripts would "provide grist for many sensational stories in the press," the President had said in his speech. He was right.

The *Chicago Tribune* reprinted the transcripts verbatim in a special section. Two paperback-book editions of the released script were rushed into print, and they sold millions. Radio and television network broadcasts offered readings in which newsmen and actors dramatized the parts of the President, Haldeman, Ehrlichman and Dean. Ziegler complained: the actors attached twists and inflections to the words. Jokes about deleted expletives made the rounds. There seemed to be no end.

Ken Clawson, meanwhile, was distributing to White House aides a list of all the radio talk shows in major cities. A covering memorandum suggested that members of the White House staff phone the stations and state the President's case.

Instead of picking up a phone, Dave Gergen picked up his pen and scribbled a note to Haig's aide, Joulwan: "Is there no way to bring these circulars under control? Many people over here find some of them offensive, others dangerous if they ever reach the press, and a few—like this one—unethical if not illegal. Does anyone really think taxpayers pay for government lines in order to have White House staffers call radio talk shows?"

ON WEDNESDAY afternoon, May 1, the Judiciary Committee voted almost exactly along party lines, twenty to eighteen, to inform the President that the transcripts did not satisfy the subpoena. Haig told the senior staff that if Republican support held, the committee would have to proceed without the tapes. The President's strategy appeared to be working. It was doubtful that an attempt to cite him for contempt could succeed. As long as the committee remained divided along partisan lines, Haig said, the President was protected.

By the close of that business day, the Government Printing Office had sold out its entire first printing of the transcripts.

The President sent one copy to David and Julie Eisenhower's home. Julie didn't want to read it. But David stayed up nights reading that week.

The President's family was upset by his decision to concede the transcripts. The cold printed words, they felt, in no way conveyed the President's hurt and concern during those awful months in 1973, the fear for his aides' futures, for his Administration. The transcripts made Nixon out to be cynical, petty, selfish. The family knew otherwise. They thought, just as he did, that his enemies would use the transcripts to tear him apart. If his enemies couldn't find anything much in the substance, Nixon had said, they would use the shadow.

David Eisenhower knew how the President talked in private, and he knew equally well that there was no way the transcripts could hide it, even with all the expletives deleted. The idiom of the White House under Nixon was hard-nosed and brutal; it had been that way in David's grandfather's day. He assured Nixon that language and tone were sham issues.

David was more concerned about the President's muddling approach to things, and his indecision. The transcripts had surprised him and he felt both relief and foreboding. They seemed to establish that the President had no advance knowledge of the Watergate break-in and espionage, but they had also shown David a President who was careless, amoral and unclear in his own mind. David wondered about his father-in-law. If Watergate had been handled that way, what about other things?

LEONARD GARMENT looked at the problem of the tapes in dramatic terms: he could not understand why Nixon hadn't destroyed them before their existence was publicly revealed. If Shakespeare had written this, Garment observed—or Pirandello, or Pinter, or even Mickey Spillane—it would be essential that Nixon undertake, but fail in, an attempt at their destruction: that he be tripped by a Secret Service agent as he ran to the incinerator, or that he be apprehended as his bathrobe caught in the door. That would at least lend authority to the drama. But for the President first to record the evidence of his own shabby complicity, and then to preserve the tapes, was an act of transcendental lunacy, Garment thought.

On Garment's stage, life was a process of being better than the worst side of oneself. But Nixon, he said, had a peculiar monster perched on his shoulder that whispered into his ear—and onto his tapes. With the release of the transcripts Nixon had allowed America into the ugliness of his mind—as if he wanted the world to participate in the despoliation of the myth of presidential behavior. The transcripts, Garment thought, were an invasion of the public's privacy, of its right not to know. That was the truly impeachable offense: letting everyone see.

CHAPTER TWELVE

ON Friday, May 3, the President took his fight to Phoenix, Arizona. Goldwater, Rhodes and the rest of the state's Republican congressional delegation accompanied him on Air Force One. Goldwater had guaranteed a warm reception, and a campaign-style rally for the evening.

The Senator wore his old Air Force flight jacket as he sat making small talk with his colleague Senator Paul J. Fannin and Mrs. Nixon. After about an hour, the President asked the Senators to join him in his private cabin for a drink. What should he talk about at the rally? Inflation seemed to be what most people were concerned about, Nixon said.

Goldwater agreed, thinking that if he replied, "Mr. President, what about Watergate?" Nixon might call the Secret Service and have him thrown out of the plane. (More than a year before, Goldwater had told the President that something about the Watergate affair smelled and that it should be aired, and he had offered his help. The President had acknowledged the offer perfunctorily.) In any case, Goldwater was loyal to the party. He stood ready still to rally public support for the President.

Nixon decided that he would talk about inflation.

Goldwater and Fannin returned to their seats in the VIP compartment and played gin rummy. Rhodes was summoned forward. Nixon talked to him about Arizona, next fall's elections, legislation. The President asked about Rhodes's children. Rhodes mentioned that his son Tom had recently graduated from law school and was having difficulty with the bar exam.

"Where is he now?" the President asked.

He was in Phoenix and would be meeting the plane.

There was no mention of Watergate. Rhodes was relieved. He too had broached the subject with the President several months before. Nixon had seemed only casually interested as Rhodes described how the House intended to conduct its impeachment inquiry.

"When do you think it will be over, John?" the President had asked, as if he were not involved.

"It might be over in June."

"June? Not before that?" The President had seemed puzzled that it would take as long as six months.

Rhodes returned to the VIP cabin after ten minutes with Nixon. Later the President joined the delegation in the rear, chatting easily. Congressman John B. Conlan mentioned how much he loathed the federally funded Legal Services project on the Navajo reservation in his district; the President needed more control over the Legal Services program. Nixon listened and agreed.

The President shifted the topic. He was finally "over the hump," he said simply. The reference required no further explanation.

The plane landed at the Arizona Air National Guard Center. It was a closed arrival, no crowds. The President was introduced to Tom Rhodes. Nixon put his arm around the young man. "Bar examinations aren't everything," he said. The President was smiling. "You can come back."

The presidential motorcade ended at the Camelback Inn, where the President was to stay in the condominium of J. Willard Marriott, owner of the resort and of the restaurant-hotel empire which bears his name. Guests at the inn, many dressed in tennis clothes or bathing suits, lined the two hundred yards from the parking lot to the President's quarters. A mariachi band of twenty high-school students in orange-and-black uniforms and sombreros played Mexican music. The President listened, trying his best to look enchanted. He started forward to say something and shake hands with some of the musicians, but the band played on. He tried again, but the band was still playing. Finally they stopped. He thanked them and walked the last fifty yards to the house, passing a large cactus dressed in an Uncle Sam outfit.

When Goldwater had promised a warm welcome, he had not anticipated the jeering demonstrators who were waiting to greet the President at the Phoenix Coliseum. The possibility of a confrontation lasted only until the Secret Service agent in charge at the rally found another entrance.

The rally was a central element in the President's newly designed effort to put Watergate behind him. It had been planned as minutely as the most important campaign appearances the President had made in 1972. The Republican National Committee had put up $20,000 to insure the rally's success.

The White House chief of advance, William Henkel, had worked hard. His lead advance man, Red Cavaney, had spent eight days making the arrangements. Worried that the indoor Coliseum, which seats 13,800, would be only half filled, the advance team had planned to distribute an extra 10,000 tickets and then turn away the overflow at the door. Local Republicans, more concerned about disappointing bona-fide ticket holders, had vetoed the idea and promised a packed hall.

The President's arrival was well coordinated: a cue was given to the platform speaker, who concluded his remarks; "Hail to the Chief" lasted twenty-eight seconds; the Tucson lawyer who had volunteered as the local advance man signaled, and three thousand balloons and five hundred pounds of confetti descended from the rafters onto the cheering crowd. The audience stomped on the balloons, *bang, bang, bang,* and roared its delight.

The President mounted onto the stage. Framed by two carnation-covered Styrofoam elephants, he waved his victory sign. The crowd was on its feet now, and it took several minutes before there was quiet. Then, as the President started to speak, 150 demonstrators began chanting, "Out now. Out now." The White House communications crew turned up the volume on the speakers nearest the demonstrators and drowned them out. The President asked the dissidents to observe the tradition of free speech. Barry Goldwater half suspected that Nixon's advance team had arranged the demonstration. Once, he had heard, the President suggested to Senator James L. Buckley of New York that he stage a demonstration against himself in which he would be physically threatened.

In his single mention of Watergate, the President said, "The time has come to get Watergate behind us and to get on with the business of America." He pledged "to stay on the job." That earned him a thunderous ovation.

THE EDITED transcripts were wholly unacceptable evidence as far as Jaworski was concerned. He wanted the President's tapes, and he thought he had a lever to get them. In the first week of May, the special prosecutor had called a meeting of his most trusted assistants. For more than two months they had been sitting on probably the biggest secret in Washington—that the grand jury had voted to name the President as an unindicted co-conspirator in the plot to obstruct justice. Now, Jaworski said, the time had come to use whatever means were at their disposal to get the tapes they needed. When the White House moved to quash the prosecutor's subpoena, it had left them no alternative. Jaworski did not need to be more explicit. They were all lawyers. They knew that the ultimate legal argument in favor of the subpoena was the secret action of the grand jury; the courts had firmly established the principle that an unindicted co-conspirator must provide subpoenaed evidence.

Jaworski outlined his strategy: The House Judiciary Committee was ready to begin formal hearings on impeachment, and disclosure of the grand jury's action would devastate Nixon's position. Twenty-three ordinary citizens had found probable cause to charge the President with participation in a crime. If that information were known, it would make it far easier for members of the Judiciary Committee, especially the Republicans and the conservative Democrats, to support impeachment.

Jaworski reasoned that the most effective way to get the tapes they wanted might lie in revealing the information not in open court, but in the White House. He was ready to bargain.

The staff discussed the plan. Perhaps they could do with fewer than the sixty-four tapes, one of the lawyers suggested; maybe ten or fifteen. A compromise might be submitted to the White House in secret . . .

Exactly, said Jaworski.

Haig was traveling with the President when Jaworski reached him by phone. "Alec, I need to talk to you. In private." Jaworski suggested May 5, the next Sunday, at the White House. "You ought to have counsel standing by," he advised. "I'll have Rick and Phil there." The reference was to Richard Ben-Veniste and Phillip Lacovara, two of Jaworski's assistants.

Haig asked him what was cooking.

"There's no need for you to speculate," Jaworski replied. "But you are going to need advice of counsel, so Jim [St. Clair] should be there."

Haig, alarmed by Jaworski's tone and his uncharacteristic vagueness, called St. Clair. The President's lawyer couldn't figure out what it might be about, either. Things seemed to be going well, St. Clair said. What the hell could be so important to drag him back to Washington on a weekend? He agreed reluctantly to come back from Boston for the meeting.

That Sunday morning, Haig and St. Clair each made network television appearances as part of the White House public-relations offensive. They emphasized the President's determination not to surrender any more tapes or documents.

Haig, fashionable in a muted plaid suit and polka-dotted tie, said, "I think the time has come for all of us to ask ourselves a pretty fundamental question. At what point in the review of wrongdoing does the review itself involve injustice, excesses and distortions which, in effect, result in the cure being worse than the illness itself?"

JAWORSKI HAD ordered a government car for the trip to the White House. Expecting a big black sedan, the prosecutor and his assistants were surprised when the driver showed up at the wheel of a small tan compact, which they barely squeezed into. At the south gate of the White House Joulwan met them and got in with some difficulty. They were taken to the diplomatic entrance of the mansion, where there was scarcely any chance of being seen by reporters. The four men piled out like clowns from a tiny circus car as Haig waited. Inside, the carpets were being cleaned and white throw rugs had been laid down every few feet. Joulwan took Ben-Veniste and Lacovara into the library, chatting along the way about the great personal sacrifices Haig had made by leaving the Army to serve the President.

As Joulwan began telling war stories in the library, Haig escorted Jaworski to the map room.* Jaworski was wearing a dark charcoal suit and looked very somber. They sat down on a high-backed sofa.

Jaworski had prepared his speech carefully. He thought it would be appropriate to speak with unusual formality on this occasion. "Alec, the grand jury, in the last week of February, authorized the special prosecutor to cite Richard Nixon as an unindicted co-conspirator in the Watergate cover-up."

Haig sat silent as he tried to sort out his feelings. He was angry: what they had done was unfair. But he also realized that he had seen it coming. The President had feared that Cox would name him a co-conspirator. It was Jaworski who had done it.

"About fifteen members of my staff have known about this and have kept it quiet out of fairness to the President," the prosecutor said. "Now you are forcing me to come out with it in a hearing—in response to the motion to quash." Jaworski paused.

Haig kept his poker face. "Where are we, then?" he asked finally.

"If the President is willing to give me fifteen or maybe eighteen of the tapes, we might be able to compromise," Jaworski said. That was the price.

Haig felt trapped. It wasn't much of a bargain, no matter how he looked at it. He wanted time to think. St. Clair would have to be consulted, and Buzhardt.

* Haig thought he owed his life to an accident that involved Joulwan. The two served in the same company in Vietnam and were bivouacked in a tent when there was a mortar attack. As they slid into a foxhole Joulwan dropped the company clipboard he was responsible for. They both bent to grab it and as they did so a mortar hit the lip of the foxhole, inches from where their heads had been. When they came to, they declared they owed their lives to Joulwan's clipboard.

Lacovara and Ben-Veniste were called in.

"I've told Alec that the grand jury has taken this action and that we are not eager to disclose this," Jaworski said. "Alec thinks—"

He was interrupted by St. Clair's arrival; the flight from Boston had been late. St. Clair shook hands and sat down. His gray pin-striped suit jacket was buttoned at the bottom, making him look even more portly. He seemed tired and drowsy.

"I've told Alec about a matter of some delicacy," Jaworski explained, and he handed St. Clair a copy of the grand-jury transcript. They were quiet as St. Clair thumbed quickly through the pages, in the confident manner of a man familiar with such material. The others watched his eyes.

"When is this secret indictment going to be announced?" he asked.

A chorus of voices answered that the President was an unindicted co-conspirator. Haig was embarrassed. St. Clair attempted to gloss it over. He asked Jaworski whether he had anything else for him. Jaworski didn't reply.

St. Clair's tone grew harsh. Jaworski, he implied, had chosen his moment because he had concluded that the President was surviving the impeachment investigation. Well, if Jaworski was hell-bent on forcing the information out, better now than later. "This is an attempt to embarrass the President," he said.

"We don't want to embarrass the President," Lacovara responded. "And we don't want the judicial process to interfere with the impeachment process. The effect will be unfair to the President only if we cannot obtain an agreement consistent with our responsibilities to get materials relevant to subpoena."

"I don't see how this is relevant," St. Clair protested.

It would seem relevant to Judge Sirica, Lacovara said. Sirica had to rule on the White House motion to quash the subpoena. The grand jury thought the President had been involved in a crime. Therefore this particular President could not legitimately exercise a claim of executive privilege.

St. Clair took issue. "The President continues to have the privilege unless and until he is displaced."

Haig interrupted the debate. "It might be in our interest to consider this. Let's talk about it."

Chastised, St. Clair asked, "What kind of compromise are you talking about?"

Jaworski was prepared to keep the grand jury's action secret in exchange for a reduced number of tapes.

This was blackmail, St. Clair said to himself. But he also thought Jaworski wouldn't be able to make good on his promise. Somehow it would get out, he was sure of that. "Before I can decide, I need to know how many tapes and which ones you are talking about," he said. "We'll have to discuss it with the President."

Jaworski was not surprised. He was aware that the lawyer had very limited authority.

The meeting came to a perfunctory end. Ben-Veniste was to inform St. Clair the next day which tapes they wanted.

As they left the White House, Jaworski and his assistants were optimistic. Haig had seemed inclined to compromise despite St. Clair's hostility.

Actually, Haig thought he had been ambushed. He told St. Clair that Jaworski's proposal was a bad bargain no matter how it was resolved—no bargain at all, really. He didn't want to have to make the decision, either. He called Buzhardt. It was a no-win proposition, Buzhardt agreed. He thought they should refuse. There was no way they could be sure the secret wouldn't leak anyhow.

Haig flew to Camp David that afternoon to tell the President. Nixon took the news passively, almost as if he had been expecting it. He would listen to the tapes Jaworski wanted. He, the President, would be the one who'd make the damage assessment, he said purposefully.

Haig had anticipated such a response. The President would make his decision based on what he heard. At about six o'clock that evening, Haig called Steve Bull and asked him to come to the President's EOB office and set up two tapes for Nixon. The President listened for several hours that Sunday night.

HAIG HAD some maneuvering to do. He was fighting two battles at once for control of the tapes. For the moment, Jaworski was disengaged, as he awaited word on a compromise. A majority on the Judiciary Committee, however, agreed with Jaworski that the edited transcripts were an unacceptable form of evidence. But Haig continued to see hope in the twenty-to-eighteen vote holding that the transcripts did not represent compliance with the subpoena. The initial vote to subpoena the tapes, in early April, had been thirty to three.

Haig consulted Timmons, St. Clair and Ziegler. They all agreed that it was essential now to place the impeachment issue in as partisan a light as possible. The Republicans on the committee had to be held. The President's decision to resist the subpoena would need the support of other influential Republicans in the House, especially those who weren't regarded as down-the-line Nixon supporters. Barber B. Conable, Jr., of New York and John N.

Erlenborn of Illinois were two such men. Conable's influence in the House, where he was the fourth-ranking Republican, was enormous. Nervous, vocal, intellectual, he was regarded by his colleagues as almost puritanical in his standards of personal and political conduct, a man of unquestioned integrity. Erlenborn, though a party man and a conservative, had a reputation for independence and was generally opposed to broad claims of executive privilege. He was highly regarded in the Illinois Republican delegation; two of its members, Thomas F. Railsback and Robert McClory, were members of the Judiciary Committee.

On Tuesday, May 7, Haig and St. Clair had breakfast with Conable and Erlenborn in the White House mess. Haig set the tone. The committee's position was extreme, he said. In addition to the tapes under subpoena, the committee had informally requested another 141 presidential recordings. Those would probably be subpoenaed too. He complained about the length of time it would take to make transcripts of all the conversations. It could take six months, even more. It would be an ordeal. To meet the terms of the request would mean a delay that no one wanted, not the President, not the committee, not the House. The President wanted to cooperate; he wanted the impeachment process expedited.

"The demands of the Judiciary Committee are unreasonable," St. Clair stressed. "What can we do not to appear to be obstructionist?"

Conable was impressed. Haig and St. Clair were talking like reasonable men trying to deal with unreasonable men. He had an idea. "Now that the President has been forced to take off his clothes in public"—the others chuckled—"the question of additional tapes can be handled like a game of Russian roulette. Tell the House committee that all the requested tapes won't be turned over, but that the committee can select at random five or ten of the ones they want the most. Those tapes, not transcripts, will be turned over. It will be clear that the President has nothing to hide. It will also preserve the principle that the committee doesn't have unlimited access to the tapes."

St. Clair said he was intrigued by the idea and promised to consider it. The meeting was going well. Neither Conable nor Erlenborn seemed in danger of deserting.

The men finished their coffee, and on the way back to the Hill the Congressmen praised St. Clair's skill and tact.

FOR ALMOST two years, Watergate had been a political nightmare for Hugh Scott, a politician accustomed to resting comfortably. Time and again the

White House had enlisted the Minority Leader's prestige in support of the President, only to undercut him with disclosures which Haig or Nixon had failed to warn him about. But Scott doubted that there had ever been so hellish a week as the one since the President had gone on television.

As he watched Nixon that night, Scott had been relieved by the President's words and by the sight of all those stacked looseleaf binders. But then he had read in the newspapers that the transcripts were scarcely vindicating, particularly the March 21 conversation that Haig had dangled in front of him in December. Consulting his copy of the blue book, Scott compared the March 21 transcript with his recollection of what Haig had shown him. They were substantially different—large segments had been left out of the transcript he had seen in December. The reporters had begun pressing him to explain how he could reconcile what was in the transcripts with his public statements.

Scott had called his staff together and expressed his chagrin. What was he going to say now? His staff was familiar with Scott's philosophy of leadership—"Don't move unless you have the troops," he often told them. Well, there weren't enough troops to justify a blast at the White House.

It had taken the help of three aides before Scott had a one-sentence statement, which did not, in any case, reflect his real opinion: "The statements I made in January seem, in my judgment, to be consistent with the full material I have read."

Later, seething at what Haig had done to him, Scott had read about two thirds of the twelve hundred pages of transcripts. Now, Tuesday morning, May 7, at the same hour Conable and Erlenborn were breakfasting at the White House with Haig and St. Clair, Scott took the elevator to his office and announced to his staff, "I have finished reading the transcripts. There is something I must do. Now. I don't want anyone to try to talk me out of it. I simply have to do it."

He rushed into his inner office and came out twenty minutes later with a statement which he read to some reporters who had been called by his press secretary. The edited transcripts, said the Senate Minority Leader, reflected "a deplorable, disgusting, shabby, immoral performance" by each of the participants.

ON THE other side of the Capitol that morning, House Minority Leader John Rhodes was hunched over his desk, reading transcripts. He had finished about half of them and was dismayed. He was now persuaded that Richard Nixon was not indispensable as President of the United States.

Aside from the amorality of Nixon's discussions, Rhodes thought they revealed a president who was not his own man, not in command. Rhodes had always thought Nixon was able. He had thought that the President's aloofness showed strength. He had always admired Nixon's ability to make tough decisions and stick by them. But no longer. "I have never read such sleaziness in all my life," he told an aide.

At a press conference later that morning, a reporter told Rhodes what Senator Scott had said. "I won't quarrel with Scott's statement," Rhodes replied.

At two o'clock, Scott walked through the Capitol to his weekly meeting with Rhodes in Room H-230. They shook hands, more solemnly than usual. For months there had been on-and-off discussions among the Minority Leaders, Barry Goldwater, and a few other influential Republicans about the possibility of going to the White House to urge resignation. There might come a point, Rhodes and Scott had agreed, when they might have to jump ship—for the sake of the country and the party. And for themselves. It had always been regarded as a last resort, as hypothetical. Now the possibility seemed suddenly real.

"Hugh, the time is coming when we may have to play the hole card," Rhodes said.

Scott nodded.

IN THE Executive Office Building, many middle-level and junior presidential aides regularly stopped by the office of Mort Allin, who was in charge of compiling the President's daily news summary. There were wire-service machines in the reception area, and the staff liked to drift through and see what was new. Today, Scott's and Rhodes's statements dominated both the news and the conversation in Allin's office. The GOP leadership's retreat was unprecedented, and profoundly depressing. And other angry remarks from traditional Nixon supporters were coming over the ticker.

Across West Executive Avenue, Haig flew into a rage when he was informed of Scott's statement. The disloyalty, the spinelessness of the man! Scott had not even warned the White House. Haig called him. "You've betrayed me," he shouted over the phone as if he were chewing out a corporal.

Defensively Scott said that his comments had not specified anybody in particular.

Bullshit. Scott knew damn good and well whom the comments were directed at, and what harm they would cause the President. The White House was trying to clear the matter up once and for all, and now this.

The conversation ended abruptly.

Scott was not Haig's major source of concern, however. The general had just received word from the President that there would be no more tapes for anybody. Period. He was not going to submit to Jaworski's blackmail, he was not going to feed the Judiciary Committee's insatiable demands. He had gone too far already.

Haig understood the implications of the President's words all too clearly. He informed St. Clair. St. Clair phoned Jaworski. "The President does not wish to make any agreement," he announced. "His decision is final."

Jaworski couldn't think of much to say. He kept thinking how St. Clair was stressing, overstressing, the fact that it was the President's decision, his decision alone. Jaworski politely acknowledged the call. The fact that the President would not negotiate further was the signal. There could be only one meaning. The tapes were incriminating. The President would rather risk disclosure of the grand jury's secret action than surrender the tapes.

At four o'clock, St. Clair moved to inform the world in general, and the House committee in particular, of the President's decision, dressing it in a cloak of presidential principle. The setting was "Cocktails with Clawson," another of the presidential communications director's public-relations innovations. Invited reporters were served glasses of soft drinks wrapped in napkins printed especially for these occasions, during which members of the Administration made themselves available for interviews in an informal atmosphere.

Sitting in a wing chair, his legs crossed and his hands extended, St. Clair said there would be no more tapes for anyone. The President had told the full story of Watergate in the transcripts he had already released. "The only basis for further requests would be a desire by some to erode the presidency, and the President is not going to stand for it," St. Clair said defiantly. If others persisted, "then we are going to have a confrontation, because the President is firm in his resolve that he has done more than is necessary."

On Capitol Hill, Barber Conable was indignant. What had become of the reasonable, conciliatory approach St. Clair had outlined at breakfast? There had been no suggestion of flat rejection. Conable now concluded that some way would have to be found to disassociate the Republican Party from Richard Nixon.

On the House floor and in the cloakrooms, late that Tuesday afternoon, Conable found a consensus that Nixon was a liability to the party. Some members were getting hysterical. Still, Conable decided to wait a few days.

THAT AFTERNOON, the President finished his listening. Cueing a tape from April 19, 1973, Steve Bull found a nineteen-minute gap in a conversation between the President and Ehrlichman. Aghast, he hurried to inform Buzhardt.

"It doesn't surprise me," Buzhardt responded casually.

PHILIP BUCHEN of Grand Rapids, Michigan, dined that evening at the Georgetown home of Clay T. Whitehead, director of the White House Office of Telecommunications Policy. Buchen spent three days a week in Washington as executive director of the Federal Privacy Commission headed by his former law partner, the Vice-President of the United States.

Whitehead was baffled by Gerald Ford. "Why isn't Ford doing something to organize himself?" he asked. "He knows that the Nixon Administration is crippled. Is the Vice-President prepared to take over?"

Far from it, Buchen said. He had known Ford for years and was probably his closest friend. "Jerry can't do anything, because it would look like he was abandoning Nixon," he told Whitehead. Ford was not the type of person to assert himself in such a delicate situation. And the Vice-President's staff was inept, Buchen said, they had done nothing to prepare for a Ford presidency. Buchen, however, had been giving the matter a great deal of thought. "I'm convinced that there is a real possibility that Nixon will resign or be impeached," he continued. And because neither Ford nor his staff could be relied on, someone had to begin planning immediately for a transition. He suggested they establish a small team.

Whitehead, a Harvard Ph.D. who got his political education in the Nixon White House, had worked on the 1968 presidential transition. He was still an official of the Nixon Administration, but his disaffection was almost complete. He had been an architect of the aggressive White House policy toward the television networks—a true believer—but for almost a year he had operated as if there were no President. Twice Haig had almost pleaded with him not to bring important matters before Nixon, citing the President's inability to act. "The President isn't in any shape to deal with this," Haig had told him once.

Whitehead looked forward to a Ford presidency. Perhaps the lost promise of the Nixon Administration could be reclaimed there. He agreed to help prepare for a transfer of power.

"Jerry can't know what's going on," Buchen stressed. "Absolute secrecy is necessary."

They discussed who might join them. Buchen called it the Whitehead Project. Whitehead called it the Buchen Project.

THE NEXT morning, May 8, Scott received a call from George Bush, chairman of the Republican National Committee. Bush was having trouble keeping the party professionals in line. A move for Nixon's resignation was developing.

Things were getting worse on the Hill too, Scott said.

"What in the world do we do now?" asked Bush.

Scott said that he didn't know, either.

Rhodes phoned next. "At least ten members have told me today that they are off the reservation."

The same thing was happening on the Senate side, Scott said.

Rhodes had talked with Goldwater about playing the hole card. Goldwater was ready to go along with whatever the Minority Leaders decided. The erosion of support for the President had been worse in the past few days than in the entire year before, said Rhodes.

The White House response to the disaffection came that afternoon from the Administration's resident Jesuit priest, Dr. John McLaughlin, a special assistant to the President. Meeting with reporters, Father McLaughlin advanced a theological analysis of the transcripts that attempted to prove that they were neither amoral nor immoral. Senator Scott's characterization, said the priest, was "erroneous, unjust, and contains elements of hypocrisy. The President acquitted himself throughout these discussions with honor."

Nixon spent most of the day by himself. At 6:30 P.M. he boarded the presidential yacht *Sequoia* for a trip down the Potomac. He sent his strip steak back to the galley because there was fat on it. A steward cut the fat off and returned the steak to the President, who sat alone at the dining table, gazing out at the shoreline.

AT A routine economic meeting with the Republican leadership at eight-thirty the next morning, Nixon exchanged pleasantries with Senator Scott, who sat next to him. The Minority Leader's remarks about the transcripts were not mentioned. The President seemed even more bored than usual. He did not engage in any of his long monologues.

After the meeting, George Bush told Barber Conable that he was considering resigning as Republican national chairman. Conable did not try to dissuade him.

Haig approached Conable a moment later. "They're getting a little testy up on Capitol Hill, aren't they?" Haig said, a sarcastic grin on his face.

"Yes," Conable answered soberly.

House Minority Leader Rhodes did not attend the leadership meeting at the White House. He was breakfasting with a group of reporters at the Sheraton-Carlton Hotel, three blocks from the White House, across Lafayette Park.

He was grim and blunt. It might be a good idea for the President to consider resignation as an alternative to impeachment. "If Nixon comes to conclude that he can no longer be effective as President, he will do something about it," Rhodes suggested. "If he should resign, I would accept it." Resignation "would probably be beneficial" to the party.

As Rhodes and his press assistant, J. Brian Smith, left the hotel by car, Smith said, "Your statement is going to make headlines."

"I did it on purpose," Rhodes said, settling into the seat. "That's how I feel." A few moments later he turned to Smith. "You can't imagine how miserable I feel when I can't support the President."

House Republican Conference Chairman John B. Anderson of Illinois, the third-ranking House Republican, also held a press conference that morning. Anderson, gray-haired and urbane, a graduate of Harvard Law and a liberal, was hated by the Nixon Administration. Convinced that the transcripts revealed a total moral collapse in the White House, he was equally disturbed at the reaction to them by most of his colleagues on the Hill, by the President's aides and even by the press. There was no acceptable alternative to immediate resignation, Anderson asserted. The March 21 tape alone established "a prima-facie case for obstruction of justice." If the President did not resign, he faced certain impeachment.

The first editions of that afternoon's newspapers played Rhodes's and Anderson's comments together. Though they had said somewhat different things, the distinction was lost and their statements seemed to suggest a major move by influential Republicans to secure the President's resignation. Editorials in that day's *Chicago Tribune,* perhaps the staunchest Republican newspaper in the country, in the conservative *Omaha World-Herald,* and in the Hearst newspapers, all called on the President to resign. William Randolph Hearst, Jr., editor in chief of the Hearst chain and for years one of Nixon's strongest supporters, signed the editorial himself.

At noon, Senate Majority Leader Mike Mansfield hurried to meet Senator Scott. They agreed that anything could happen now, and they decided that they should meet with Ford as soon as he returned from a speaking tour in Illinois.

Even Ford seemed to step back from Nixon that afternoon. Speaking at Eastern Illinois University, he told the class of 1973, "While it may be easy to delete characterization from the printed page, we cannot delete characterization from people's minds with a wave of the hand. That is why I am speaking frankly on the subject, perhaps more so than some of my colleagues might wish."

AT 1:08 P.M., Chairman Peter Rodino brought down the gavel to open the House Judiciary Committee's formal hearings on impeachment. The ceremony, following seven months of staff investigation, was carried live on national television for twenty minutes. Then, after a brief debate, the committee voted, thirty-one to six, to close its doors for business—consideration of the evidence. Two thick binders were placed on each member's desk. Committee counsel John Doar began reading from the first volume in a monotone that seemed to drive part of the committee to distraction and put the rest to sleep.

St. Clair was permitted to remain to hear the evidence against his client. As he entered he had told reporters, "The President will not be impeached. The House of Representatives will not impeach." Then, as he took his seat at the counsel's table in front of the two-tiered platform where the thirty-eight members of the committee sat, St. Clair heard what sounded like a thousand cameras clicking. He thought once again of the Army–McCarthy hearings. He was relieved that the hearings were beginning. At least he'd know where he'd be each day for the coming weeks, maybe months. The hearings might be a pro-forma exercise, but being there was preferable to being at the beck and call of Haig and the President. St. Clair would get a call some mornings to come to the West Wing and would wind up spending eight or nine hours there, mostly waiting around. He would return to his desk in the EOB in the evening exhausted from the frustration. He was tired of it all. On the few occasions when he had been permitted to see the President, Nixon had rambled on about nothing, often making little sense.

After the Judiciary Committee adjourned that afternoon, reporters asked St. Clair for his reaction. "On balance," he said, "I'd rather be back in Boston practicing law."

ANDERSON HAD a four-o'clock appointment with Scott. They sat on one of the gold-brocade couches in the Minority Leader's office. Anderson argued passionately that a delegation should be sent to the President to urge him to resign.

"I do not favor that now," Scott replied. "Each person should make his own judgment. Certainly no collective action is timely now. The time will come, but it is not now."

The troops still weren't there in sufficient numbers.

Anderson thought that Scott lacked courage.

A LIGHT rain fell through most of the day. The President met a delegation of Vietnam War veterans, several favored Congressmen, five departing staff members, and Bruce Herschensohn, one of the antimedia writers on his staff, and Herschensohn's parents. Two people from Louisiana presented petitions of support to the President.

Ziegler told reporters about the President's "mood of determination." Deputy press secretary Gerald Warren elaborated, "Let me restate what I thought I made clear yesterday. The President has every intention to complete the work of his Administration. He is determined to remain in office despite the discussions by some and attacks by others."

Bebe Rebozo, who was testifying before the staff of the Senate Watergate Committee, described the President as in "high spirits." Nixon would never resign, Rebozo told reporters, because "he is confident he has done nothing wrong."

White House communications director Clawson stated, "The President will not quit, even if hell freezes over—no matter what."

ALL AFTERNOON, Rhodes's office was swamped with phone calls objecting to the Minority Leader's remarks on resignation. Some of the callers threatened his life. An FBI agent was sent to his office to stand guard. That evening, at a party on Capitol Hill, Rhodes went through a receiving line in which the First Lady was standing. Approaching her, Rhodes summoned the brightest smile he could manage.

"How are you, Mrs. Nixon?" he asked.

A photographer asked them to pose for a picture. "Oh, yes," Mrs. Nixon said. "Let's smile as if we liked each other."

"Mrs. Nixon," Rhodes said, "it isn't the way you heard it."

"Yeah," she shot back, "that's what they all say."

HAIG WAS finally convinced that the White House lacked a coherent strategy. Father McLaughlin—whom Haig detested—speaking about morality, and Ken Clawson talking about hell freezing over weren't going to do the job. Timmons, Clawson, Buchanan, Gergen, and some of the lawyers had been urging for weeks that a strategy committee be established to coordinate the

President's legal and public-relations defense. Haig had another Gergen memo on his desk: "Organizing for Impeachment." This time Haig did not toss the advice into his wastepaper basket. Instead he read: "It is time we faced up to the fact that this operational work is a full-time task; *it can no longer be done with the left hand.*"

Gergen was right, Haig decided. He summoned Dean Burch, the White House liaison to the Republican Party, to head the committee. They agreed that Buchanan, Timmons, Clawson, Gergen, Garment, and Buzhardt should serve on it.

Burch called the members to his office that day, Friday, May 10. Their first task was to contend with the rumors that were sweeping the city—including one that the President's resignation was imminent. Nixon had met privately with Vice-President Ford for fifty-five minutes that morning, contributing to the waves of speculation. Not all the rumors predicted resignation. One held that Nixon was going to issue a statement. Another, that he would call a news conference. A third, that he would address the nation on television. A fourth said Nixon was turning over all the tapes under subpoena. Another had the Cabinet being assembled in an emergency session to hear the President. Yet another had Secretary of State Kissinger flying back from the Middle East to accept the President's resignation letter.

The Burch group was bewildered. There seemed to be no solution other than to deny the rumors, and Jerry Warren had been doing that all day.

The pressure became so intense that Ziegler finally called the *New York Times* with a statement: "The city of Washington is full of rumors. All that have been presented to me today are false, and the one that heads the list is the one that says President Nixon intends to resign. His attitude is one of determination that he will not be driven out of office by rumor, speculation, excessive charges or hypocrisy. He is up for the battle, he intends to fight it and he feels he has a personal and constitutional duty to do so."

That evening, the President decided to take a ride on the *Sequoia* again. He left with his wife, David and Julie shortly before six. David had just finished an exam and they were out to celebrate. It was a warm, pleasant evening. The breeze was refreshing. The four went topside and, sitting in the wicker chairs, sipped drinks.

There had been another "Bebe" story in the papers that day. It said that Rebozo was under investigation for an unreported $50,000 political contribution he had collected in cash.

Such stories almost always altered the President's mood and made him even more withdrawn than usual. Nothing seemed to sting the President as much as watching his friends being consumed by the scandal. As the yacht cruised downriver, a military aide approached the President. Photographers were waiting on the pier for the *Sequoia* to return, he said. More were lined up on the Potomac bridges in the hope of getting a picture as the boat passed underneath.

Nixon left his chair abruptly and started pacing. They were trying to get a picture of his *face,* goddammit. They were attempting to discover how he was handling the pressure.

He picked up the ship-to-shore telephone. "Crown, get me Ziegler."

Crown was the code name for the White House switchboard. The President was using an unsecure line. Anyone else listening could have heard only half of what was being said, however, because the send and receive ends of the conversation were on two different frequencies.

Ziegler came on the line.

Goddammit, Nixon shouted into the phone, why was the press always hounding him? Why couldn't he get a few private moments? How had it leaked out that he was aboard the *Sequoia*? Goddammit, he hadn't wanted it discovered. Why couldn't Ziegler control the press? Goddammit, goddammit, oh goddammit.

All week David Eisenhower had noticed a strange, wavering quality in the President's voice. David was looking for signs of collapse in his father-in-law. He concluded there was no way to calm Mr. Nixon with words. Quickly he climbed up to the bridge to talk to Lieutenant Commander Andrew Coombs. Something had to be done. There was no way of knowing who would be waiting at the Navy Yard to witness the President's anger. They must outfox the press and dock elsewhere.

There were only two alternatives, the skipper told David: to cruise to Mount Vernon and order a helicopter to take them back to the White House, or to dock at the old Anacostia pier. But two Navy tugs were berthed at Anacostia and it might be difficult to get them cleared out of the way.

David went back to check on the President. He was talking quietly to the others now, and he seemed calmer. In just a few minutes the fit of anger seemed to have subsided. David went topside again. He told Coombs that it would be all right to dock at the usual location. Half an hour later, the boat slid into its berth at the Navy Yard and the President rushed into the waiting limousine before photographers could get a glimpse of him.

THE DAYS of May 1974 were lonely ones for Mrs. Nixon. There was an occasional reception or a tea—Military Wives of the Year, the Women's National Republican Club, a tea for visiting high-school students from

Ohio, the Senate wives luncheon, a breakfast for the wives of former members of Congress; saying hello to the Veterans of Foreign Wars' poppy girl. Almost invariably, Mrs. Nixon's appearances were short. She would arrive, shake a few hands, smile, allow a few photographs, and leave.

The few times she lingered were when small children visited the White House. Then she would become animated, the joy in her face evident. Members of her staff marveled at how children always seemed to seek her out, even in a crowded room.

Most of the First Lady's days were spent in her pale-yellow bedroom on the second floor of the mansion. Her room, and the blue sitting room adjoining it, overlooked the south grounds and offered a spectacular view of the Jefferson Memorial and beyond. A devoted letter writer, she spent hours on her correspondence. And she did a lot of reading, including the thin inspirational volumes on friendship and love which rested on the night table next to her canopied bed. These were her rooms, and she had her privacy.

Around 11 A.M., she would write out her lunch order, most often a chef's salad, soup or a sandwich, and coffee, to be served at one o'clock. More often than not, these days, the tray came back to the kitchen with the coffee gone and the food untouched.

When she and the President dined alone, there was always a great rush to get the food from the kitchen to the table. Often the Nixons had been seated for only a minute before the butlers started pressing to serve them.

Why the big rush? a member of the kitchen staff had asked.

"A minute is a long time when you're not talking," a butler had explained.

On Camp David weekends, the President and his wife hardly saw each other. When they did, silence usually prevailed. Backstairs their distance was an open secret. Marine Lieutenant Colonel Jack Brennan, the President's military aide, joked that his duties included briefing Nixon on how to kiss his wife.

Mrs. Nixon had always hated being a political wife. Since Nixon had come to Washington as a Congressman, she had yearned to return permanently with her husband and children to California and live like an ordinary American family.

She and her husband had not really been close since the early 1960s, the First Lady confided to one of her White House physicians. She had wanted to divorce him after his 1962 defeat in the California gubernatorial campaign. She tried, and failed, to win his promise not to seek office again. Her rejection of his advances since then had seemed to shut something off inside Nixon. But they had stuck it out.

Watergate, and the tapes particularly, widened the gap. Despite the rein she kept on her emotions, the transcripts had visibly disturbed her. "How foolish to have tapes," she told her few friends and several chosen assistants. She would then smile or laugh nervously. The tapes were like love letters, she said. They should have been burned or destroyed.

The White House physicians were worried about the First Lady. She had returned from a South American trip in April 1973 distraught and even more underweight than usual. She was becoming more and more reclusive, and drinking heavily. On several occasions members of the household staff came upon her in the pantry of the second-floor kitchen, where the liquor was kept, in the early afternoon. Awkwardly, she had tried to hide her tumbler of bourbon on the rocks.

Helen Smith, Mrs. Nixon's press secretary, tried to get the First Lady out to more parties and receptions. But wherever there was a gathering, there were reporters with Watergate questions. "Why bring it up?" Mrs. Nixon asked dejectedly when reporters caught up with her on a trip or on one of the family's dinner outings to Washington restaurants.

Smith had a tough job. Delicate and generous by nature, she had felt cruelly pushed around by Haldeman. Now Ziegler commanded her like a drill sergeant, oblivious to either her wishes or the First Lady's. He ignored Smith's memos and almost never asked her opinion on Mrs. Nixon's public appearances. The President himself insisted on picking the menus and the guest lists, and on supervising the seating arrangements for state dinners at the White House. Ziegler and the President also concerned themselves with the slightest details of Mrs. Nixon's few public appearances. Mrs. Nixon's attitude toward such events was principally one of resistance. When Smith tried to schedule interviews or television appearances, the First Lady usually refused, saying, "Dick's too busy." Tricia Nixon Cox, called "Dolly" by her mother, also hated public appearances and avoided interviews scrupulously. So Julie Nixon Eisenhower, the younger daughter, became the family link to the outside world. In the days following release of the transcripts, Helen Smith was bombarded with requests for interviews with someone in the family. Julie and David agreed to meet reporters on Saturday, May 11.

It was a big event. Julie, wearing a polka-dot blouse, and David, in a Lacoste tennis shirt, stood before separate microphones in the East Garden. The noonday sun was brilliant.

Question: "Do either of you foresee any point at which the President would resign?"

"Absolutely not, no," David replied.

"He is stronger now than he ever has been in his determination to see this through," Julie added.

The next question came from Robert Pierpoint of CBS: "Mrs. Eisenhower, may I say first of all that I feel I have to apologize for addressing these questions to you, since in our system we do not hold the sins of the fathers against the following generations, and we don't have a monarchy in which you are going to inherit the power. I am not quite sure why you are here to answer these questions."

Julie was visibly agitated. "Mr. Pierpoint, I am going to try to control myself in answering the question, because it really does wound me. . . . I have seen what my father has gone through, and I am so proud of him that I would never be afraid to come out here and talk to any members of the press about resignation or anything else, even though it goes against my grain because I know he does not want me out here because he does not want anyone to construe that I am trying to answer questions for him."

Her voice was quivering. "I am not trying to answer questions for him. I am just trying to pray for enough courage to meet his courage. Really."

Another questioner asked Julie how her mother was bearing up.

"She is able to take things with a grain of salt," Julie replied. "She is philosophical and I guess she finds she can hold up under all this because she loves my father and believes in him."

As the interview neared its end, the President's daughter observed, "He is not shackled by Watergate. If you look at his appointment schedule, if you see the things he is doing, the people he is meeting with, it all confirms the message."

The White House switchboard was flooded with calls praising Julie's performance. Later that afternoon, Smith encountered the President going up in the elevator and mentioned the response. He just stood there, silently. He does not look well, Smith thought; he does not look strong or vigorous. Nixon's faced looked damp from sweat. She thought, This man is not in control of the situation. As she turned away, she saw tears in his eyes.

FEW OF the President's men were as shocked by the transcripts as the senior academic-intellectual members of the Nixon Administration: Arthur F. Burns, the chairman of the Federal Reserve Board; Daniel Patrick Moynihan, ambassador to India and formerly an adviser on domestic policy; George P. Shultz, formerly the President's principal economic counselor. They read the transcripts in different parts of the world. They heard a Richard Nixon they had never been exposed to.

Whatever Nixon's failings, these men had often been impressed by the President's strength, his competence and the keenness of his mind. The Nixon of the transcripts was weak, insecure, indecisive, inarticulate, uncomprehending—even incompetent at times.

The conspiratorial nature of the discussions surprised them less. In their minds, Watergate had always seemed characteristic of Nixonian excess. They knew the President could be petty, vicious, vindictive, unprincipled—particularly when he was with Haldeman and Ehrlichman. Heretofore they could only guess at the hidden side of his personality. Now, as they read the thick blue volume with its deleted expletives and coarse, cynical language ("candy-ass," "the hang-out route"), the guesswork was ended. There were basic elements of the Nixon character which the President could not bring himself to show them, they concluded. They were men he regarded as lofty thinkers, whose respect and approval he coveted and courted.

Burns, the President's chief domestic aide and counselor during the first two years of his administration, was especially shocked. Nixon had spoken clearly, decisively, grammatically and even eloquently to him. He had rarely sworn beyond a mild "goddam." The transcripts were full of presidential grunts, unfinished sentences, meandering thoughts which began almost nowhere and finished someplace else. Burns had never heard some of the expressions. He thought, "Here is a Dr. Jekyll. A split personality. What does it all mean? Does Nixon live a double life? Is he a great actor?"

Henry Kissinger was less amazed. He was in the Middle East when the transcripts were released. Copies of the blue books were forwarded to the Secretary's plane. At night, in his hotel, and shuttling by air between capitals, he had time to read. He put aside the material that had been packed for him—a book on chess, some thrillers and a pornographic novel—and turned to the transcripts with morbid fascination.

Around Kissinger, Nixon was proud, even arrogant. Here the President seemed full of self-loathing, oblivious to bullying and disrespect from his subordinates. Ehrlichman talked to the President like an exasperated parent addressing a stupid child. The language was baffling. Sure, the President occasionally referred to someone as an "asshole" after a few drinks, but never much more than that. In Kissinger's presence, Nixon was almost prudish—prissy even, the Secretary thought.

Nixon's greatest personal asset, Kissinger had thought, was his willingness to make big decisions himself, seeking consultation with only a few people—an ability to "take big bites of a problem," as the Secretary phrased it. But here, with Haldeman and Ehrlichman—"the fanatics"—it was all different.

Watching the conspiracy unfold in the taped conversations confirmed what Kissinger had suspected. "Of course, that's how it must have happened and evolved," he told his aides. "This explains why Nixon refused to cut his ties with Haldeman and Ehrlichman even after their resignations."

The transcripts would be Nixon's undoing. Even if he clung to office, how would he govern after this? All moral authority was gone, Kissinger said. The deletions and denigrating characterizations suggested something else, long concealed, about the Nixon character. Rumors and some reliable reports circulated that Nixon regularly employed ethnic slurs, particularly anti-Semitic ones, and that some had been deleted from the transcripts. Was Nixon a racist? An anti-Semite?

For his part, Kissinger was convinced that the President was anti-Semitic. He had believed it for years. As the son of German Jews who had fled the Nazis, he was particularly sensitive to what he regarded in Nixon as a dangerous brand of anti-Jewish prejudice born of ignorance. He saw in the President an antagonistic, gut reaction which stereotyped Jews and convinced Nixon that they were his enemies. Many times Kissinger returned from a meeting with Nixon and told his deputy, Lawrence Eagleburger: "That man is an anti-Semite." The remark by Nixon which most often unsettled Kissinger was well known to the President's close associates: "The Jewish cabal is out to get me." The meaning of the often-repeated comment was a source of debate within the Administration. Many believed that it reflected hostility more to intellectuals than to Jews.

Late in 1971, Nixon had summoned the White House personnel chief, Fred Malek, to his office to discuss a "Jewish cabal" in the Bureau of Labor Statistics. The "cabal," Nixon said, was tilting economic figures to make his Administration look bad. How many Jews were there in the bureau? he wanted to know. Malek reported back on the number, and told the President that the bureau's methods of weighing statistics were normal procedure that had been in use for years. Later, there was another suspected "Jewish cabal" in another department.

Malek, a young West Point and Harvard Business School graduate who had been brought into the Administration by Haldeman, knew that these tirades were not reserved for Jews. The President had once told him he did not want any more "fucking academics" or "goddam Ivy Leaguers" appointed to high positions. They were wrecking his programs; most if not all of the problems in government could be traced to them. Haldeman had directed Malek to ignore presidential orders which suggested departmental purges or quotas, and Nixon did, in fact, continue to approve appointments of academics, even Ivy League ones and Jews.

Arthur Burns, himself a Jew, was convinced that Nixon was not truly anti-Semitic. There were, however, ugly strands of prejudice in the man, Burns had concluded, and he was not surprised that there were, apparently, anti-Semitic remarks on the tapes. The President really didn't have much love for humanity, Burns believed. Why should Nixon love Jews any more than Japanese or Italians or Catholics? Nixon regularly employed epithets for whole sections of mankind, he knew.

Burns and Kissinger had often discussed the question. Burns used to point out that the President greatly admired Israel, and that a large number of Jews served in his Administration. What disturbed Burns was something he considered apart from anti-Semitism: if the President perceived that Jews or Israel, or anyone else, for that matter, got in his way, he was prepared to stomp them. Burns vividly recalled a 1973 White House meeting during which the President had a tantrum about an amendment to his trade bill; the amendment would have restricted business with the Soviet Union if Russia did not ease its persecution of Jews. "Members of the Jewish community" were causing him difficulties, Nixon had said, because of their support for the amendment. A wave of anti-Semitism might descend on American Jews if they persisted, he predicted. Burns watched Nixon very closely on that occasion, and he was impressed by the President's fury. Burns felt that Nixon was saying that Jews might suffer for thwarting his will.

AFTER A year of dealing with Nixon, Fred Buzhardt had learned to discount the President's diatribes. Nixon said vile things about everybody—about bureaucrats, Congressmen, reporters, lawyers, Russians, Democrats, Easterners, ethnic groups, his own staff.

Just after David and Julie's press conference that Saturday, Fred Graham, a CBS television reporter, called the White House press office for comment on a story scheduled for that evening's news. Graham had information that in two of the tapes the President had made disparaging remarks about Jews and had called Judge Sirica a "wop." When he was asked by Ziegler, Buzhardt insisted to the press secretary that he had heard no such thing on the tapes. Ziegler tried but couldn't talk Graham out of the story, so he moved to kill it. He told two of his secretaries to get hold of CBS correspondent Dan Rather. Failing that, they were to reach Walter Cronkite or the CBS Washington Bureau chief or the producer of *The CBS Evening News,* or the president of CBS, Arthur Taylor. None could be reached. Ziegler blamed the secretaries and started shouting at them when the story went on the air. "Ron, we can only place the calls," responded Anne Grier. "If you think you can do any better, then be my guest."

The next morning, a similar story by Seymour M. Hersh ran in the Sunday *New York Times.* Hersh cited conversations between Nixon and Dean on February 28 and March 20, 1973. Both the White House and James Doyle, chief press officer for Special Prosecutor Jaworski, had tried to call Hersh off the story. Doyle had checked transcripts of the two conversations Hersh referred to, and he couldn't find the references.*

There *were* ethnic references on the same tapes—including some that might be regarded as anti-Semitic—but Buzhardt knew they were not the remarks cited in Hersh's account. The President had, in fact, said on one tape that it was not going to be his policy to have a Jewish seat on the Supreme Court, as it had been for some other Presidents. Jews, he said, were intelligent and aggressive and were everywhere in the government. If any minority group needed a leg up, it clearly was not the Jews. Nixon had then praised his liberal foe on the Court, Justice William O. Douglas, and had made disparaging comments about his own appointees.

Now Haig, Ziegler and Buzhardt felt they finally had an opportunity to strike back at the opposition. The President had been unfairly accused. On Sunday morning, Buzhardt appeared on an interview show to denounce the news accounts.

"There have been fabrications," he said. "There have been attempts to portray remarks that are on the tapes as racial slurs, and they are not. And I wonder, you know, it's clear that a concerted campaign has been made to cause these to be publicized." He clasped his fingers together to denote the interlocking nature of the conspiracy. "And that is one of the problems. It bothers many of us. Obviously this type of material is not relevant to the question of whether the President has committed treason, bribery or high crimes or misdemeanors. I can only characterize this as malicious and vicious attempts to poison the public mind against the President by any means."

On Monday morning, at the Burch group meeting, Buzhardt argued forcefully for some countermove to the stories. Garment, a Jew, agreed to listen to the relevant tapes and then, if justified, to go out on the White House lawn to refute the *Times* and CBS accounts, in front of cameras.

At ten o'clock one evening that week Garment got a call at home from Julie. "Daddy wants to see you." Garment drove back to the White House

---

* The problem, it was later discovered in the White House, had been caused by transcription errors. One of the original transcripts ascribed the phrase "Jewish boys" to the President. A corrected version put it in Dean's mouth. And an initial, and therefore uncorrected, version of the other transcript in question indeed had the President calling Judge Sirica a "goddam wop." But Nixon's actual words, which sounded similar on the scratchy recording, had been "That's the kind I want," a reference to tough judges like Sirica.

and went to the Lincoln Sitting Room. Julie got beers for the men and left.

He was upset about the stories, the President told Garment. He wasn't what they were saying he was.

Garment replied that he didn't need convincing. It was absurd to call Nixon an anti-Semite. Look at all the Jews he had appointed to high posts.

"The stories are very unfair," the President concurred, "and they should correct them."

That would not be simple, Garment explained. The only way would be to make the relevant portions public. Would the President allow him to do that?

He would.

They had another beer and talked for an hour about the distinctions between what people, even Presidents, say and what they actually mean. In anger or frustration things are said that are not meant. The taping system had etched inconsequential presidential remarks in stone.

The next day, Garment called Clifton Daniel, the *New York Times* Washington Bureau chief, and offered to let him listen to the relevant portions of the tapes. Daniel said that he would agree if he were allowed to listen to the full conversations.

Garment realized that Daniel was making him an offer that the White House could not but refuse. Garment had listened to the two tapes and he certainly could not recommend that anyone—especially the *New York Times*—be allowed to hear them. There were things that would prove highly embarrassing to the President. And Garment never appeared on the White House lawn to refute the stories.

Later, Ziegler informed the President that he was certain that a member of the White House staff had helped the *Times* and CBS develop the accounts. Ziegler thought he knew who had done it.

"I want him fired in five minutes," the President shouted into the phone. "And I want a progress report in three minutes."

Ziegler tried to reach the suspect.

Two or three minutes later, the President was back on the phone. Where was the progress report?

Ziegler said he was trying to locate the culprit.

The President hung up. He was soon served his dinner, and the matter was dropped.

Ziegler told him later that he wasn't sure any longer that he had in fact found the right person. No one was fired.

ON MONDAY afternoon, May 13, the President gave a ninety-minute interview to Rabbi Korff for a book that was to be published by the clergyman's anti-impeachment crusade.

Nixon leaned back in his chair. The sun refracted through the three-inch-thick bulletproof windows behind him, the beams of light bouncing off his highly polished desk.

"How do you stand up under this kind of vilification and attack and savagery that has gone on for the past year and a half?" Korff asked. "What enables you to persevere?"

"Part of it is inheritance," the President said. "A strong mother, strong father, both of whom worked hard and were, incidentally, deeply religious. And a very strong family, my wife and my two daughters, and my two sons-in-law, all of whom stand like a rock against the attacks. . . . But in more personal terms, it gets down to what the Quakers call peace at the center.

"The individual cannot succumb to the attack, or take the easy way out, like resigning the office, as I could have on other occasions, by not running for the office in the first instance, taking the easy way out after a defeat or thinking, 'Well, I will go out and make money,' which is very easy for me, being a fairly accomplished lawyer. . . .

"I don't change at the center. I don't go overboard when we win and I don't get terribly depressed when we lose. I don't go overboard when things are good, I don't go overboard when they are bad. And it is keeping on an even keel. The Midwesterners had a term. They say, 'Stay steady in the buggy.' . . . but the most important factor is that the individual must know inside, deep inside, that he is right. . . .

"As people look back on the years of the seventies, Watergate will be written about as being something very difficult to understand, particularly coming in the campaign of an individual who is supposed to be a political pro, which I am.

"I believe that when it is all sorted out in the end, it will be found that there has been harassment on a massive basis of innocent people, that many without guilt have had their reputations badly damaged, and I fear, too, that it will be found that many who have been charged with guilt have been charged on flimsy indictments.

"I am not the press's favorite pin-up boy," Nixon told the rabbi. "If it hadn't been Watergate, there would probably have been something else. So now they have this. But I will survive it and I just hope they will survive it with, shall we say, as much serenity as I have."

CHAPTER THIRTEEN

THAT evening, Clay Whitehead reviewed a list of problems Gerald Ford would face immediately if he became President. Under the heading "Taking the Reins," the first listing was: "Designate Haig Replacement."

The Vice-President was still unaware of Whitehead and Buchen's planning sessions. His belief in Nixon's innocence remained steadfast: Watergate was a political vendetta conducted by Nixon's old enemies in the press and the liberal wing of the Democratic Party. The impeachment drive was not motivated by considerations of law or justice or principle.

Ford's public defense of Nixon often ignored the recommendations of the Vice-President's staff and advisers. Buchen, Ford's political aide Robert Hartmann and Mrs. Ford had all urged him for months to carve a political identity that would separate him from Nixon's fortunes. To Mrs. Ford in particular the President was anathema. Ford, however, persisted in his unequivocal proclamations of the President's innocence. Even the edited transcripts didn't alter his basic view. He had read them on a plane going to Michigan. He was disturbed at the conspiratorial nature of some of the conversations. But Nixon's actions were essentially harmless, if tactically flawed, he told Hartmann. Only once, at Eastern Illinois University, had the Vice-President's support of his Chief seemed to waver. But at his next stop in Chicago he had resumed his zealous defense.

Still, behind his placid exterior the Vice-President was showing signs of uneasiness. He hadn't planned to become President, and he wouldn't plan for it now. He had wanted to be nothing more than Speaker of the House, and he had accepted the Vice-Presidential nomination largely because it seemed a fitting way to end his political career. Now events were spinning out of control. Though the reality of the situation pressed itself on his logical mind, emotionally he succeeded in pushing it away.

At noon Tuesday, May 14, Ford met with the Majority and Minority Leaders of the Senate, Mike Mansfield and Hugh Scott, at the Capitol. The meeting, which had been sought by the leaders, increased Ford's discomfort.

A Senate trial now seemed very likely, the leaders told him at the outset. Rules and regulations were already being considered.

At that, Ford's uneasiness became acute.

The leaders sought to reassure him. They wanted merely to keep him informed because he was president of the Senate, Scott told him. If the House voted impeachment, it would be appropriate for a president pro tempore, and not Ford, to preside until the trial began and the Chief Justice took over. Matters relating to the trial would be coming to the floor.

Ford readily agreed. He didn't want any part of it, he said. If the House voted impeachment, he probably wouldn't come near the Senate until the trial was over. He hated even to discuss it.

Mansfield wanted the trial to be carried live on television. Americans had lost faith in their country's institutions. It was crucial that the denouement take place in the open, he said, for all to witness. The Majority Leader's manner was grave. Clearly, he did not approach the subject with any enthusiasm. Scott too favored televising the trial, and Ford seemed to agree.

The leaders were concerned about the Senate's image. Everything would have to be done with dignity. All the proceedings must be scrupulously fair. As the Democratic leader, Mansfield assured Scott and Ford that the President's wishes with regard to procedure, and to the rules of evidence, would be accorded great weight. Mansfield then left.

"Jerry," Scott now said, "there's a better than a fifty-fifty chance that you will be President before long."

Ford said nothing.

"I urge that you conduct a completely open presidency," Scott said. He waited for Ford to respond.

"Hugh, for me there simply can't be any other way," the Vice-President said finally.

Rather inappropriately, Scott lectured him. "Success in dealing with Congress will often depend on the feeling which members develop toward you. 'Mr. President' it should be whenever others are around; but in private with Mike, Carl [Albert] and the rest, insist that they call you Jerry."

Pleased with the way he was developing his theme, Scott contrasted his vision of a Ford presidency with Richard Nixon's White House. Nixon and the men around him were aloof, unapproachable, contemptuous of people like Ford and himself, Scott said.

The Nixon Administration had been a disaster for Scott. He had been sure that he would play a major role in Administration policy, share in the big decisions, have a place in the sun. He hadn't gotten it. He did not want the same thing to happen again.

Ford reassured him. He recalled their closeness during the years when "Hugh and Jerry" had been their party's leadership team in the two houses. "Hugh, we've always been on a first-name basis, and that must continue—with all those I'd have to work with. If it comes to my being in that position, I'll want to rely on you particularly, because we know each other's problems. I'll continue to count on you, whatever happens. Your advice has helped me a lot."

Scott was pleased.

FORD'S SUCCESSOR as Minority Leader in the House, John Rhodes, called a meeting of the House Republican leaders the next day. He was having second thoughts. He faced a tough reelection campaign in November. Since his statement about the desirability of resignation, he had been besieged by letters and telegrams. The response had been markedly pro-Nixon, by about ten to one. Back-pedaling, he shared his doubts with the other leaders, among them Conable, Anderson, and Robert Michel, chairman of the House Republican Campaign Committee.

Every member of the House had to run in November, Rhodes noted. That was less than six months away. Republican prospects were awful. Campaign money was difficult to raise. If George Bush resigned, and it seemed likely that he would, the White House couldn't get anybody of stature to take his place. This might not be the time, Rhodes suggested gently, for Republicans in Congress to declare themselves independent of the Republican in the White House. Nixon had the support of millions of hard-core party loyalists who could make life miserable for Republicans who stood against their President.

John Anderson was angry. The future of the Republican Party didn't lie with die-hard Nixon loyalists, he asserted, and the party leadership should not bend to them. Rhodes, he implied, was bowing to a knife at his own neck. The time for real leadership had arrived.

Rhodes replied hotly that Nixon was still President, still the leader of the party. Watergate had not changed that, not for the moment. The party would self-destruct if the leaders didn't recognize the support that Nixon still had in the country. Rhodes had seen it and heard it. The support was real, not some fake letter-writing campaign dreamed up in the White House.

The others tried to find a middle ground between Anderson's demand that the leadership call for resignation and Rhodes's rally-round-Nixon. After a stormy hour, they settled for caution. They would quietly poll the House Republicans. Each would talk to about twenty-five members.

The message—and it came back very fast—was political: Above all else, an overwhelming majority of House Republicans were terribly worried about their political futures, and the last thing they wanted to see was a march on the White House by their leadership. They didn't want to vote on impeachment until after the election, they didn't want to vote on impeachment, period. They needed hard-core Republicans to win in November. They needed the people who run local campaigns, ring doorbells, raise the money. Nixon's fight was their fight. Those people saw Nixon as an underdog, a man under attack by their own enemies—the press and the congressional liberals.

The message was clear: Cool it.

Word of the poll soon reached the White House. Haig, Burch and Timmons were comforted. The House leadership was at bay. The basic strategy to divide the impeachment battle along party lines was working where it most counted. Haig was less sanguine about the Senate. Only a third of the membership was up for reelection. Something had to be done to keep the key Senators in line, most particularly Scott and Goldwater.

That week Buzhardt invited Scott to lunch. They met on the Hill. At first Buzhardt was indirect, talking generalities in his most gracious Southern style. Watergate was creating a certain investigatory atmosphere, he drawled —pervasive, uncontrollable, frivolous. If it were not brought under control, there would be others, not just Nixon, who might get swept up. There were rats' nests all over Washington, he cautioned, and they might be discovered.

Scott fidgeted. He was not naïve.

For example, Buzhardt continued in his friendliest manner, Senator Scott himself was involved in a series of appointments to government jobs which had bypassed Civil Service regulations. In fact, Scott was the worst offender on the Hill, Buzhardt noted—particularly with regard to the General Services Administration. GSA chief Arthur Sampson was Scott's man. The two of them operated the GSA as if they were running a private employment agency, Buzhardt observed.

Scott listened carefully and silently. Buzhardt recounted some more unfortunate history. Firms okayed by Scott had been awarded GSA contracts in various irregular ways. Of course, much of this was simple politics, Buzhardt agreed—just as a lot of Watergate had been. There was a lot of tough talk in Washington, and it wasn't confined to the President's tapes. That was part of the business of politics. Everybody was vulnerable. Buzhardt had a list of all the appointments and grants that Scott had promoted.

SENATOR GOLDWATER was a bigger problem. He was much more unpredictable, so unpredictable that Dean Burch, who had once been his administrative assistant, had been brought to the White House almost for the sole purpose of keeping tabs on him. The Senator not only got the appointments he wanted, he sometimes got more than he had counted on.

J. William Middendorf II, the Undersecretary of the Navy, had approached Goldwater several weeks earlier to solicit support for appointment to the vacant secretaryship. Middendorf had worked in Goldwater's 1964 presidential campaign, and afterward had served for five years as treasurer of the Republican National Committee, before he was appointed ambassador to the Netherlands.

Goldwater had told Middendorf that he really didn't care whether he got the secretaryship. An ambassadorial post and a tour as Undersecretary of the Navy were about par for the course, the Senator had observed.

Eventually, after a lot of pushing, Goldwater had promised his support. If Middendorf wanted it so badly, why not let him have it? Goldwater told Burch. And Burch was accommodating, as always.

Secretary of Defense James Schlesinger was opposed and phoned Goldwater.

"Okay, you're the boss," said Goldwater. "I don't care."

Deputy Defense Secretary William P. Clements, Jr., amplified Schlesinger's objections. Goldwater replied that he was not committed to Middendorf, not in the least. The last Goldwater heard of the matter was a call from Burch a few days later. Middendorf had the job.

A few Senators never even thought of straying. Some of them were Southern Democrats. Senator James O. Eastland of Mississippi renewed a pledge that he would never vote to convict the President in a Senate trial. Not under any circumstances. When it came to appointments or other matters of privilege or patronage, Eastland always got his way. "I get any damn thing I want," he boasted.

JUDGE JOHN Sirica set aside a Friday afternoon in mid-May to hear the arguments in open court on St. Clair's motion to quash the special prosecutor's subpoena. The grand-jury minutes, recording the citation of the President as an unindicted co-conspirator, remained in a special safe in the special prosecutor's office. Members of the staff were under strict instructions to refrain from discussing the matter outside the office. Now, as he was preparing himself for the oral arguments on the motion to quash, Jaworski called St. Clair to tell him what he had decided. To reveal the grand jury's action while the House Judiciary Committee was considering the evidence would be unjust. He would join with St. Clair to request that the hearing be held *in camera.*

St. Clair praised the special prosecutor for "an act of legal statesmanship."

Inside Sirica's chambers, St. Clair argued forcefully that Jaworski had no claim to the tapes. The special prosecutor was an employee of the executive branch and subject to the President's instructions. He lacked legal standing to subpoena the President for tapes or any other evidence.

Jaworski was truly outraged. The argument was flatly contrary to the pledge he had received from Haig, he said, almost stammering. When he had been asked to take the job, he had been guaranteed by Haig the right to sue for tapes, and that understanding had been ratified by the Senate Judiciary Committee. It was his charter.

After the lawyers left the judge's chambers, St. Clair spoke to Jaworski. The issue of standing was the President's best argument, and St. Clair was going to pursue it regardless of what Haig might or might not have promised Jaworski. Haig had made no promises to the court. If Haig ordered him not to use the argument, St. Clair said, he might quit.

Jaworski phoned Haig and accused St. Clair of abrogating the understanding of the previous October. The special prosecutor's office had kept the President's status as an unindicted co-conspirator secret, and look what he was handed in return. The President's lawyer had strayed from the bounds of fair play. Jaworski had no choice but to go to the Congress, to the Senate Judiciary Committee, to report that the White House was tampering with the special prosecutor's charter and undermining his ability to conduct a real investigation. He was informing Haig of his intention even though the general had not extended him the same courtesy by telling him in advance of their new tack.

Haig did not suggest that any compromise was possible.

"There's nothing I can do other than report it," Jaworski said.

"I understand," Haig replied.

ON MAY 20, Jaworski registered his protest in a letter to Senator Eastland, the chairman of the Senate Judiciary Committee. "Under Mr. St. Clair's approach," he wrote, "this would make the assurance of the right to take the President to court an idle and empty one. Counsel to the President, by asserting that ultimately I am subject to the President's direction in these matters, is attempting to undercut the independence carefully set forth in the guidelines which were reissued upon my appointment with the express consent of the President."

St. Clair read about Jaworski's letter in the papers. (Haig, as was his way, had neglected to forewarn him.) He hurried over to see Eastland.

"What do you think Leon is trying to do?" the Senator asked in his Mississippi twang. "Is he laying a foundation to quit?"

Yes, said St. Clair. The President's lawyer was sure that Jaworski had made a tactical error and was looking for a face-saving way out. The subpoena for the tapes was a trial subpoena; it had not been issued by the grand jury investigating the case. By tradition, trial subpoenas carry less weight than those issued by grand juries. Jaworski would have one hell of a time demonstrating a compelling need for the tapes now. The White House was in a strong position. St. Clair was confident that Jaworski's blunder would cost him the tapes.

Judge Sirica was less impressed than Senator Eastland by St. Clair's argument. That day, he denied the motion to quash and issued an order directing the White House to turn over the sixty-four tapes. The President had until May 31 to produce the tapes or file an appeal.

Neither the President nor Haig nor St. Clair was surprised. They had expected Sirica to rule against them. They saw their chances on an appeal, going over Sirica's head.

The next evening, May 21, Nixon invited Haig, St. Clair and Buzhardt to a supper cruise on the *Sequoia*. They arrived by limousine at the Navy Yard just after six o'clock and climbed the stairs to the *Sequoia*'s upper deck. The President told the stewards to bring drinks. Buzhardt—"the Baptist," as Nixon called him—asked for a ginger ale.

As the yacht steamed out for the thirteen-nautical-mile trip down the Potomac to Mount Vernon, they sat apparently relaxing in the breeze. But the talk was business—impeachment, Sirica, Jaworski, tapes. It was impossible to escape Watergate, even for a few deliberate moments of relaxation. The general and the lawyers too knew that their careers, their reputations and their futures rested in large measure on what happened to the Nixon presidency. Haig in particular had cast his lot. He was a soldier, yet here he was, irredeemably politicized as a Nixon general. The lawyers at least were there in accordance with the traditions of their profession; everyone is entitled to a lawyer. Military men, of course, had served Presidents, but never under quite the same circumstances. Haig felt that he had burned his bridges. Increasingly he was counting on Buzhardt to lead him through the legal thicket, to keep them from crossing the line of legality—a line that many others who had tried to serve this President had crossed.

The President indicated that he would fight the case for his tapes up to the Supreme Court, if necessary. His attitude matched St. Clair's and Buzhardt's judgment that the problem was the tapes case, the courts, more than the impeachment inquiry, the Hill.

Nixon seemed unusually tense, even after a couple of shots of his thirty-year-old Ballantine Scotch. St. Clair didn't know him well, but he was surprised that this most disciplined man could not force himself to relax. Nixon seemed to try to reach out to St. Clair, to get to know him better. There was something touching about the President's awkwardness, St. Clair thought. He felt sorry for him. Nixon had had two years of bad legal advice. That was what had gotten him into all these Watergate problems.

After nearly two hours they were at Mount Vernon, where George Washington had lived and was buried. It was dusk. The four men walked down to the bow of the *Sequoia* for a ceremony prescribed by Navy regulation. As they stood in the wind, the boat's bells tolled eight times at five-second intervals. Taps was played. A recording of the national anthem was broadcast.

The President turned to St. Clair and said, "They pay you nickels and dimes, but this is what makes it worth it."

His voice carried very clearly. Haig, and the lawyers, and members of the crew looked away in embarrassed silence.

A few minutes later the boat docked and the President and his party walked two hundred yards to a helicopter that was waiting to take them back to the White House. St. Clair sat next to the President, across from Haig and Buzhardt. As they flew, Buzhardt broached the possibility of asking Charles Alan Wright to come back to work on the Supreme Court briefs and arguments.

Wright's briefs had been impressive in the initial tapes case, Buzhardt thought. St. Clair was only a hired gun; he had been brought late into a case he had not really had time to master. And St. Clair didn't have a feel for government, for the political arena, the press, the city of Washington, or Richard Nixon. He was certainly not accustomed to having his clients call the shots.

Wright had left when the President decided not to take his case on the tapes to the Supreme Court the previous fall. They should persuade him to return. True, Wright hadn't stood up well to pressures. He was dismayed by hate mail; one letter he received had said, "I pray six times a day that you are going to die." But he was a scholar, and arguments to the Supreme Court are scholarly exercises. Buzhardt couldn't get a commitment from the President to bring Wright back.

JAWORSKI WAS sure the President wanted to avoid a test in the Supreme Court. The Cox firing, Haig's compromises about allowing the special prosecutor to listen to certain tapes, the surrender of seven of the tapes in November, were all indications that the President did not want the case to go to the high court.

Jaworski wanted to force the matter. It seemed unlikely that the special prosecutor could get a Supreme Court decision on the tapes before the justices took their summer recess. Unquestionably, the White House would appeal Sirica's decision to the Court of Appeals. That could take weeks, months. Jaworski was sure he'd win there, but that would mean that the Supreme Court would not get the case until fall. The cover-up trial would have to be postponed still later, to the spring of 1975.

Even then, if Jaworski won and got the tapes, it would take weeks to screen and transcribe them. The witnesses in the cover-up trial were already going stale. If there were such a delay, James Neal, the crack Tennessee trial lawyer, had already said he would not be available to prosecute the cover-up case.

It was enormously complicated. Jaworski felt that, as a lawyer, it was his responsibility to do what was in his power to expedite the impeachment inquiry. The country had a criminal President. Delay was Nixon's weapon. The courts were, by their nature, playing into the President's hands.

Technically, it was possible to file directly to the high court, leapfrogging the Court of Appeals. In such a motion, Jaworski could include the still-secret information that the President was an unindicted co-conspirator. That might persuade the justices that they were needed to step in and force an early resolution. A suspected criminal in the White House might jar them into action. But that very information could also precipitate inaction. Jaworski thought about that too as he walked to his rooms in the Jefferson Hotel at night. It was risky. Very, very risky. Suppose he filed a direct appeal to the Supreme Court, simply asking for a hearing. Suppose the justices said no. Suppose it was an angry no. Suppose it was a sarcastic reminder to Jaworski that there is a Court of Appeals for just such a reason, and that no one receives special treatment. Not the President, and not an arrogant special prosecutor.

Such a slap could be fatal; the psychological victory to the White House would be immeasurable. The clerks at the Supreme Court were saying that the Court had fallen behind in its calendar. It would be difficult to persuade the justices to take a case so late in the term. There were strong and sound precedents for the Court to shun "political" cases. And there was nothing more political than Watergate, it would seem. The nub of the White House defense was that the President was being strung up for political conduct.

For Jaworski, the issue in the tapes case was a criminal matter, which was why he wanted it decided in the courts where it belonged. He hoped that the justices would see it that way. It was as close a call as he would have to make, he thought. He told Phillip Lacovara to prepare the motion for the Supreme Court.

Normally, Jaworski's inclination would have been to call Haig to warn him, but not this time. The White House had undercut him. Haig had broken his promise—the very basis on which Jaworski had accepted the job. He had been kicked in the ass. He was not about to broadcast his intention to kick back.

At 4:15 P.M. on Friday, May 24, St. Clair filed an appeal from Sirica's decision in the Court of Appeals. As soon as Lacovara got word, he called Supreme Court clerk Michael Rodack to tell him he had a request for an expedited hearing before the justices. Lacovara obtained the docket number of the Court of Appeals case and had it typed on the prosecution's papers.

The Supreme Court closed at 6 P.M., but Jaworski wanted his request for an expedited hearing filed that evening. Haig, and the White House, must not be permitted time. Surprise. For once, from his end. He wanted to throw them off guard.

Between 4:30 and 5:15, Lacovara and four of his colleagues sat collating and stapling the papers together, and at 5:20 Lacovara got into a staff car. Caught in the rush-hour traffic, he just made it to the Supreme Court at the dot of six. Rodack was there waiting in his shirtsleeves.

Done.

"Big casino," James Doyle, Jaworski's spokesman, called it.

CHAPTER FOURTEEN

T HE small man with thinning hair and a scholarly, meek look sat behind the cluttered desk in the West Wing of the White House. His slightly rumpled suit, inexpensive white Dacron shirt and drooping black socks seemed out of place in the exquisitely furnished office. Around him were the historic keepsakes of five years of whirlwind diplomacy. Contemporary art hung on the walls, and marvelous Oriental rugs lay on dark-blue wall-to-wall carpeting. Foot-high stacks of papers bulged from folders marked "Top Secret." They were piled all across the desk.

It was the office of Dr. Henry A. Kissinger, Secretary of State of the United States and national-security adviser to the President. The gentleman sitting at Kissinger's desk was Air Force Major General Brent Scowcroft, one of the Nixon Administration's most powerful men.

As Kissinger's deputy at the National Security Council, Scowcroft used Kissinger's White House office whenever it was vacant. His own office was tiny by comparison, so small that, given the height of the West Wing ceilings, it was neither as long nor as wide as it was tall.

Scowcroft used Kissinger's office, with its comfortable blue sofa, matching armchairs and conference table with six chairs arranged around it, to hold meetings, greet visitors and conduct the routine business of international affairs in Kissinger's absence. He operated at the very center of power in the Nixon Administration. No one had closer or more regular contact with Nixon, Haig and Kissinger. When Kissinger was out of the country, Scowcroft conducted the President's daily briefing, keeping him posted on Kissinger's dealings abroad and on diplomatic and military developments.

Scowcroft was in almost constant touch with Haig. When Haig had left as Kissinger's deputy to become Army Vice-Chief of Staff in January 1973, Scowcroft, who was then the President's military aide, had succeeded Haig at NSC. Since he had returned to the White House, in May 1973, as the President's chief of staff, Haig had taken pains to keep Scowcroft well briefed about those aspects of the decision-making process which the President and Kissinger were unwilling to disclose. Remembering the usefulness of his own direct ties to Haldeman during the first four years of the Nixon Administration, Haig knew how valuable that sort of information could be. Kissinger's highly personalized, secretive style often cut his deputy out from important developments and plans. Independent lines of communication were essential.

Scowcroft picked up the phone. It was Kissinger. On May 29, 1974, he was well into his thirty-second day in the Middle East and had endured a month of grueling shuttles between Damascus and Jerusalem, seeking disengagement of the Israeli and Syrian forces in the Golan Heights.

The phone line was not secure, so Kissinger chose his words carefully, but he made it clear to Scowcroft that he had very good news. A top-secret teletype message would follow at once.

Without waiting for the coded message, Scowcroft walked to the Oval Office to alert the President. It was just before 9 A.M. The Middle East negotiations had been successful at last. Among other things, this meant that Nixon could soon embark on his trip to the Mideast.

For more than a month, Scowcroft had been dealing with the contingency that the President might visit Israel and the Arab States. He had chaired secret meetings with the White House advance team, who could now begin the arrangements. The meetings were so secret that the first had been held in the military situation room in the West Wing basement. For a month the trip had been on one moment and off the next, just as the prospects for a settlement had risen and fallen. The President had awaited each development with unusual concern. He wanted a respite from Watergate, an opportunity to display himself as the statesman, the peacemaker, rather than an embattled President struggling against impeachment. Now, with the success of the negotiations, it was at last possible.

Six blocks west of the White House, in a wood-paneled suite next to Kissinger's State Department office, Lawrence Eagleburger was getting the same good news that morning. As Kissinger's principal deputy at State,

Eagleburger too would begin to make the formal arrangements for Nixon's trip, laying the foundations through the appropriate diplomatic channels. Eagleburger, forty-four, was a career foreign-service officer whom Kissinger found to have the right blend of intellect, loyalty, decisiveness, experience and social grace to be his executive assistant. Eagleburger also had the ability to say, "Henry, you're full of shit." Eagleburger coordinated the day-to-day operations of the State Department in Kissinger's absence. He and Scowcroft maintained the foreign-policy empire which had been built by Kissinger over the previous five and a half years.

Scowcroft and Eagleburger protected Kissinger—better even than Haig had when he had been Kissinger's deputy. A code of silence was upheld rigidly by those near Kissinger, the same way a Capitol Hill staff might protect its alcoholic Congressman boss. Protecting Kissinger didn't involve shielding his private life from public view. It meant keeping Kissinger's personal view of Richard Nixon secret—from the public, from the press and from the President's own staff. Though mitigated by admiration for certain elements of the Nixon character, Kissinger's basic attitude toward the President was one of loathing and contempt. Both Eagleburger and Scowcroft knew that that secret was perhaps more significant than those that were stored in Kissinger's safes. Its disclosure could destroy Kissinger, they felt, and the country's foreign policy as well. As the Watergate crisis intensified, keeping Kissinger in office came to be viewed by some—and that included Kissinger, Scowcroft and Eagleburger—as essential to the national security.

The three of them doubted that Nixon could handle foreign affairs without Kissinger. They believed that the key to America's foreign policy was not only Kissinger's experience and intellect, but also his stature. It was a balancing force against Nixon. If Nixon were to run foreign affairs without Kissinger, they reasoned, the sloppiness that marked his handling of Watergate, particularly the cover-up, would leave its mark on foreign policy.

Neither Eagleburger nor Scowcroft thought that all of Kissinger's negative feelings toward the President were justified. His frequent descriptions of Nixon as irrational, insecure and maniacal could at times just as easily apply to Kissinger as to the President, they believed. But at least Kissinger was not sloppy. Even at his worst, Kissinger was less *dangerous*.

Each knew the strange history of the Nixon-Kissinger relationship intimately. What they hadn't heard from Kissinger himself they had picked up from Haig and others at NSC and State. Yet not even their knowledge was sufficient to explain the incomprehensible behavior of these two men.

IN THE beginning, the summer of 1968, when Nixon received the Republican presidential nomination, Kissinger was bitterly disappointed. His mentor, Governor Nelson Rockefeller of New York, had failed to win the nomination. Kissinger had told friends and associates that Nixon was "unfit" for the presidency, "dangerous," capable of unleashing nuclear war. Then, three weeks after his election in 1968, Nixon had asked Kissinger to serve as his national-security adviser. Meeting with the President-elect, Kissinger shifted his assessment. The man whose approach to foreign policy he had regarded as hopelessly shallow and unsophisticated appeared to him now far more subtle and complex. Kissinger detected in Nixon a pragmatism which might conquer the ideological rigidities that had marked the politics of this coldest of cold warriors. He had discussed the matter with Rockefeller. Rockefeller didn't like Nixon personally, but he urged Kissinger to accept. That way, both men could keep their feet in the door. The forty-five-year-old Harvard professor took the job.

Though William P. Rogers, an old Nixon friend, had been named Secretary of State, Kissinger was in control of most of the foreign-policy and national-security paper flow to the President. Installed in the West Wing basement, Kissinger aspired to a personal relationship with Nixon similar to the one he had with Rockefeller, in which two men guided by the same general philosophy and approach to foreign affairs reached decisions jointly.

Instead, Kissinger found himself screened off from the President by the bureaucratic stops that Haldeman had created at Nixon's direction. Just like every other member of the new Administration, Kissinger dealt with Nixon primarily on paper, not in the easygoing, informal kind of conversations he had enjoyed with Rockefeller. Both Haldeman and Ehrlichman, he complained, were determined to keep him at a distance from Nixon. The President's two principal aides were "idiots" and "Nazis," he said. What kind of man would surround himself with such imbeciles? For their part, Haldeman and Ehrlichman openly ridiculed Kissinger; he could not be trusted because of his liberal friends. Ehrlichman half jokingly insinuated that Kissinger was "queer," and wondered aloud to Kissinger assistants whether Henry, a divorced bachelor, would know what to do with a girl at a Georgetown cocktail party. "Were there any boys at the party for Henry?" Ehrlichman once asked, pleased with his own joke.

In his meetings with the President, Kissinger was almost never able to get a decision on the spot. Instead, the President listened to his presentations impatiently and told Kissinger that he would inform him in due course of whatever actions he wished to take. Often Kissinger returned to his office shaken, chewing his nails, worrying and waiting. It was a dangerous system, Kissinger believed, particularly with Haldeman taking the notes. The President's mind wasn't sophisticated enough to reach these kinds of decisions alone.

And without Kissinger, who would help Nixon? Haldeman? Ehrlichman? They would go along with any crazy thing that came into Nixon's head, Kissinger complained. There was no coherent policy developing; Nixon was apt to conduct foreign affairs by whim. Only his own superhuman efforts, Kissinger implied, were preventing catastrophe. "If the President had his way, we'd have a nuclear war every week," he said on several occasions in those early months. On other occasions Kissinger railed that the President was not tough enough, especially in conducting the war in Southeast Asia. "If Nelson were President, we'd crack 'em," he said. The contradiction—complaining at one moment about Nixon's severity and in the next about his weakness—seemed to say more about Kissinger to some of his aides than it did about Nixon.

The national-security adviser regularly ridiculed his chief's intellect and ability. "You tell our meatball President I'll be there in a few minutes," he once snapped to a secretary who had summoned him to a meeting with Nixon. "Wasn't our leader magnificent on that," Kissinger said sarcastically of Nixon's early public statements on the war in Vietnam. The President deserved a B-plus or a C or even a C-minus, he would say. But to the President's face Kissinger offered only high praise.

He instructed one of his National Security Council aides, John Cort, to prepare a briefing book on the North Atlantic Treaty Organization for the President. When he received it, Kissinger said that it was brilliant, but that it must be simplified because Nixon wouldn't understand it. "Don't ever write anything more complicated than a *Reader's Digest* article for Nixon," he directed.

Meeting with his closest associates, he would imply at times that the President was a wild man, almost uncontrollable. Part of the problem, Kissinger maintained, was that Nixon too often reacted to foreign-policy questions out of personal anger, or for domestic political considerations.

At first, very little direct information got back to the staff to corroborate Kissinger's unflattering and alarming portrait of the President. But there was some supporting evidence. Early in 1970, the President returned a National Security Council briefing paper on the visit to China of Laotian Premier Souvanna Phouma and other Southeast Asian leaders. The President's margin notation was clearly written. "Bomb them," it said. On another occasion, Nixon was presented a serious NSC option paper on Korea that contained a series of mutually exclusive alternatives, and he had checked all of them. This time it was Haig, Kissinger's chief deputy, who expressed concern. "What are you supposed to do when the President screws up?" he asked.

Meeting with India's Prime Minister Indira Gandhi, Nixon made it evident that he did not know where one of India's principal states, Bengal, was. Kissinger cited the incident as one more example of Nixon's "second-rate mind."

Still, Kissinger's assistants knew his habit of making scathing, derogatory comments about nearly everyone. Each had heard himself called "a second-rate mind" or worse. The security adviser had referred to one colleague as a "psychopathic homosexual." This had caused Leonard Garment to say, "Henry's characterizations are like his girl friends—affectations."

In the National Security Council offices in the White House basement, there was a continual flow of nasty comments about people—many from Kissinger. But he felt the intense pressure, too. "I have a constituency of one man," Kissinger told his aides. Reaching out to Nixon, Kissinger sought admission to the inner circle.

In 1969, one issue dominated all others: Vietnam. Elected on a pledge to end the war, Nixon meant to operate on all fronts, and Kissinger opened up secret peace negotiations in Paris with representatives of North Vietnam. At the same time, Nixon and Kissinger were secretly formulating a plan to escalate the war.*

As THE President paid more attention to the war and spent more and more time reviewing options, Kissinger's influence grew. He fought to bring most major State and Defense Department decisions through the National Security Council. That gave him absolute control over the paperwork—which in turn increased his control over more and more of the President's meetings.

Kissinger was more willing to do the President's bidding than were Secretary of State Rogers and Defense Secretary Melvin R. Laird. He asked how, not why. If the President wanted a plan that included the most minute details of conducting an all-out war in Southeast Asia, Kissinger came up

---

* Kissinger developed a top-secret plan: the "November Option." It called for mining the harbor of Haiphong and bombing North Vietnam on a massive scale. He labored personally over the most minute details. He calculated the exact times for bombing certain facilities when the fewest number of civilians would be endangered. Implementation of the plan, Kissinger said, would be a "brutal blow" to the enemy. But the President, concerned about the powerful antiwar movement that had savaged Lyndon Johnson, held back and did not put the plan into effect until much later.

with it. If Nixon decided to shelve the plan and send Kissinger secretly to Paris to negotiate peace, Kissinger did it. Nixon's inconstancy, combined with Kissinger's unwillingness to take a stand, confused Kissinger's staff. There was no apparent policy. The President seemed to change his mind so often, and in such extreme ways.

"Nixon is a man who can't be pushed too far," Kissinger warned his associates. Those who looked for more evidence to corroborate Kissinger's portrait of the President found it. Almost from the beginning, Kissinger had secretly had all his telephone calls, including those with the President, monitored and transcribed. The conversations gave Kissinger's assistants enough information about the President to alarm them. Nixon rambled, he made thoughtless remarks and suggestions about people and policy, he sometimes slurred his words as if he had been drinking heavily. His ignorance of important subjects suggested he was lazy and unprepared for the kinds of decisions which require thoughtful consideration. His nasty references about the inferior intelligence of blacks revealed a deep prejudice.

Like Kissinger's personal view of Nixon, the existence of Kissinger's clandestine monitoring system was a zealously guarded secret. The practice had begun simply enough in 1969, with a secretary listening to each of Kissinger's phone calls and transcribing in shorthand. A special switch enabled the secretaries in Kissinger's outer office to deactivate the microphone on their telephone extensions. Early in 1970, the system became more elaborate and Kissinger began tape-recording his telephone calls. An IBM Dictabelt machine, housed in the credenza behind his secretary's desk and hooked into his telephone, was automatically activated when the telephone receiver was picked up. Eventually, several Dictabelt machines were plugged into the phone system, insuring that there were always standby recorders if one failed or ran out of tape.

Kissinger took the monitoring very seriously. There were to be no slip-ups. Diane Mathews, one of the secretaries, was assigned to watch the Dictabelt carefully and signal one of the other women in the office to take shorthand notes if the belt ran out in midconversation. Kissinger's appointments secretary or Haig also listened regularly to important calls and took notes, especially if the conversations were with the President. On some calls, the unsuspecting party might be talking simultaneously to Kissinger, Haig, a transcribing secretary and the appointments secretary. In his basement office in the White House, eight other phones were connected to Kissinger's direct line with Nixon, to facilitate monitoring and transcribing. Haig rigidly enforced the rule that each day's calls be transcribed and typed before the secretaries went home at night—until, eventually, a special night crew of secretaries was assigned the task of finishing the transcribing. Only Kissinger's most personal calls with Nancy Maginnes, whom he later married, escaped transcription.*

Nixon was often on the phone with Kissinger for fifteen minutes or longer. The President was repetitive, sometimes taking minutes to come to a point, or he might suddenly shift to another topic without finishing whatever he had been discussing. If a conversation was especially important, Haig usually rushed out of his office, saying to the secretaries, "Can we get that right away?"

Kissinger occasionally came out of his office after such calls. "Who was taking that?" he would ask.

One of the four women stationed in the small outer office would raise her hand.

"Wasn't that the worst thing you ever heard in your life?" Kissinger would ask. Before the secretary nodded assent, Kissinger would turn, shake his head and grumble to himself.

During one call, the President drunkenly relayed to Dr. Kissinger the Vietnam military policy of his friend Bebe Rebozo. Kissinger told his aides about the call, and for a while thereafter Haig referred to Nixon as "our drunken friend."

During another call, Kissinger mentioned the number of American casualties in a major battle in Vietnam. "Oh, screw 'em," said Nixon.

Kissinger took care to see that complete transcripts of his calls with the President were preserved in the personal records being accumulated for his memoirs.

Eventually, he became so concerned about the security of his papers and files that he moved some of the most sensitive to Rockefeller's Pocantico Hills estate. He intimated to associates that he feared Haldeman and Ehrlichman might try to steal them. When a legal adviser reminded him that it was against the law to store classified documents outside government facilities, Kissinger had the files returned to the White House.

Despite his personal assessment of the President, the forces both of Kissinger's personality and of circumstance combined to establish gradually the relationship he desired with Nixon. Kissinger's closest aides were more than familiar with his fundamental approach to dealing with Nixon. He had genuine respect for the President's tough view of what American foreign

* The secretaries listened to her calls, however, and sometimes took notes, in case mention was made of a social engagement; Kissinger often forgot such things. The staff's duties included handling his personal finances and his social schedule.

policy should be, and he appealed to it directly, providing the intellectual framework and negotiating skill to make it operational. The Russians, the Chinese and the Communists of Southeast Asia must all be made to believe, Kissinger insisted, that the United States was willing to escalate the war in Southeast Asia far beyond existing parameters if America were to achieve its objectives.

By the spring of 1970, Nixon, Kissinger and the NSC staff faced a crisis. Cambodia was being used as a staging area by Communist troops. The possibility of invasion was discussed and an invasion plan was developed. Many of the liberal academics on Kissinger's staff—among them Morton H. Halperin, Anthony Lake and William Watts—were strongly opposed. "Don't worry about it," Haig advised them. "The Old Man will never go through with this. I've seen him come up to these decisions and then back away."

But the President did give his approval. Haig was elated. The others weren't. Kissinger called them his "bleeding hearts."

Watts went to see Kissinger alone to state his objections.

"Your view represents the cowardice of the Eastern Establishment," Kissinger told him.

Furious, Watts got up out of his chair and moved toward Kissinger. He was going to punch him. Kissinger moved quickly behind his desk. He was not serious, he said. Watts, whose selection as the NSC aide coordinating the Cambodian invasion had just been approved by the President, resigned.

"You've just had an order from your Commander in Chief," Haig said. Watts could not resign.

"Fuck you, Al," Watts said. "I just did."

Kissinger called his staff together in the Executive Office Building to plead for their support of the decision. "We are all the President's men," he said, "and we've got to behave that way."

AMERICA'S WILLINGNESS to expand the war in Southeast Asia was also evidenced in secret diplomatic threats and by American bombers. Kissinger could control the President on such issues as the bombing of Cambodia, he boasted to his aides. And, by assuming a posture designed to appeal to Nixon's own tough self-image, Kissinger ingratiated himself with the President on other matters.

At one point, the Senate Foreign Relations Committee attempted to obtain a copy of the Pentagon Papers, months before their existence became publicly known. Haldeman, Ehrlichman, Kissinger, and presidential assistants John Scali and Richard Moore met in Ehrlichman's office. "Refuse the request," Kissinger recommended, "by telling them these papers are essential to the national security."

Scali demurred. The intimation that Congress could not be entrusted with information that affected the national security might not be too well received on the Hill, he said. He suggested they turn over the papers and avoid a confrontation. Kissinger pronounced Scali's position "a craven policy," and thereupon got up to leave.

"Wait a minute, Henry," said Haldeman, "we haven't finished discussing this yet."

"Well, I have," said Kissinger. "I know what our President will do." He walked out of the meeting.

The bureaucratic walls which had barricaded Kissinger from Nixon fell slowly but steadily.

As THE pressure of events drew the President and Kissinger closer, Kissinger became increasingly alienated from many of his own staff. Some who were disillusioned with both the Kissinger policies and his personality left his service, convinced that the problem was as much Kissinger as the President. He seemed to thrive on trouble, hysteria, fright, uncertainty. He raged at the secretaries. He appeared to take pleasure in humiliating his aides, once excluding his ranking deputy, Helmut Sonnenfeldt, from a ceremonial picture-taking session with the words "Not you, Hal, you're not important enough." He made appointments with reporters and visiting academics, then accused his assistants of overscheduling him.

Coleman Hicks, one of a series of appointments secretaries who quit, became so frustrated that he had Kissinger approve all appointments in writing. "You have indicated you want to see the following people and they will be scheduled if you want," said a memo form devised for the purpose. "Please check the appropriate box—approve or disapprove." But even when Hicks pulled out the appropriate memo with Kissinger's check marks beside the names of unwelcome visitors, Kissinger accused him of keeping him from important business by haphazard scheduling.

Kissinger seemed singularly obsessed with his own prestige and image. If he had a long list of telephone messages, he would often call back Nancy Maginnes first, then Governor Rockefeller, then movie stars and celebrities, and *then* the President. He was enormously sensitive to criticism in the press; he assigned his aides the distasteful job of heading off negative stories and lodging complaints about those that made it into print. The job was especially difficult because the offending stories were often true; Kissinger himself was, at times, the unwitting source. He let information slip as he courted many of Washington's most influential journalists.

Kissinger counseled his aides that deviousness was part of their job. "You systems-analysis people have too much integrity," he told one of them. "This is not an honorable business conducted by honorable men in an honorable way. Don't assume I'm that way and you shouldn't be." If an aide was particularly sensitive to deviousness, Kissinger would try to lighten the impact of some of his starker deceptions by making jokes about his own methodology and his disinclination to give the same version of events twice in a row.

On occasion he expressed enthusiasm at the size of the bomb craters that American B-52s left in North Vietnam, and he once bragged to Elliot Richardson that they would "reduce Le Duc Tho to tears." When Anthony Lake, his executive assistant, questioned the bombing policies, Kissinger ridiculed him. In a long discussion that grew heated, Kissinger said that Lake's approach to the war was "not manly enough." Lake was so upset by the conversation that he went into a hallway in the West Wing and pounded the vending machines with his fists. Haig talked him out of quitting on that occasion and on one other, but Lake did soon resign.*

Kissinger's inability to manage either personal relationships or staff organization ("He couldn't even recognize his own senior staff members on the street," Coleman Hicks once remarked) became an accepted fact of life in the White House basement. It was Haig who kept things running smoothly, walking a tightrope between the staff and Kissinger and between Kissinger and the Oval Office. Haig managed the paper flow. He worked longer hours than anyone else in the office. He insulated the staff from Kissinger's wrath. He knew the cable traffic perfectly. He was gregarious, personable, likable. He wore a dinner jacket as comfortably as an Army uniform. He assiduously avoided the intellectual and ideological debates which scarred the NSC staff. He tolerated with superhuman strength the abuse that Kissinger heaped on him.

"Only someone schooled in taking shit could put up with it," Hicks observed to his colleagues.

In Haig's presence, Kissinger referred pointedly to military men as "dumb, stupid animals to be used" as pawns for foreign policy. Kissinger

---

* Lake was one of the aides whose telephones were secretly tapped with the approval of both Kissinger and Haig. In 1973, when Lake learned of the tap, he phoned Kissinger to discuss the matter. Kissinger said he knew nothing about the tap, paused and added, "in any detail."

often took up a post outside the doorway to Haig's office and dressed him down in front of the secretaries for alleged acts of incompetence with which Haig was not even remotely involved. Once when the Air Force was authorized to resume bombing of North Vietnam, the planes did not fly on certain days because of bad weather. Kissinger assailed Haig. He complained bitterly that the generals had been screaming for the limits to be taken off but that now their pilots were afraid to go up in a little fog. The country needed generals who could win battles, Kissinger said, not good briefers like Haig.

On another occasion, when Haig was leaving for a trip to Cambodia to meet with Premier Lon Nol, Kissinger escorted him to a staff car, where reporters and a retinue of aides waited. As Haig bent to get into the automobile, Kissinger stopped him and began polishing the single star on his shoulder. "Al, if you're a good boy, I'll get you another one," he said.

Haig bore silently any resentment he felt. He had always been able to avoid friction with his superiors. In the Johnson Administration his tireless work and smooth, easy manner had impressed his influential bosses at the Pentagon, Joseph Califano and Army Secretary Cyrus Vance. Haig had come highly recommended to Kissinger, who had installed him in the White House basement as his military aide at the start of the Nixon Administration.

One of Haig's early assignments was to prepare the daily NSC intelligence report, which was based on vast amounts of information that flowed into the White House situation room. His access to virtually every piece of intelligence that reached the White House was unique, and he quickly acquired a superior knowledge of each NSC project and component. He handled the immense volume of paperwork adroitly, sometimes placing his own memos on top of the stacks that went to Kissinger. As he became more confident, he sometimes rewrote memos submitted to Kissinger by other members of the staff. On other occasions he sent memos back to their authors with instructions that Kissinger wanted them done differently. No one knew for sure if the desired revisions reflected the preference of the President, Kissinger or Haig. As Haig asserted his growing managerial role on the staff, others who saw themselves as the brightest stars in the Kissinger constellation of aides were eclipsed.

Though some resented Haig, few questioned his authority. He had complete access to Kissinger, and Haig assured his colleagues that he was acting in their own interests. If it happened rarely that someone balked at having his memo rewritten, Haig would explain that he was merely tailoring it to suit the idiosyncrasies of its recipient. It was better for all concerned, said Haig, that he deal with "those shits"—Kissinger, Haldeman, Colson and the rest. He claimed no political ambitions. "I've got to get out of here," he would remind Kissinger's civilian aides—back into the *real* Army, away from this temporary duty that could only screw up his military career.

Still, the key to Haig's ascent was Kissinger, because Haig was almost indispensable to him. He provided order, discipline, predictability. Without Haig there would be chaos. Pure military decisions bored Kissinger. Haig handled them for him. He served as the NSC liaison to the Pentagon brass and kept their feathers unruffled. ("Al, I'd invite you to this meeting, but the Army doesn't have anything at stake here," Kissinger would half joke.)

Among Kissinger's principal aides, Haig alone stayed on after the Cambodian invasion, and in June 1970 he was formally appointed as Kissinger's deputy. Though Kissinger was wary of granting any aide too much power, he was convinced he could control Haig. Haig was loyal, at least the most loyal of Kissinger's subordinates. ("It is clear that I don't have anybody in my office that I can trust except Colonel Haig," Kissinger told a senior FBI official in 1969 as he reviewed the wiretapped conversations of several other aides.)

Richard Nixon was also an admirer. If the President stopped by the NSC office and found Kissinger gone, he would sit talking with Haig. Sometimes Nixon called Haig to his office to discuss military questions which Kissinger was unable to answer or which he had bucked to his deputy.

Nixon began to test Haig, making vague negative comments about Kissinger, expressing concern that Henry was off on his own or that he was not following policies and procedures they had agreed upon. He wanted Haig's opinion. Delicately, Haig managed to defend Kissinger, at the same time making it clear that his ultimate loyalty was to the President.

Kissinger began to be obsessed about what Haig and Nixon said to each other when they were alone. Kissinger regarded himself as a conservative in foreign-policy matters, but Haig, he observed, was a right-winger. And Kissinger was concerned that Haig might establish a private relationship with the President that would diminish his own influence over Nixon in foreign affairs. Gradually Kissinger concluded that he had handed Haig too much power. Haig was devious, duplicitous, he sometimes said now. Kissinger worried that Haig spied on him for the Pentagon and, worse, for the President.

Kissinger's insecurities concerning his deputy finally reached such a pitch that he called in one of his secretaries, Julie Pineau, to ask her who was the most impressive person she had met on the job. Who was the best member of the NSC staff, the most competent? He was relieved, visibly, when she named Winston Lord, a Kissinger favorite.

When he was around Kissinger, Haig took great care not to flaunt his relationship with Nixon. He was determined to succeed with both men. To Kissinger and his aides, Haig sometimes referred to the President as an inherently weak man who lacked guts. He joked that Nixon and Bebe Rebozo had a homosexual relationship, imitating what he called the President's limp-wrist manner. And around the men he cultivated in the Pentagon and the White House, Haig implied that Kissinger was too often the barrier to definitive military action. He complained about Kissinger's temper tantrums, his dishonesty, his disorganization, his reluctance to offend the weak-livered eggheads he had associated with in academia. These men thought Haig trusted them, because he was willing to share such harsh judgments with them.

As the negotiations to end the war in Vietnam progressed, relations between Kissinger and Haig almost disintegrated. Nixon sent Haig to Southeast Asia to make independent appraisals of the military situation. Haig was the President's line to the battlefield. Returning, Haig argued successfully that the American withdrawal of troops should be conducted at a pace slower than that recommended by Kissinger. Kissinger felt that he had been undermined.

Nixon sent Haig to Paris to observe Kissinger's bargaining with the North Vietnamese, and Haig counseled the President to take a harder line than Kissinger was pursuing at the bargaining table. Kissinger reacted with alarm and fury. Neither military nor diplomatic realities justified Haig's position, Kissinger said. Their arguments grew heated and personal. Kissinger was certain that Haig's intervention was making a settlement more difficult, particularly the settlement the President himself wanted—one which could be announced before Election Day, 1972.

On October 26, less than two weeks before the election, Kissinger was able to announce that "peace is at hand" and that terms for a settlement had been agreed upon. When the prospect of settlement collapsed after the election, he blamed Haig. Kissinger was nearly certain that Haig, during his travels to Southeast Asia, had persuaded Vietnamese President Thieu to hold out for better terms than Kissinger had negotiated.

In December 1972, while Kissinger was negotiating in Paris, Nixon was closeted at the White House with Haig and Charles Colson. The peace talks were deadlocked. Both men told him Kissinger was once more taking too soft a negotiating position. The options cabled back to Washington by Kissinger included resumption of bombing in the North. Haig urged the President to take decisive action to finally bring the North Vietnamese to their knees.

Nixon weighed his choices and acted. Haig informed John Scali of the President's decision: "This man is going to stand tall and resume the bombing and put those B-52 mothers in there and show 'em we mean business."

IN JANUARY 1973 Haig became Vice-Chief of Staff of the Army, after Nixon had promoted him over 240 higher-ranking officers. He was given his fourth star. Four months later, the departure of Haldeman and Ehrlichman from the White House underlined the changing realities of the second Nixon administration—for Nixon, for Kissinger, for Haig. As the President's popularity, his power and his grasp on his office declined, Kissinger's was rising. It was no longer he who needed Nixon, Kissinger told his aides; now it was Nixon who needed him. Kissinger wanted to be Secretary of State. Nixon promised him he would have the appointment.

Kissinger explained to his aides why he wanted the job. Adding the State Department to his domain would complete his control of the foreign-policy bureaucracy. As both Secretary of State and national-security adviser to the President, he could protect diplomacy from the corrosion of Watergate. It had not escaped Kissinger that Nixon might destroy American foreign policy by trying to use it as a means of his own survival. It might fall to Kissinger to protect that policy from a President who was growing increasingly irrational and unpredictable, he said.

And his appointment would bring along with it another particularly pleasant prospect: the humiliation of Secretary of State William Rogers. Kissinger hated Rogers. He thought him stupid, inept, weak. Kissinger enjoyed demeaning Rogers, keeping information from him, hurting him. Haig often spoke of Kissinger's amusement at seeing Rogers excluded from the process of making important diplomatic decisions.

In the late spring of 1973 Rogers did not want to relinquish the secretaryship, especially to Kissinger. As Nixon considered whether to appoint Kissinger or John Connally to State, Rogers' tenure was extended several times. The President preferred Connally and expressed distrust of Kissinger to Haig among others. Kissinger used his leverage. He threatened to resign from the Administration unless Rogers was banished and his own appointment as Secretary announced. Nixon capitulated, though unhappily. He was unable to bring himself to tell Rogers personally; their friendship went back to the Eisenhower Administration. (In 1952, Rogers had been one of the few Eisenhower men who had defended Nixon against charges of maintaining a secret slush fund during the election campaign.)

Nixon sent Haig to convey the message to Rogers and get his resignation.

Rogers, his pride already sorely wounded, was deeply offended. "Tell the President to fuck himself," he said. He refused to either resign or be fired by Haig. If he was to be dismissed, he wanted the request for his resignation to come from the President personally. "I am sorry," he told Haig; there was no other way. Haig was angry and dumbfounded; he could not imagine a Cabinet officer, or anyone else, for that matter, refusing an order from his Commander in Chief. Nixon stalled and fretted and looked for a way to avoid confronting Rogers.

When, on July 16, 1973, Alexander Butterfield revealed the existence of Nixon's taping system, Kissinger was outraged. How did the President dare to tape their meetings without his knowledge? He professed incredulity. The irony could hardly be lost on his aides. Yet Kissinger persisted. From an historical point of view alone, the President's taping system was "insane," he said. It was *indiscriminate*. "To tape eight years of conversation would take eight years to listen to!" He was contemptuous. "To leave yourself to the mercy of historians like that is unbelievable irresponsibility," particularly since Nixon conducted meetings "with such fantastic indirection."

For weeks Kissinger turned to his closest friends and aides for advice and gave free rein to his anger, raising questions about Nixon's mental stability. Perhaps he should refuse to accept the position of Secretary of State and get out of that man's Administration once and for all, while he still had a chance to emerge with his reputation intact. It was the first time that those who were closest to Kissinger believed he was serious about quitting.

But Rogers, having reconsidered, was by then ready to leave the Administration. He was disgusted with what he regarded as Nixon's specious claim of executive privilege in withholding the tapes. In August, Kissinger was nominated as Secretary of State. The appointment was confirmed in the Senate in September.

By late October, after Cox had been fired, Kissinger's anxieties about the President had become more acute. "Sometimes I get worried," he said. "The President is like a madman." Kissinger was deeply pessimistic. He had looked to the second Nixon administration as a once-in-a-century opportunity to build a new American foreign policy, to achieve new international structures based on unquestioned American strength, détente with the Soviets and China, a closer bond with Europe.

It seemed no longer possible. Watergate was shattering the illusion of American strength, he said, and with it American foreign policy. He decried "the brutal puritanism of the age." Whatever Nixon's transgressions, those who were attacking the President, especially the press, had no idea of the damage they were inflicting on international order, he said. Congress now felt free to interfere in foreign policy. Foreign leaders, allies and enemies alike, seemed perplexed by the President's inability to deal decisively with his own troubles, to make Watergate go away. America's ability to make good its commitments was in serious doubt throughout the world. Indochina would be the first great Watergate casualty, Kissinger predicted bitterly. The Congress, the press and the people would never permit the Administration to demonstrate the resolve needed to save it. When Vietnam fell, American foreign policy would be reduced to a myth. What good is strength without the will to use it? Kissinger asked rhetorically. The specter of the United States as a "pitiful, helpless giant" aptly described the Watergate America of Richard Nixon, Kissinger believed.

Kissinger adapted his negotiating strategies to fit his perceptions of the moment. In talks with the Russians, the Israelis, the Arabs and others, he sometimes alluded to Nixon's precarious position at home and tried to turn it to the advantage of his own negotiating stance. The President's troubles had made Nixon more determined than ever to take a tough line with potential adversaries. Kissinger portrayed himself as more reasonable, more flexible. He could understand the other side's position and would lend a sympathetic ear. But Nixon, he would imply, was beyond control and should not be tested too severely. If the other side could yield just a little ground, he, Kissinger, might be able to go back and convince the President to take a softer line. The stratagem usually worked, Kissinger and his aides believed, but they doubted that it would do for long.

Scowcroft and Eagleburger reinforced Kissinger's belief that world leaders were relying on him more than the President: it was Kissinger who was the symbol of American legitimacy and continuity, not Nixon. Kissinger relished such stature. Yet ultimately, he said, his position was not very much more stable than the President's. That realization served to heighten his ambivalence toward Nixon. "That SOB has got to go," he exploded frequently in the early months of 1974. "He's going to have to resign. It's inevitable." Then, after reflection, he would tell his aides, "No, he shouldn't do it."

Then the month-long Middle East negotiations and the release of the edited transcripts pushed Kissinger still further from the President. Nixon was so desperate to obtain a Golan Heights agreement for domestic political purposes, Kissinger maintained, that he was undermining Kissinger's strategy and endangering the whole Middle East peace initiative. During one impasse in the talks, Kissinger told the Syrian President that unless immediate progress was forthcoming he would break off the negotiations.

"If this isn't settled by Monday, I'm going home." It was a risky tactic. Kissinger's sense of timing told him it would work.

In Key Biscayne, Ziegler told reporters that Kissinger was under orders from the President not to leave the Middle East until there was a settlement. Fortunately, news of Ziegler's statement did not reach Damascus until after President Assad had made the desired concession. The negotiations moved quickly toward a settlement.

Kissinger was infuriated. Nixon, he said, was determined to foster the illusion that he was in charge of the negotiations, to save his neck. "I'm the one who knows the placement of every goddam soldier on the Golan Heights —not him," he complained.

Chapter Fifteen

FROM Washington, Nixon viewed the situation differently. The Middle East settlement was a result of his own work, he told his family. "Henry wanted to come home, and I kept him on the job." The negotiation was successful because the leaders in the Middle East knew they could rely "only on my word." It was essential that he visit the Middle East now to demonstrate that his personal commitment would prevent another outbreak of war there.

At 1:02 P.M. on May 29, Nixon came into the White House press room to announce, on live television and radio, that there was a settlement. He looked worn and haggard. "It is obviously a major diplomatic achievement," the President said, "and Secretary Kissinger deserves enormous credit for the work that he has done, along with members of his team. . . . As far as the United States is concerned, we shall continue with our diplomatic initiatives, working with all governments in the area toward achieving the goal of a permanent settlement, a permanent peace."

That night, on the *Sequoia,* the President entertained eleven Congressmen, most of them Southerners. The guests ate beef tenderloin and heard Nixon's elation at the Middle East cease-fire. He spoke about the settlement in terms of his Administration's continuing foreign-policy triumphs. He listed past achievements and speculated on those to come. Haig sat quietly at the table. Mississippi Congressman G. V. "Sonny" Montgomery, touted by the press as Nixon's "favorite Congressman," asked the President what help he needed on Watergate.

"If I thought I was guilty, I'd quit," the President responded. There were, he told his guests, some tapes containing national-security material so sensitive that he would never give them up. "Never."

On the morning of the thirty-first, Friday, Nixon breakfasted with Haig, Scowcroft and Kissinger. He greeted the Secretary—who had just returned from the Middle East—with nervous laughter.

"Where have you been, Henry?"

Kissinger was not amused.

THAT SAME morning the justices of the Supreme Court were meeting to consider the special prosecutor's petition that they decide the tapes case without prior review by the Court of Appeals. St. Clair had filed his opposing brief the day before, urging the justices not to "rush to judgment," because hearing the case this term could prejudice the House impeachment inquiry. Buzhardt had checked the Supreme Court docket and was confident they would prevail. The calendar was full. The justices would have a ready excuse to sidestep the issue.

But the White House underestimated the degree to which Nixon's conduct had offended the Court. The President's appointees Chief Justice Burger, Harry A. Blackmun and Lewis F. Powell, Jr.,* had all expressed their disgust to varying degrees—to their clerks and to each other. Nixon appeared to be willing to flout the rule of law openly in the expectation that they would rescue him. They felt he had put them on the line, and they were wary.

The conference began with the justices seemingly split in their positions: Potter Stewart, Powell and Douglas favored taking the case; the Chief Justice, Blackmun and Byron R. White were opposed; Thurgood Marshall and William J. Brennan, Jr., held back while the others debated. They were well aware that if they failed to expedite their hearing of the case the impeachment proceedings would take place without the congressional committee having a chance to get the disputed tapes.

Justice Stewart's presentation was strenuous: the Court had a responsibility to resolve the issue as soon as possible, not sidestep it; the principle involved was fundamental. The opposition argued that the importance of the issue was so great that the case merited full judicial review and thus should first be heard in the Court of Appeals.

Justice Marshall, whose position was never seriously doubted by the rest,

* Justice William H. Rehnquist, the fourth Nixon appointee, had disqualified himself from the case because he had served as an Assistant Attorney General under John Mitchell.

and Justice Brennan too, came down squarely on Stewart's side. St. Clair's brief, it seemed, was based on a fundamental misreading of the situation. He was arguing that, as a matter of law, the Court was precluded from considering a case that might affect the outcome of impeachment. His argument was insulting, several of the justices felt. As a practical matter, he might have a point, but they doubted there was support in the law for his view.

At 3 P.M. the Court announced that it would take the case on an expedited basis, bypassing the Court of Appeals. The Chief Justice laid out a timetable for briefs and oral argument. A ruling was possible before August.

Buzhardt read the decision as a clear signal that the Court intended to rule against the President on the merits. St. Clair disagreed. They would still win, he predicted.

The President was meeting with his senior political counselors, Dean Burch, Anne L. Armstrong, Roy Ash and Kenneth Cole, when the Court's action was announced. He asked for ideas on the 1975 State of the Union Message and the 1975 legislative program. "I want to know what Cabinet officers feel, so I can make a determination what we get into and not," he said.

ST. CLAIR was back in district court on Monday morning, June 3, to oppose the attempts of Colson and Ehrlichman to get White House files that related to the Ellsberg burglary case. Judge Gerhard A. Gesell had had his fill of stalling. He had warned St. Clair in their last encounter that unless the President turned over the subpoenaed files the case against Colson and Ehrlichman would have to be dismissed and he would hold the President personally responsible for aborting the trial.

"I don't give a damn," Nixon had responded to his lawyers. It wasn't fair in the first place that a man like Ellsberg should be free and his former aides on trial, he said.

The courtroom was packed with spectators and reporters. St. Clair was nervous waiting to find out whether Gesell would make good his threat and hold the President of the United States in contempt. Colson walked over and whispered something, but St. Clair couldn't hear it above the clamor of the spectators. St. Clair had gotten his introduction to Watergate through Colson, in 1973 when Colson had retained him briefly to represent him in his own troubles. Colson had later passed St. Clair's name on to the President with praise. Now, as St. Clair watched, Colson approached the bench. He was speaking very softly to the judge. Something was happening. The courtroom became quiet.

"I plead guilty, your honor," Colson said. There were audible gasps, including St. Clair's. Collecting himself, St. Clair fished a dime from his pocket and handed it to his assistant Jack McCahill. He wanted deputy press secretary Jerry Warren to have at least a moment's warning.

THAT AFTERNOON, St. Clair took the young lawyers on his staff to the Oval Office. They were upset that they had never met their client, and finally the President had agreed to see them. They gathered around the edge of the deep-blue oval carpet, judiciously considering its gold-stitched presidential seal. Someone noticed that the floor was covered with linoleum, a bad imitation of wood grain. The President tried to make small talk. The White House photographer took a group picture of the client and his lawyers. After ten minutes they were ushered out.

LEON JAWORSKI was by now convinced that the President had erased most, if not all, of the missing eighteen and a half minutes of conversation on the June 20 tape. But he lacked proof. On June 6 Steve Bull was recalled before the Watergate grand jury. Aside from Rose Mary Woods, he was the only member of the President's personal staff known to have handled the tape. Bull could not seem to shake the public stigma of Watergate, though the special prosecutor's office had never regarded him as suspect.

The five-hour session was grueling. Jaworski's assistant in charge of the grand jury, Ben-Veniste, did not even break for lunch. But Bull had no more details about the gap than when he had testified the previous fall. Ben-Veniste turned to the President's most recent review of his tapes, in May.

Bull gave him a file containing his cueing notes. The tapes were listed on unnumbered pages in the order in which the President had listened. Now Ben-Veniste had what he wanted—a list of the tapes the President considered most important. He now knew which tapes Nixon had studied immediately before rejecting the compromise offer to keep his status as an unindicted co-conspirator secret.

That the President had been named by the grand jury was no longer secret. There had been huge headlines in that morning's *Los Angeles Times* and the *Washington Post*. *Times* reporter Ron Ostrow had gotten the story from one of the lawyers for the men indicted in the cover-up.

St. Clair's response neither confirmed nor denied the report: "The evidence before the grand jury does not support and, indeed, contradicts such an allegation by the grand jury. Furthermore, the evidence before the grand jury on the Watergate matter relating to the President is before the House committee and, together with information furnished subsequently by the President to the House committee, proves the President's innocence."

BULL WAS not the only member of the President's staff to be subjected to rigorous interrogation that day. Henry Kissinger held a press conference. He was expecting a docile, even congratulatory reception. It was his first meeting with the reporters since he had returned triumphant from the Middle East. But the reporters were more interested in the Administration's wiretapping than in shuttle diplomacy. During his confirmation hearings the previous fall, Kissinger had downplayed his role in wiretapping reporters and White House aides. Under oath, he had maintained that he had merely provided others with the names of his assistants who had had access to leaked information. He had sworn that he never recommended that anyone be tapped.

Now Kissinger was faced with new accusations. The House Judiciary Committee had prepared an unexpurgated transcript of a conversation between John Dean and the President which undermined his claim. Discussing the origins of the wiretapping program, Nixon had said on February 28, 1973, "I know that he [Kissinger] asked that it be done."

The reporters' sharp questioning upset the Secretary.

Had he recommended that his aides be tapped?

"I did not make a direct recommendation." His lower lip jutted out defiantly.

Then what sort of recommendation had he made?

"This is a press conference and not a cross-examination," Kissinger snapped. "I have attempted to serve this government in an honorable manner for five and one half years. I do not conduct my office as a conspiracy."

Had he retained counsel "in preparation for a defense against a possible perjury indictment?"

Kissinger tried to control himself, working his hands furiously behind him. Even his closest aides had never seen him so angry. No, he answered.

Kissinger was seeing his worst fears about the corrosive effect of Watergate confirmed. For the next two days he fumed at the affront to his honor, his integrity. On Saturday morning he discussed the matter over breakfast with Senate Majority Leader Mike Mansfield. The viciousness of the press was making it exceedingly difficult for him to conduct foreign policy, he told the Montana Democrat. If suspicion continued to hang over him, it would become impossible for him to carry out his responsibilities. He might have to resign. Mansfield sought to reassure the Secretary, telling him not to even think about the matter, not to be goaded.

The next morning's *New York Times* contained more information about the taps that contradicted Kissinger's claim that he played virtually no role in the program of surveillance.

Kissinger called Mansfield at home. He was so disturbed about the rash of stories that he might not accompany the President to the Middle East, he said. His presence might diffuse the focus of the trip.

Again Mansfield sought to calm him. "Don't you dare think that way. You go. You're needed. You can be extremely helpful. The country depends on you," the Majority Leader said.

Chapter Sixteen

AT the White House, the announcement of the President's journey to Egypt, Saudi Arabia, Syria, Israel and Jordan had been made in five separate press releases to meet traditional Arab objections to appearing on the same piece of paper as Israel. Bill Henkel, chief of the advance crew, was in the Middle East, trying to cram several months' preparations into a week. The precautions for the trip had to be extraordinary. Secret Service and CIA intelligence indicated that terrorists might try to kill the President.

From Nixon's vantage point, the Middle East looked better and better compared to Washington. All he needed now was a good sendoff. That had been left in the hands of his friend Rabbi Korff. Fourteen hundred people were gathered in the Regency Ballroom of the Shoreham Hotel on Sunday afternoon, June 9, for a testimonial luncheon sponsored by the National Citizens Committee for Fairness to the Presidency. As they waited for the President to arrive, Republican Senator Carl T. Curtis of Nebraska told them, "The get-Nixon crowd, including those who conduct a trial by press, are in for a big surprise."

The audience cheered lustily.

The ambassador to Italy, John Volpe, brought them to their feet. "You just look at this Nixon family," he said. "They are a close-knit family."

Pins were presented to the Nixon daughters. Mrs. Nixon was honored as a defender of the American family. Tricia told the audience, "You will be in our hearts all the days of my father's presidency—nine hundred sixty-five more days."

At 3:05 P.M. the President arrived and was welcomed by thunderous applause. He proceeded carefully. He built his case for support of the presidency, not of himself. "Tomorrow, as you know, Mrs. Nixon and I will start a very long journey of fifteen thousand miles in which we will visit five nations, four of which have never been visited by a President of the United States before." The rally on the eve of that journey, he said, would "be long remembered, not only by the President but by all future Presidents for whom you are working."

He listed past triumphs: ending the Vietnam War, opening relations with China, achieving détente with the Soviet Union. He turned to his even greater ambitions. "I can assure you that the hope for building a peaceful world rests in the leadership of the United States, and that leadership, of course, rests in the hands of whoever may be President. . . . I shall do nothing to weaken this office while I am holding this office."

He was interrupted by cheering. "God bless Nixon," the crowd shouted.

"One final personal thought," the President said, and he quoted a letter written to a White House stenographer by her boss: " 'We have been together ever since we came to Washington in 1969 as part of this great adventure, on January 20 of that year, and we shall leave together only when we have completed our service, and we shall leave heads high on January 20, 1977.' "

The crowd roared. Tricia and Edward Cox stood to his left, Rabbi Korff on the right. He lifted his right arm and formed the familiar victory sign. As he left the podium, he was limping slightly.

THE NEXT morning, as Air Force One headed for Salzburg, Austria, Henry Kissinger was still brooding. He was with Eagleburger and Scowcroft, in the spacious staff quarters just behind the President's private cabin. They could see how terribly worn Kissinger looked. Scowcroft thought Nixon's trip should have been postponed for six weeks or so, to give Kissinger time to recover from his exhausting month in the Mideast. The wiretapping accusations had frazzled him. But the President wanted to get out of the country to strike the pose of world peacemaker. Kissinger's problems would just have to wait.

But the allegations were serious. The House Judiciary Committee now had copies of all the FBI's raw files about the taps. They contained memos that were bound to implicate Kissinger even further. Some quoted Haig as saying that Kissinger had requested certain taps personally, and that Kissinger had told the FBI that whoever leaked information to the press should be destroyed. Kissinger had visited bureau headquarters to read transcripts of the tapped conversations.

Aboard the plane, Kissinger told his aides that he saw an endless attack being mounted against him. Eagleburger and Scowcroft both recognized that Kissinger had shaded the truth in his testimony. They searched for a solution. Eagleburger had already proposed to Kissinger that he hold a press conference to denounce the stories and threaten to resign, if necessary. Scowcroft had opposed it. There had been relatively few stories he said; threatening resignation would indicate that Kissinger was overly sensitive on the subject; it would suggest that he was covering up. But Kissinger was coming around to Eagleburger's view. He couldn't ignore the attack; sooner or later it would have to be answered. In the hands of the thirty-eight members of the House Judiciary Committee, the FBI documents would be leaked in the most unfavorable light. Perhaps it was time to go on the offensive.

"Henry, then do it," Eagleburger told him.

Kissinger went forward to see Haig. "I've had enough, it's got to be met head on," he told the general. He did not mention that he might threaten resignation, only that he was considering a press conference.

Haig took the matter to the President. When he came back, he indicated that Nixon was concerned that a press conference might distract attention from the President's mission. Perhaps Kissinger should think it over.

Ziegler was even less pleased and suggested that Kissinger take the standard White House line of denial—"I won't dignify it with comment."

But when the plane landed in Austria, the party learned of another unfavorable story, as well as an editorial in the *New York Times,* and the State Department press office saw more coming. Boiling, Kissinger stayed up until nearly dawn, talking with Eagleburger and Scowcroft and with advisers back in Washington. His mind was made up. They all recognized that if the stories continued full tilt he might have to make good on a threat. A public threat to resign could be made only once.

Kissinger needed to break the continuing chain of accusation and denial, he needed a grace period from attacks in the press. Mansfield had told him that he would be called before the Senate Foreign Relations Committee to answer the new charges. Kissinger decided to preempt the committee: He would demand publicly that it open an inquiry into the accusations against him; that would force the attackers to pause. Hearings could not take place until after the Middle East trip. Kissinger's staff would have time to assemble the memos and documents that could be used to answer each of the accusations and support the Secretary's version of events. He would be in an extremely sympathetic forum, with Senators who supported him and his policies. He drafted a letter to the Foreign Relations Committee.

At 5 A.M. Salzburg time, members of the press-office staff began knocking on the doors of reporters' hotel rooms. There would be a press conference first thing before breakfast. Filing into a cavernous room in Kavalier Haus, most of them expected Kissinger to hold forth on his expectations for the presidential journey.

He walked to the microphone. "Last Thursday, a number of you commented on the fact that I seemed irritated, angered, flustered, discombobulated. All these words are correct," he said. He read his letter to the committee and expressed concern that he hadn't had an opportunity to respond fully to the accusations.

"The impression has been created that I was involved in some illegal or shady activity that I am trying to obscure with misleading testimony." He laid out the situation from his perspective:

In 1969 he was conducting sensitive negotiations; leakers were endangering those negotiations; some of his aides were suspect because of their ties to the previous Administration; he had been told that prior administrations had conducted wiretaps to protect the national security. Accordingly he had provided information on who had access to data that had been leaked. He had known that they would probably be tapped. But the President, not he, had initiated the wiretapping program. Though he found it distasteful he had accepted it.

He appealed for understanding. "All of you in this room know from your profession that the truth very often has intangible aspects." And he deplored the climate in which "unnamed sources can attack the credibility and the honor of senior officials of the government without even being asked to identify themselves."

His aides cringed at that reference. They were all aware that Kissinger's credibility had been called into question by FBI memos signed by Director J. Edgar Hoover himself, and by the President's own taped words, not by unnamed sources.

Kissinger seemed on the verge of tears and his voice choked as he talked about his place in history. "When the record is written, one may remember that perhaps some lives were saved and that perhaps some mothers can rest more at ease, but I leave that to history. What I will not leave to history is a discussion of my public honor. I have believed that I should do what I could to heal division in this country. I believed that I should do what I could to maintain the dignity of American values and to give Americans some pride in the conduct of their affairs. I can do this only if my honor is not at issue and if the public deserves to have confidence. If that cannot be maintained, I cannot perform the duties that I have exercised, and in that case I shall turn them over immediately to individuals less subject to public attack."

The questions from the reporters indicated that they were skeptical.

"I want to make absolutely clear I am not making this as a threat in order to gain support," Kissinger responded. "I am stating an objective fact. It is impossible and incompatible with the dignity of the United States to have its senior official and to have its Secretary of State under this sort of attack in the face of the dangers we confront and the risks that may have to be run and the opportunities that may have to be seized. This is a fact. This is not a threat."

One reporter wondered aloud if the same standard might be better applied to the President.

"The President is the only nationally elected official," Kissinger replied. "For a President to resign under attack would raise the most profound issues of national policy, and in my judgment a President can leave office only according to the constitutional processes that have been foreseen for it. . . ."

Finally Kissinger, Haig and Ziegler strode in step from the room, their bearing grim and military.

Minutes later, Ziegler stormed into his staff quarters. He hadn't wanted Kissinger to have a press conference, let alone threaten to resign. It was an inauspicious start for the President's trip. Goddammit, he shouted. Again the focus was on Kissinger, not the President. Once more the attention was on Administration scandal. How the hell could they divert attention from Watergate with Kissinger dragging it across the seas?

Haig reported back to Kissinger on Nixon's reaction. "Good job, and the President won't accept your resignation," he said.

Haig was disturbed, however. This business was hurting his own credibility. He was the Kissinger deputy who had implemented each of the taps through the FBI. Kissinger's denials were bound to focus further attention on his own role. Clearly he would be the key witness before the Senate Foreign Relations Committee. The central question would be who had initiated the taps—the President, Kissinger or Haig? Watergate was engulfing the President, and now it was threatening Kissinger and himself.

That evening Kissinger dined with Scowcroft, Eagleburger and Peter Rodman, his personal aide. The press conference had been cathartic. He replayed it between bites of Wiener schnitzel. Was it the right thing to do?

Had he said the right things? What would the reaction be? What would the Russians think?

The reassurance of his aides helped. For the first time in his career, Kissinger had taken the sort of public gamble that had succeeded over the years for Richard Nixon. He sensed that it was Nixon's almost demonic courage that had made the President what he had become. Nixon was often as careless with power as a tightrope walker who downed three drinks before walking across the canyon, Kissinger thought—that was the quality of Nixon's leadership that he both admired and feared. Now he had adopted the same precarious stance himself.

WHILE MOST members of the presidential party concerned themselves with Richard Nixon's political life, Major General Walter Tkach, his personal physician, was worried about the President's life, period. During Nixon's years as Vice-President and President, Tkach had examined his principal patient regularly. Nixon was a healthy man generally, not given to complaining about minor discomforts. Tkach relied on those around the President, particularly his valet, Manolo Sanchez, for information. It was unusual for the President to summon him on the spur of the moment, as he did this day. Tkach hurried to Nixon's sitting room.

The President greeted him perfunctorily and pulled up his left pant leg. Tkach could see that the leg was inflamed and swollen. He examined the leg more closely, then went through a series of checks which confirmed his fears. A blood clot had formed in a vein in the leg, he explained. Phlebitis. The clot could break loose and go to his heart or lungs. That could be fatal.

Continuing the trip was a senseless risk, Tkach told him. Strain from extended standing, climbing stairs, long walks, even crossing his legs might free the clot. He recommended that the President be hospitalized immediately and, after enough rest to insure that the clot had stabilized, that he fly back to Washington for further treatment.

The President rejected the advice. "The purpose of this trip is more important than my life. I know it is a calculated risk." He was obligated to finish what he had started.

Tkach gave him a support hose. Nixon tried it on. It was too uncomfortable, he said.

The physician told him the only good news he could think of. His diet, at least, was proper for the illness.

Leaving his patient, Tkach hurried to Haig's room. He shook as he told him the diagnosis. "I am going to order him to go home," Tkach said, and he bolted for the conference room, where Bull and Henkel had established a temporary office. It was ornately decorated, with pictures of Hitler hanging on the walls; the Führer had used the room during the war, carving up Europe on a map.

Tkach did not pause for pleasantries. "Does the President have a lot of standing to do? Will he have to go on any long walks? Will he encounter a lot of stairs?"

The schedule called for Nixon to be on his feet extensively. The next day's schedule—Cairo, Henkel said—was particularly rough. There was a lot of standing, walking, climbing.

"Is there any way we can change this?" Tkach sounded scared.

"No, it's too late," said Henkel.

They paced back and forth, to avoid being overheard by others in the room. Tkach said that Nixon belonged in a hospital; he should never have made the trip. "The President has a death wish," he said. "He won't take my advice. He won't listen to me." He explained how death could be instantaneous if the clot broke free.

Usually Henkel and Bull made light of Tkach's concern about the President's health. He was easily alarmed. They preferred to take the advice of Nixon's other physician, Lieutenant Commander William Lukash. One White House joke held that Tkach carried two cures in his medical bag—a bottle of aspirin and Bill Lukash's phone number. But the President, meanwhile, had quietly summoned Lukash. It was the first time both doctors had accompanied him on a trip. Though he was sensitive to the danger of offending his senior physician, Nixon had more confidence in the younger man. Lukash seemed more precise and more sure of himself.

His diagnosis was the same, and his warning equally dire. He too tried to convince the President to terminate the trip. Nixon was just as adamant with him. He issued his own order: no one was to mention his condition; it had to be kept absolutely secret. Its disclosure would further harm the objectives of his presidency.

IN WASHINGTON that evening, Whitehead and Buchen met with the new members of the transition team for the first time: Brian Lamb, Whitehead's assistant at the Office of Telecommunications Policy; Larry Lynn, a former aide to Kissinger at the NSC; Jonathan Moore, formerly an assistant to Rockefeller and then to Elliot Richardson. The five men sat around Whitehead's dining-room table, drinking Cokes.

Buchen stated the problem. Some groundwork had to be done for Ford in the event that he had to take over the presidency on short notice. Ford himself would have nothing to do with such preparation. Accordingly, Buchen was acting on his own. Ford was not aware of the existence of the group. Buchen spoke of Ford as an old friend—decent and honest, but very limited in his knowledge of the presidency. Ford would literally need a notebook, Buchen said, one with tabs that would specify in simple steps each decision and action required of a new President.

There was another problem. If Ford became President, he would be besieged by old political friends, each of them with ideas and advice on how to proceed. Ford had always been susceptible to such pressure, Buchen said.

Former Secretary of Defense Laird's name was mentioned. Articulate, charming and intelligent, all agreed. But he was also an incorrigible schemer who would approach the new President—if it ever came to that—with grandiose plans, they were certain. The transition group should find a way to shield Ford from his influence.

Haig was still another obstacle. Already Ford had come to like and trust the Nixon chief of staff. Lynn and Moore in particular were concerned about this. Haig could not be trusted, Lynn said. The general's capacity to beguile, and his position in the Nixon White House, could pose dangers for Ford. Haig was the chameleon bureaucrat. Moore elaborated: The general was tired; he would quite naturally be preoccupied with justifying past behavior and associations. Men like Haig would never be able to give their total allegiance to the new President.

The group decided that each member would write short papers on their areas of expertise—economics, National Security Council, the departments, etc. They estimated they had until early September to complete their work.

There was one last item on the agenda—Nixon's legal future. They agreed that Ford needed to be protected from entreaties that Nixon receive preferential legal treatment upon leaving office. The outgoing President should be accorded respect, not harassment or vengeance; but the potential that someone might approach Ford for a deal was dangerous. The new President would have to be warned that such an attempt should be rebuffed.

Whitehead walked Buchen out to his car to talk privately. What would happen if Nixon were impeached and convicted and then refused to leave office? Maybe the notion of the President resisting removal was not so absurd. Suppose he went crazy and tried to use the military to retain office. The two men wondered if perhaps they should raise the question with the Secretary of Defense, James Schlesinger. What if it became necessary to remove the President through the Twenty-fifth Amendment's provision relating to incapacity to govern?* They decided they were obliged to consider every possibility, no matter how remote, how unthinkable.

ON THE morning of June 12, the President and his entourage made the three-hour-and-forty-five-minute flight from Salzburg to Cairo. Their motorcade entrance into the capital was jubilant. Several hundred thousand people lined the curbs, rooftops and balconies. For three quarters of an hour Nixon stood in an open limousine with Egyptian President Anwar Sadat. Cheering workers, soldiers, schoolchildren—trucked to their stations by the thousands —waved placards which hailed the President as "a man of honor" and proclaimed both leaders great statesmen dedicated to peace and progress.

Sadat was the perfect host. His welcoming remarks seemed to grasp Nixon's purpose: "The role of the United States under the leadership of President Nixon is vital to promote peace and tranquillity in the area. It is a great challenge, but I am convinced that with goodwill and determination, statesmen of the stature of President Nixon are apt to meet it."

Nixon thanked Sadat privately for the huge crowds.

"Wait until we get to Alexandria," Sadat said.

Henkel, in charge of advance, had vigorously opposed making a stop there. Having the presidential party overnight in Alexandria meant additional security arrangements and hosting a formal banquet without benefit of a resident embassy. The American ambassador was also opposed; he was offended at Nixon's preference for public appearances over substantive meetings. But the President overruled them both. The trip to Alexandria, by train, was politically important to Sadat, he said.

As promised, the crowds were spectacular, even before they reached the port city. Every mile of the route was lined with peasants, soldiers, workers. Women crowded close to the passing train, expressing their approval in the Arab high-pitched warble of prayer. A magnificent white stallion, mounted by a soldier carrying the flags of both countries, raced beside the tracks. The horse reared and threw its rider, then kept the pace alone. Ziegler estimated that two million people had turned out.

The President's party rode in a luxurious rail coach that had been built in the nineteenth century. Many drank strong dark beer from quart bottles. Dr. Lukash read the best-seller *Jaws*.

---

* Under the Twenty-fifth Amendment, the Vice-President and a majority of the Cabinet can declare that the President is "unable to discharge the powers and duties of his office," whereupon the Vice-President would become President. However, if the President maintains that no inability exists, both Houses of Congress decide the issue. A vote of two thirds of the members of each house would be required to remove the President.

A Secret Service agent interrupted him. "You are wanted up front."

Lukash was horrified when he reached the President. Nixon, in total disregard of his physicians' advice, was standing in the open-sided Victorian observation car waving to the crowd. The President and Sadat shifted places from one side of the open car to the other, acknowledging the cheers, each holding on to the overhead brass railing to keep his balance.

Lukash could see that the President was doing his best to disguise great pain. The physician took a seat on the red leather banquette in the rear of the car. The full-length green curtains dividing the coach kept him out of sight of the camera crews up front. He reached into his medical bag.

A few minutes later, Nixon limped into a private compartment in the front of the train, where Lukash joined him. The physician gave him a pain killer and pleaded with him to keep off his feet. Nixon went back to stand with Sadat.

Secret Service agents scanned the crowds almost desperately. Reports were coming through of a terrorist raid on an Israeli kibbutz, in which three women had been killed. In Beirut a Palestinian terrorist group was taking credit for the attack. "That is how every Arab should receive Nixon, the chief imperialist in the world," its communiqué said. Despite the massive presence of heavily armed Egyptian security forces, the President's exposure to the huge crowds seemed a senseless risk to his Secret Service contingent.

Dr. Tkach sought out Dick Keiser, head of the presidential-protection unit of the Secret Service, and expressed his alarm at Nixon's behavior.

"You can't protect a President who wants to kill himself," Keiser responded.

Shortly before reaching Alexandria, Nixon and Sadat spoke informally with several of the 126 reporters aboard the train. Nixon moved again to the open side of the railroad car, calling their attention to the size and enthusiasm of the crowds.

Sadat pointed to one of the many banners: "We Trust Nixon." "He has fulfilled every word he gave," Sadat said.

Encouraged by the White House advance office, Egyptian officials in Alexandria had mobilized a campaign-style greeting. By the time the presidential party arrived, more than a million people stood on the sea walls and in the streets. Some had climbed lampposts.

The official party traveled by motorcade to the Ras El Tin Palace, where the President hosted a banquet for Sadat. It was as luxurious a residence as Nixon had ever seen, magnificently opulent. It had taken King Farouk thirty years to build. As he toasted Sadat, the President again remarked on the crowds. "There is an old saying that you can turn people out but you can't turn them on," he said. "They have touched our hearts, and I'm sure the hearts of millions of Americans who saw that welcoming on television."

Kissinger turned to Eagleburger and Scowcroft. "It's too bad that such crowds can't be turned out in the United States," he said. The three men laughed.

THE NEXT day, June 14, the President helicoptered to Giza and, defying his doctors again, toured the Great Pyramids on foot with Sadat. Returning to Cairo, the two leaders announced a joint agreement for economic cooperation—including a United States pledge to sell nuclear reactors and fuel to Egypt. As a surprise token of his friendship, Nixon gave Sadat the two-million-dollar helicopter in which they had flown. Members of the presidential party joked to the pilot that he would be the President's next state gift.

On the motorcade to the airport, the President emerged from his Lincoln convertible, waded into the masses and was mobbed. Secret Service agents, incredulous at his recklessness, flailed at the faceless bodies until they could establish a cordon around him. Then, as gently as possible, they pushed him back into the car and whisked him away. Relieved at the close call, the security men asked each other why Haig didn't intervene; it was the chief of staff's job. Haldeman had sometimes let the President take small risks in motorcades and crowds, but never anything like this. What was wrong? Couldn't Haig talk sense to the President?

But Nixon continued to chart his own course, ordering that whatever free time his schedule called for be devoted to more public appearances, particularly if they might involve large crowds. That afternoon, after crossing the Red Sea by plane to Saudi Arabia, he rode from the airport to Jidda in King Faisal's Rolls-Royce. The Secret Service, which always prefers that a President use his own limousine with an agent at the wheel, was horrified. The President seemed to be doing everything he could to make his protection more difficult.

The following morning the President refused to be driven in anybody's car. In spite of the pain in his leg, he insisted on making the five-minute walk across the Al Hamra Palace grounds to his meeting with the King.

At the departure ceremony that afternoon, Faisal's farewell message went beyond pro-forma tribute-paying. "What is very important is that our friends in the United States of America be themselves wise enough to stand behind you, to rally around you, Mr. President, in your noble efforts, almost unprecedented in the history of mankind, the efforts aiming at securing peace and justice in the world. And anybody who stands against you, Mr. President, in the United States of America or outside the United States of America, or stands against us, your friends in this part of the world, obviously has one aim in mind, namely that of splintering the world . . . the bringing on of mischief."

The President flew east once more, to Damascus, Syria. Again he was ignoring the advice of those responsible for his safety. They had been insistent that this part of the trip be canceled. Syria had broken off relations with the United States in 1967. The absence of diplomatic facilities made it impossible to secure adequate intelligence about terrorist activities. The extraordinary number of Palestinian refugees was gravely worrisome to the Secret Service. Worse, the limited American intelligence available was skeptical of President Assad's ability to control either the government or the population of revolutionary Syria.

Thirty minutes out of Damascus, the President's plane was cruising at fifteen thousand feet. George Joulwan, Haig's assistant, noticed two Russian-built MIG jets approaching on the left. "Look," he shouted, "we've got fighter escorts."

Somebody else pointed out two more jets closing from the right.

Brent Scowcroft knew that the advance team always prohibited any such escort. "Wouldn't this be a hell of an ending," he said.

Henkel got up to investigate. As he turned, the plane suddenly began a nose dive and went into a series of rolls. Henkel was thrown across the aisle into the seat next to Scowcroft. He looked up at Scowcroft's soft gray eyes. They were bulging like two silver dollars.

Colonel Ralph Albertazzie, the President's pilot, took the giant jet through a series of evasive turns and steep banks for seven minutes while he sought assurance that the four Syrian aircraft were friendly. Finally convinced, Albertazzie resumed his approach pattern and landed.

As the plane taxied to a halt, Syrian security men were still confiscating handsomely printed leaflets distributed that morning throughout the low-income districts of Damascus: "Was all the war, all the blood that was shed under American bombs, all the dead we suffered, so that Nixon and the prophet of imperialism, Kissinger, could visit Damascus and give us a hundred million dollars?"

The twenty-eight-mile route to the city was lined with soldiers armed with Russian-made AK-47 automatic rifles. As the crowds grew thicker, the President insisted that the roof of the limousine be opened. He stood smiling and waving. The spectators were subdued for the most part, more curious than enthusiastic. "Revolutionary Damascus Welcomes President Nixon," the signs said.

His meeting with Assad was instructive. As they talked, Assad's young son turned to his father and said, "Isn't Nixon the one you said on TV is a foreign devil and the friend of the Jews? Now you are having him here. Why?"

Assad said to Nixon, "That's my son, that's also my people. So you see my problems."

On the afternoon of Sunday, June 16, the two leaders announced the resumption of diplomatic relations between their countries. Then the President jetted off to Israel to promise the Israelis the same nuclear-power capability he had offered Egypt. Nineteen thousand armed troops and security agents provided the toughest security ever afforded a foreign visitor. The road to Jerusalem was lined with workers and children who had been given the day off. Their placards proclaimed mixed feelings: "Blessed Be Your Welcome"; "Don't Sell Us Out"; "You Can't Run from Justice"; and "Welcome, President *Ford.*"

After a visit to Jordan on June 17, the President headed for home. Aboard Air Force One, he emerged from his cabin in a red plaid sports coat and strolled back to the staff section, stopping to talk with everyone except the members of the press pool. He was tanned, but he looked tired. In nine days he had traveled 14,775 miles and had met with seven heads of state. Reaching speech writer Dave Gergen, he lingered. "I used a lot of your stuff," he said. "Not all of it, of course. You understand."

Gergen nodded.

"Now that you've had this experience, would you like to be an ambassador?" Nixon asked.

Gergen, thirty-three years old, didn't know what to say. The idea was preposterous.

The President asked him if he spoke French.

"Not very well."

"Then I'll have to send you to Iraq," Nixon said.

The President's blue-and-white helicopter landed on the south lawn at 4:29 P.M., Wednesday, June 19. Vice-President Ford, members of the Cabinet, two hundred teenage Republicans and most of the White House staff were waiting. They waved small American flags and chanted, "Two more years. Two more years."

Welcoming the President home, Ford quoted an Arabic saying: "May Allah make the end better than the beginning."

CHAPTER SEVENTEEN

JUNE 21 was the Nixons' thirty-fourth wedding anniversary. That day, the President's former special counsel, Charles W. Colson, was sentenced to a one-to-three-year term in the federal penitentiary. Reading from a prepared statement, Colson implicated the President in his crime. Nixon had "on numerous occasions urged me to disseminate damaging information about Daniel Ellsberg," the same act for which Colson was going to jail. He was convinced that the President "believed he was acting in the national interest," Colson added.

Nixon was at Camp David for three days' rest and to prepare for his trip to Russia. Though the swelling in his leg had eased somewhat, his doctors pleaded with him to postpone the trip. He refused. The press, which had finally learned of his illness, was told that he had suffered "a mild case of phlebitis" on the last journey, but that it had abated.

The crew of Air Force One had barely time to apply a coat of Turtle Wax to the fuselage before the President flew away from Watergate again, bound for Brussels and then the Soviet Union. He crossed the Atlantic with his left leg elevated to reduce the pain. He was looking forward to his meeting with Brezhnev. The Secretary General of the Communist Party was his friend.

The thirty-six hours in Belgium were given over largely to ceremonial meetings, called to assure America's NATO allies that the President would make no agreements with the Soviet Union until they had been consulted.

At Vnukovo Airport, Secretary Brezhnev bounded across the tarmac to greet Nixon, leaving his translator behind for the moment. As they drove to the Kremlin in Brezhnev's black Zil limousine, they talked animatedly, pausing to wave to respectful Muscovites gathered at prearranged points along the route. Many of the spectators held small Soviet and American flags.

The President was genuinely fond of his Soviet colleague. Brutal politician though he might be, Brezhnev could also be jovial, sentimental, gregarious and a marvelous raconteur. He had the elemental qualities of the crude, rough-talking, heavy-drinking comrade, Kissinger observed in a private moment—qualities that Nixon himself lacked but was drawn to.

Regardless of the warm greeting, the President knew he could expect only so much from Brezhnev. The Soviet press had largely ignored Watergate. When the matter was referred to, it was portrayed as a plot to destroy détente. But the Kremlin understood the precarious nature of Nixon's position. KGB agents stationed in Washington under journalistic cover had been canvassing American politicians and reporters about the likelihood of the President's finishing his term. Pointedly, Soviet officials told Western journalists that they expected no dramatic results from the Moscow summit conference. Rather, they hoped to "traditionalize" the principle of top-level meetings, no matter who was President.

The President had his usual present for Brezhnev—an American automobile for the Secretary's extensive collection. Their first two summits, in 1972 and 1973, had yielded two $10,000 models, a Cadillac limousine and a Lincoln Continental. This time it was a $5,578 Chevrolet Monte Carlo, not very impressive in a garage that already housed a Citroen-Maserati speedster, Rolls-Royce and Mercedes sedans, and Brezhnev's favorite, a new Mercedes 300SL roadster. But Brezhnev had learned that the Monte Carlo was named "Car of the Year" by *Motor Trend* magazine, and he had let it be known that he would like one.

The Nixon-Brezhnev summit of 1972 had resulted in a treaty limiting each country's defensive and offensive nuclear-missile systems—the top jewel in the crown of the Administration's foreign-policy agreements. Their summit in 1973 had kept John Dean on ice for a week, as the Senate Watergate Committee suspended its hearings in deference to Brezhnev's visit to the United States. Now the 1974 summit was suspect in Congress, where fears were widespread that the President might somehow "sell out" in desperation to get an arms-limitation agreement which would improve his public standing.

Nixon and Kissinger were of one mind in believing that limiting the expansion of nuclear-weapon systems and maintaining parity in the balance of nuclear terror were the key to a successful détente with the Soviet Union. And, in their grand strategy, the American-Soviet relationship was the key to world peace. United States influence in every area of the world was predicated on a delicate, cooperative relationship with the Russians. Every major diplomatic move was viewed in relation to the prospective Soviet reaction. The ability of the United States to promote peace in the Middle East—or to fight in Vietnam—hinged on an at least tacit acceptance by the Russians. Because so much was premised on the balance of nuclear force, no treaty was regarded as more important by Nixon or Kissinger than a permanent strategic-arms-limitation (SALT) agreement.

The President had often confided to Kissinger his most telling reason for slowing down the nuclear-arms race. He feared that the United States would lose it. Continued military competition was too expensive. The country might not be able to sustain the costs of a prolonged cold war. America, the President felt, was too likely to buckle under the pressure. Besides the economic weakness of the country, Nixon perceived a weakness of will. Too many of the same political critics who were pushing him to the wall on Watergate would not support a tough posture toward the Russians, he said.

The President and Kissinger regarded the stakes in the 1974 summit as especially high. If they offered the kind of tough proposal they preferred, its rejection would almost inevitably escalate the arms race. If they offered a less ambitious proposal which the Soviets were more likely to accept, Nixon would be accused by critics of selling out for a cheap, Watergate-motivated deal. Both Kissinger and the President had decided to lean in the direction of making the Soviets a more palatable offer and taking a chance with the critics at home. They were in agreement that their proposal served American interests well. But Kissinger calculated that the prospects of any satisfactory agreement were substantially reduced by Watergate. The Soviets were likely to test how far the President would bend. Kissinger was less than absolute in his confidence that Nixon could withstand the pressure.

His concern went beyond the question of Nixon's will, however. The President had not done his homework, and he seemed distracted. Unless he mastered his briefing book in a matter of hours, Kissinger feared, Nixon would never be able to grasp the essential details of the complex negotiations.

Normally, Kissinger would have taken his concern to Haig. But there was little time left, and, besides, Kissinger was loath to talk with the general. During the planning for the trip, Haig had been assigned quarters adjacent to the President's suite in the Kremlin Palace. Kissinger, who had wanted them, had registered a bitter protest through Scowcroft. Haig had responded that the White House chief of staff needed to be at the President's side. The battle over the suite lasted several days, and conflicting instructions had gone to the advance team. White House communications agents installed, removed, replaced, removed again and reinstalled special communications equipment as the prospective occupant changed again and again.

Scowcroft could see how short Kissinger's fuse had become. He was drawn and tense, even more snappish than usual. Haig finally won the contest for the room; technically, the advance staff worked for him. Kissinger, unwilling to expose his interest any further, did not appeal the decision to the President. But his attack on Haig continued. The summit was a diplomatic trip, he told his aides—why in hell did the chief of staff, nothing but a bureaucrat in essence, have to be close to the President? It was he, not Haig, who was to mastermind the summit strategy. It was he, not Haig, who would keep the President from making a serious error. It was he, not Haig, who would actually conduct the business when the President finished with his ritual toasts and posing for pictures. Haig knew nothing about the summit.

"General Haig is out for himself and when it comes to the crunch he puts himself first," Kissinger said.

AT THAT night's dinner in the Granovit Hall of the Kremlin, the President used the first exchange of toasts to attribute existing arms agreements to the relationship between Brezhnev and himself. He raised his glass. The agreements, he said, "were possible because of a personal relationship that was established between the General Secretary and the President of the United States. And that personal relationship extends to the top officials in both our governments. It has been said that any agreement is only as good as the will of the parties to keep it. Because of our personal relationship, there is no question about our will to keep these agreements and to make more when they are in our mutual interests."

The following morning *Tass*, the Soviet news agency, translated the President's toast differently. "Personal relationship" became "the relations that have grown up between us"—implying that détente was premised on the mutual interests of two nations, not of individuals. Reading the account at breakfast, Robert Kaiser, Moscow correspondent of the *Washington Post,* noted the distinction. He asked Jerry Warren about it. Warren's jaw seemed to drop, and he hurried to tell Ziegler.

James K. W. Atherton, The Washington Post

THE INNER CIRCLE: *above,* chief of staff
Gen. Alexander M. Haig, Jr. (left), with
Leonard Garment, counsel to the President;
left and *below,* James D. St. Clair and J.
Fred Buzhardt, White House special counsels
for Watergate. Opposite: *above,* General
Haig; *below left,* Rose Mary Woods, the
President's personal secretary; *below right,*
Ronald L. Ziegler, press secretary.

Joe Heiberger, The Washington Post

Associated Press

THE PRESIDENT'S SPEECH WRITERS:
above, Raymond K. Price, Jr.;
below, Patrick J. Buchanan.

Dirck Halstead

James K. W. Atherton, The Washington Post

FOREIGN AFFAIRS AND NATIONAL
SECURITY: *above,* Secretary of State
Henry A. Kissinger; *left,* Lawrence
Eagleburger, assistant to the Secretary
of State; *below,* Lt. Gen. Brent
Scowcroft, deputy assistant to the
President for national security affairs.

THE INVESTIGATION: *above,*
Watergate Special Prosecutor
Archibald Cox; *right,* House
Judiciary Committee counsel John
Doar (left) and Chairman Peter W.
Rodino, Jr.; *below,* Watergate
Special Prosecutor Leon Jaworski
speaks to reporters and spectators
outside the Supreme Court after
the Court ruled unanimously that
Nixon must surrender the
Watergate tapes.

Associated Press

KEY REPUBLICANS IN CONGRESS: *above,* Charles E. Wiggins of California, the President's chief defender on the House Judiciary Committee; *left,* Thomas F. Railsback of Illinois, a member of the "fragile coalition" on the H.J.C., regarded as a litmus test of the impeachment vote; *below* (left to right), Senate Minority Leader Hugh Scott of Pennsylvania, Senator Barry Goldwater of Arizona, and House Minority Leader John J. Rhodes of Arizona.

James K. W. Atherton, The Washington Post

Frank Johnston, The Washington Post

Dirck Halstead

Above, Mrs. Nixon, the President, David and Julie Eisenhower cruising the Potomac aboard the *Sequoia.* Opposite: *above,* Rabbi Baruch Korff, chairman, Citizens Committee for Fairness to the Presidency, presides at a luncheon in honor of Mr. Nixon on the eve of the President's trip to the Middle East in June 1974; *below left,* Mrs. Nixon, the President and Charles G. (Bebe) Rebozo; *below right,* Julie and David Eisenhower at a press conference in the East Garden of the White House, May 11, 1974.

Dirck Halstead

Larry Morris, The Washington Post

Official White House Photo

Above, President Nixon and President Anwar Sadat of Egypt are greeted by crowds in Alexandria in June 1974. Opposite: *above,* President Nixon and Secretary Leonid Brezhnev during Nixon's trip to the USSR, June 1974; *below,* Mrs. Nixon, in Russia, watches her husband deliver a televised address.

Official White House Photo

Dirck Halstead

Craig Herndon, The Washington Post

Above, Robert Hartmann (left), Vice-President Ford's chief of staff, and Philip Buchen, Ford confidant and coordinator of the presidential transition team. *Below,* presidential aide Stephen Bull congratulates King Timahoe as Lt. Col. Jack Brennan, military aide to the President, looks on.

Official White House Photo

Official White House Photo

AT THE WHITE HOUSE, AUGUST 7, 1974,
AFTER THE PRESIDENT HAD TOLD HIS FAMILY
HE WAS GOING TO RESIGN: *above,* the
family—Edward and Tricia Cox, the
President, Mrs. Nixon, Julie and David
Eisenhower; *below,* the President embraces
his younger daughter, Julie.

Dirck Halstead

AUGUST 9, 1974: *above,* President
Nixon says farewell to the White House
staff; *below* and *opposite,* he waves
goodbye from the steps of the helicopter
that will take him to Andrews Air
Force Base on the first leg of his
journey to his estate in San Clemente,
California.

Dirck Halstead

Wally McNamee, Newsweek

AUGUST 9, 1974: Vice-President and Mrs. Ford watch as the carpet is rolled up outside the President's helicopter, and then turn to walk back to the White House.

That afternoon Ziegler told reporters that there had simply been a mistake made in translation and that it would be corrected in the evening editions of *Izvestia*. He introduced Leonid Zamyatin, director of *Tass,* who said carefully, "General Secretary Brezhnev and President Nixon have repeatedly emphasized the importance of their personal relationship." Ziegler beamed. But the evening's edition repeated the mistranslation, and Soviet sources told selected Moscow correspondents of American newspapers that the distinction was scarcely accidental.

As the formal talks went on through the day, the Soviets carried on a game of keeping the President and his staff in the dark about the schedule. Meetings were postponed while Brezhnev napped, then suddenly a protocol deputy would appear at the entrance to the President's quarters and announce that a meeting was imminent. The pattern continued through the first few sessions. Nixon and his staff were irritated, but they accepted the tactic. The Soviet strategy was to weaken their resolve.

The psychological battering continued on Saturday, June 29. Brezhnev insisted that the President fly with him to his retreat on the Black Sea. Then the trip was delayed, ostensibly because of the weather, then was rescheduled for a later hour. Next it was moved back—to take advantage of a break in the weather, the Russians said. Then it was postponed once more, and minutes later the Americans were informed that departure would be in half an hour.

Brezhnev and Nixon snacked on caviar aboard the Secretary General's Ilyushin-62 airplane. After a ninety-four-minute flight, they drove to Brezhnev's cliffside dacha in Orleans.* Brezhnev escorted the President to the edge of the cliff and then into a Plexiglas elevator, in which they descended to the beach below. As the two leaders gazed at the sunset, Ziegler remarked how similar the Russian leader's plush vacation spa was to Nixon's San Clemente estate.

Next morning the two men walked down to the beach and its seaside swimming pool. They climbed to the top of the cliff on which the dacha perched, walked through the lush gardens and admired the lily ponds. Haig, Kissinger and a retinue of Brezhnev's deputies tagged along.

Then, unexpectedly, the President insisted on meeting with Brezhnev

---

* Orleans is a district of Yalta, only three miles from the center of the larger city. When the Russians had initially suggested Yalta as one of the negotiation sites, the American advance team had objected. They were concerned that Yalta, scene of the historic 1945 meeting of Roosevelt, Stalin and Churchill, remained a symbol of an American "sellout" to the Russians. The advance team referred the question back to Washington, and the President responded that if Brezhnev wanted it, so be it. The Soviets, in turn, agreed to refer to the meeting site as Orleans.

alone. The two leaders headed for a meeting room between the main and guest dachas, while the others waited at the swimming pool. Kissinger had been scheduled to be with the President through all his meetings that day; the negotiations were entering their most crucial phase. He was furious at being excluded. Usually the President acquitted himself well with Brezhnev, but Nixon still hadn't mastered the briefing book, and Kissinger thought he was no match for Brezhnev, who was always extraordinarily well briefed. Brezhnev routinely mastered details that the President was accustomed to leaving to his aides. Kissinger worried that the President might make a major slip, get into unfamiliar areas, give something away accidentally.

Kissinger was sweating. An hour passed. He paced up and down the length of the swimming pool. An hour and a half. He voiced his concern to his aides. Nixon and Brezhnev had never been alone together for so long. Two hours. Kissinger could see the two sitting at the pale-wood conference table, an assortment of beverages spread on trays next to them.

Finally the others were summoned to the meeting. As the formal talks resumed, it seemed as if the two leaders had not discussed the substance of the negotiations at all. The agenda picked up exactly where it had been, as if nothing had happened. Kissinger and Haig were profoundly troubled. So was everybody else in the presidential party. They had no idea of what the two had discussed. But whatever it was, it became apparent that the President had made no commitments which would compromise the American bargaining strategy. As the talks got more technical, Nixon deferred to Kissinger. Brezhnev continued to conduct the Soviet side of the negotiations, using two Soviet generals as messengers to shuttle in and out with charts of missile-strength levels.

Then, abruptly, Brezhnev announced that there could be no agreement on limiting offensive nuclear weapons. Nothing was possible without greater American concessions, he said. The Americans must allow the Russians a greater number of missiles as compensation for long-range U.S. bombers in Europe and multiple-warhead missiles.

The President seemed perplexed. Kissinger was stunned. They had expected resistance, but not to this degree. Brezhnev was adopting an extremely hard line.

They tried again.

Brezhnev could not be moved.

The President sat gazing out the windows, looking toward the sea. He desperately wanted some sort of agreement to take back to Washington, but he could not make any further concessions without sacrificing U.S. strategic interests. He had no card left to play. He held firm.

THAT EVENING, the presidential party had dinner aboard a 115-foot yacht of the Soviet Navy. Nixon and Brezhnev moved aft, drinking as they sailed across the Black Sea in the shadow of the sheer cliffs of the Yaila Mountains. Brezhnev, wearing sunglasses, chain-smoked Russian cigarettes. The left sleeve of his blue-gray coat slipped above his tanned wrist, exposing an expensive gold watch. The President, dressed in gray slacks and a maroon sports jacket with the customary American-flag pin in the lapel, stared out over the water, wistfully at times, a few strands of hair blowing forward across his face.

The next day Brezhnev and Kissinger returned to Moscow, and the President traveled to Minsk.* He visited Katyn, where 149 Russians had been forced into a barn and burned alive by Nazi troops on March 22, 1943. He walked through a huge open field, then stopped at the statue of a man carrying his dead child in his arms. He sat down alone at a small table and signed the guest book. The only sounds were the tolling of the memorial bells every fifteen seconds and the clicking shutters of the photographers. The press-office staff worried about the eerie, lonely image of the President.

Nixon returned to Moscow Monday evening and conferred with Kissinger. The Secretary of State had spoken with Brezhnev and had then spent five hours bargaining with Foreign Minister Andrei Gromyko. They had finally worked out an alternative to the seeming impasse on an agreement to limit offensive nuclear weapons. Both sides would sign a protocol committing themselves to eventual negotiation of an agreement that would extend to 1985. It was nothing more than an agreement to agree at some future time. Kissinger usually detested such arrangements; they limited future bargaining options, he felt. But the two sides agreed it was preferable to acknowledging that the momentum of détente had been broken. So they would have this appearance of an agreement, as well as the settlement of two much less important issues: limitations on underground testing and installation of defensive missile systems. The President's disappointment was obvious. He had hoped for far more.

He joined Brezhnev later that evening for a final exchange of toasts. Brezhnev remarked that the agreements "could probably have been wider." The President reemphasized the great importance of, variously, his "personal relations," his "personal friendship" and his "personal relationship" with Brezhnev. The Soviet leader was unresponsive to the overture. He spoke

---

* The press plane flying behind the President lost a tire on takeoff and an engine during the flight. The navigator of the Soviet craft walked into the passenger section and poured himself a shot of vodka, then two more to take back to the cockpit.

of the "feelings of respect and friendship" between the American and Russian peoples.

The signing ceremonies took place the next morning. Ziegler struggled to give the summit a public-relations coloring beyond its substantive progress, praising the agreements in the hyperbole of history. Throughout the trip he had been insistent that Kissinger be excluded from the ritual picture-taking sessions. The pictures were to be of the President and Brezhnev. In all but one instance, the photos of the major ceremonies showed the two leaders alone.

During the nine-and-a-half-hour flight back to the United States, the President worked on a speech ("The process of peace is going steadily forward . . .") to be delivered on live television when he stopped in Maine. From there he would fly directly to Key Biscayne. He didn't want even to visit Washington.

Vice-President Ford presided over the televised welcoming in Maine. "I cannot escape the conclusion," he said, "that the Biblical injunction 'Blessed are the peacemakers' has again been confirmed."

Chapter Eighteen

PETER Rodino and his counsel, John Doar, had taken care to conceal their sentiments and conclusions as the impeachment process went forward. Every public statement and private maneuver was measured to create an illusion of neutrality. It was a necessary pose. They saturated the committee with a catalogue of evidence of the crimes by the Nixon White House—all without comment. Their strategy was designed to create a nonpartisan majority for impeachment composed of the committee's twenty-one Democrats and perhaps half a dozen Republicans.

Returning from the hearing room to his office for lunch on June 27, the chairman was on edge. After six weeks of closed hearings, he was under intense pressure to expedite the proceedings. Republicans were charging that the majority was deliberately dragging out the hearings. The Democratic leadership, sensitive to the charge, was growing uneasy.

He stopped by a small alcove office where his administrative assistant, Francis O'Brien, sat chatting with three reporters—Sam Donaldson of ABC television and Paul Houston and Jack Nelson of the *Los Angeles Times*. The press had been exceedingly gentle with Rodino—Congressman Everyman from Newark, unpretentious, fair, judicious.

How did the chairman think the committee vote was shaping up?

Rodino's guard was down, and he said what he thought: All twenty-one Democrats on the committee would vote to impeach; he hadn't taken a formal count, but he was pretty sure. The twenty-one votes were sufficient to take impeachment to the floor of the House, but he deemed it essential to pick up at least five Republicans and make a strong showing.

Nelson, an experienced Washington reporter, had no reason to assume that Rodino's comments were off the record. His front-page story in the next morning's *Los Angeles Times* said that Rodino had told unnamed "visitors" in his office that he expected all twenty-one Democrats to vote to impeach, and it named the six Republicans whom Rodino thought most likely to join the majority—William S. Cohen of Maine, Caldwell M. Butler of Virginia, Hamilton Fish, Jr., and Henry P. Smith of New York, and McClory and Railsback of Illinois. The *Times* account said Rodino had concluded that the evidence was sufficient to justify a Senate trial. It was a "background" story—Nelson had reported the facts without naming Rodino as a source or quoting him directly.

Late the next morning, O'Brien handed the chairman a clipping of the story, and Rodino turned ashen. His offhand comments could destroy his carefully constructed image of impartiality and with it all hope of bringing Republican votes over.

At the White House, Clawson wasted no time. If the *Los Angeles Times* account was true, he said, Rodino should be dismissed as chairman and replaced by a fair-minded Democrat.

Speaker Albert phoned Rodino, urging him to defend himself on the House floor. Rodino went to the floor and told his colleagues, "I want to state unequivocally and categorically that this statement is not true. There is no basis in fact for it, none whatsoever."

In that evening's telecast, Sam Donaldson said that he had believed Rodino's estimate to be off the record, but since it had been reported and denied, he felt obliged to confirm the accuracy of Nelson's account.

The next day, Clawson described the Judiciary Committee inquiry as a "partisan witch-hunt," and Father John McLaughlin called Rodino a "crude political tactician" who ought to disqualify himself.

Unnerved by his blunder, Rodino found himself suddenly on the defensive, his credibility with the so-called swing votes (the committee's moderate Republicans and Southern Democrats) strained.

Rodino was most concerned about one member of the minority, Thomas Railsback of Moline, Illinois. Railsback was the barometer of impeachment, Rodino believed. He could take two to four other Republicans with him. An undistinguished legislator, Railsback normally had little influence over his colleagues, but on impeachment he was genuinely conscience-stricken, and everyone knew it. If Railsback were finally to vote against the President, it could make impeachment acceptable to the Jaycees and Rotarians of America.

The impeachment investigation had become all-consuming for Railsback. His evenings were spent discussing the evidence with fellow committee members or listening to the tapes. He had listened so often that he had pinpointed several errors in the text of the committee's transcripts. Railsback shunned the Washington social life as conducted in Georgetown parlors, and so he was surprised when Joseph Alsop, the prominent political columnist, invited him to lunch at his home. Alsop's call sounded almost like a command. Railsback reported on schedule.

Alsop traveled in the sophisticated circles that Railsback rarely encountered. A confidant of Kissinger and Haig, he had come to believe the President was "ninety-nine percent nutty as a fruitcake." "The armpit of humanity," he called Nixon. But, like Kissinger and Haig, Alsop reeled at the specter of impeachment; he dreaded its effect on the political system, on Kissinger's delicate foreign policy, on the struggle in Indochina. Grievous and permanent national harm would come if a President were routed from office. All Presidents stretched the law, he believed—necessarily so. It was Nixon's misfortune to be so personally unappealing that he was being held accountable for it.

Impeachment, Alsop told Railsback, would be a catastrophe. It would shake the foundations of a strong presidency. It would be a triumph for the political fringes. The issue was not Richard Nixon, Alsop stressed, but the survival of American strength and tradition. Alsop mocked the prospect of Ford becoming President—the absurdity of a man elected from a single Michigan congressional district, totally without experience in foreign affairs and without any concept of executive authority, occupying the White House.

Railsback was surprised at Alsop's undisguised advocacy; it seemed indecent, pompous, even outrageous. Yet he found Alsop fascinating. Alsop invited Railsback back—for breakfast, and then for another lunch. At their last meeting, in early July, Railsback secured Alsop's assurance that the conversation would be absolutely confidential and revealed his position. He was *not* going to vote to impeach Richard Nixon.

Alsop thought the Republic was safe.

ST. CLAIR's burden was immense: representing his difficult client in the Supreme Court; defending him before the Judiciary Committee, coordinating each move with the White House public-relations machine. In addition, Buzhardt had suffered a heart attack in mid-June and was recuperating at home.

Buzhardt read through the briefs submitted to the Court and was appalled at their quality. St. Clair's arguments for withholding the tapes were thin, sometimes amounting to little more than nitpicking. There was no hint of the articulate scholarship that Charles Alan Wright had brought to the first tapes case. St. Clair, who had never argued a case in the Supreme Court, had left much of the work to his even less experienced assistants.

Jaworski and Lacovara, on the other hand, had paid careful attention to the preparation of their briefs and their arguments. They had decided to divide the oral argument before the Court. Jaworski's presence in court would in itself underscore the momentous nature of the case; Lacovara was more familiar with the legal intricacies. They agreed to remind the Court at every opportunity that they represented the government and that Richard Nixon stood before it not as President, but as an individual. They would therefore insist on sitting to the right of the bench, the side reserved for the government.

Another matter of protocol presented difficulties for Jaworski. Government attorneys traditionally wear formal cutaways before the Supreme Court. But Jaworski, years ago, had once gone to the Court in a borrowed cutaway that didn't fit. He thought he had looked like a penguin, and he wasn't going to repeat his mistake. Lacovara got out a treatise on Supreme Court practice, photocopied the section on attire, and sent it to Jaworski. He got a note back saying, "You should be pleased that I'm not going to show up in cowboy boots and buckskins."

On Monday, July 8, Jaworski wore a dark-blue business suit. As the government sedan pulled up to the Supreme Court Building just after nine, a cheer went up from the crowd waiting in line to get inside. "Give'm hell, Leon baby," and "Go, Leon," people shouted. Jaworski, Lacovara and James Neal had to struggle to get through.

Inside, they waited uneasily for about half an hour in the room normally used by the Solicitor General. To break the tension, they speculated about how they would argue to each of the justices in the old paintings that lined the walls. Just before ten, they took their seats at the table to the right of the bench. St. Clair was at the other table.

At two minutes after ten, the eight black-robed justices filed in. The jammed courtroom was silent as Chief Justice Burger announced the case. "You may begin whenever you are ready, Mr. Jaworski."

Jaworski seemed nervous. He spoke awkwardly as he slowly recited the history of the grand jury's proceedings. He noted that the grand jury had named the President an unindicted co-conspirator, and then he moved haltingly to the heart of the matter: Who is the arbiter of the Constitution?

"Now, the President may be right in how he reads the Constitution," Jaworski said. "But he may also be wrong. And if he is wrong, who is there to tell him so? And if there is no one, the President, of course, is free to pursue his course of erroneous interpretations. What then becomes of our constitutional form of government? . . . This nation's constitutional form of government is in serious jeopardy if the President, any President, is to say that the Constitution means what he says it does and that there is no one, not even the Supreme Court, to tell him otherwise."

Justice Stewart had some questions on the point. Jaworski summarized the argument: "What I am saying is that if he is the sole judge, and he is in error in his interpretation, then he goes on being in error in his interpretation."

"Then this Court will tell him so," Justice Stewart said. "That is what this case is about, isn't it?"

"Well, that is what I think the case is about, yes, sir," Jaworski readily agreed.

He then challenged St. Clair's basic claim. Under the conditions of his appointment as special prosecutor, the case did not involve an internal dispute within the executive branch. Jaworski cited the assurances of Haig, Bork and Attorney General William B. Saxbe, Richardson's successor, as to his indisputable right to take the President to court on the question of executive privilege. It was up to the Court, he said, to decide who was right, on the merits. His standing was not at issue.

In contrast to Jaworski, St. Clair was affable and relaxed as he began his presentation. He pressed his contention that the Court did not have jurisdiction to settle a dispute within the executive branch. Though some powers had been delegated to the special prosecutor, the President was still the President, and the Court could not alter that fact. Jaworski was subject to the President's orders and decisions, like any employee of the executive branch. If the Court ordered the President to surrender his tapes, they would inevitably make their way to the House Judiciary Committee. That action would involve the Court, however indirectly, in an impeachment proceeding, a power the Constitution specifically reserved to Congress.

St. Clair was interrupted 217 times by the justices' questions. But their skepticism did not seem to daunt him. They seemed dubious about his claim that executive privilege was absolute and that the President, not the courts, was the ultimate arbiter of what evidence should be surrendered, even in a criminal case.

St. Clair insisted that the privilege was essential to protecting the President's privacy, whatever the circumstances. As an example, he cited privileged conversations the President might have about the appointment of a judge.

Justice Marshall detected a flaw in that reasoning. "Don't you think it would be important . . . if an about-to-be-appointed judge was making a deal with the President for money?"

"Absolutely," St. Clair responded.

But by St. Clair's reasoning, Marshall noted, the President would not be obliged to turn over a tape of such a conversation.

"I would think," St. Clair replied, "that that could not be released, if it were a confidential communication. If the President did appoint such an individual, the remedy is clear, the remedy is he should be impeached."

"How are you going to impeach him if you don't know about it?" Marshall asked.

"Well, if you know about it," St. Clair said, "then you can state the case. If you don't know about it, you don't have it."

"So there you are. You're on the prongs of a dilemma, huh?"

"No, I don't think so," St. Clair persisted.

Marshall tried to explain. "If you know the President is doing something wrong, you can impeach him, but the only way you can find out is this way. You can't impeach him, so you don't impeach him. You lose me someplace along there."

The audience broke out into laughter.

A few minutes later, Lacovara offered the rebuttal argument on behalf of the United States. He had scarcely begun when Justice White urged him to focus on the matter of executive privilege.

Lacovara was delighted. He wanted to emphasize a key point Jaworski had failed to make about the relevancy of Nixon's status as an unindicted co-conspirator. "This President is not in a position to claim this public privilege, for the reason that a prima-facie case showing can be made that these conversations were not made in pursuance of legitimate governmental processes or the lawful deliberations of the public's business. These conversations, as we showed in our forty-nine page appendix, and as the grand jury alleged, were in furtherance of a criminal conspiracy to defraud the United States and obstruct justice."

As to St. Clair's argument that the Court must not be involved in a political dispute, Lacovara cited occasions when the Court had decided cases with political implications, beginning with *Marbury v. Madison*. The Court had a duty to interpret the Constitution. "That's all we ask for today. That's all Judge Sirica has done. We believe he has done it correctly. . . . And we submit that this Court should fully, explicitly, and decisively . . ." he paused, "and *definitively* uphold Judge Sirica's decision."

St. Clair did not use his fifteen minutes to rebut Lacovara. He conceded that the Court often decided cases with political overtones. But this case was different, he argued, in that it would affect the impeachment proceeding.

".... The President is not above the law. Nor does he contend that he is. What he does contend is that as President the law can be applied to him in only one way, and that is by impeachment, not by naming as a co-conspirator in a grand-jury indictment, not by indictment or any other way. ...."

It was just after 1 P.M. when the arguments concluded. St. Clair came out smiling. He chatted with reporters and signed autographs. "I think it went very well," he said. Jaworski seemed less sanguine, but he smiled to the crowd, acknowledging its cheers. In the prosecutor's press office, James Doyle was getting reports from the other lawyers on the staff. Jaworski had not done a very good job, St. Clair had done better; but Lacovara had rebutted brilliantly. Buzhardt received a similar assessment from his sources.

St. Clair met with Nixon for forty minutes that afternoon. It had gone well, he told the President, very well. They had a good chance. He firmly believed it.

The President was scheduled to spend the week in Washington, his first full week in the capital in two months. He had a busy schedule—meetings with Cabinet officers, economic advisers and congressional leaders, and assorted ceremonial occasions. The meetings would demonstrate that the country had a leader who was active in domestic affairs as well as leading the world. Nixon seemed to be reinvigorated by his travels, and by St. Clair's assessment. A poll showed that fifty-three percent of those questioned thought media coverage of Watergate was excessive.

ON TUESDAY afternoon, July 9, Rodino shattered the President's show of business as usual. He released the Judiciary Committee's version of eight tapes. There were awesome differences between what the White House had managed to transcribe and what the committee staff, using superior equipment, was able to hear on the same recordings. To Rodino, the differences demonstrated that the cover-up was still in progress, with the concurrence of Haig and of Nixon's lawyers. The staff had prepared a 131-page side-by-side comparison of the texts. Nearly a hundred major discrepancies and omissions were noted. The White House editing proved to be predictable. Changes seemed tailored for St. Clair's claim that the President knew nothing of the cover-up until March 21, 1973, and then had acted to end it. According to the White House version of the meeting of March 22, 1973, the President told his aides that John Mitchell was recommending "that now we use flexibility in order to get off the cover-up line." The committee transcript said that Nixon quoted Mitchell to the opposite effect, that "we use flexibility . . . in order *to get on with the cover-up.*"* Nixon's order that day to Mitchell, which Haig, St. Clair and Buzhardt had tried to hide from the committee, was also there: "I don't give a shit what happens. I want you all to stonewall it, let them plead the Fifth Amendment, cover up or anything else, if it'll save it—save the plan. That's the whole point."

St. Clair tried to justify the omissions and discrepancies. That section had been left out, because it was not deemed relevant, he told reporters. It concerned the Senate Watergate Committee and technically did not involve an obstruction of justice, since it referred to a congressional, not a Justice Department, investigation. The subpoena had called for a conversation among Nixon, Dean and Mitchell. The omitted conversation occurred after Dean had apparently left the room, and it was therefore outside the bounds of the subpoena, St. Clair said.

What about the other discrepancies? the reporters asked.

"I would not look upon this as sinister. My experience has been that if you give these tapes to three people to listen to, you get three variations."

Ziegler tried to deflect the impact of the disclosures. He called in reporters from the two major wire services and charged that the release was a "hyped public-relations campaign" by Rodino, Doar and the Democrats. "They have chosen the public-relations route which will focus the news media on only one section of the tapes. They should release the full body of evidence all together, all at once and not in piecemeal fashion."

THE HEADLINES in the next morning's editions of the *Washington Post,* July 10, read "Transcripts Link Nixon to Cover-up." At ten o'clock the President and Kissinger met in the Cabinet Room with the congressional leadership of both parties to brief them on the trips to the Middle East and the Soviet Union.

Beginning with a long monologue, Nixon observed that his tough posture in the Middle East and with the NATO leaders in Europe had been enough reason to expect a cool reception in Russia. "It did not turn out that way. Of the three summits, discussions we had there were the fullest and least belligerent. . . . We made progress, progress that would have been considered monumental two years ago, but now, with so much done, it doesn't seem so important perhaps."

He turned to the specifics of the nuclear-weapons agreement. Senator Mansfield and Senator Robert E. Byrd, the Democratic whip, appeared to

---

* Emphasis added.

be asleep. Nixon reminisced about earlier summit meetings. "In 'seventy-two we went out to one of the dachas, and I sat for four and one half hours with three Soviet leaders. I took a rough beating on Vietnam. Very rough. Brezhnev paced the floor and pounded the table. In 'seventy-three, I went to bed at eleven P.M. Henry woke me up at twelve and said, 'Brezhnev wants to talk.' We sat up from twelve to three-thirty. This time they gave me a beating on the Mideast. If we had crumbled either time, we would have made no progress overall. But we stood tough."

The President glanced around. "For the U.S., the choice we have is either to make an agreement that is adequate for our purposes and for theirs—"

Kissinger, watching intently, picked up. "One interesting thing which emerged is that they calculate our weapons strength from the perspective of—"

Nixon interrupted. "It was a tough discussion, but not one that ended in impasse. They're going back to talk to their people and we're going back to ours. I talked to Grechko [Andrei Grechko, the Soviet Defense Minister] and found he was not nearly so lacking in agreement. We can see that they will go balls out."

"Go what?" inquired Senator Stennis, who was hard of hearing.

"Go balls out! Balls out!" the President said loudly. There were snickers. "And if so, John, you'll have to vote more money for arms in your committee."

Kissinger mentioned China. "We calculate that by 1978 to 1980, China could be in a position to kill millions of Soviets in any exchange."

The President interrupted. "We believe China would accept the loss of half their population."

France. Kissinger said, "Pompidou was on so much medication the last year that he couldn't think straight."

Kissinger was beginning to dominate the discussion. "One of the biggest problems in East–West relations is excessive talk in the United States of our approaching inferiority. We had to address that question everywhere. Therefore we have to be concerned that our debate at home does not go overboard."

He continued his report, country by country.

Italy. Kissinger told them that the country was "in very bad shape. Forgive me, but dealing with them is like talking to a group of Harvard professors." There was laughter. "You just don't feel like anything will come out of it."

Germany. The new leader, Helmut Schmidt, "doesn't suffer from this vapid sentimentality that afflicted Brandt at the end," Kissinger said.

The Russian summit meeting. "The key session was Sunday afternoon in the Crimea, where the President and Brezhnev exchanged intelligence estimates. If I can be excused for saying so, anyone else would have been arrested for handing out information like that."

The Secretary of State did not mention Brezhnev's refusal to reach any agreement with Nixon, but still the President seemed nervous about where Kissinger's frankness might take the discussion. Nixon offered his own interpretation of Soviet-American relations: "Why have the Soviets stood aside and allowed us to settle Berlin, Vietnam and the Middle East? One, because the United States is big, mean and tough as hell and they know it. Two, the obsession with peace in the USSR. Twenty million Russian people were killed during World War II. We must have the fear elements working, but also the hope element."

THAT EVENING the President entertained ten conservative Congressmen from both parties aboard his yacht. Rain drove them belowdecks, where Nixon offered another monologue about his trips to the Middle East and Russia.

He dwelled on the crowds, especially the ones in Egypt. How friendly they had been. How they cheered as their leader, Nasser—no, Sadat, of course . . . How the Egyptians were willing to act contrary to what the Russians wanted. That was a relationship to nurture, the friendship with Nasser. This time he did not correct himself, and later he referred again to Nasser.

The Congressmen glanced at each other uncomfortably. The President rambled on. The Russians were "obsessed" with peace. He had had to sit through a long Russian movie about the slaughter during World War II.

There was beef tenderloin for dinner. The President had become something of a wine buff during his New York City days, and the *Sequoia* was stocked with his favorite, a 1966 Château Margaux which sold for about thirty dollars a bottle. He always asked for it when beef was served. And he had issued orders to the stewards about what to do when large groups of Congressmen were aboard: His guests were to be served a rather good six-dollar wine; his glass was to be filled from a bottle of Château Margaux wrapped in a towel.

TRIM AND well tanned, John Dean arrived in the Judiciary Committee's hearing room just before ten o'clock on Thursday July 11. He smiled and shook hands with St. Clair, then took his seat at the witness table.

The President's allies had waited a year for an opportunity to question Dean under oath. To the White House, Dean was the tricky, conniving, "bottom-dwelling slug" (as columnist Joseph Alsop had called him) who had dragged the President into the cover-up. St. Clair was ready. This would be the major Watergate bout—a classic battle between a great cross-examiner and a great witness. During the Army–McCarthy hearings, St. Clair had watched as Joseph Welch destroyed McCarthy in one burst of righteous anger. He hoped for a similar triumph.

Doar was first, and Dean's responses were cool, refined and detailed. He was in full control of the chronology of events, remembering details as precisely as he had the previous summer at the Senate Watergate Committee hearings.

At 2:10 P.M., St. Clair began his questioning. He focused immediately on the linchpin of his defense—that Nixon had *not* approved the $75,000 payment Howard Hunt received on March 21. He looked at the committee as he spoke, a technique used by trial lawyers to unnerve a witness and remind the jurors of their duty.

In his research, St. Clair had come upon an astounding statement made by Dean to the Senate committee, a statement that by itself, he was convinced, was sufficient to take the President out of the chain of events leading to the $75,000 payment. He picked up the green paper-bound volume of Watergate Committee testimony and read from page 1423. It referred to the President's meeting with Dean on March 21.* Dean had testified, "And the money matter was left very much hanging in that meeting. Nothing was resolved."

"Do you recall testifying to that?" St. Clair asked.

"Yes," Dean said, "with regard to—"

St. Clair interrupted. "Is that the truth?" he asked sharply.

"Yes, it is," Dean replied, "with regard to the raising of a million dollars. I didn't think there was anything resolved as to how to raise a million dollars."

St. Clair had erred: There had been *two* money issues discussed during that meeting—the possibility of eventually raising a million dollars to pay off all the burglars, and Hunt's immediate demand for $120,000, of which $75,000 was paid the same day. Dean had never claimed that the issue of raising the million dollars was resolved.

But St. Clair, still confused, repeated Dean's quotation from the green volume. "Is that the truth?" he demanded again.

---

* When Dean testified before the Watergate Committee he mistakenly said that the meeting had taken place on March 13.

"I will stand on my last answer, Mr. St. Clair." Aware that he had turned the point to his advantage, Dean rubbed it in. Until his meeting with the President, he said, he had refused to take part in any decision leading to payment of more money to the burglars.

"I had gone in with the intent of trying to turn off the payment to Hunt," he explained. "I came out having been turned around . . . The President felt it was desirable."

The questioning proceeded. Dean continued to demonstrate his superior knowledge and understanding of the record. Several times he corrected St. Clair on dates or names. At one point, St. Clair asked Dean about a question John Mitchell had raised with the President.

"Well," Dean corrected, "I testified that Mr. *Ehrlichman* raised the question—"

"It would be a lot easier if you would just answer yes or no, if you could," St. Clair snapped. "You know, time marches."

"I understand," said Dean.

"Thank you," St. Clair responded coolly, as if he had finally won a point.

"But," Dean interjected, "I want the committee to have the full information I have."

"I gather that," St. Clair said. "Now just answer the question!"

Several members of the committee raised objections to St. Clair's manner; he was attempting to browbeat the witness.

St. Clair became defensive. "My only point is, Mr. Chairman, [that] the answers have been very extensive and to a great extent not responsive. But I will not raise the point. I will go ahead."

To St. Clair it seemed ludicrous that a witness as important as Dean would be cross-examined for only half a day. Now he was getting speeches from Dean but no answers. Dean's a smart little bastard, St. Clair said to himself, but let us endure his speeches, and eventually he'll put his foot in his mouth.

The chair asked St. Clair to repeat his question.

"I must apologize," he said. "May it be read? I don't recall the question."

Dean was ready. "I can save time," he said. "I recall the question and the answer I was going to give."

"Is that satisfactory, Mr. St. Clair?" asked the chairman.

"Yes," St. Clair answered helplessly.

Dean repeated the question and answered it.

St. Clair tried to pick up the thread. Did Ehrlichman report the conversation in question to the President on the afternoon of the twenty-first?

"That conversation had occurred on the morning of the twenty-second,"

Dean corrected him again, "so it would be impossible to report it on the afternoon of the twenty-first."

The question was not terribly important, but St. Clair realized he had been outfoxed. He could only say, "I am sorry. I misspoke."

The President's lawyer never recovered. At 4:35 that afternoon he completed his interrogation. It was now the members' turn. As they questioned Dean for five minutes each, St. Clair sat slumped in his chair, his head tilted back, staring at the ceiling. He closed his eyes several times. He had lost his chance to give his Joe Welch speech and crush John Dean.

Chapter Nineteen

DAVID EISENHOWER liked to play games. During the first Nixon term, he and the President frequently played a game of pocket billiards they called Golf. Balls were set before each of the six pockets and one on the cue spot, and the object was to sink all seven balls in as few shots as possible. Once the President had done it in three. But he had stopped playing in 1971.

As the second Nixon term progressed, David played games more and more. He would get a whiffle-ball game going on the White House tennis court with some of the staffers. The object of the game, called Home Run Derby, was to hit the ball over the fence. Sometimes he could convince Julie to play. David and Julie also played a lot of bridge. And David loved the board game Diplomacy, which he always won.

But his favorite was the American Professional Baseball Association game, a computer-designed contest in which the participants served as the team managers. Complicated sets of cards listed the hitting, fielding and pitching averages for players of every American and National League team, dating back to the 1950s. By adjusting the lineups, knowing the real teams' weaknesses and strengths, David was able to win ten or fifteen more games in a given season than the actual team had won. He often played alone or with his law-school classmate, Brooks Harrington, a six-foot-two former college football player who was a political liberal. In the late spring and early summer of 1974, David was spending up to three or four hours a day playing APBA baseball.

His fascination with baseball—he had spent the previous summer as a sports writer for a Philadelphia paper—was regarded with derision by many on the White House staff. Seeing him walk through the mansion in the late afternoon with a stack of law books under his arm, Tom DeCair of the press office joked, "David's home from Little League practice." Some of the others called him Jughead.

But whatever the cost in esteem, the long hours over the baseball game or Diplomacy seemed to help keep the President's son-in-law at a certain distance from the problems of Watergate, which was what David wanted. Harrington, who became David's closest friend, didn't press him about Watergate, though the subject came up inevitably. When the edited transcripts were released in April, David said to him, "You and I both know how this is going to come out." During those same weeks, when David was trying not to read the news magazines, Harrington would mention an article and David would ask to see it. He would go off with a copy of *Time,* read it, and come back shaking his head.

David told Harrington, an ex-Marine, that he was thinking about going back into the Navy. He wanted to get away. He also mentioned it to his grandmother Mamie Eisenhower. "She almost leaped out of bed, she was so happy," David said.

But that was really no better an escape than the hours playing games, he decided. David was coming to grips with something he hadn't fully realized when he married Julie: that he had become not only a member of the Nixon family but a member of the Nixon Administration. The luxuries, the travel, the status of serving as an unappointed presidential adviser, had come with the marriage. Now that the Administration was coming apart, so was everything else.

Julie was so wound up in her father's defense that it was straining their marriage. Her devotion to her father was uncomplicated. Each damaging development was a technicality in her eyes and she would tell David not to bore her with the facts. The President turned increasingly to Julie for her love and devotion and sustenance.

David resented the situation. He wanted his wife back. He thought her illness earlier in the year, a tubular pregnancy, was psychosomatic; it had happened because she had gotten herself so worked up over what was happening to her father, David told Harrington.

Mrs. Nixon was unhappy with David. "Why aren't you giving Julie support?" she wanted to know. Julie was out in the front lines defending her father, Mrs. Nixon said, while David was in the library stacks studying or off somewhere playing Diplomacy. There had been shouting once, and David had stormed out of the room.

He was fighting hard to draw a line where politics could stop, where family loyalty could stop and his own personal morality and his own life could begin. It was hard to find that place.

The President had wanted David to go on the trip to Russia and assist in briefing the press. But David declined. Instead he took six weeks off after the spring semester to see if he and Julie could have a life of their own.

He felt strongly that Watergate was going to have an unhappy ending, but he could not get the message through to Julie. Her unquestioning loyalty made it impossible to deal with events on their basic, real level, he thought. Her stubbornness was difficult to contend with. At times he imagined her as the heroine of a movie, the devoted daughter defending her embattled, innocent father. David, part of him at least, wanted to help prove her right.

David's feelings about the Nixon Administration were intensely personal. In 1968 he had written a memo to Nixon saying why he should run for President. The '68 victory was euphoric. But the 1972 victory celebration was not. David and the rest of the family knew that Watergate was doing something to the President. Something awful. In 1973 they watched it eat away at him. Being President ceased to be fun after Haldeman and Ehrlichman left, Nixon said. The next year was worse. For David too.

"We're innocent," the President told him many times. And David was sympathetic to Mr. Nixon, as he always called him. He thought he could relate to the President's problems through an experience of his own, when he was in the Navy. As a lieutenant junior grade aboard the U.S.S. *Albany,* he himself had once covered up a matter.

One of David's collateral assignments on the ship had been to act as intelligence officer. When he took the job he had signed for hundreds of classified publications; his signature attested that he had received the documents from the officer he relieved. There had been no time to check and see if they were all aboard, let alone to page-check each one as was normally required.

When David had less than a month left on board, his immediate superior insisted that a full accounting of the four-hundred-odd publications be made. On his first check, David was missing thirty of them. After a full search of the ship, there were still ten missing. It was the worst three weeks of his life, he told his friends—filled with haunting visions of Portsmouth Prison as he searched and searched. Finally he found all but one. It was a secret publication about Russian infrared devices. He had signed for four printed copies and could find only three. Desperate, David and another officer devised a complicated scheme to deceive the authorities. They burned an extra onionskin copy of the publication and said it had been one of the originals. Then they witnessed the proper report, saying that the missing copy had been routinely burned according to the regulations for disposing of extra classified material.

Since David never knew what he had signed for—never knew if there were in fact four copies originally—he persuaded himself that it was possible he had done nothing wrong. Neither, perhaps, had his father-in-law.

ON THE evening of July 11, Brooks Harrington and his wife, Carol, a Navy lieutenant junior grade who was executive assistant to the head of the Navy race-relations unit, joined the Nixons, the Coxes and the Eisenhowers aboard the *Sequoia*. It was a beautiful evening, with the temperature in the upper seventies. They all sat topside, sipping drinks.

The President asked Carol Harrington where she and Brooks had met.

It had been Guantánamo Bay Navy Base in Cuba, a fact which seemed to interest the President.

How was the base set up? he wanted to know. Had there been any incidents with the Castro government? How many civilians worked there? Did Navy ships use it a lot? Was it good duty? Was it secure from attack?

"Dick," Mrs. Nixon said finally, "tell them about the Russian trip." The boatride had been arranged for that purpose.

He spoke enthusiastically—especially about his personal relationship with Brezhnev, which he asked them not to discuss elsewhere. He painted a picture of two world leaders who shared certain conservative values—about their own societies, about the nature of political leadership. He and Brezhnev were the only two members of the most exclusive club in the world. Only they could understand each other. Only they could understand the burden and weight of leading the two superpowers.

Brooks winced. He thought the two leaders sounded like two Bull Moose Republicans who had been to a Kiwanis lunch.

"The Russians missed you," the President said pointedly to David.

David felt guilty.

Nixon mentioned a boatride he had taken with Brezhnev and how he had almost frozen, it was so cold. He became momentarily distracted, lost in thought.

The *Sequoia* continued down the Potomac and went under a bridge. Mrs. Nixon pointed out that there were—happily—no reporters lining the railing this time.

Julie hovered around her father. "Do you feel okay, Daddy?" she asked. "Is the sun in your eyes?" "Do you want another drink?"

He seemed to recede deeper into his own thoughts, acknowledging her questions only perfunctorily.

Harrington asked the President whether politicians in Russia had to court the military to gain power. The question reawakened Nixon's interest.

No, he said, and he began talking about the nature of the military. When you make a suggestion or proposal to the American military, he explained, they say no, they say they can't do it. He cited the 1970 invasion of Cambodia as an example. The military had wanted to hold back, he said; they had thought the operation was too risky and of limited value. He was the driving force, Nixon said, the one who had to say, "Do it."

The conversation was relaxed and pleasant as the *Sequoia* continued downstream. Then David inadvertently alluded to the disclosure of the President's taping system. The Nixon daughters flinched. The President withdrew again, and the discussion became awkward. Fortunately, it was time for dinner.

The President walked to the head of the table and pointed to his left. "Julie here," he said. Then he directed Brooks to sit on his right.

The stewards served steaks. The President was still lost in his own thoughts, staring into his plate.

"Daddy, eat your steak," Julie said.

He took a bite.

"Isn't this good steak?" she asked.

The others began talking uneasily about beef prices, watching for some reaction from the President. He continued to look at his plate while he picked at his food.

A steward asked what they wanted for dessert.

Julie turned to her father. "Have some apple pie."

He shook his head no.

"Have some ice cream, Daddy."

No.

She turned to the steward and said that the President would have some ice cream with chocolate sauce.

Acquiescing, the President ate it.

"Wasn't the food good?" she asked.

"It was okay," he said. "Not as good as last time."

After dinner, they retired to the after cabin for more talk. A year earlier, the President had ordered that no magazines or newspapers be kept aboard. (At the White House, only the sports section of the *Washington Post* was left each morning on the table by his door.)

The President asked Brooks and David what they thought of their generation. He was concerned that young people might want to quit making sacrifices.

Brooks had worked to organize blacks and Indians in Oklahoma. But after the draft ended, everyone seemed to lose social consciousness, he said. No one wanted to give himself to anything larger than himself. The President nodded.

David cited his classmates at Amherst. They had never complained about the war until they had gotten a low draft number.

The President expressed concern about businessmen who apologized about being businessmen as if it were no longer a reputable profession. Too many Americans lived off government handouts, he said. Self-reliance might be outdated.

Julie suggested that Brooks run for Congress.

Both Brooks and David ought to run for Congress, the President said. He would vote for them both. He asked Brooks how old he was.

Twenty-six.

"Wait until you're thirty-two and then make a move," Nixon advised.

Chapter Twenty

O N Friday, July 12, the House Judiciary Committee released its evidence—3,888 pages. In stark chronological fashion, Doar and his staff had catalogued without commentary the abuses of power in the Nixon White House.

The front pages were filled with damning excerpts.

By noon, Jerry Warren was besieged. Already that morning, St. Clair had said publicly that he expected the committee to vote to impeach. It was the first such acknowledgment by the White House.

What was the President's assessment? reporters shouted at Warren.

The President, said Warren, also expected the committee to report a bill of impeachment.

The reporters ran to the phones.

A few minutes later, Ziegler was at the podium to soften the impact.

"The President recognizes that this is a political process and he would not be surprised by a committee vote against him," Ziegler said. "He does feel strongly that the House will not vote impeachment."

At four o'clock the President took off aboard Air Force One for what the White House described as a working vacation at the Western White House. He had been airborne for scarcely an hour when more bad news arrived: John Ehrlichman had been found guilty of conspiring to violate the civil rights of Daniel Ellsberg's psychiatrist, and of three additional counts of lying to the FBI and the grand jury.

Aboard the plane, Ziegler was getting more details from his aides back in the Washington press office, who wanted to know what to tell reporters.

He didn't know. Check the files, he directed; see what the response had been when other members of the staff had pleaded guilty or gone to jail or been convicted.

In Washington, the staff found a statement issued in the President's name after the conviction of Dwight L. Chapin, his former appointments secretary. It expressed Nixon's concern and feelings for Chapin's family. Ehrlichman's name was substituted and the statement reissued.

LEON JAWORSKI was making preparations. Not even his most trusted staff was fully aware of his intentions. He called his friend from LBJ days, Joseph Califano. The subject was so important he needed to test the alternatives on an old hand. Jaworski knew that Califano was in touch with Haig. For months the general and the prosecutor had each used Califano to sound things out.

Jaworski was now sure that the President was in trouble so deep that he would not be able to get out of it. Once Nixon saw his situation more clearly, things might change overnight. Even the proudest man would make a deal when his back was to the wall. It was not at all inconceivable that Richard Nixon would soon be ready to plea-bargain. Jaworski was ready to discuss the terms.

There was no area more sensitive for the prosecutor. The only public criticism that had been leveled against him had been for allowing some of Nixon's men to plead guilty to reduced charges. What could the President trade? Could Jaworski ask him to give up his office? Did anyone have the right to ask that of a President? Would the special prosecutor be interfering in the impeachment process? Could Jaworski insist on getting Nixon's testimony against the other cover-up defendants? The President turning state's evidence—it sounded ludicrous. Should Jaworski make the first overture? How could he let them know he was ready to deal?

Jaworski wanted to look at the national interest in the broadest sense. He thought it was important to finish Watergate as quickly as possible. His inclination was to let the President bargain his office away. It would save the country an ordeal and end the uncertainty. Haig's comments of late were unusually disturbing. Haig had indicated to Jaworski that the President was unstable—in fact, out of control. This was a time, Haig had told him, when the real national interest, perhaps the real national security, was most at stake.

But there was another factor. Jaworski was convinced that he could never bring Nixon to trial. The House would vote impeachment, and the Senate would convict. The trial of the cover-up defendants would begin in the fall. With all the resulting publicity, it would be impossible to give Nixon, a former President, a fair trial. By plea-bargaining, Jaworski would not be giving much away.

It was a very hypothetical discussion. Jaworski and Califano reviewed the issues, the priorities, the questions of fairness and equal justice. Jaworski had no alternative but to await developments, Califano suggested. They agreed to keep in touch.

That Tuesday, July 17, Senators Scott and Mansfield met in the Minority Leader's office. They agreed that preparation for a Senate trial should begin immediately. Ken Davis, Scott's aide, was directed to start the machinery. A committee on procedures was to be formed. Tickets were to be printed. The television networks were to be contacted secretly to make arrangements for live coverage.

St. Clair was preparing for the final arguments that he was to deliver before the House Judiciary Committee on July 18. On the evening before his presentation, he dined with several members of his staff at Jenkins Hill, a restaurant a few blocks from the Judiciary hearing room. They reviewed the situation.

"What did Hauser do about that transcript?" St. Clair asked McCahill.

"It's ready," McCahill replied.

"Get him on the phone and tell him to bring it up here," St. Clair directed.

Hauser appeared shortly afterward. The transcript was two and a half pages long, a portion of a conversation between Nixon and Haldeman on the morning of March 22, 1973. St. Clair was still trying to extricate the President from the charge that he approved the $75,000 hush-money payment. There was one line in the transcript that he wanted to get into the record; two sentences from the President to Haldeman: "I don't mean to be blackmailed by Hunt. That goes too far."

"It looks pretty good to me," St. Clair concluded.

Larry Speakes, St. Clair's press aide, thought otherwise. The snippet came from a subpoenaed conversation which the President had withheld from the committee. Presenting the transcript at this late date would be a public-relations disaster, Speakes felt, but St. Clair was a $300,000-a-year lawyer and he must know what he was doing. Speakes kept his advice to himself. Malcolm J. Howard, another of St. Clair's assistants, was equally concerned, but he cautioned against arguing with St. Clair. "Once Jim's got his mind made up, that's it," he said.

The next morning St. Clair was having second thoughts. Riding with Speakes and Howard to the Hill, he said he was not sure it was a good idea to introduce the transcript. "I don't know . . ." His voice trailed off.

Speakes saw the opening. "Well, Mr. St. Clair, I think—" Howard, sitting between them in the back seat, shoved an elbow into Speakes's ribs, and the sentence went unfinished.

Rodino called the session to order at 10:25 A.M. St. Clair, expecting to begin his presentation immediately, was surprised when the chairman called on Doar for several last-minute items of business. Doar told the committee that the President had rejected its latest subpoena for tapes. The committee had also asked the White House for Ehrlichman's handwritten notes of his meetings with the President. In his solemn monotone, Doar described how, in a mix-up, the committee had received two sets of Ehrlichman's notes— one from St. Clair and the other from the special prosecutor's office. The set from St. Clair consisted of 175 pages, 88 of them blank; there were 643 lines of notes. The version of the same material that the special prosecutor's office had obtained from the White House contained twice as many lines of notes.

St. Clair fumed as Doar let the committee arrive at the conclusion that he was intentionally withholding relevant material. He had already told Doar that it was a simple mix-up, that there was no deception intended on his part. Buzhardt's heart attack had left St. Clair confused as to what had already been provided to whom. He resented this sour prelude to his own presentation.

At last Rodino called on him to offer his final argument.

St. Clair spoke from very few notes, almost extemporaneously, his manner cordial, even friendly. His attention was focused on the two tiers of seats where the members sat. "I think I would be less than candid if I didn't indicate to you the enormity of the responsibility that I feel in regard to this matter, representing the President of the United States . . ." But the enormity of the committee's responsibility to make a decision was even greater, he said.

A vote to impeach could be justified only by evidence that was "clear and convincing"—"because anything less than that, in my view, is going to result in recrimination, bitterness and divisiveness among our people. And this will not be good for the United States of America."

There was really just one allegation of criminality against the President to warrant impeachment, St. Clair suggested—the payment of hush money to Hunt. "Mr. Dean set in motion the events that resulted in payment of Mr. Hunt's attorney's fees. And I submit he could have gone out and played tennis rather than meet with the President on the morning of March twenty-first, and the same result would have happened."

Since the President didn't order or authorize the payment, then the only question left, St. Clair said, was whether or not the President knew it had been made. He would prove that the President had not known.

"The President has authorized me to distribute to and disclose to this committee a portion of a transcript of a conversation he had with Mr. Haldeman on the morning of March twenty-second . . . Keep in mind, now, this is the President on the morning of March twenty-second with Mr. Haldeman. And he says, among other things, 'I don't mean to be blackmailed by Hunt. That goes too far.' "

There were furious objections to the introduction of this new, eleventh-hour evidence. But Rodino cut off the protests and asked St. Clair to continue.

How had the President responded to Dean's revelations of March 21? His decision was not a flash of light, St. Clair said, but it came. By the end of April Richard Nixon had obtained the written resignations of Dean, Ehrlichman and Haldeman.

The lawyer's cadence became more rapid.

Was there an obstruction of justice? No. All testified before the Senate committee freely. All testified before the grand jury. There was a new Attorney General. A special prosecutor.

"The President urged Mr. Dean to tell the truth. He urged Mr. Magruder to purge himself of perjury. He told Mr. Mitchell"—a pause, this part was more difficult—"the President was preparing to let the chips fall where they may, that Mr. Mitchell should not keep quiet on his account. And ultimately all of these gentlemen were indicted by a grand jury and are now prepared to stand trial on these issues, so that if you want to judge the pudding by the eating, the process has worked. Maybe it should have worked days earlier. I don't know. I don't pretend perfection on my part or even on the part of the President. . . . I am sure that if every time our associates were charged with wrongdoing we fired them, we would never have anybody work for us. . . . What would you have done that was substantially different? If there was a delay in terms of days, was there any real prejudice developed for the people of the United States by reason of that delay?"

When he had concluded, a storm of protest again erupted over St. Clair's introduction of a new transcript. It was only two and a half pages, whereas the conversation had lasted an hour and twenty-four minutes—and all of the conversation was under subpoena.*

St. Clair promised to pass the members' objections along to the President.

"I want to thank you very much for having been as courteous as you have been," Rodino told St. Clair. "And we appreciate the fact that you have had a very, very difficult time, and we excuse you."

The chairman managed to hide his anger. He was incensed at St. Clair's conduct throughout the investigation. Months earlier, he and St. Clair had talked privately. "There is something here bigger than all of us," Rodino had told the President's lawyer. "I'm not talking about a particular client or a particular committee, but about the country and the Constitution." St. Clair had agreed. Now Rodino was sure St. Clair did not see his point. His list of grievances against St. Clair was long: rejected subpoenas; incredibly sloppy, almost criminal editing of the transcripts; the lawyer's failure to listen to all the tapes himself; his willingness to make representations to the committee without having reviewed the evidence in the White House.

Rodino knew that St. Clair was embarrassed to admit that he had limited access to his client, the tapes and other evidence. The President, Rodino reasoned, was making the legal decisions himself. St. Clair was a puppet—another arm of the bankrupt public-relations apparatus in the White House. Rodino thought that a self-respecting lawyer in St. Clair's position would have quit.

St. Clair gathered his papers together, then pushed his chair back and rose. He walked over and shook hands with Doar and minority counsel Albert Jenner.

He thought he had the case won—not in Judiciary probably, but more likely on the House floor; and if not there, definitely in the Senate. He had stopped the stampede, he was sure; he had circumscribed the issue so that Republicans on the committee would hang on; maybe the three Southern Democrats would join the seventeen Republicans and kill impeachment in the committee by a vote of twenty to eighteen. That part was doubtful, maybe overly optimistic, yet he felt good. The safe, cautious vote would be to acquit, especially in the Senate. He had gotten the two-and-a-half-page transcript into the record; that would be helpful in a Senate trial. A very good day, he decided.

---

* The transcript also quoted the President as saying in reference to Hunt, "That, uh, judge gave him thirty-five years." The sentencing of the Watergate bugging conspirators did not take place until March 23—the day after the purported date of the transcript—and Hunt had indeed received a provisional sentence of thirty-five years. Thus it appeared the President was commenting on an event that had not taken place. Disclosure of the contradiction cast doubt on the validity of the transcript itself, and the House committee opened an investigation into the matter, which was never resolved.

Caldwell Butler, still undecided which way to vote, recorded in his diary that evening: "A very masterful presentation. . . . If the Judiciary Committee were a jury that had to retire and deliberate and conclude its deliberations immediately . . . St. Clair would have carried his day."

THE NEXT day it was Doar's turn. For months he had meticulously avoided any suggestion of advocacy. Now the monotone was gone and he spoke with a passion that reflected his frustration, anger and deeply held conviction.

St. Clair, he said, had things upside down. "When you get to the proof . . . you find yourself in the labyrinth of the White House, in the Byzantine Empire where 'yes' meant 'no' and 'go' was 'stop' and 'maybe' meant 'certainly' and it is confusing, perplexing and puzzling and difficult for any group of people to sort out. But that is just the very nature of the crime—that in executing the means, everything will be done to confuse and to fool, to misconstrue, so that the purpose of the decision is concealed.

"My judgment is that the facts are overwhelming in this case that the President of the United States authorized a broad, general plan of illegal electronic surveillance, and that that plan was put into operation by his subordinates. . . . Following that, I say . . . the President made the decision to cover up this shortly after the break-in on June seventeenth and he's been in charge of the cover-up from that day forward.

"What he decided should be done following the Watergate break-in caused action not only by his own servants, but by the agencies of the United States, including the Department of Justice, the FBI, the CIA and the Secret Service. It required perjury, destruction of evidence, obstruction of justice, all crimes. But, most important, it required deliberate, contrived, continued, and continuing deception of the American people."

St. Clair, who had not been present for Doar's summary, picked up a copy of the afternoon *Washington Star-News* at a newsstand outside the White House. The headline, "Doar Calls for Impeachment," surprised him. He had thought Doar would not go so hard. But he realized someone had to answer his argument of the day before. In all, he empathized with Doar. It was unfair to force Doar to stay neutral to the very end and then to have him cram all his advocacy into one afternoon. That, he decided, must account for Doar's basic mistake: the story said that Doar had told the committee that the President had "directed" the cover-up. An extreme position, an unsupportable statement, a strategic error, St. Clair thought. It was another sign that the President would win, if not in the committee, then in the end.

At the President's seaside villa in California, Ziegler issued a blast in response to Doar's presentation. He called Doar "partisan," "radical" and "biased." Ziegler said Doar apparently thought he was working for a "kangaroo court."

St. Clair arrived at the presidential compound in San Clemente at 9 A.M. on Monday, July 22, three days after Doar's presentation. He intended only to brief the President and maybe get in some golf. But Ziegler had scheduled a televised press conference for him to rebut Doar's charges against the President. St. Clair met with Nixon and Haig for nearly two hours and spent the rest of the day preparing.

The reporters were far more interested in St. Clair's thoughts on the forthcoming decision of the Supreme Court, however, than on the past week's Judiciary proceedings. They wanted to know if Nixon would obey an order to turn over the tapes.

St. Clair, trying to hide his own concern, ducked the question as best he could. The fact was that he didn't know what Nixon would do if the ruling was adverse. The President had ordered that no one on the staff say whether there would be compliance. A promise to comply would tempt the Court to rule against him, Nixon had said. If the justices thought he was prepared to defy them, they might be less inclined to rule against him. Defiance would undermine the very basis of the Court's authority and create a constitutional crisis. And Nixon wanted to convey that threat.

St. Clair had bowed to the President's strategy. He realized how bad he looked. It was inappropriate, he kept insisting to the reporters, for him to comment on a pending court case.

THE PRESIDENT had invited Robert Finch, his old friend and former Secretary of Health, Education and Welfare, to visit him that day at San Clemente. Finch thought that Nixon looked very tired. The President seemed fatalistic about his prospects; there was no hint of what he might do to avoid impeachment. The country had become so consumed by Watergate, Nixon said, that foreign affairs and the economy were being neglected. He could not just abdicate his position of leadership—resign—in the face of the unstable world situation.

Finch was struck by the force of the President's words, the conviction behind them. He had arrived thinking that perhaps Nixon wanted to ask him to come back to Washington and help with the defense. But that was not the purpose of the invitation, though Finch was not sure what the purpose was, even after they had spent forty-five minutes together.

The President rambled. The governments under tight martial law in the Far East, he said, were much better prepared to take hard measures to remedy their economies than were the Western European governments which existed on thin parliamentary majorities. He reviewed the global picture. The oil problem, the Middle East, the Far East. The power of China, the economy of Japan. Relations between the Chinese and the Japanese, between the Russians and the Chinese. Watergate was making it difficult for the United States to compete internationally, he said.

Abruptly, the President changed subjects and expressed his regret that Finch had not run for the Senate or for the governorship of California. It was an awkward moment. Finch had abandoned his campaign plans when it became obvious that his long association with Nixon made it impossible to win at the polls. The economy, Finch lied to the President now, had made it too difficult for him to run this year.

But Nixon seemed to know better. He spoke of the loyalty of his old friends and how tough it was for him to see them suffer because of Watergate.

On his way out, Finch encountered Ollie Atkins, the official White House photographer, and said he was puzzled about the purpose of the meeting. Atkins told him that the President had wanted someone there to whom he could reach out and touch. Nothing more.

IN WASHINGTON, a bipartisan majority on the Judiciary Committee was at last taking shape. The key to consensus still lay with the "undecideds"— three Southern Democrats and the small group of Republican swing votes. Rodino had spoken with Alabama Democrat Walter D. Flowers, several times over the last few weeks, each time prodding him to get the undecideds together and hammer out some agreement. But no meeting had taken place. They were all in casual contact, occasionally reviewing each other's position on the evidence, but they had yet to sit down as a single group. Time was running out. The committee's final, televised deliberations were to begin in two days, and there still was no agreement on acceptable articles of impeachment. At the lunch break on Monday, Rodino went to see Flowers again.

Over the weekend Flowers had finally decided for sure that he would vote to impeach. "I'll check with Tom [Railsback] and try to set up a meeting," he told Rodino.

Railsback had just returned from a weekend in Illinois, where he had again reviewed the evidence, the lawyers' summaries, his notes. In the three weeks since he had told Joseph Alsop that he would not vote to impeach, he had been moving steadily away from the President. It was hard to escape the conclusion that, directly or through Haldeman, Richard Nixon had given the orders.

Railsback was angry at the committee's minority leadership. Hutchinson, the ranking Republican, regarded members of the party as duty bound to save a Republican president. The position was offensive.

Railsback remembered back to the early spring, when he had received a call from William Hewett, chairman of Deere and Company, the giant farm-equipment manufacturer headquartered in his home district. Hewett had said that Peter M. Flanigan of the White House had called him twice and wanted him to talk to Railsback about his posture on the House Judiciary Committee. Railsback resented that Richard Nixon ran the White House that way. The impeachment evidence, viewed in that light, seemed that much clearer.

Railsback had decided he wanted to take a stand against it all—the dissembling, the stonewalling, the concealing, the lying, the cheating. Besides, he rationalized, the vote wouldn't put Nixon in jail. It was just a vote about whether he should remain in office. He told Flowers that afternoon that he would sound out Cohen, Fish and Butler. Flowers would contact James R. Mann and Ray Thornton, his fellow Southern Democrats.

At eight o'clock the next morning, Tuesday, July 23, the seven Congressmen gathered in Railsback's office over coffee and danish pastry. There was agreement that the articles of impeachment drafted by John Doar were unacceptable and that they should try drafting a compromise set to submit to the committee as a whole. The meeting went on for an hour without anyone actually saying he would vote for impeachment. Finally Flowers sought some commitment. "Knowing what we know now," he asked the others, "does it justify the extreme action of removal from office?"

Everyone seemed to nod assent—they were all going to vote to impeach.

Flowers joked with Butler, "Caldwell, do you realize that every pickup truck in Roanoke is going to be up here after you by nightfall?"

PART II

Wednesday, July 24

JAWORSKI and Lacovara sat quietly in a government sedan in the Washington traffic. They were confident that the Supreme Court had decided in their favor. The real gamble had been in May, when they had asked the high court to bypass the Court of Appeals. The only question now was whether they had all eight justices who were voting. NBC reporter Carl Stern had called an hour earlier with a tip that the Court was unanimous, but Jaworski, cautious by nature, was waiting to hear it directly from the justices.

Turning south down First Street, they passed the Senate Caucus Room, where, a year and a day before, Senator Sam Ervin had read to the gallery and a national television audience a letter from the President about the tapes. "Before their existence became publicly known," Nixon had written, "I personally listened to a number of them. The tapes are entirely consistent with what I know to be the truth and what I have stated to be the truth."

Across the street from the Supreme Court Building, two men wearing Nixon and Kissinger masks held a large banner that quoted Nixon's remark to Mitchell from the March 22 tape: "I don't give a shit what happens. I want you all to stonewall it. Let them plead the Fifth Amendment, cover up or anything else that will save the plan. That's the whole point."

Jaworski and Lacovara, having pushed their way through a crowd of reporters, photographers and cheering spectators, entered the courtroom shortly before 11 A.M. White House assistant counsel Jerry Murphy was sitting at the counsel table to the left. They took their places at the table on the right, reserved for the government.

Some time earlier, they had agreed they would probably get a five-to-three decision and that William O. Douglas, the most liberal of the justices, would be likely to draft the majority opinion. Lacovara was recalculating when the court marshal interrupted: "The Honorable, the Chief Justice, and the Associate Justices of the Supreme Court of the United States."

The packed room was quiet as the black-robed justices filed in. Lacovara fingered the thread hanging from the "lucky suit" he had worn in all his appearances before the Court.

Chief Justice Warren Burger took his seat in the center of the elevated bench and slowly and deliberately began to read. Jaworski and Lacovara knew instantly that the decision must be unanimous—the Chief Justice was delivering it.

Only the justices and their clerks knew how total the agreement was. On July 9, just a day after the oral arguments, the justices had unanimously decided against the President. Burger had assigned himself to draft the opinion. He shared some of the President's sentiments about executive privilege and wanted to establish a constitutional standard for the doctrine. The other justices, however, found his opinion inadequate and suggested major revisions. Burger worked hard to stitch the suggestions into a consistent whole, but he still did not produce a satisfactory opinion. Some of the clerks remarked privately that Earl Warren would have had an opinion within three hours of the first conference. Finally Justice Potter Stewart undertook to coauthor the opinion. Gradually, the other justices returned the working drafts with fewer changes. The day before the decision was to be announced, the justices accepted a final version which acknowledged a constitutional basis for executive privilege but rejected the President's particular claim as "generalized" and "undifferentiated." In careful but clear language, the Court ordered the President to turn over the tapes of sixty-four subpoenaed conversations to Judge Sirica.

Murphy heard Burger conclude, "Accordingly, the judgment under review is affirmed." Standing as the justices filed out, he was thinking about how to get to the nearest phone.

At the White House, Buzhardt's assistant Richard Hauser dashed to his boss's office, muttering, "Eight-zip." "What does 'zip' mean?" Jane Thomas, Buzhardt's secretary, asked as Hauser swept by.

Buzhardt was not surprised. He and Haig had long been reconciled to an adverse decision. As soon as the Court bypassed the Appeals Court, they were fairly certain the President would lose. When Buzhardt had heard that the Chief Justice was drafting the majority opinion, he called Haig in San Clemente to tell him that the decision not only would be adverse, but would possibly be unanimous. That would make things difficult. If there was no minority opinion, there was little room to maneuver for partial compliance. And the President would have lost the support of his own appointees—men who supposedly shared his judicial philosophy.

Haig had heard the warning, but hadn't wanted to talk strategy; he would wait and see. Now Buzhardt was calling to say they couldn't wait any longer. He required instructions. How were they going to react?

First, Haig said, he would have to inform the President. He would check and get back soon.

Haig's aide Charles Wardell brought him the wire-service copy, and the general took it over to the residence. It was early in San Clemente, only a little past eight-thirty. The President was not yet in his office.

When Haig called back, Buzhardt was finishing another cup of the black coffee that he drank almost addictively. Now he would get his instructions. But the President himself came on the line. Buzhardt was surprised; he hadn't talked to the President for a long time.

"There might be a problem with the June 23 tape, Fred," Nixon said.

Buzhardt thought the President must be referring to some national-security matter.

"Get right on it and get back to Al," Nixon instructed.

ZIEGLER WATCHED the televised announcement of the Supreme Court decision from his suite at the Surf and Sand overlooking the Pacific. As the morning breakers crashed a hundred yards below his window, he scratched some notes on a yellow legal pad. He knew he would be spending the morning with the President, fashioning some response. Nixon would drown him with requests for more and more information, for alternatives.

He rode a borrowed Honda to the Nixon compound, arriving just after 9 A.M. Despite a California tan, Ziegler looked white and tired to Connie Gerrard, his secretary. Accustomed to his imperious manner, Gerrard carried a suit coat, shirt, tie and dress shoes into his office. She shared with the other secretaries the chore of transporting her boss's dry cleaning and dirty laundry, and shopping for his clothes. Sometimes she selected several pairs of new shoes, waited as he tried them on, advised him on the color and style, and then took back the rejects to the store. Ziegler had recently lost thirty pounds. That meant he had needed a lot of new clothes. His staff accepted these menial chores with varying degrees of tolerance, recognizing that the demands he made on them were extensions of the pressures the President put on him. His temper tantrums were excused on similar grounds. Nixon raged at Ziegler, they knew, and Ziegler raged back at whoever was handy.*

Gerrard gave him the morning newspapers, already marked in yellow to spot important material, and waited to be sure he hadn't lost the motorcycle key again. Ziegler didn't even glance at the papers. He shouted for his coffee, made a couple of notes on a legal pad and charged out the door, heading for Building A.

Haig's secretary, Muriel Hartley, was in no mood to see Ziegler, now or ever. As he stormed by her toward Haig's office, she tried unsuccessfully to stop him. "The SOB muscles his way in on everything," she had once complained. "Even Dr. Kissinger asks first." She had suggested to Haig that he put a lock on his door which could be released from a buzzer on her desk. Haig had said no. She knew, though, that Haig often didn't want Ziegler in there.

Perhaps today might be different. The general had gone to the residence forty-five minutes earlier to brief the President and had just come back, his mouth set in a tight line. He was in his office with St. Clair and Joulwan, and they all looked very grim. The door between Haig's office and the President's was closed as Ziegler joined them, though the President hadn't yet arrived.

Nixon had exploded when Haig told him of the Court's unanimous decision. How could the men he had appointed—Burger, Blackmun and Powell—not follow their conscience, fail to support him? For Nixon, the question of compliance was still an open matter; he was not prepared to make a snap decision. He wanted to weigh the alternatives carefully. Maybe he'd finally follow through on his often-repeated threat—he would burn the tapes and resign.

* The press-office staff was less tolerant of Ziegler's insistence that his coffee be served in a cup and saucer identical to the President's—cream-colored Lenox china with a silver presidential seal—and that his Scotch be poured only into a cocktail glass embossed with the presidential emblem. Combining resentment and jest at the way Ziegler treated them, his staff took to adding the Filipino suffix *Chon* to their names (the President and his family were served by Filipino stewards). Thus, the regular duties of Anne "Chon" Grier included pickup and delivery of Ziegler's laundry at the Golden Star Valet, four blocks from the White House; Karin Chon Nordstrom was assigned to scout Ziegler's littered hotel rooms for underwear and other items he left behind at checkout time; Judy Chon Johnson set up his desk each morning with a pack of Marlboros, a matchbook embossed with the presidential seal, a roll of Certs and a day's supply of Titralac; Connie Chon Gerrard spent hours on the phone trying to arrange tennis matches with partners of sufficient White House rank not to offend Ziegler's sense of protocol, but with skill enough to challenge his on-court abilities; summer intern Tim Chon Smith took Ziegler's shoes to the Carlton barbershop for their regular shine.

As Ziegler listened to Haig he knew what he was in for. The President needed to let off steam, and the assignment of taking the heat was going to fall to him. Haig took his share, but he readily deferred to Ziegler whenever possible. Often Ziegler would sit for hours alternately listening to the President's intemperate and garbled tirades and then to endless questions and requests for information. At times it was almost overwhelming.

The President had always despised small talk, but lately he would interrupt the conversation and ramble, usually about his past triumphs. Then suddenly, he would seem to be jolted to the present and would offer preposterous alternatives, make ridiculous suggestions. Ziegler accepted these remarks as offhand challenges. They were not to be taken literally, and he did not take them so. Like Haig, Ziegler had learned to simply ignore Nixon's more outrageous orders. Haldeman had once said that it was a staff officer's duty to ignore any clearly inappropriate demand, even if the President had insisted on it.

Ziegler's rapid rise, after Haldeman and Ehrlichman had departed, at first found him poorly equipped to accomplish such sidesteps, and he had passed along some of the President's more ill-considered notions. Gradually he had learned to deflect most of them, however. As he became more confident, he said that he had never realized what yes men Haldeman and Ehrlichman had been. Often the President only needed time—sometimes just a few minutes—to cool off.

The President seemed to trust Ziegler more each day and found relief in sitting and rummaging through his thoughts with him. Ziegler was impressed by his complexity and sensitivity. If only the world knew the real Richard Nixon, he often remarked, the public would appreciate him so much more.

Over the last year, Ziegler had become a counselor to the President in the most fundamental sense—his confidant and alter ego. Each tiny move the President made was run through Ziegler again and again. Ziegler watched the painful deterioration of the President's popularity and political strength and, with it, the deterioration of his spirit. Still, at times Nixon could be extraordinarily thorough and alert. He hungered after facts, information, approaches, alternatives.

The President's demands on him took all of Ziegler's days. He had no time but to sit and listen, go out and try to implement, and—before he was halfway through his tasks—answer a call from the President to come back and listen some more. He had learned to dodge some of the calls; he instructed his secretaries to develop alibis for him.

Ziegler had begun to see himself as the crucible through which the President's decisions were forged. He had become sophisticated in anticipating demands. He would have Sawyer and Gannon prepare lists of positive suggestions on every conceivable aspect of the situation. Then, at the appropriate moment, he would slip them into the conversation as if they had been the President's ideas. He watched Nixon's decision-making curve move up and down, and waited for the right moments to press his points. He offered his advice cautiously, fearful that it might be interpreted as too bold or too harsh. A number of aides had fallen into disfavor for offering painful advice.

The details of running the country had been left to General Haig as the President withdrew more and more into himself to reflect on his Watergate options. Nixon had lost interest in domestic affairs, and he gave only occasional bursts of attention to foreign policy. Haig might remind the Chief that it was time to make a decision, but it fell to Ziegler to sit and listen to the convolutions of the President's laborious debates with himself.

Today, a decision would have to be made.

As ALWAYS, Buzhardt moved methodically. He located the reference to the June 23 conversation on the special prosecutor's subpoena. The Presidential log and diary verified that the meeting with Haldeman had taken place in the Oval Office between 10:04 and 11:39 A.M. Buzhardt called a Secret Service agent and requested the reel. As he waited for the tape to be brought from the EOB storage vault, he prepared his listening equipment. The erase button on his Sony 800B recorder was already electrically disconnected, but he took the extra precaution of jamming the mechanism by placing a plastic block under the erase button, making it impossible to depress. He felt that his precautions were well taken, since there were no copies of this tape. This was the original of a tape that the President himself had described as a "problem."

The word "problem" was frequently a presidential euphemism for disaster, but it could also be a signal of overreaction. Buzhardt thought the President was oddly lacking in judgment about certain matters. He did either too little or too much. When there had been leaks, he had gone beyond all reason: he had created the Plumbers, he had approved the Huston plan. He had underreacted to John Dean, failing at first to see the damage Dean could do him; then he had overreacted to the fact that Dean had squirreled away a number of documents. When Haldeman and Ehrlichman were implicated in the cover-up, he had overreacted to the demands for an intensified investigation and had allowed a special prosecutor to be appointed. The Saturday Night Massacre was another exaggerated response. Nixon had miscalculated about the tapes—he should have burned them straightaway, Buzhardt believed; the ferocious battle to keep them had riveted public attention, had created a national obsession. Afterward the President had shifted suddenly and given up a batch of them. Then he had dumped twelve hundred pages of transcripts on the public, but, by editing them indiscriminately, lost whatever advantage he might have gained from the act. Nixon could not seem to grasp the fact that there would be a public reckoning.

Len Garment was right, Buzhardt thought. Watergate was a series of discrete, unrelated transactions. There had been no grand strategy, just consistently bad judgment. For some time, Buzhardt had been half waiting for something that would totally undermine the President's defense. He had brought himself around to the notion that maybe it wasn't in the tapes of Nixon's Watergate discussions. He still thought that, technically at least, the President had not broken the law in the cover-up. If there was a problem, Buzhardt thought, it was more likely in the area of his finances or in the abuses of the Internal Revenue Service.

In June, the President had asked him how the Supreme Court would deal with matters of national security on the tapes, indicating that there might be some problem in that area. "They've got to give us some room on national security," Nixon had said. "How's that going to work, Fred?" Buzhardt said he had no idea how the Court might treat such matters. Perhaps Buzhardt was now going to hear that national-security problem. That must be why the President wanted him to listen. Buzhardt knew the date June 23, 1972, well. In his statement of May 22, 1973, the President had denied any political motivation in his instructions to Haldeman on June 23.

It was forty minutes before the reel arrived. Buzhardt removed it from its cardboard box and threaded it into the machine. He put on the large headphones. He had little trouble finding the beginning of the conversation, since it was the first on the reel. He was used to having to thread through hundreds of feet of tape.

There was a period of silence and then he heard Haldeman's voice. It was a routine chat between him and the President—setting up a meeting with Secretary of State William Rogers. Then Haldeman said, "Now, on the investigation, you know, the Democratic break-in thing, we're back in the problem area, because the FBI is not under control, because Gray doesn't exactly know how to control them, and they have—their investigation is now leading into some productive areas, because they've been able to trace the money, not through the money itself but through the bank, you know, sources, the banker himself. And, and it goes in some directions we don't want it to go."

Buzhardt realized that he was one of the few people to listen to a tape of a conversation that had taken place so soon after the break-in. Apparently, the only earlier reference to Watergate on a subpoenaed tape had been on the infamous June 20 recording—in the obliterated eighteen and a half minutes of conversation between Haldeman and the President.

Buzhardt thought Haldeman was giving a pretty full and knowledgeable explanation of the early Watergate investigation. What did he mean by being "back in the problem area"; by "the FBI is not under control"; by "leading into some productive areas"? Perhaps these were references to national-security matters, perhaps not.

Haldeman continued: ". . . Mitchell came up with yesterday, and John Dean analyzed very carefully last night and concludes, concurs now with Mitchell's recommendation, that the only way to solve this—and we're set up beautifully to do it—ah . . . that the way to handle this now is for us to have Walters call Pat Gray and just say, 'Stay to hell out of this, this, ah, business here, we don't want you to go any further on it.' That's not an unusual development—and, ah, that would take care of it."

Buzhardt recognized the connection. The President had acknowledged fourteen months before that Haldeman and Ehrlichman had contacted CIA Deputy Director Walters, to "ensure that the investigation of the break-in not expose either an unrelated covert operation of the CIA or the activities of the White House investigations unit [Plumbers]."

But the President had also declared in his statement of May 22: ". . . it was certainly not my intent, nor my wish, that the investigation of the Watergate break-in or of related acts be impeded in any way."

Buzhardt's spirits fell. The tape established that Haldeman intended to use the CIA to impede the investigation of Watergate. Furthermore, it laid the origin of the plan to Mitchell. Perhaps the President would bring up a legitimate national-security consideration. That might muddy the waters. They had faced a similar difficulty with the tape for March 21, 1973, when Nixon had appeared to authorize the payment of hush money to Hunt. The President's lawyers had argued that in fact Nixon had turned off the proposal later in the same conversation, though Buzhardt had always been dubious about that claim. Things looked grim this time, but Buzhardt was one to hold out hope.

"What about Pat Gray—you mean Pat Gray doesn't want to?" Nixon asked.

"Pat does want to," Haldeman answered. "He doesn't know how to, and he doesn't have—he doesn't have any basis for doing it. Given this, he will then have the basis."

Buzhardt listened as the President asked questions about the investigation and Haldeman explained how the Dahlberg and Texas money had left a trail.*

Gradually, the President got Haldeman's point. Referring to the money his campaign aides had sent to the laundry, he asked, "What do they say? They were approached by the Cubans? That's what Dahlberg has to say, the Texans too. Is that the idea?"

"Well, if they will. But then we're relying on more and more people all the time. That's the problem. And they'll stop if we could—if we take this other step," said Haldeman, returning to Mitchell's cover-up plan.

"All right, fine," said the President.

"And they seem to feel the thing to do is get them to stop," said Haldeman.

"Right, fine," said Nixon.

"They say the only way to do that is from White House instructions. And it's got to be to [CIA Director] Helms and, ah, what's his name—Walters," said Haldeman.

Buzhardt felt that here was a potential smoking gun. The President had personally approved an initial step in the Watergate cover-up, not from ignorance but after an explanation of the political pressures, in order to cover a money trail that led back to his reelection committee.

"And the proposal would be that Ehrlichman and I call them [the CIA officials] in," continued Haldeman.

"All right, fine," Nixon said impatiently. "How do you call him in? I mean you just— Well, we protected Helms from one hell of a lot of things."

"That's what Ehrlichman says."

"Of course, this is Hunt, that will uncover a lot of things," Nixon said. "You open that scab, there's a hell of a lot of things, and we just feel that it would be very detrimental to have this thing go any further. This involves these Cubans, Hunt and a lot of hanky-panky that we have nothing to do with ourselves."

---

* Kenneth H. Dahlberg, a Nixon campaign fund raiser, collected $25,000 in cash contributions, converted the funds to a cashier's check and turned it over to the Nixon reelection committee in Washington. The check was then deposited in the bank account of Bernard Barker, one of the Watergate burglars; it provided investigators with the first link between the burglary and Nixon campaign cash.

Manuel Ogarrio, a Mexican lawyer, served as a conduit for contributions from Texas donors to the Nixon campaign. The money was "laundered" through his bank in Mexico City to make the funds untraceable. In addition to the Dahlberg check, four checks drawn on Ogarrio's account and totaling $89,000 were deposited in Barker's account.

Now Buzhardt saw how the President had been able to sell himself the national-security justification.

"Well, what the hell," Nixon said, "did Mitchell know about this thing to any much of a degree?" The reference was to the Watergate bugging.

"I think so," Haldeman responded. "I don't think he knew the details, but I think he knew."

This exchange, Buzhardt was painfully aware, undercut the President's claim that he had known of no Watergate involvement by his assistants until John Dean came to him the following March. It put Nixon right in the middle of the cover-up. It gave him a reason to cover up: he was concealing the involvement of his campaign manager, Mitchell. And the tone disclosed even more. There was no surprise or indignation. "Did Mitchell know about this thing to any much of a degree?" the President had asked. He either knew of or had strongly guessed at Mitchell's involvement.

Nixon continued: "He didn't know how it was going to be handled, though—with Dahlberg and the Texans and so forth? Well, who was the asshole that did? Is it Liddy? Is that the fellow? He must be a little nuts."

"He is."

"I mean he just isn't well screwed on, is he? Isn't that the problem?" asked Nixon.

"No, but he was under pressure, apparently, to get more information, and as he got more pressure, he pushed the people harder to move harder on—"

"Pressure from Mitchell?" asked Nixon.

"Apparently."

"Oh, Mitchell," Nixon said. "Mitchell was at the point that you made on this, that exactly what I need from you is on the—"

"Gemstone, yeah," Haldeman said.

It wasn't absolutely clear to Buzhardt, but it sounded like "Gemstone"— the secret code name for Gordon Liddy's espionage plan that included electronic eavesdropping and break-in at the Watergate. Certainly Haldeman was not holding back from the President.

"All right, fine," the President said abruptly, "I understand it all. We won't second-guess Mitchell and the rest. Thank God it wasn't Colson."

Haldeman told the President that the FBI, after interviewing Colson, had concluded that the break-in was not a White House operation, but probably a CIA scheme—Cubans and the CIA. "So the CIA turnoff would—" he said.

"Well, not sure of their analysis," Nixon interrupted. "I'm not going to get that involved. I'm . . ." Buzhardt couldn't hear the rest of the sentence.

"No, sir, we don't want you to," said Haldeman reassuringly.

"You call them in," ordered Nixon.

"Good deal," Haldeman responded.

"Play it tough. That's the way they play it and that's the way we are going to play it."

"Okay. We'll do it."

There had been no mention of national security. The President and Haldeman were using the claim to persuade the FBI, through the CIA, to back off from the investigation. Buzhardt sipped his coffee. National security was a ruse.

The President and Haldeman then shifted to other business—the resignation of the chief of protocol, lobbying action on a pending revenue bill, international finance, Italian monetary problems. ("I don't give a shit about the lira," Nixon remarked.) As the reels slowly turned, Buzhardt heard the two men discuss press coverage of recent Administration decisions, and a statement being drafted on busing. But they came back to Watergate. The President carefully told Haldeman how to handle Helms and Walters:

". . . Say, 'Look, the problem is that this will open the whole, the whole Bay of Pigs thing, and the President just feels that'—ah, without going into the details. Don't, don't lie to them to the extent to say there is no involvement, just say, 'This is a comedy of errors,' without getting into it, 'the President believes that it is going to open the whole Bay of Pigs thing up again.' And, ah, 'Because these people are plugging for keeps,' and that they should call the FBI in and say that we wish for the country, 'Don't go any further into this case, period!' "

At that, the two men turned back to Oval Office business. Buzhardt stopped the recorder. He rewound the reel and listened again. A second hearing did not change his impression. The tape was devastating. Buzhardt was overwhelmed. He had heard the President approve the plan, he had heard him suggest the exact wording. Buzhardt had found the "smoking pistol." He had heard the President load it, aim and fire.

Buzhardt removed the earphones from his aching ears. He sat gazing at the files all over his desk. School's out, he thought.

Only one week before, St. Clair had rebutted the House Judiciary Committee's charge that the President had interjected the CIA into the FBI's investigation in an effort to impede it, and he had argued on the basis of the May 22 statement. He had quoted it at length and offered the conclusion that the President had mentioned the CIA only to prevent exposure of an unrelated covert CIA operation. St. Clair's brief had further claimed that "the President had no prior knowledge of an alleged plot to obstruct justice by such means as the attempted use of the CIA to thwart the FBI's Watergate investigation."

They had misled the House committee.

Buzhardt picked up the phone. "Give me San Clemente," he said. A few moments passed as he waited on the line for the White House operator to reach California and get Haig.

"Well, we've found the smoking pistol," he began. His voice was calm and emotionless.

"Are you sure?" Haig asked.

"Yes, it's the ball game. Bob told him a lot that day."

Haig accepted the information coolly. He registered no surprise as Buzhardt outlined how the President had authorized Haldeman to contact the CIA. Buzhardt told him Haldeman had opened the conversation by telling the President, ". . . we're *back* in the problem area, because the FBI is not under control." An obvious reference to an earlier conversation, Buzhardt said, perhaps to June 20, to something said in the obliterated eighteen and a half minutes.

That could mean only one thing, Haig said. The President himself had erased the eighteen and a half minutes. Unfortunately, it all added up.

Buzhardt underlined the gravity of the new problem. As head of the executive branch, the President was of course in charge of the FBI and the CIA. So the instruction to Haldeman was probably not, in the most technical sense, an obstruction of justice. But it was certainly an abuse of power or an abuse of agency. By almost any definition, it was an impeachable offense.

"Well," said Haig, "what do you think we ought to do?"

Buzhardt had given it some thought. "Well, we've got the Court decision to think about also. I think the President ought to think about his options." If there had been no smoking gun he would have recommended that they supply transcripts rather than the tapes to Judge Sirica and make the argument that that constituted compliance, but that option was now closed. To do so now could make them all party to a crime.

The President could turn over the tapes and hope for the best, but the more realistic choice was to turn over nothing, Buzhardt said. This could be done only if the President resigned. Resignation would abort the Judiciary Committee's impeachment investigation and thus end the committee's need for the tapes. As for the special prosecutor, the only way to end his need for the tapes would be to stop all prosecutions—by pardoning everyone. Refusal to comply with the Supreme Court decision, Buzhardt reiterated, would pretty much have to involve both resignation and pardons. He was inclined to favor the idea.

There was another strong reason for the President to resign, Buzhardt added. The brief that had been submitted to the House Judiciary Committee had included a serious misrepresentation about what happened on June 23, 1972. Buzhardt reminded Haig that if a lawyer has been party to misleading a court, he is obligated to get his client to change his plea or correct the misrepresentation himself. Resignation would constitute a change in plea before the House inquiry. The only other choice was to disclose the tape at once.

Haig told Buzhardt that he and St. Clair would go over to see the President soon. "We'll get back to you."

JUST AFTER 1 P.M. Buzhardt walked across West Executive Avenue to the West Wing to join Timmons, Burch and Garment for lunch in the White House mess. Their expressions were grim. They were discussing the Court's decision, and, as he sat down at the table, Buzhardt offered no hint of what he knew.

Timmons was arguing that the President had to resign. He was proceeding on the assumption that the tapes were bad, otherwise the President wouldn't have fought so hard to keep them. He suggested that Nixon resign over the issue of preserving the confidentiality of presidential conversations. He felt that the President was better off pleading an ultimate executive privilege, refusing to turn over any tapes—burning them, if need be—on the grounds that to turn them over would irreparably damage the presidency. That way he would leave on principle, instead of being hauled out. Timmons had asked Haig that morning, "How much consideration are you giving to resignation?" Haig had been noncommittal. He had replied simply that every option was being considered.

Timmons' arguments were better received now, at lunch. Buzhardt and Burch agreed with him. Garment shifted in his chair and expressed surprise that they wanted to throw in the towel so quickly. He said he had talked with Charlie Wright that morning. Wright had urged that they not allow a precedent in which the Congress drove a President from office without a vote in the constitutionally mandated manner. There was a certain purity in taking it through to the end, Garment argued. The others were unpersuaded.

After lunch, Garment and Buzhardt strolled back across West Executive Avenue to their offices. As they walked into the early-afternoon sun, Garment asked, "What's up?"

Buzhardt straightened slightly and squinted at him. "It's bad, Len."

Garment didn't press for details. He anticipated the worst.

BUZHARDT'S MIND was focused on the question of pardons. Ever since he had become counsel to the President he had been cautious about recommending the use of the presidential pardon power. Now he was contemplating pardons for a whole category of men who had been, or might become, Watergate defendants. He had his staff review all those who would have to be pardoned if the President resigned and refused to turn over the tapes. It was a long and varied list—over thirty men, ranging from Herbert L. (Bart) Porter, a minor official of the Nixon reelection committee (who had pleaded guilty to lying to FBI agents), to Howard Hunt, Haldeman, Ehrlichman and Mitchell. The last three had not yet even been tried. The President could not pardon some and not others.

DAVE GERGEN sat alone in his office drafting a wire to Haig. He suggested that the President might turn his Supreme Court setback into an advantage by announcing, in a dramatic personal statement to the nation, that he would comply. It was important to turn over to Sirica as many original tapes as possible within hours. A date for the completion of the transfer should also be set. "Let's take the suspense out of this thing for a change," Gergen wrote. He recommended also that the President give the tapes to the House Judiciary Committee.

Gergen did not know what was going on in San Clemente or what the President's response might be, but he thought it important to shift public attention away from a reclusive President who might or might not relinquish the tapes to a reasonable and cooperative President who felt himself bound to obey the law.

HAIG WALKED across the San Clemente compound to the President's office in the den of the residence. He could predict the effect that Buzhardt's conclusions would have on Nixon.

Nixon looked up at him from his reclining chair. Calmly Haig outlined Buzhardt's interpretation of the June 23 tape and his analysis of the available options.

The President seethed. Buzhardt was completely off base, he said. Everything that was on the tape had been disclosed in his previous statements, including May 22, and in the testimony of Haldeman and Ehrlichman before the Senate Watergate Committee, and most completely in the CIA memcons. *He* knew what *he* meant, the President protested, and what *he* had meant was that Haldeman should insure only that the FBI not jeopardize long-buried CIA secrets left over from the Bay of Pigs operation. Then, as he had so often done, the President stared penetratingly at Haig and insisted that he was innocent—he had been concerned about national security.

The President attacked his lawyer's judgment—Buzhardt was probably tired, he was still ill from his recent heart attack; besides, he was given to panic. He had panicked in November when he and Garment had recommended resignation. He had been wrong then, and he was wrong now. No, the President concluded, Buzhardt could not render a reasoned judgment. What about St. Clair?

Haig called St. Clair and asked him to come over.

St. Clair had already talked with Buzhardt and knew his assessment. As a precaution, he had called the Secret Service in Washington to make sure the tapes were secure. But St. Clair had been more immediately concerned about the Supreme Court decision and didn't want to jump to any conclusions about the contents of the tapes. Was there any way to avoid turning them over? He had fidgeted as he waited for the text of the decision to come over the White House wires. *United States v. Nixon* was the biggest court case of St. Clair's career, and he had thought he'd won it. He was shattered that he had lost. When he read the decision, it became clear to him that the tapes would have to go to Sirica.

"The President is not above the law. Nor does he contend that he is," St. Clair had told the Court. He hoped that the President understood what that meant. Nixon had never told him exactly what he would do if there were an adverse decision, but St. Clair knew that his own legal advice to the President had to be unqualified compliance.

When St. Clair arrived at the residence, he told the President and Haig that he advised full compliance. The President was not convinced. He wondered if, in fact, to preserve the power of his office, he didn't have a constitutional duty to reject the court order.

Both Haig and St. Clair observed that defiance would mean certain impeachment and conviction.

Even so, the President said, he might have an obligation to carry this battle into the impeachment forum. The consequences to the office of the presidency were grave, and therefore the matter must be given all possible tests and full public argument. Hadn't St. Clair, after all, argued to the Court that "as the President the law can be applied to him in only one way . . . by impeachment"?

The conversation continued for two hours before the President appeared to accept the notion of some form of compliance. Characteristically, he had arrived at a decision without actually having made it.

St. Clair tried to explain to his client what Judge Sirica and the special prosecutor would probably expect.

There must be some exception for national-security material, Nixon insisted.

It was Sirica who would rule on claims of national security, St. Clair said. Just as he had with the first batch of tapes.

The President wanted time to review all the tapes himself. There was to be no wholesale turnover. He instructed St. Clair to inform Sirica that they would need time—weeks, perhaps longer—to do a thorough job.

"I can't get that," St. Clair said. He reminded the President that Jaworski's consistent strategy had been to get the tapes quickly, so that the cover-up trial could take place, as planned, in the fall. Certainly Sirica would support an immediate turnover. St. Clair, caught in the middle, sensed that he was being used in a frivolous attempt at one more stall. His professional reputation would be damaged further.

Nixon's anger flared again. He had difficulty enough with the Court telling him *what* to do, he said. They were not going to tell him *when* to do it. And St. Clair was his lawyer, he had better secure the necessary delay. He, Nixon, wanted it. That was that.

St. Clair was insulted. His client was instructing him again on how to handle the case. He didn't want to argue anymore. The President had agreed to compliance, of a sort.

THE DRAMA of Buzhardt's conclusions about the June 23 tape was, for the moment, pushed into the background. Absorbed by the pressure to offer public assurances that the tapes would be forthcoming, Haig, St. Clair and Ziegler went to Haig's office to work on a statement of compliance.

Haig called Buzhardt and told him that Nixon disagreed with his analysis. The President was insisting that the June 23 tape was "not that bad." He had decided to announce that he would comply.

Buzhardt said the decision was premature; it meant only postponing the inevitable consequences. When those consequences were weighed, the non-compliance-and-resignation option looked attractive. It might represent the President's last chance to stand on principle and to leave office without suffering devastating exposure. And God only knew what was on the rest of the tapes.

Haig reiterated that the President had decided to comply. Resignation, noncompliance, pardons—all of it was too much to consider that day. The President was in one of his black moods. June 23, the impact of any disclosure—those judgments would have to be put off.

Buzhardt gave up. The President was really taking the easy course; an announcement of compliance would delay the larger issue. But the issue was still there, and Buzhardt knew it would surface quickly. Then there would be no easy way to dispose of it. In the meantime, there were those who would have to be alerted. Timmons had told him that House Republican Minority Leader Rhodes had pledged to lead the fight against impeachment. Buzhardt phoned Timmons and told him that there was a bad tape; he suggested that Rhodes be warned not to do or say anything until he heard from Timmons again. Timmons agreed.

RAY PRICE had arrived at his office in the San Clemente compound early that morning to work on the President's speech on the economy. It was scheduled for the next day. He had barely settled down to work when the news of the Supreme Court decision came over the Associated Press wire. Price jotted down some ideas for a suitable response, sent his suggestions over to Haig and Ziegler, and went back to work on the speech about the economy. A short while later, he was interrupted by Haig, who wanted to discuss the language of the President's response. Using Price's draft, Haig, St. Clair, Ziegler and Price got a statement ready for the President.

JERRY WARREN was waiting for word from Ziegler. The press had been badgering him all morning, running in and out of his office at the Surf and Sand. Would the President comply? Would he defy the law of the land? When would there be an announcement on the President's decision? If he complied, when would the tapes be released?

Warren had no answers. He was dependent on Ziegler for any information. Ziegler had been phoning constantly, but it was to find out how the press was reacting, how it was reporting the Court's decision and the delay in an announcement from the President. Warren knew that these were the President's questions.

Warren asked Ziegler when an announcement would be made; he was concerned by the delay. Some reporters seemed to think that the President would tell the Court to shove it, he said. There were news stories going out over the wires that began, "President Nixon, isolated here at his seaside villa . . ." The staff was getting edgy, too. This was Warren's quiet way of urging some response. Ziegler was necessarily noncommittal; he was protecting the President's options. Everything possible was being done to get a statement ready, he said.

Tom DeCair, one of Warren's aides, asked about the delay. "Ron will tell us when the time is right," Warren responded coolly.

Finally Ziegler phoned Warren to say that St. Clair would hold a press briefing at 4 P.M. There was some question about where it would be. The San Clemente Inn was unavailable. The owner had booked the usual briefing room to a local concern. Local business was more lucrative and permanent, he had said.

Warren and Ziegler talked about using the cafeteria at the Concordia Elementary School in San Clemente, but relocating the cameras and equipment was impractical. Nor did they relish the image of the President's lawyer coming live to America from the cafeteria of an elementary school. Finally they found suitable space at the Surf and Sand. Warren was relieved to have something to announce.

Haig called Muriel Hartley into his office to take down the statement that St. Clair would deliver. St. Clair, Ziegler, Price and Joulwan listened as Haig recited the text. It had gone through so many drafts that Haig was able to rattle it off—at times too fast for Hartley. Haig became impatient when she missed a word.

A few minutes later, he picked up the typed statement and walked over to show it to the President. He returned shortly. The President had approved it. Ziegler rushed out to his office in B Building, called the press office and dictated the three-paragraph statement to Shirley Browne, Warren's secretary. When he had finished, Ziegler and St. Clair drove over to the Surf and Sand.

Price did not see them go. He was talking to the President about the next day's speech. Having incorporated suggestions from other advisers, he had taken the latest draft to Nixon at about 2:30 P.M.

The President was pensive. At first he seemed to want to talk about the Court's decision. He felt that things looked less than optimistic. But then he tried to buck up his senior speech writer. They spoke in generalities for a few minutes, and then the President got down to their business.

Price appreciated the strategic importance of making a major domestic address. It would show that the President was not crippled by the Court's decision—that despite the decision and the press's morbid concern with Watergate, the President was squarely facing the country's major dilemma.

THE WHITE House sedan sped north along the highway, past the luxurious seaside apartments of Laguna Beach, and up the ramp to the Surf and Sand parking lot. Reporters rushed to meet the occupants—St. Clair and Ziegler —but the two men went straight to the press office.

Ziegler asked Judy Johnson to fetch his shaving kit for St. Clair. As they waited, he tried to ease St. Clair's nervousness. Clawson joined in, happy to be finally included and anxious to enter the press conference as a participant in this historic occasion.

When St. Clair had finished shaving, he emerged from the office and walked slowly into the Surf and Sand's Mai Tai Room. The podium, designed for Ziegler and Warren, was too high, and he looked straight into the lights.

"I have reviewed the decision of the Supreme Court with the President," he began. "He has given me this statement, which he has asked me to read to you: 'While I am of course disappointed in the result, I respect and accept the Court's decision, and I have instructed Mr. St. Clair to take whatever measures are necessary to comply with that decision in all respects.' "

At the same time, Nixon laid claim to a victory in principle: "I was gratified . . . to note that the Court reaffirmed both the validity and the importance of the principle of executive privilege—the principle I had sought to maintain."

St. Clair laid down his paper. "As we all know, the President has always been a firm believer in the rule of law. . . . In accordance with his instructions, the time-consuming process of reviewing the tapes . . . will begin forthwith."

Once back in Ziegler's office, St. Clair collapsed into a chair, exhausted from the tension. It had been a traumatic day. Now, away from the clamor of the briefing room, he began to unwind. Ziegler decided to forsake his liquor-free diet and sent Johnson to the top-floor bar for a pair of double Scotch-and-waters.

"Judy, what did you think?" he asked her when she returned.

Johnson was accustomed to Ziegler's constant need for feedback. Part of her job was to circulate in the press room and report back on the reactions of key reporters. She hadn't had time today, so she offered her own opinion. "You were very serious," she told Ziegler, who had done little more than introduce St. Clair.

"Was I too serious?" Ziegler asked. "Did I look depressed?"

"No," she said, "just very serious."

As she turned to leave, St. Clair asked, "What do you think the reaction will be?"

"Public or press?"

"Both."

"Relieved."

St. Clair snapped alert. "What do you mean? Do you think they really felt that the President of the United States would not abide by a Supreme Court ruling?"

Johnson looked him in the eyes. "They may not have thought it, but it was a relief to hear someone say it."

THE FRAGILE coalition of House Judiciary Committee members met again in Railsback's office that morning to search for the right language for an article of impeachment charging the President in the Watergate cover-up. The charge—Article One—would have to show exactly what Nixon had done to warrant impeachment. If direct actions could not be shown, it would note simply that the President had "condoned" or "acquiesced" in the activities of others. Mann and Flowers explained that Rodino and the pro-impeachment Democrats were willing to accept a version drafted by the coalition. The coalition was intent on making a conservative charge. Whenever one of them made a suggestion for moderation, the others agreed quickly. Railsback was thinking how uncertain of themselves they were; their commitments to impeachment were shaky.

At 7:45 that night Rodino called the Judiciary Committee to order in Room 2141 of the Rayburn House Office Building. All thirty-eight members were present. Millions of people watched on television.

"Before I begin," Rodino said, "I hope you will allow me a personal reference. Throughout all of the painstaking proceedings of this committee, I as chairman have been guided by a simple principle, the principle that the law must deal fairly with every man . . . It is now almost fifteen centuries since the Emperor Justinian, from whose name the word 'justice' is derived, established this principle for the free citizens of Rome."

While writing this out, Rodino had thought back to the time he had received a personal note from President Nixon. It was in the fall of 1973, after Rodino had received an award from the Justinian Society. A messenger had brought an envelope from the White House: a note of congratulations signed with the President's personal "RN." That was a few days before the Saturday Night Massacre.

Railsback had spent almost the whole day working on the draft of Article One and had devoted little time to preparing an opening statement. He had only a few notes. With the television cameras focused on him, he appeared nervous and agitated, and at times out of breath, as he expressed his concerns and uncertainties. "Let me say that I am one of those that have agonized over this particular inquiry . . . Richard Nixon, who has twice been in my district campaigning for me, that I regard as a friend, that only treated me kindly whenever I had occasion to be with him."

He narrated the sequence of events, getting most of the dates right and some of them wrong: the attempt to contain Watergate, the payment of hush money, the lying, the withholding of evidence, the misuse of the FBI and the CIA, the turning over of grand-jury testimony to Haldeman. "I just can't help but wonder, you know, when you put all of this together in that kind of perspective—I am concerned, and I am seriously concerned. I hope the President—I wish the President could do something to absolve himself. I wish he would come forward with the information that we have sub-poenaed. I just am very, very concerned."

Thursday, July 25

THE following afternoon, the President boarded his helicopter for the flight to the FBI helipad in downtown Los Angeles. He was to deliver Price's speech on the economy before a business group. The address would be televised, and the White House was billing it as a major presidential message. Haig and Ziegler hoped the speech would get both the President's and the country's minds off Watergate, at least briefly, but no one had high expectations. Gergen had sent Haig a memo arguing against making it. "A thirty-minute speech in this atmosphere and with the present content of the speech has precious little chance of success," he had written. Gergen thought the speech was laughably simplistic and would bring ridicule upon the White House. But Nixon was determined to go through with it.

As the presidential party passed the demonstrators in front of the Century Plaza Hotel, Steve Bull thought they looked like the same people who had gathered during the 1972 campaign. Their banners were different, though: the signs had shifted from the war to a simpler theme—Nixon.

The President was escorted to a suite on the nineteenth floor. Although he had shaved an hour before, his beard gave his face the same grayish cast that had caused him trouble during the televised debates with John Kennedy in 1960. Nixon sent a military aide for an electric razor, and a hotel steward produced one. The President shaved hastily. When he entered the Los Angeles Room, where seventeen hundred business leaders were waiting, he appeared nervous.

282

Price had written a classic Nixon speech. It opened with a series of assumptions about the causes of inflation: the decline in grain production, the oil embargo by the Middle East countries, an economic boom in the industrialized countries. It dismissed unpalatable solutions: swift spectacular actions such as wage and price controls, higher taxes, lower taxes. There followed another catalogue of accepted wisdoms, which the President also rejected. Then, finally, a solution: the President asked each American to cut his consumption by one and a half percent and save the difference.

As Gergen had feared, the speech was greeted with almost universal scorn. If everybody saved one and a half percent of his income the recession would deepen, if not lead to depression, most economists seemed to feel. One editorial called the President's approach "Biting the Cotton Bullet."

In Washington, the House Judiciary Committee opened another ten hours of televised debate on the impeachment charges. Each of the thirty-eight members was allotted fifteen minutes.

The third member to speak was Caldwell Butler of Virginia. He had stayed up the night before until about 3 A.M., working on his statement at his dining-room table. It had been typed in his office that morning, but he had refused to release it to the press, afraid that he might have a change of heart. He began to speak quietly about Nixon. "I have worked with him in every national campaign in which he has taken part . . . And I am deeply grateful for the many kindnesses and courtesies he has shown me over the years. I am not unmindful of the loyalty I owe him."

He continued for a few minutes without revealing his position. Then he said, "There are frightening implications for the future of our country if we do not impeach the President of the United States . . . If we fail to impeach, we have condoned and left unpunished a course of conduct totally inconsistent with reasonable expectations of the American people.

"The people of the United States are entitled to assume that their President is telling the truth. The pattern of misrepresentation and half-truths that emerges from our investigation reveals a presidential policy cynically based on the premise that the truth itself is negotiable.

"It is a sad chapter in American history, but I cannot condone what I have heard; I cannot excuse it, and I cannot and will not stand still for it."

He would vote to impeach for obstruction of justice and misuse of power, "but there will be no joy in it for me."

FRIDAY, JULY 26

WHEN St. Clair got back to Washington on Friday morning, he had little to be optimistic about. Just before leaving San Clemente, he had argued with the President again, trying to make clear that Judge Sirica wouldn't tolerate abrasive maneuvers that seemed simply to play for time. Nixon had become abusive: he wasn't going to be pushed around by the courts or by his lawyers. St. Clair had sought solace from Haig, who listened sympathetically; but the instructions held: Get more time.

Riding with McCahill to the courthouse, St. Clair told his assistant that the President was intent on not turning over any tapes until he had reviewed them personally. The President was willing to tell Sirica to shove it, St. Clair said—unanimous ruling and promised compliance notwithstanding.

McCahill expressed some wonder that the President thought he could impose conditions on a case that he had lost unanimously. It did not seem to be an option that they possessed.

St. Clair gazed nervously out the car window. McCahill had never seen him so distant, distraught and edgy.

"We lost the case," McCahill continued. It seemed obvious. "Let's comply."

That was for the President to decide, St. Clair said. He himself was caught between the President and the court. Somehow, he aspired to accommodate both. "If Sirica pushes him too hard, the client may not turn over anything." They were on the thin edge.

At the courthouse, St. Clair got out and slid into what his assistants dubbed "the St. Clair shuffle." Normally he walked at a brisk pace, but when there were cameras, microphones and reporters around he slowed to wedding-march time. His aides had tripped on his heels until they had caught the rhythm.

As St. Clair made his way toward the entrance, ABC newsman Sam Donaldson mentioned to him that he was scheduled to appear on the *Issues and Answers* program on Sunday.

St. Clair, maintaining a smile, replied curtly, "No way."

Uncertain that he had heard correctly, Donaldson asked him whether he intended to appear on Sunday.

"No way."

Larry Speakes, St. Clair's press aide, was confused. St. Clair had agreed to appear. Didn't he intend to appear? he asked.

"No way," St. Clair repeated.

St. Clair glided past the cameras and into the courthouse. His smile faded as he entered the chamber. He didn't indulge in his customary banter with the press or the attorneys from the special prosecutor's office. He had an unpleasant task to perform, and he wanted to get it over as rapidly as possible.

He explained to Judge Sirica that the Secret Service had begun making copies of all the tapes the previous morning. He assured the judge that the original reels as well as copies of the subpoenaed conversations would be furnished. However, he would *not* be able to promise all tapes in "x number of hours."

McCahill cringed at the negative.

The White House lawyers would have to sift through the material and index each claim of executive privilege, St. Clair said. More important, the President wanted to listen to the tapes he had not previously heard. "The President feels quite strongly that he . . . should know what it is he has turned over to the court."

Sirica pointed out that his original order of May 20 had called for the sixty-four taped conversations to be produced, along with the White House index, in eleven days. St. Clair had appealed the order; the Supreme Court had found against him. Had not the Supreme Court upheld his order "in all respects"? Sirica inquired of St. Clair.

Forcing a smile, St. Clair agreed that the Court had upheld Sirica by a vote of "eight to zero."

Sirica replied that he wanted the tapes as soon as possible. He instructed

St. Clair and Jaworski to go into an adjacent jury room and reach an agreement on a timetable. If they could not, he would impose one.

St. Clair's televised remarks from San Clemente about "the time-consuming process of reviewing" had served warning to Jaworski. He was weary of empty White House promises of deliberate speed which meant weeks and months of stalling, and he had the court on his side. He told St. Clair he wanted something immediately. Surely the twenty conversations that had already been released in edited form had been fully reviewed. Why could they not be produced at once? Next Jaworski wanted the tapes which the President had listened to in May. He counted. Of those sixteen conversations, thirteen were under subpoena. They would come next. Thirty-one conversations would remain to be delivered.

St. Clair pointed out that, as always, there was very little certainty about the tapes. Nothing was known about those thirty-one conversations. Some might not have been recorded. Gaps might have occurred as tapes were changed. A conversation might have taken place on a phone that was not tied into the automatic recording system.

Jaworski responded that they could deal with the uncertainties later. He wanted the first batch by Monday.

"I have no authorization to promise you'll get tapes by Monday," St. Clair said flatly.

Gradually they reached an agreement, with the stipulation that the President himself must approve it. St. Clair had no power to bind him. In the courtroom, St. Clair told Sirica that the first twenty tapes would be produced by 4 P.M. the next Tuesday. St. Clair would deliver within a week the conversations that the President had listened to in May. The rest would be delivered as they were prepared, even if that meant one or two at a time.

Uncomfortably, St. Clair repeated that nothing could be final until it was approved by the President; he himself had no authority.

Sirica reminded him that he would do everything in his power to prevent any delay of the Watergate cover-up trial. He reserved the right to prod the White House if this agreement failed to produce the tapes. Staring directly at St. Clair, the judge insisted that the lawyer himself listen to the tapes.

St. Clair was taken aback. The Judge couldn't be serious, he didn't understand the problem, surely he knew what a task he was imposing—it would take weeks. But he realized that Sirica was making him personally responsible for getting what the court was supposed to get. Sirica's implication was clear: For months the lawyers had assiduously avoided listening to tapes that the President didn't want them to hear. No longer.

St. Clair was concerned about becoming a potential witness if any material was not complete or if it had been tampered with. He knew from Buzhardt that at least one tape contained devastating information which had been withheld from a legally constituted authority. He stood facing the judge, playing with his fingers, his eyes set at a middle distance, and tried to beg off, calling himself "a poor listener."

Sirica insisted.

St. Clair reluctantly agreed. He was deeply disturbed by Sirica's order. Once again he had been humiliated.

"All right, now I think we're getting somewhere," Sirica said at last.

SOON AFTER St. Clair returned to his office at the White House, Buzhardt came in. St. Clair complained to him about the way both the President and Judge Sirica had treated him. Buzhardt was more interested in getting a second opinion on the June 23 tape. He expected St. Clair to listen immediately. It was, after all, the most devastating piece of evidence against his client to date.

St. Clair refused. He would not listen now.

Buzhardt was incredulous.

St. Clair, chafing from the events of the last several days, said that he was tired and that he was planning to catch an early-afternoon plane back to Boston. He had an important engagement.

Buzhardt said all right, but there was no way he was going to work alone over the weekend to prepare the first batch of tapes.

Okay, St. Clair said, and he departed.

St. Clair had not only abandoned the tape problem, he had left McCahill and his other assistants to contend with the House Judiciary Committee hearings and the expected vote the next day. His engagement was a golf date—the member-guest tournament at the Eastward Ho Country Club on Cape Cod.

DAVE GERGEN, anticipating that the Judiciary Committee would approve at least one article of impeachment and that a lengthy and damaging debate on the House floor would follow, addressed an "eyes only" memo, "The Option Two Arguments," to Dean Burch, who was heading the White House strategy committee. Gergen suggested that the President preempt debate with a dramatic speech in which he would request an immediate pro-forma vote in the House for impeachment.

It should improve RN's chances of survival and would ultimately be better for the country and the Republican party. Here's why: 1. The pro-impeachment vote is snowballing and there appears to be no stopping it. . . . Lying ahead are more indictments, more tape disclosures, the Watergate trial, bad economic news and uncertainties abroad. In short, there is very little good news in prospect.

Gergen guessed there would be a two-to-one or even a three-to-one margin in the House, and consequent disaster in the Senate. A move by the President to encourage a Senate trial would give him the psychological advantage of having brought himself to judgment rather than having been dragged to it by a runaway House. A Senate trial would be conducted on firm rules of evidence. It would give the White House its best chance to present a case and to attack the relevancy of wide-ranging, vaguely worded accusations of undocumented presidential abuses. "RN needs a ten-strike with the public now," Gergen wrote. "He needs to get back on top of this issue, and only a dramatic move can do it."

Gergen's memo found a receptive audience in the White House. The senior staff, isolated except for occasional phone calls with Haig and Ziegler in San Clemente, was demoralized; they had lost confidence in their ability to serve. Burch's strategy group convened.

Timmons had watched forlornly as the President's support in the House Judiciary Committee eroded. He was revising his optimistic projections on impeachment. The pro-impeachment Republicans were persuasive. Their anger and indignation in a nationally televised floor debate could demolish what was left of the President's support. Timmons urged serious consideration of option two: concede the House and go to the Senate.

Pat Buchanan was opposed. Like Nixon, he thought that most members of Congress were eunuchs. If the President had to go down in the House, he should take some Congressmen with him. "We should hold those mothers' feet to the fire," he said. To take the pressure off the House would only add to the momentum in the Senate. "We've been too nice to those guys, and what has it ever gotten us?"

It was Burch who cut through the fog. To debate options was absurd. They didn't have any options until they knew what was in the tapes that were going to Sirica. Selected portions were bound to dribble out, during either a House debate or a Senate trial. How could they defend the President on the Hill when they were themselves ignorant of the evidence that was about to be offered the court?

Timmons was of the same mind. There was no escape from the President's long, confused and poorly explained obsession to keep the tapes to himself. It was folly to think that, with Nixon's credibility in tatters, they could muster another round of support. Members of both houses would demand proof that there were no more bombshells.

This was not the first time they had discussed the problem. They were approaching the President on his most sensitive side, no one needed to be reminded of that. He had refused adamantly to give anybody on his staff except Buzhardt access to the tapes. Even Buzhardt, usually overly optimistic, was troubled. The President wasn't going to give them unlimited access. Still, they had to know *something* more if they were going to mount any kind of defense. They had to have a representative to listen to the tapes.

It would have to be a political realist. All agreed on Buchanan. He knew the charges, the defense, the testimony, and he had been around long enough to be familiar with the personalities and the code words. More importantly, the President trusted him more than any of the others. Pat Buchanan was hard-nosed, he wouldn't hedge.

Saturday, July 27

BUZHARDT was convinced that the June 23 tape completely undermined the President's position, but he couldn't get any support. Haig wasn't sure. The President disagreed categorically. And St. Clair had not only refused to listen but had remarked blandly that he was confident he had sufficient evidence to refute any allegation that the President had obstructed justice or abused his authority in the single act of sending Haldeman to talk to the CIA.

On Saturday morning, Buzhardt asked Buchanan down to his EOB office. Haig had instructed him to feel out Buchanan on the June 23 tape without precisely telling him what was in it.

When Buchanan arrived, Buzhardt hedged. What would happen if there was a serious problem about the contents of one of the tapes? "Al told me to ask you," Buzhardt said.

Buchanan wanted to know what he meant.

"Well, what would you say if there was something that showed the President knew of the cover-up earlier than he said?"

"Is it an early tape or a late tape?" Buchanan asked. Before Buzhardt could answer, Buchanan finished the thought. "If it's something ambiguous, we can handle it. If it's in March, well, it means he was wrong by a week or so. But if it's in June or July of '72, then that's the smoking gun."

Buchanan pressed for more information, but Buzhardt would say only, "It's pretty serious."

IN SAN Clemente, the President began a typical working day with briefings from Haig and Ziegler. Later he and his chief domestic adviser, Ken Cole, met with Housing and Urban Development Secretary James T. Lynn. The Secretary, with Cole's support, was seeking agreement to back a House version of a revenue-sharing housing bill over the Senate version; the House version would cost $1.2 billion less.

Lynn and Cole had been scheduled to meet with the President the day of the Supreme Court decision, but they had been put off for three days. They were rested and tanned. Cole had found time for some golf and tennis.

They thought the President looked tired as they began to present their arguments. Nixon was familiar with the material; he had already read Cole's briefing paper. In fact, the whole enterprise was canned—it was a ritual, the decision had already been made. Both the President and Cole knew it. It was the way Nixon did business. Lynn didn't know he was part of a prepared script.

The President gave his approval and changed the subject to the 1975 State of the Union Message, scheduled for the following January. During the discussion that followed, there was a reference to certain drafts of suggestions which were due in the fall. Nixon smiled faintly and started to say something, but then he halted abruptly; his eyes glazed over. He glanced away; the smile flickered. The President seemed to find something irrepressibly amusing about the future.

For the first time, Cole thought the President might not finish his term.

Lynn tried for a note of cheer. "You've got a lot of people out there who support you strongly."

"Do you really think there are?" the President inquired.

"Yes, sir," Lynn said forcefully.

The President waited for more words of encouragement, but Bull came back in to tell him that he was due at a presentation of a Medal of Freedom. Through the office window, they could see the press gathered outside.

The President stood up and said, "Well, keep up the good work, boys."

Bull handed the President the briefing folder. "What's this fellow's name?" the President asked.

Bull began to sum up routinely as the President thumbed through the folder. "This is going to be Dr. Charles L. Lowman. There is a discrepancy as to his age, either ninety-three or ninety-four. You speak first, and Brennan gives you the medal for him. Just put it around his neck. He responds with a few remarks."

The President had some trouble with the name, repeating it several times to Bull and stumbling each time. Bull was accustomed to helping the Presi-

dent with names. He stood patiently by until he was sure the President had
it right. The President often confused the names of close aides and even
Cabinet members. He had once addressed Secretary of Agriculture Butz as
Wally instead of Earl.* At first he had some trouble remembering his son-
in-law Ed Cox's name. The President's personal aides used to refer to Cox
as "the New Boy."

Bull remembered an occasion when the President was working a large
crowd at an airport. A little girl had waved to him vigorously, shouting,
"How is Smokey the Bear?" (Smokey resided at the Washington Zoo.) The
President smiled at her and turned away, but she kept on waving and in-
quiring. Unable to make out what she was saying Nixon turned to Bull, who
whispered, "Smokey the Bear, Washington National Zoo." The President
walked over, took her hand and said, "How do you do, Miss Bear?"

The President asked Bull to invite Dr. and Mrs. Lowman into his office
for the customary warm-up. The ceremony on the lawn just behind his office
went smoothly, although several reporters thought the President was ill at
ease and stumbled over his words more than usual.

Ollie Atkins, who was photographing the ceremony, had just snapped
pictures of the same medal being presented to another recipient. Bull and
Brennan had gone behind the low office building, and Atkins had taken a
picture of Brennan, convulsed in laughter, watching Bull present the medal
to the President's Irish setter, King Timahoe.

AFTER LUNCH the President took Tricia and Ed Cox to secluded Red Beach
for the afternoon. He was limping slightly, but seemed oblivious to the
debacle that was building in Washington.

The press office was another matter. Ziegler didn't trust the news reporting, so he had directed his secretaries to monitor the Judiciary Committee
proceedings and report to him every fifteen minutes. On that Saturday, as
the committee moved to its first formal vote, he insisted that his most
trusted aide, Diane Sawyer, do the job.

On television all that afternoon, a number of the members, reading aloud,
supplied the carefully prepared "specifics" that Nixon's staunchest defenders
on the committee had demanded, the specifics that spelled out how it had
all happened: the conversations, the game plans, the details of the cover-up.

At last Republican Congressman Charles W. Sandman, Jr., of New
Jersey, whose voice had been the loudest in calling for "specificity," wanted
it called to a halt. "Please, let us not bore the American public with a re-

---

* Wally Butts had been head football coach at the University of Georgia.

hashing of what we have heard. You've got twenty-seven votes. Let's go on with our business."

But it was too late, and the recitation—intended for the television audience—droned on. It was almost seven in the evening when Rodino called for the vote on Article One. As the camera moved from one member to the next, down the order from senior to junior, each face was an emotionless mask.

Sandman had counted accurately. The impeachment forces had exactly twenty-seven votes.

In San Clemente, Sawyer cried out, "The poor President, oh, the poor man," and ran to tell Ziegler. Ziegler was shaken, and he didn't even know exactly where the President was. The switchboard reached Manolo Sanchez at a trailer at Red Beach. Ziegler had not intended to talk to the President; he was just checking on his whereabouts. But before he could explain, Nixon was on the line, and Ziegler blurted out the news.

The President reacted calmly. He would stay at the beach a while longer and then come back to the office.

Caldwell Butler, dictating his taped diary later, said of the vote:

> I was never more moved by any experience that I've had. I'm quite sure that if I hadn't been in public view I would have cried or shed a few tears . . . There were no loud voices, no loud votes—no way to cast your vote quietly in an atmosphere as quiet as that. I cast my vote. There just wasn't any way to describe how I felt at the time except just a complete abdication of any kind of—a complete drain or abdication, I guess, is as good a word as any—of desire to do anything except just get out of there.
> . . . I knew the implications of it for the country and [had] this absolute feeling of sadness about the whole thing, that we've come to this but— And that's about it—just a total feeling of sadness for the country. And with all due respect to those who think that there were those of our colleagues that were happy with it, I don't think so.

After the vote, Rodino went back to the committee offices, and Ken Harding, the sergeant at arms, told him he had received a call saying that a kamikaze pilot had just left National Airport and was heading for the committee room. A few staffers looked out the window. John Doar sat on a couch, Francis O'Brien across from him in a chair. Rodino, his arms folded, leaned on a desk as they discussed drafting the report which would be given to the House.

The talk stopped. Rodino's body started to shake. Then his small hands clutched his arms, and tears streamed down his face. Weeping quietly, he left the room, went to a washroom and then to the counsel's office, where he called his wife at home.

"I pray that we did the right thing," he said to her. "I hoped it didn't have to be this way."

Sunday, July 28

I N the morning, Haig put on the best face he could. The newspapers were saying that the White House had no strategy to resist impeachment. One story said the President's top aides had given up. Haig had to counter that impression. Both the general and the President shared the opinion that Haig could speak for the Administration with greater force and credibility than anyone else.

While the rest of the presidential entourage made preparations for the trip back to Washington, Haig went up to Los Angeles to be interviewed for CBS television by Mike Wallace. They had already taped an interview to be shown on that evening's installment of Wallace's popular show *60 Minutes.* But Wallace wanted new material, and he moved right to the point: "General, it's been a devastating week for the President: a unanimous Supreme Court decision against him, and then, last night, a vote in the House Judiciary Committee—impeachment against him. How is the man bearing up?"

Haig's answer was striking. "The man's own—own inner strength, his own perception of his vulnerabilities and his guilt or lack of guilt, has sustained him during these difficult periods, and will continue in the weeks ahead." Haig did not stop to elaborate. The idea was to make the President's eleven votes look like a victory. The Judiciary Committee was packed with liberals and predisposed to move against the President, he said. Back in February, the White House had expected to hold only three or four of the seventeen Republicans on the committee.

"Wait a minute," Wallace said.

Haig insisted. Yes, there had been discussions then in which the resident political experts concluded that only three or four could be held. "We're quite confident that the vote will come out the other way in the full House."

Wallace resisted: "General Haig, White House estimates on Watergate have been consistently wrong through the last couple of years. Why should anyone believe that you're not just whistling past the graveyard again?"

"Well, this is serious business, Mike."

"And you're stonewalling it," Wallace answered. "I can't say I blame you for doing it . . . And one wonders what the strategy of the White House is, if indeed there is any strategy, to keep it from happening. You've got to do more than take Southern Congressmen out on the *Sequoia* on the Potomac at night to stroke them."

Haig attacked the committee's investigation. "With a great array of talent aligned, with the full-time preoccupation and, indeed, the objective of finding some semblance of wrongdoing, of course they have succeeded! How could it be otherwise? I've been here for over twelve months now with the President—I didn't come in at a happy time . . . There were those that told me, 'Don't do it! If you want the helm of the *Titanic,* have at it!' I don't find that. I do know there are men down in the woodwork of any staff or any organization that, when the going gets tough, are looking for reasons. They can't understand why difficult things occur and why everything isn't one round of merry successes.

"Of course we have a strategy," he went on. "That strategy is to have those bodies that are dealing with it deal with the facts in the evidence, and to hopefully avoid the emotionalism, the kinds of groundswell of opinion that foreclose and prejudge issues. We feel—with the hard litmus test and evidence at hand—that the case for impeachment is not there."

"Is it not possible," Wallace asked, "that the President, to save the country the trauma of a Senate trial, might resign?"

Haig chose his words carefully. He left the door open. The criterion would be "the best interest to the American people. That will be the criterion on which Richard Nixon rules, governs, if you will, continues in office or might decide not to."

HAIG RETURNED to San Clemente to supervise the move back to Washington. It was more complicated than usual, since more than the customary complement of aides had made the trip. Many lingered in their farewells to members of the housekeeping staff. Mrs. Nixon seemed even more withdrawn than usual, pale and unsmiling as she boarded the plane.

Air Force One departed El Toro Air Base for Washington at 2:26 P.M. The mood on board was somber. Haig and Ziegler were forward in the President's cabin. Both went back to speak with the reporters in the press section, emphasizing the line they had adopted since the Judiciary Committee vote. There had been reverses, a "triple whammy," Haig conceded, but they had not given up on the vote in the full House. The President, Ziegler maintained, was disappointed with recent developments, but not discouraged. Haig did not foresee resignation. How could he rule out the possibility? reporters pressed. The President always "decided these things in the best interests of the American people," Haig said.

By the time the President arrived at Andrews Air Force Base, congressional reaction to the House Judiciary Committee vote had hardened. Few Congressmen seemed to agree with Haig and Ziegler about Nixon's chances. Even Rhodes appeared prepared to concede, saying publicly that a full-scale televised defense on the House floor of the President's conduct in office was the "only viable possibility" for the President to avoid impeachment.

The President called Julie just after he arrived at the White House. He had spoken with her almost every day for months. "Chins up," he said. He sounded strong, refreshed and optimistic as he tried to reassure her. "Keep your spirits up," he told his daughter.

Julie's optimism, however, had ebbed. St. Clair had told her two days before the Supreme Court ruling that the President had a good chance to win. On several occasions she had told her father she thought his lawyers were inept, and St. Clair's mistaken estimate only served to reinforce her opinion. David had never shared her optimism. When he had heard the Court's decision, he had remarked matter-of-factly to his friend Brooks Harrington, "What else could it be?" By the time of the first House Judiciary vote, Julie too was becoming fatalistic. She didn't watch it on television, and when David told her the outcome she did not seem surprised.

Late Sunday evening, the President returned to his bedroom. The room, furnished simply but elegantly with antiques, was exactly as he had left it. A pair of blue-and-white striped pajamas hung on the inside of the door to the bathroom. His tobacco and pipe were on the small writing desk. Six books, either history or biography, were on the nightstand next to the four-poster bed. One was about Churchill. Another was David Halberstam's *The Best and the Brightest,* an account of the intellectuals around Kennedy and Johnson who had led the country into the Vietnam War.

MONDAY, JULY 29

DAVID Gergen had just settled behind the desk in his corner office in the EOB when the phone rang.

"The general wants to see you," Haig's secretary said crisply.

Gergen always moved quickly when Haig called. Besides, he was relieved to have the President and his senior aides back in Washington; when they were in California, Gergen felt even more than usually cut off from the center. As he crossed West Executive Avenue he wondered why Haig wanted him. Perhaps the President would be going on television to defend himself. A speech? A statement? A strategy meeting? More bad news?

As he entered the general's green office, Gergen saw that Haig was angry. The chief of staff was standing alone by his big table, drumming his fingers on a copy of Sunday's *Washington Post,* and he did not look up. Finally Haig shoved the paper aside. He ordered Gergen to sit down and directed his attention to two stories on the *Post's* front page. One, datelined San Clemente, stated without qualification that the President's closest aides (presumably including Haig) were telling each other that Nixon could not survive in office. The other story, from Washington, pictured a presidential staff in disarray and a President who was removed from reality and from the momentum of impeachment. Nixon's aides, the story reported, were acknowledging privately that they had failed to develop a strategy to prevent the President's removal. The sources cited were White House staff members who handled congressional liaison, public relations and speech writing for the administration.

Haig was furious. The stories contradicted the theme he and Ziegler had been carefully emphasizing since the Judiciary vote: yes, there had been certain reverses, but they were confident that the President would prevail.

The general wanted to know where the stories were coming from. This wasn't a plumbing operation to find leakers, but he had to know who these people were. The last act of the Watergate drama was about to unfold, and members of the President's staff who made negative comments to reporters would not help resolve it. As the chief of staff, he could not and would not tolerate such conduct. The problems had to be worked out logically and responsibly—in fairness both to the President and to the country.

Haig didn't accuse Gergen directly, though he knew Ziegler thought Gergen was a chronic leaker. He wanted to know if there were any "weak sisters" on Gergen's speech-writing staff who should be gotten rid of. Who were the ones who couldn't stick it out? They should leave now.

"I'm probably the weakest of all," Gergen replied. Weeks, months, almost two years of frustration now showed. Yes, he had talked to reporters. Gergen picked up the paper and scanned the Washington story. "Here I am; this is me." He pointed to two paragraphs:

> In what appears to be a minority view on the White House staff, one presidential aide said Friday that "it is tempting to overstate the problem because the best time to respond and develop a strategy is after the House Judiciary Committee votes."
>
> But the same aide expressed the opinion that the White House had handled Watergate poorly for two years, and he voiced some doubt about the ability to devise a coherent plan at this late date.

Gergen put the paper down and looked at Haig. Things were bad, Gergen said. There wasn't any coordination and, yes, it was true, he was not optimistic about the chances of organizing successfully to defend the President at this late date.

The general reminded him that the *Washington Post* was not the proper forum in which to voice his frustrations. Haig doubted the ability of the liberal press to handle such information fairly, to refrain from sensationalizing it. There was a question of loyalty, even of patriotism, he said sternly, and that applied to each member of the staff.

Gergen said that he understood, but that he felt foolish trying to keep up an optimistic façade. He had been doing it for months; he had told acquaintances in the press over and over that the President had turned the corner on Watergate. He had compromised himself.

"What do you think about me?" Haig shot back. He was the one out on the front line, sticking his neck out. His own doubts ran deep, very deep. "He's guilty as hell," Haig said.

Gergen was startled. Haig was the ultimate loyalist.

The chief of staff drew a deep breath. He still had to keep the ship together, he said. Again, it was a question of loyalty and patriotism. He had made his decision and he would see it through. Everyone on the White House staff should do the same or they should get out.

There was nothing more to be said. Gergen got up to leave, thinking that for once Haig had leveled with him. His respect for Haig had risen considerably. As Gergen walked out of the office, he saw Clawson waiting— the next in line to be questioned on the subject of leaking.

TIMMONS AND Burch also came in to see Haig, but not about leakers. They wanted Haig to know how dire the situation was—not just in Congress but in the White House as well. There was danger of disintegration at both ends of Pennsylvania Avenue, they warned him.

Before the President had left for San Clemente, Timmons had found cause to believe that things were looking up. The shock of the transcripts seemed to have worn off a bit, and the President's foreign trips had helped to divert attention from Watergate. But then Ehrlichman had been convicted and the Supreme Court decision had come down. The House Judiciary Committee had gone on television, and the crazies, as Timmons called the President's chief critics on the committee, hadn't acted crazy. In fact, Timmons thought, the televised hearings had been a public-relations bonanza for the President's opponents, convincing the public that the committee was in no way a kangaroo court.

While the President, Haig and Ziegler vacationed in San Clemente, the strategy group, without direction from the top, had been stalled. Some of its members were bitter about being left alone to spin their wheels while their chiefs ruminated among themselves in California.

Timmons and Burch told Haig what they would require if they were to continue a rearguard action in the House to hold down the vote for impeachment. First, they must have a quick damage assessment of what was on the tapes. The rest of the political staff, especially those in Timmons' congressional-liaison office, were gun-shy, and they were not going to risk their own reputations further unless they had some idea of what the evidence was. They felt compromised. Second, Timmons and Burch wanted a personal commitment from the President that he would be front and center in his own defense—that he too would make a personal effort, maybe get on the phone and do some lobbying.

Haig respected both men. He did not dispute their political judgment. He understood their reluctance to lobby for the President in the dark, but he could not assure them that their requests would be met. He would talk with the President and let them know.

THIS MORNING, Ron Ziegler was closeted in his office with one of the suspected leakers whom Haig had personally ordered wiretapped in the first Nixon administration, William Safire, a former Nixon speech writer who had left the White House to become a columnist for the *New York Times*. Safire discerned in Ziegler a mood of "edgy confidence and frustration," as he described it later.

They were interrupted by a phone call. After a few seconds, Ziegler, listening, closed his eyes. John B. Connally, Nixon's first choice to succeed Spiro Agnew as Vice-President, had just been indicted for allegedly accepting $10,000 in illegal payments and for conspiracy and perjury in connection with the rise in milk supports.

Ziegler hung up the phone. Turning back to Safire, he asked helplessly, "Do people know what's going on in this country?"

Ziegler was sure the indictment had been timed to arrive as the Judiciary Committee completed its deliberations on impeachment.* It was an outrage, he said.

Outside Ziegler's doorway, the news was received in the press office with disbelief, anger and gallows humor. "Ten thousand dollars is like one dollar to John Connally!" Sawyer observed. She shook her head. It was inconceivable that Connally, with his millions, would take $10,000.

"It's too bad Nixon didn't choose Connally for Vice-President," another staffer said. "Then we could have a clean sweep."

The indictment was but one more trial for Jerry Warren. At the daily briefing he was battered with questions about the President's future. There would be no resignation, he insisted, even if the full House were to vote to impeach. Besides, the President was confident that the House would not impeach. "There is no focus of attention here in the White House on . . . anything to do with the Senate; we do not feel that it will go to the Senate."

---

* In fact the timing was the result of an agreement between the special prosecutor and Connally's attorney. Jaworski consented to hold off the indictment until the first court day after Connally's son was married. The wedding had taken place on Saturday, July 27. Connally was later acquitted of the charges.

BUT SENATORS Mansfield, Scott, Byrd and Griffin met quietly in the Capitol a few minutes after Warren's remarks, to begin arrangements for the first trial of a President in 106 years. The basis of their conversation was a draft resolution defining the rules and procedures. There were also the matters of tickets for the galleries, television coverage and the duties of the Senate sergeant at arms. Senator Scott's aide, Ken Davis, had been working directly with the networks and was pleased that, so far, the preparations had escaped public notice, except for a one-sentence reference in *Newsweek*.

When Scott left the meeting, he walked to his office to talk with John Rhodes. The House Minority leader was grim. The situation was deteriorating rapidly, he said. It was possible that the vote for impeachment would be upwards of 300 out of 435.

Rhodes had still not committed himself publicly. His press secretary, Jay Smith, had recently given him a thirteen-page memo that dealt with the politics of the situation. It pointed out, among other considerations, that Rhodes stood to lose his position as Minority Leader if he voted for impeachment. "You left one thing out," Rhodes had told him. "How the hell are we going to put the wheels back on the Republican Party after this is over?" In an attempt to slow the stampede, Rhodes was setting up informal "rap sessions" with GOP Congressmen over the next few days. The old idea of a pro-forma vote in the House to hurry the issue over to the Senate was gaining ground, he told Scott.

Scott and Rhodes reviewed the most recent defections; there was serious erosion among conservatives. That morning, Howard Phillips, Nixon's former director of the Office of Economic Opportunity, had announced the formation of a group called Conservatives for Removal of the President. And John M. Ashbrook, the conservative Ohio Republican Congressman who had unsuccessfully sought the party's presidential nomination in 1972, had announced that he now favored impeachment.

The Minority Leaders agreed that impeachment by the House was inevitable.

Things weren't looking good in the Senate either, Scott said. He thought there were already sixty votes against the President, only seven short of the necessary two thirds needed for conviction. That was bad at this stage, and it looked as if it would get worse, especially if the tapes contained damaging material.

As FOR the President, he was alone with his tapes again. Since 11 A.M. he had been in his EOB office, listening. Bull was in the anteroom, cueing for him. Just after five o'clock, Nixon summoned St. Clair and Buzhardt. He told them he had reviewed the first group of twenty conversations, the ones St. Clair had to turn over to Sirica tomorrow, Tuesday.

That took care of the immediate issue, but Buzhardt had another problem: June 23.

The President asked Buzhardt if he had listened to the other two conversations he had with Haldeman on that day.

"No," Buzhardt replied. He had listened only to the first conversation.

"Well, I'm going to check those," said the President.

A little before six, the direct phone from the White House in Bull's home rang. Bull had arrived home only a few moments before and was tired. Who the fuck is this? he wondered as he picked up the receiver. He waited for the operator to identify the caller, but the voice on the line was the President's. Nixon wanted Bull to come back in at about eight and set up one or two more tapes for him.

Then the President joined his wife and Julie for a cruise on the Potomac. It was one of the shorter trips of the season, an hour and fifteen minutes, and one of the most subdued. Lieutenant Commander Coombs thought Julie seemed maudlin.

The *Sequoia* docked at seven-thirty and the President returned to the White House for his rendezvous with the tape recorder. Julie joined David at their apartment. The phone rang shortly after she arrived. David answered. It was Ben Stein, suggesting that David turn on the television set because Sandman and Representative Charles Wiggins of California were putting forward a spirited defense of the President. "They're saying really good things," Stein said. "You ought to turn it on, because it may be the last time you hear anybody saying good things about the President."

"How do you think he's doing?" David asked.

"Badly."

"Very badly," David offered. He put Julie on the line and went to turn on the television.

"How are things going?" she asked.

Stein never knew what to tell her. Throughout the spring and summer their frequent conversations had followed a pattern. Stein always tried to think of something positive to say. Partly to have something else to talk about, he had given Julie a copy of Joan Didion's collection of essays, *Slouching Toward Bethlehem*. She had liked it immensely. Tonight Stein counted himself lucky: he could tell her about Sandman's and Wiggins' arguments.

But Julie wasn't very cheered. As she had done several times of late, she asked Stein if he thought the White House staff would stay in line.

"I think so," Stein answered, trying to sound confident. "How's your father?"

"Oh, he's all right," she said, not too convincingly.

Stein tried one more time to cheer her, praising her parents. "They're so strong," he said. "Like pioneers, even like Lincoln."

Julie always accepted such praise without question.

As they were talking, the House Judiciary Committee approved a second article of impeachment that charged the President with abusing his power and with repeatedly violating the constitutional rights of citizens. This time, the vote was twenty-eight to ten. Another Republican, Robert McClory of Illinois, had joined the majority.

The President listened to tapes until late into the evening. Finally he removed the oppressive headphones and rose from his captain's chair to summon Bull. His fatigue was evident on his face.

"I've heard enough," he said.

Tuesday, July 30

DESPITE his weariness, Nixon had had difficulty sleeping. It was a problem that occurred ever more frequently, and it was beginning to cause concern in the family. For years Nixon had maintained the same schedule rigidly, but all through that spring and summer his cycle had become erratic. Staff members who knew or sensed the problem, particularly Haig, Ziegler and Bull, had constantly to readjust the President's calendar to accommodate his unpredictable hours.

This morning he had an eleven o'clock meeting with Secretary Simon, Scowcroft and Kenneth Rush, his new economic adviser—his only appointment for the day. When he had not come down by ten-thirty, Ziegler sent Judy Johnson to ask where he was. The one person who was sure to know, Sanchez, said the President was still asleep. The meeting was postponed until three. But by noon Nixon had gone to the Lincoln Sitting Room to hear more tapes. He was still listening at three.

St. Clair was due in Sirica's courtroom at four o'clock with the first twenty tapes. Although these conversations had been reviewed before the edited transcripts were released, it was taking a long time to index the first batch, as well as to prepare a list of the parts the President desired to be withheld on the grounds of national security or executive privilege. An inordinate amount of time, St. Clair thought. As the deadline approached, he lost his patience. "I haven't got all day," he shouted into the phone at Hauser. "I've got to be in court. Get that list over here."

St. Clair's pressed staff was also involved in an exhausting search for any notes that Haldeman, Colson or Ehrlichman had made during or after the conversations. The notes were also under subpoena.

St. Clair got neither the list nor the notes in time. The person most familiar with the documents, Buzhardt, was unable to help look. As unofficial personal counsel to Haig, Buzhardt had accompanied the general to a hearing of the Senate Foreign Relations Committee, where, for three hours, Haig was grilled about what he knew concerning the Administration's wiretapping activities. Buzhardt's assistance was scarcely required; Haig himself fielded and skirted the questions quite deftly.

It was after three-thirty when St. Clair and a retinue of aides left by car for the courthouse. As they approached the building, St. Clair contemplated the reporters crowding around the entrance. "Look at those vultures," he sneered.

Dan Popeo, one of St. Clair's assistants, told the driver to go around the back way. "No, no, no," St. Clair contradicted. "Go in the front way."

As the car braked at the entrance, St. Clair fashioned his broadest smile. "Okay, we'll play their game," he said, and he got out to greet the vultures.

At twelve minutes to four, the President's lawyer turned over the twenty tapes and explained uncomfortably that a search for the notes was continuing. The printed matter—notes, index and list of privileged material—would be delivered the next day, he assured the judge.

THE PRESIDENT at last kept his appointment with Simon, Rush and Scowcroft to discuss international economics and Simon's recent trip to the Middle East. He appeared to focus on the issues. To Scowcroft, it seemed like business as usual. Simon felt that he had rarely seen the President so calm and confident. After the hour-long meeting, the Treasury Secretary effusively told reporters that the President was as strong as he had ever seen him.

Nixon was still relaxed, almost cheerful, when Buzhardt entered the presidential office in the EOB early that evening.

The President asked him again if he had listened to the other two June 23 conversations.

Buzhardt had not.

Well, said the President, *he* had. And they proved his contention that the FBI had been sidetracked for legitimate reasons of national security, not for political considerations.

Buzhardt said he would listen immediately. Taking the President's copies, he headed back to his office. He threaded the magnetic tape to the second Nixon-Haldeman conversation of the day—from 1:04 to 1:13 P.M.—and adjusted the headphones.

"Okay, just postpone," he heard the President say, but he couldn't make out the rest. He heard scratching noises, as if the President were writing as he talked. The scratching stopped. "Just say," the President continued, and he added something which was unintelligible. And then, "very bad to have this fellow Hunt, ah, he knows too damn much, and he was involved—we happen to know that."

Buzhardt stopped the machine. The allusion wasn't too bad, he decided. The President knew about Hunt's involvement. That was never covered up. Buzhardt pressed the playback mechanism and heard Nixon talking in vague terms about Hunt's being "likely to blow the whole Bay of Pigs thing." The President seemed to be considering what excuse or cover story might be fed the CIA. "I don't want them to get any ideas we're doing it because our concern is political," the President said.

"Right," Haldeman answered.

"And at the same time, I wouldn't tell them it is not political. . . ."

"Right."

Was that what he had heard? Buzhardt rewound the tape and listened again. Yes.

Buzhardt let the conversation run to the end before he took off the earphones. There were, as the President had insisted, references to the CIA and national security, but it sounded as if Nixon and Haldeman were solidifying the cover they had agreed upon earlier that day. Rehearsing their lines? Buzhardt went to the next Nixon-Haldeman conversation, an EOB meeting that took place between 2:20 and 2:45 that afternoon. It was elliptical, but it also implied strongly that the CIA was being used to stop the FBI for political reasons.

Buzhardt put the headphones down and walked back to the President's office.

"Now, doesn't that clarify it?" Nixon asked as Buzhardt walked in.

"No." The two conversations made things worse.

Nixon insisted. They demonstrated that national-security purposes were real.

"The tapes don't show that," Buzhardt replied. "They make it clear that the security business was the cover story."

"I know what I meant," the President almost shouted, "and regardless of what's on the tapes, it was done for national-security reasons."

"What were they?"

The President didn't really reply.

Buzhardt repeated his conclusion.

The two men stared at each other. Finally Nixon broke the silence. "I disagree," he said emphatically, and he walked out of the room.

Buzhardt collected himself slowly. As he walked down the hall to his office, he thought about how many times he had gone home from work and told his wife, "I think the President thinks if he can convince me, everything will be okay." There was no convincing the lawyer this time.

More certain than ever that the June 23 conversations were fatal, he called St. Clair. He told him about his latest discussion with the President, and now he insisted that St. Clair listen to the tapes.

St. Clair was anxious as he came in to listen. In San Clemente, he remembered, the President had told him that the initial tape was "not that bad." Hearing the conversation now, he had trouble understanding its meaning. Among other things, he did not recognize some of the players in the scenario and really didn't know the whole history well enough. Patiently, Buzhardt identified Dahlberg and Ogarrio and explained their significance to events.

St. Clair asked to hear it again. But a second hearing failed to persuade him that the President's assessment was mistaken. The legal case was still not there. The conversation was not conclusive, St. Clair said.

Buzhardt explained that the conversation was a direct contradiction of what the President had said in his May 22 statement. That construction of events was basic to the President's defense—a "flare point," Buzhardt called it. Any significant evidence which undermined the May 22 statement was probably fatal. For two years the President had clung to a basic story, had denied that he had sought to cover up. On the surface the tape might not sound so bad, but in the context of those specific denials it undercut the President and Haig and Buzhardt.

Buzhardt reviewed the background of the May 22 statement. When it had been constructed, Haig and Buzhardt, and the President as well, were aware that it was the bottom line. It had to stand definitively. It had stood, Buzhardt said, until now. They were lawyers and they had to be practical. If the President had lied about this, what was on the other tapes?

St. Clair said he was not persuaded, though he saw a large problem.

Buzhardt's frustration was evident. Put it in another context, he suggested. The tape plainly contradicted St. Clair's own presentation to the Judiciary Committee.

Now St. Clair seemed to understand. He listened to the tape a third time and weighed it against his flat assertion to the committee that national security was the single motivation for the orders to the CIA. His own position was untenable. The tape proved that the President had lied to the nation, to his closest aides and to his own lawyers—for more than two years. Even if the tape did not prove legal guilt, it would certainly mean impeachment and conviction. St. Clair saw that now. He wanted time to think things over. He had his own options to review at this late date.

THAT EVENING Mrs. Nixon went to dinner at David and Julie's with her old friend from California, Helene Drown. David had never seen her so distant. Julie and he tried to draw her out, but she remained very quiet, distracted, uncommunicative. She didn't want to talk about the Judiciary Committee. She really didn't want to talk at all.

THE COMMITTEE was completing its task. It passed the third article of impeachment, for the President's defiance of its subpoenas. The vote was twenty-one to seventeen. Two additional articles, accusing Nixon of illegally concealing the bombing of Cambodia and of committing tax fraud, were rejected by votes of twenty-six to twelve.

The last vote having been recorded, Rodino gaveled the committee's deliberations to a close just after 11 P.M. The leaders of the House had agreed to begin floor debate in about two weeks, after completion of the committee's final report. Ziegler had watched the proceedings with Sawyer in his office. As usual, he sent Warren out to offer the official response: The White House remained confident that the full House would not vote to impeach.

In truth, the President's aides were shattered—they had lost confidence in the outcome of the House vote, in the President's innocence, in his ability to govern, and in each other.

Burch and Timmons had spent most of the day canvassing the Hill. Nixon would be lucky to get a hundred floor votes in the House, even his strongest supporters were advising. The televised impeachment hearings had been ruinous. There was much to be said for getting the matter over to the Senate as quickly as possible.

Both Burch and Timmons had been angered by Haig during the senior-staff meeting that day. The chief of staff had continued to allude to a "problem" on the tapes, but had refused to tell the men in the trenches what it was. Worse, Haig had deferred to St. Clair and ruled that Buchanan would not be permitted to listen to the tapes. Buchanan was not a lawyer and would therefore not be protected by attorney–client privilege.

Timmons, seeing the choices narrow, pushed Haig on option two. Shunting the issue over to the Senate was Nixon's best, perhaps only, chance. Timmons tried to extract a promise that the general would take the proposal to the President. At last Haig agreed.

WEDNESDAY, JULY 31

IN the morning, St. Clair met on the Hill with the Chowder and Marching Society, a group of Republican Congressmen regarded as friendly by the White House. (Congressman Nixon was a charter member when the club was formed in 1949.) St. Clair was coming to grips with the fact that the President's defense was more a political than a legal battle. It was a rough session. Chowder and Marching's members were under pressure from their constituents. They seemed to place the blame on St. Clair as much as on the President. Finally Tom Railsback came to St. Clair's defense. The lawyer, he stated, had done an excellent job on a tough case.

St. Clair left shaken. The last twenty-four hours had been brutal. At last convinced of the inevitable repercussions of the June 23 tape, he was tired and depressed and was looking for some way to get out of the case. The process of getting the President out of office had to be expedited, whether it was by resignation or by impeachment and conviction. To St. Clair, resignation was preferable. It would be quicker and more dignified. And it would save St. Clair the professional embarrassment and frustration of arguing a hopeless case in the House and then in the Senate.

He went to see Buzhardt, who welcomed St. Clair's overnight conversion. Resignation was the preferred route, Buzhardt agreed readily. Both lawyers considered taking a recommendation to the President, but decided they had better see Haig first. The chief of staff would have to agree with them if their judgment was to carry much weight with the President. Haig would be reluctant to confront Nixon, Buzhardt knew. But he thought the general was beginning to share in the sense of fatalism.

The lawyers walked over to Haig's office. The general was busy but he sent out word that he would see them shortly.

"Al," Buzhardt began when they were finally seated inside, "Jim and I want to see the President."

Haig looked serious and said nothing. The lawyers stated their position: Even if they could somehow show that the tape was insufficient evidence of obstruction of justice, its disclosure would enrage the public and Congress. The tape demonstrated that the President had lied for two years about his participation in the cover-up. Legally, the tape might not be any worse than the March 21 conversation; politically, the President didn't stand a chance once it was released.

"Al," Buzhardt said, "it's going to kill him."

Haig did not dispute their assessment. Somewhat nervously, the attorneys explained their obligations as lawyers. They had to set the record straight. Buzhardt paraphrased the canon of ethics and repeated the point he had made a week before: If a lawyer found that a client had withheld evidence, he was obliged to disclose the evidence or get the client to change his plea. In this case, resignation would constitute a change of plea.

Haig seemed not to disagree. The question was no longer if but how the President would leave office, he admitted finally. Haig leaned toward resignation. Yesterday, he confided, the President had seemed on the verge of deciding to resign. But today Nixon had changed his mind and had told Haig he was determined to fight to the finish.

Haig was fairly certain the impeachment process should not run its course, but he was not at all clear about the best way to proceed.

Haig and Buzhardt had discussed the problem before. The general had expressed grave doubt that it was his and Buzhardt's job to force a President to resign. He had even questioned the propriety of recommending resignation. That too would be a form of pressure. There were constitutional considerations as well as moral ones, and there were dangers. He and the lawyers had access to the President, they really had undue influence over him. They were only staff men, after all. Nobody had elected them. The President was elected by the people. Suppose an ex-President were to accuse his aides and their congressional allies of forcing him out of office? Were they brushing perilously close to *coup d'état?*

There was also the question of whether they could make such a recommendation effectively. The President was not even likely to listen. They would not intimidate the President by threatening to resign. They had promised him that long ago, to assure him that he could trust them with the truth—that no matter how bad it was, they wouldn't run out on him.

The President had not been truthful with them, of course, but Haig was certain that the President felt he had been honest. Richard Nixon was in touch only with his private reality, Haig was sure. To attempt to compete with his private view of reality was an impossibility.

Haig now put forth the notion that Nixon must make the decision. It must be perceived that way—by the President, by the country, by the historians. "It has to be a willing act on his own part," Haig insisted. "We can't force him." If asked their opinion, the President's advisers might, at the right psychological moment, be able to recommend resignation as an attractive choice, but never must they be on record as telling Nixon that he lacked other alternatives. It was, admittedly, a subtle distinction.

Meanwhile, events had to be slowed somehow, preparations had to be made, others had to be brought into the picture. Particularly Price and Buchanan. They would write whatever had to be written for the President, and there was no question that some important writing was going to be required eventually. Also, Price and Buchanan were excellent sounding boards. The President trusted them. Haig trusted them.

If there was going to be no hard recommendation that the President resign, there would still have to be some conditioning. Someone would have to get through to Nixon, help him see the realities, let him know just how bad the tape made things.

"Al, you shouldn't have to carry the burden alone," Buzhardt said. "We'll carry the message."

Haig agreed to take them to the President. They did, after all, have an obligation to let their client know just how untenable they thought his situation had become. But if it got down to a definite recommendation to resign, Haig warned, he would not join them.

Haig left the West Wing and walked over to the President's office in the EOB to tell him that Buzhardt and St. Clair wanted to see him.

"There is no need to talk to them," the President snapped.

Haig said that they merely wanted to offer their assessment personally.

Nixon was firm. He did not want to hear from them. He was well aware of their views. They wanted him to resign, they thought it was somehow all over.

Haig crossed the street to carry the message back to St. Clair and Buzhardt. Once again the President would not see his lawyers.

Now what? Buzhardt and St. Clair realized that it was up to Haig. He would have to convince the President that his case was lost, that he would have to go, Buzhardt said.

"I'm not going to push him," Haig repeated. "He has got to make these decisions himself." And right now, Haig said, the President was convinced that his lawyers were wrong.

"Should I listen to the tape?" Haig asked.

"No, don't listen to any tapes," Buzhardt advised once again. But a transcript should be prepared immediately, so that Haig could get a clearer idea of the breadth of the problem. And the lawyers could advise Haig better how to deal with the President if they had a transcript.

Haig agreed. He went back across the street to ask permission to make a transcript. This time his meeting with the President took longer than before. Nixon saw no need to make a transcript. Haig argued with him. It would be difficult to mount a rebuttal without a transcript, he said. Reluctantly, the President agreed.

Haig returned with the okay. Now, who would transcribe the tape? Rose was definitely out. Who could be entrusted with the sensitive job? Finally they settled on Patricia McKee, Haldeman's former secretary. She had the best ear for the voices. The lawyers returned to their offices.

Haig remained in his office pondering what to do next, puffing steadily on one cigarette after another. He got up and wandered over to Kissinger's White House office. He found Scowcroft there. Kissinger wasn't in.

Scowcroft saw trouble on Haig's face. "What's going on?" he asked.

Haig sat down. "You wouldn't believe my problems," he told Scowcroft. "The President refuses to see his lawyers. We have another problem, and in this climate we can't sustain it."

Scowcroft didn't press. He suspected that the "problem" Haig referred to was on the tapes. He recalled a conversation he and Kissinger had had in the spring. "There must be real dirt on the tapes," Kissinger had said to him, "otherwise the President wouldn't be fighting so hard." Scowcroft had suggested that perhaps the President was fighting for the principle—to preserve the confidentiality of the office. It was true, Kissinger had replied, that the President cared about the office. "But he would gladly sacrifice the principle to save Richard Nixon. He cares about the office, but he cares about Richard Nixon more." Now it appeared that Kissinger's suspicions about the tapes were well founded.

Haig got up to go search for Kissinger. He certainly didn't want to give Kissinger this news on the telephone. There was no way of knowing how many people would be listening.

Haig located Kissinger a few minutes later and, in his oblique fashion, sketched the latest developments. Their mutual distrust was apparent. Haig was almost as vague with Kissinger as he had been with Scowcroft. There was a bad tape, he said, not necessarily fatal, but some of the lawyers thought it was. There had been bad times before, he suggested, and the lawyers sometimes tended to panic. But the tape "makes it clear that the President was involved" in the Watergate cover-up.

Kissinger was hardly startled, but he chose to play things cautiously with Haig. The Secretary had certain interests to protect. Watergate was already battering his foreign policy. The prospect of a Senate trial, even a short one, summoned nightmarish visions. It had to be averted at almost any cost. The President would be incapacitated for months.

Kissinger didn't share these thoughts with Haig. He wanted to have a position on both sides of the fence—to show that he recognized the gravity of the situation but at the same time that he was not among those deserting the President. Kissinger didn't trust Haig with a frank assessment. Any remark he made might well be carried back to the President. Haig always looked out for himself.

Haig trod with equal caution. He carefully advanced the view that the President must not be overthrown. It was the chief of staff's job, and Kissinger's, to keep the government going until there could be a calm resolution.

Kissinger was thinking that everyone was going to have to summon extraordinary restraint; the situation was highly explosive. He and Haig might never be able to level with each other. Even so, they might be able to work together.

EARLY THAT morning, Buchanan had received a phone call at home from Timmons. Haig had apparently kept his promise to take up option two with the Old Man. "There was receptivity in the Oval Office," Timmons informed Buchanan.

In spite of his personal opposition to the plan,* Buchanan said he would float the idea to reporters. He was due soon at the "Sperling Breakfast," a weekly journalistic ritual organized by Godfrey Sperling of the *Christian Science Monitor*. These on-the-record breakfasts allowed politicians to test the political waters with ten to twenty reporters.

That morning Buchanan remarked to the newsmen that the White House

---

* The plan was also called the Frey plan, after Representative Louis Frey, Jr., a Florida Republican who had unsuccessfully proposed it five months earlier to speed up the impeachment investigation.

was weighing a concession on the House vote and considering moving its case directly to the Senate. It was the first public acknowledgment by the Administration that the President was going to be defeated in the House.

Buchanan's "news" was on the wires by 10 A.M. On Capitol Hill, it was received with anger and disbelief, particularly by the President's supporters on the House Judiciary Committee. Wiggins was infuriated. "I don't care if Nixon called me and said that's what he wanted. I don't think it's right." By early afternoon, Buchanan was busy puncturing his own trial balloon. "The Old Man's people on the Hill are appalled," he reported back to Timmons. As the fallout worsened, Dean Burch got word from the President, "Kill the plan."

The White House had not only miscalculated the mood in the House but was also failing to pick up on what was happening in the Senate. Burch and Timmons had calculated an unshakable base of between thirty-five and forty Nixon Senators there. In his office that day, Senator William E. Brock III of Tennessee, regarded in the White House as a certain pro-Nixon vote, marveled to a reporter at the "dream world" the President and his men seemed lost in. There was only one way Richard Nixon could win in the Senate, Brock figured, and that was "some new exonerating evidence." And after fifteen months of watching the President's defense crumble under the weight of Nixon's own actions, he said, "There's no realistic way I can see to support acquittal—and that's the view of a lot of Republicans they're counting on. At least half the Republicans on this side are already gone. Nixon's maximum hard-core support in the Senate is twenty to twenty-six votes." He needed thirty-four and the talk in the cloakroom that day was of resignation. Many of the Senators on whom the White House was banking wanted a quick end.

"I don't think the President can avoid considering it when he finally sees the numbers in the Senate," Brock said. "But if he says, 'I want a trial,' God, he'll get it and it will be a fair trial. There is no longer any hesitancy or fear," the House Judiciary hearings had seen to that. "There is a growing feeling that a pro-conviction vote is good for the country—and a safer vote."

Brock doubted that a delegation from the Hill would march on the White House to urge resignation, however. "He wouldn't listen anyhow. Everybody has tried at one time or another to help him—begged, pleaded—and he doesn't listen. . . . The President has put too many people out on a limb too many times . . . The White House has used up all its goodwill and credibility."

The same reporter encountered Barry Goldwater in the Capitol subway. Goldwater agreed with Brock's assessment. "There's no one individual who can stop this now, there's not even one group of people who can stop it. If the President wanted to listen, he would have listened already," Goldwater said. The Nixon presidency was finished.

Two other influential Republican Senators in the "certain" column, Robert Dole of Kansas and John G. Tower of Texas, were also moving toward convicting. Tower explained his reasons: "I suppose there is a certain amount of amorality that almost all politicians will tolerate. But there is also a threshold, and that is the President's problem. . . . The Senators feel very strongly about the historical magnitude of this thing, and very few . . . will be willing to undercut their duty—especially for Richard Nixon."

Dole, as Republican national chairman, had been badly burned by his consistent defense of Nixon during the 1972 presidential campaign. His bitterness, this day, was apparent. "Everything Nixon touches seems to turn to ashes. But now the trauma is gone . . . The argument that the country can't stand the strain is no longer a consideration. Fifty-eight to sixty votes are already pretty solid for conviction." Without new evidence, the rest would come easily, he said.

LATE THAT afternoon, Haig met in his office with the senior staff. Timmons, Burch and Gergen had been urging him for days to lead some organized defense. "Everyone is talking about preparing carefully documented, factual briefs rebutting the articles of impeachment, but no one is actually doing anything," Gergen said.

Haig was finally ready to mobilize. There were about a dozen selected staff members present—speech writers, lawyers and congressional-liaison men. They would construct a defense against each article of impeachment, first for the House floor, and then—it now appeared certain to them—for a Senate trial. Neither Haig nor Buzhardt mentioned the tape.

The mobilization, said the general, would be supervised by himself, Ziegler, Buchanan, Price, Timmons, Buzhardt, St. Clair, Burch, and Charles Lichenstein, Burch's deputy. They would provide the strategy, supplanting the old Burch strategy group. Joulwan would "sit in" with his clipboard. Their decisions would be implemented by separate task forces for each impeachment article, with a lawyer and a speech writer on each team.

Clawson, whose zeal was limitless, summoned his task force immediately. He seemed invigorated by the prospect of battle. He reminded some in the room of a football coach exhorting his team after a disastrous first half. Okay, you assholes, he seemed to be saying, let's go out there and break some heads.

BUZHARDT HAD said virtually nothing during the meeting in Haig's office. He had little desire to get involved. He went home early and told his wife that the President would be out of office very soon. "He might resign on Friday."

ST. CLAIR went to seek Leonard Garment's counsel. In emotional terms, he described the impasse at which he found himself—the tape, a client who first lied to his lawyers and then refused to see them, members of Congress who seemed to blame him rather than the President. What were the responsibilities of a lawyer in such a situation? He had made false and misleading statements to the Judiciary Committee and to the courts. Were there not higher obligations now than defending the client? Maybe he should resign.

Garment sipped his coffee, listening quietly and reflecting on his own experience. The ordinary standards of lawyer–client relationship could not be reasonably applied to this case, he suggested finally. This case was too extraordinary, bound up with unprecedented responsibilities. Somehow, the President's lawyer had simultaneously to serve the office, the man and the national interest. St. Clair's resignation, especially now, would serve none of these, Garment said. This was a time of "terminal responsibilities," a time for special care and empathy—for the sake of the client and the institution. Everyone involved was now "fanning the fading embers of survival," Garment observed. Each had to play out his own role.

In the end, St. Clair would be respected for seeing it through, Garment assured him. It was especially important that the President's lawyer remain calm, that he be a stabilizing force. Otherwise there would be chaos. The mood of the country, the Congress, the press, was hostile, bitter. If the Constitution was to work, the presidency must not be destroyed in the process.

St. Clair was steadied by the advice. It nourished his calmer instincts. Winding his way through the White House, studying documents and reading testimony, he had concluded that there was little about this case that was black and white. Many events which at first seemed the result of deliberate action by the President or his assistants were not, in fact, deliberate. Garment was right. Things could get out of hand. There might be a crisis. It was delicate. Of course he would stay.

IT WAS nearly six o'clock when Haig finished briefing the President about his morning's conversation with Kissinger. The President left the EOB for the Oval Office, and Haig walked with him as far as the driveway, where the general was met by St. Clair's press aide Larry Speakes and a limousine.

For months Speakes had been urging Haig to meet with Senator James Eastland of Mississippi. It was Speakes's contention that Eastland, his old boss, was the key to handling a Senate trial successfully. In June 1973, when he accompanied the President to the dedication of a memorial to the late Senator Everett M. Dirksen in Illinois, Eastland had told Nixon, "I don't care if you're guilty or innocent, I'll vote for you."

Speakes led Haig to the Senator's office and introduced them. There were few formalities. They talked for about thirty-five minutes. Eastland agreed that the President's choices were grim. His chances for survival were not good.

HAIG HAD consulted with people whom he thought the President might ordinarily have turned to for advice: Kissinger, Eastland, the lawyers. None seemed resistant to the idea of resignation. Whatever was going to happen, he wanted the Vice-President to be kept abreast. The President had agreed that Ford should be briefed. Now, alone in his office at 7:30 P.M., Haig placed a call to Ford.

The Vice-President had already left, however, and Haig spoke to Robert Hartmann, Ford's chief of staff. Haig had a low opinion of Hartmann, a former newspaperman whom he judged a heavy drinker and a leaker. Haig didn't want to give Hartmann any impression, however remote, that he was calling about anything extraordinary; such a message would be telegraphed to a good number of anti-Nixon reporters. The general asked, matter-of-factly, whether the Vice-President could see him for a few moments the next morning. Hartmann entered the appointment on Ford's schedule.

As Haig and Hartmann spoke, Buchen and Whitehead were continuing their preparations for the transition from a Nixon to a Ford presidency. Both now were almost certain that they were planning for a reality.

DAVID EISENHOWER thought that events were moving beyond the President's control. Twice that week, his father-in-law had said that he definitely wanted Julie and David to be at Camp David for the weekend. The unusual urgency of the request made David and Julie sure that something important was happening.

That afternoon, David had lunched with Pat Buchanan, but Pat had said nothing concrete. On the contrary, Buchanan had taken a very tough line, arguing that the President should admit nothing in the House debate, that

Nixon's supporters should portray him as a man besieged by the press and by partisan enemies, persecuted for the same sins that were countenanced under his predecessors.

David had argued vigorously with Buchanan. "In light of the Judiciary vote his only choice is to effectively plead nolo contendere," he said, and admit his "mistakes." David believed deeply that Mr. Nixon was less in trouble for what he had done than for his repeated denials. "The reality of the transcripts" undercut too much, David said. He suggested that the President should "admit his participation" in the cover-up and acknowledge he was guilty of woeful misjudgment—but not of criminal conduct. Contrition, even at the eleventh hour, would carry Mr. Nixon a lot further than contention, David believed.

The discussion was resumed that evening as the Eisenhowers and the Buchanans dined at Father John McLaughlin's Watergate apartment. Buchanan, uncomfortably aware that the President's daughter was at the table, had little taste for the exercise. But David seemed hell-bent on raising the question "What does the evidence show?" and answering it. He said it showed that the President had been involved in the cover-up. Julie, incensed, turned her anger on David. Undeterred, he argued that "the basic reality of Mr. Nixon's abuses should be conceded" in the House debate. His wife seethed through the rest of the evening.

RICHARD NIXON too was gripped by anger that night. He had spent most of the day with Ziegler, once again the bearer of bad news: John Ehrlichman had been sentenced to twenty months to five years in prison for his role in the burglary of Daniel Ellsberg's psychiatrist—"a shameful episode in the history of this country," the judge in that trial, Gerhard A. Gesell, had called it.

Ziegler's talks with the lawyers that day had profoundly depressed him. The President's choices were narrowing, the tapes were obviously devastating. Haig seemed convinced that the lawyers were right, that the President would be forced to resign or face conviction in the Senate.

But Nixon refused to see it that way, and this evening, alone with Ziegler in the Lincoln Sitting Room, he was in no mood to hear what his aide was telling him. Ziegler was in the role he most disliked, identifying bleak alternatives which the President refused to face, plowing new ground, isolating grim choices, pointing out unfortunate facts. The drastic options now before the President were not the work of his enemies, Ziegler said. This time it was the lawyers, Haig, maybe even himself, who could see no easy way out.

The President's reaction was not unlike Julie's to David that night. To father and daughter, David and Ziegler seemed to be saying things that should not be uttered by those who believed in the President, things that were almost disloyal, words that seemed to abrogate the contract of faith which bound them all.

Ziegler was exasperated. He only wanted the President to understand how dire things were, to recognize the hard choices fast closing in on him. But the President would not even accept the meaning of the words on the tapes and refused to believe that his lawyers were acting in his interest.

Nixon rose and told Ziegler to get out.

Ziegler was incredulous. Nixon was so angry, so consumed by rage, that Ziegler thought the President might never again speak to him.

"Out!"

Thursday, August 1

T
HE Vice-President arrived in his office on the second floor of the
EOB early in the morning. He had returned the day before from
another of his long tours, defending the President in Muncie, Canton
and Las Vegas. He was still persuaded that the President was innocent of
an impeachable offense, and he was about to depart again on Saturday to
speak up for him in Louisiana and in Mississippi.

Ford was discussing the trip with Hartmann when Haig arrived. He did
not ask Hartmann to leave. Haig's doubts as to Ford's abilities and judgment
had been weighing heavily on him. That Hartmann was permitted to remain
during the discussion did little to build the general's confidence.

Haig was even more circumspect than usual. There was new evidence
on the tapes that were to be handed over to Sirica shortly, he said—evidence
that contradicted the President's version of events. Without explaining
exactly why, Haig told Ford that it would likely tip the vote in the House.
St. Clair, he added, was very upset that he had been allowed to misrepresent
the President's case before the Judiciary Committee.

Neither the Vice-President nor Hartmann interpreted Haig's visit as a
call to general quarters. After twenty-some minutes, Ford cut the meeting
short; he had an appointment on the Hill. The conversation had not been
terribly sensational or particularly alarming. Ford formed the impression
that Haig was saying, in essence, "The road ahead may be more difficult
than we've been thinking."

Haig went to his office in the West Wing. Buzhardt arrived soon after with the transcript that McKee had just finished typing. Though Buzhardt and St. Clair had described the June 23 conversation to Haig in considerable detail, its full impact had not yet registered. Haig read. "Good God!" he exclaimed. The contradiction between the actual words and the President's claim of innocence was stark. For fifteen months, as White House chief of staff, Haig had dreaded this moment. He had spent half the time waiting for it. The rest of the time he had been sure Nixon could hold on. Now Haig wondered if he had played this all wrong. He asked Buzhardt what he should do next.

Buzhardt argued that the transcript had to be released as soon as possible, at least to the Judiciary Committee. St. Clair was getting frantic because the committee was preparing its report and the ten Nixon loyalists couldn't be permitted to issue a dissenting report without this new evidence. It was bad enough that St. Clair had let the committee vote on impeachment in ignorance of the new tape. There was still time to argue that St. Clair had not heard the tape when the committee voted, that he had known about it only in the most general terms. But that story wouldn't wash unless the White House took the initiative now and volunteered the tape quickly. To let impeachment go to a floor vote without the evidence was unthinkable. Sirica would have the tape in a matter of hours; it was scheduled to be turned over that day. Jaworski would make sure it got to the House. There would be no doubt then that the President's aides *had* known of the evidence.

Haig agreed. The transcript had to be made public or at the very least given to the committee. They'd all be hung—St. Clair, Buzhardt and Haig— if they withheld the evidence any longer.

Buzhardt and Haig talked strategy. Haig would need the President's permission to release a transcript to the committee. There was also the question of when to make it public. For sure, Price would have to be brought into the picture now, Haig said. Probably Buchanan too. "Ray can keep a secret and knock off a good speech," Buzhardt added. Haig and Buzhardt agreed again that the President's options were limited. Impeachment was certain, and conviction almost as likely. Haig told Buzhardt about his meeting with Ford, but that Hartmann had been present. Now, Haig indicated, it was urgent that he get back to Ford. The man might be President soon. He had to be forewarned. But first Haig had to see Nixon.

HAIG HAD for months regarded himself as a surrogate President. Every damn thing landed on his desk, not Nixon's. As chief of staff to a preoccupied President, it was he who held the ship together. He decided what to take to the President and which presidential decisions to make himself, in the name of the office. It was too much for a staff man. The burden was unfair, he sometimes said.

But something else weighed heavily on Haig as he went to see Nixon. Once the tape became public, Nixon would no longer be able to govern effectively. Nixon had become increasingly unstable, obsessed, exhausted. Until now, at least the appearance of orderly government had been maintained. The presidency *seemed* to function. If the President clung to office after the tape was released, any semblance of moral authority would vanish. A Senate trial would be a nightmare. The very legitimacy of the government would be called into question.

What about Haig himself? He had propped it all up. He had made prolonged concealment possible. He might tell himself that he hadn't known. He had been careful not to participate. But there had been hints and signs everywhere, all along the way. Still, he hadn't known of a specific tape or a document. Not until the day of the Supreme Court decision. He had never been sure. *"What did he know and when did he know it?"*

As always, Haig turned to the practical problems. He did not linger over moral questions.

THE PRESIDENT had arrived in the Oval Office at about nine o'clock. His anger of the previous night seemed to have dissipated. He spoke briefly to Woods and Ziegler before going over to the EOB to listen to tapes. An 11 A.M. meeting with his top economic advisers was postponed to four.

Again Haig crossed over West Executive Avenue to the EOB. Gravely, he told the President that he had read the transcript and that he agreed essentially with the lawyers' assessment. The tape was probably fatal.

"It's all in the testimony," the President replied. He conveyed the impression that he was tired of going over this simple point again and again. It was utter nonsense to make such a big deal of this. It had all come out fifteen months before when the Walters memoranda had been turned over. Haldeman, Ehrlichman, everyone had testified about it. National security. Period.

No, Haig said. The conversation about the cover story, about the political considerations, undermined it all. It was clear from the transcript.

"But I told Pat Gray ten days later to conduct a full investigation," the President replied, waving his arm as if he were clearing off a table.

Haig's frustration boiled over. "Goddammit, it's not all in the testimony." This evidence was new, different and, in the present climate, insurmountable.

The President was calm. He tried once more to explain. In his mind, there was nothing new.

Haig refused to agree with him. The problem was deeper—the tape made clear that the President was aware of Mitchell's involvement almost immediately. All those months of denials were shot to hell.

It was a grueling session. Haig was pushing, insisting, constantly trying to assure the President that he didn't want to look at the situation this way, but that he had no choice. It was all said right there in the transcript. Now it would have to go to the committee for a judgment. Buzhardt and St. Clair were insisting on it.

The President seemed finally to understand. He withdrew, despondent. Almost by rote, he asked Haig to review the options, to draw up a list. What could be done?

Haig said that he wanted to think about it and talk to the lawyers. It was essential to get back to the Vice-President.

WHEN HAIG got back to his office, Buzhardt was there waiting for him. The general was satisfied that he had conveyed his own view, even if he hadn't stated it explicitly: The President and the nation would best be served if Nixon resigned.

At once, Haig called Ford—this time without going through Hartmann—and requested another appointment. The Vice-President was not immediately available; Haig would have to wait until three-thirty.

Haig and Buzhardt worked on options. If one assumed that the transcript would be released, there weren't many. The President could try to ride it out, allow the impeachment process to take its course, and fight it every step right through a Senate trial. They shuddered at the thought. Or the President could resign. They listed some variations:

1. The President could step aside temporarily under the Twenty-fifth Amendment.

2. He could wait and see, delaying a decision on resignation until some further point in the impeachment process, after the House vote perhaps.

3. He could try to get by with a censure vote. That would fail, Buzhardt and Haig agreed, but maybe Timmons or Burch could get someone to introduce a censure motion. It was worth listing.

4. The President could pardon himself and resign.

5. The President could pardon Mitchell, Haldeman, Ehrlichman and all the rest and then resign.

6. He could resign and hope that Ford would pardon him.

Could the President pardon himself? Haig asked the lawyer.

Yes. Buzhardt had researched the issue. The President could pardon himself. Or Ford, once he became President, could pardon Nixon.

Could Ford pardon him even before Nixon had been charged with a crime?

As far as Buzhardt could determine, under the presidential pardon powers, Ford could.

At about three-thirty, Haig went back to the EOB to see Ford. Hartmann was not there, so Haig got right to the point. The June 23 tape was serious. The President's lawyers had listened to it. Haig described it.

Ford listened in silence.

The tape was devastating, Haig said, catastrophic. The impact would be immediate and clear. The tape changed everything. *Was Ford prepared to assume the presidency within a very short time?*

Ford was stunned. This was unbelievable. A year ago, he had been a Congressman from Michigan. Now the President's chief of staff was asking him if he was ready to take over. The anti-impeachment position Ford had assumed for months was shattered.

Haig inquired whether Ford would be willing to recommend to the President what course he should follow.

Ford wanted to hear more.

It looked like resignation, Haig said, but he could not be sure. What were Ford's thoughts on the timing of a resignation, if that was the President's eventual decision?

Ford was hesitant. Haig drew him into a discussion of transition problems that might have to be dealt with—schedules, organizational considerations. With delicacy, the general began to review the options he and Buzhardt had outlined, stating that he was not advocating any particular solution. Haig raised the question of pardons—whether the President should pardon himself, whether others should be pardoned, whether the President should be given a pardon if he resigned. Haig asked for Ford's reactions to each choice.

Ford inquired about a President's pardon power.

"A President," Haig said clearly—his tone emphasizing that what he was saying applied to any President—"has the power to grant a pardon." It was an unrestricted power that could be exercised before criminal charges were brought. As a nonlawyer, Haig said, he was obviously in no position to offer any definitive opinion on the matter of law. He had been informed by a White House lawyer.

Ford appeared confused, almost befuddled at moments, during the forty-five-minute conversation. Finally he told Haig simply that he would have to think about things. He needed time before he would offer any advice. He wanted to talk to his wife, and he would also like to consult St. Clair. Most of all, he wanted to sort things out in his own mind.

NIXON WAS secluded in his EOB office all through the afternoon. The rescheduled meeting with his economic advisers was canceled. For the fourth or fifth time, he reminded his family about their weekend plans. He wanted everyone at Camp David—Pat, Julie, Tricia, David and Eddie.

By the end of the afternoon, the President wanted to get out of the White House for a while, to have some time to think away from the phone, away from Ziegler and Haig, from everyone who was pressuring him. His friend Bebe Rebozo was due in from Florida that evening, and they were planning to have dinner alone on the *Sequoia*.

Rebozo was scheduled once again to appear before Senate Watergate investigators the next day. He arrived at Washington's National Airport in the early evening, went straight to the White House and left immediately with the President for the Navy Yard.

Lieutenant Commander Coombs cast off at 7:30 P.M. The evening was hot and humid even though there was a breeze. When the stewards had cleared the dinner table, Rebozo, as he usually did, went off to chat with the crew, leaving the President to his thoughts.

As THE President and his friend sailed the Potomac, Haig was meeting in his office with the groups that were organizing the defenses for the three articles of impeachment. At this juncture, Burch and Timmons were firm that, if not they, at least Buchanan be allowed to read the transcripts that were going to Judge Sirica. It was their right, they had an obligation to the President's supporters on the Judiciary Committee and to the entire minority who intended to join in the defense. The President could not sabotage his supporters with any more nasty surprises. The issue was no longer the fate of one President, but of the Republican Party. No sensible Republican could be expected to stand up for the President without a damage assessment. Haig had alluded to "problems." What were they? How serious? Why could not the President's own staff be trusted with the truth?

Buzhardt sat in uneasy silence. It was surely not the first time he had sat through this same discussion. Whenever the issue was raised, heads turned toward him, watching for a signal. He would not, and could not, give it. This was the second echelon, and Haig was insisting that they be excluded until the President said differently.

Lichenstein thought that Buzhardt's demeanor typified the lunacy of trying to conduct a defense from the darkness, and he was enraged. If the staff had only Buzhardt's interpretation to rely on, they might all end up facing criminal charges. He was still quaking from Buzhardt's misreading of all the other tapes, and of the edited transcripts. Buzhardt, he thought, heard the same words but understood meanings that ordinary mortals did not. Burch shared his deputy's apprehensions to some extent, but he did not share Lichenstein's feelings of animosity. The mere mention of Buzhardt's name could put the even-keeled Lichenstein in a state. "Literally crazy . . . insane . . . he apprehends a reality that is not the same as ours," he said of the lawyer.

While Buzhardt kept his own counsel, Haig was unyielding. He instructed Burch and Timmons, and all the rest, to concentrate on a rebuttal of the charges, using whatever information was in the record. But his mind was elsewhere, and he adjourned the meeting abruptly.

Moments later, he called Price back in. Buzhardt was still there. Price sat down with them at the table. The meeting had been confusing, he confessed.

"It was largely for cover," Haig replied. This was the real business. The "problem" was indeed serious. Haig told Price what was in the June 23 tapes, and Buzhardt handed him the partial transcript.

Price read it quickly. "It's a dead end," he said.

Haig nodded. Here was the situation: A complete transcript of the tape would soon be released to the Judiciary Committee and made public as well. The President had agreed that it would be disclosed, and he would, of course, make a statement. Price was to draft it. After that, it was up in the air, it seemed. The President was considering his options. "A resignation is possible," Haig said solemnly. If it came to that, Price would write the resignation speech. A resignation might coincide with the release of the new transcript, or it might come later. Price's draft would have to both explain the new transcript and serve as the basis of a resignation speech. "You'd better start working on it," Haig told him. Buzhardt would brief him more fully.

Before he set to work, Price had some time to reflect. What had happened? He felt no bitterness toward the President, only sadness, and empathy. He was sure that Nixon's memory had not failed him over these two years. The President had simply chosen to believe in the better side of himself, the side he favored when he was with men like Arthur Burns,

Henry Kissinger and Patrick Moynihan. But Price knew the other side as well. He had never deluded himself about Nixon's darker instincts, his paranoia, the capacity for hatred, the need for revenge, the will to crush anyone he perceived as an enemy. But whatever Nixon had done, it was not commensurate with this ignominy, Price believed. He remembered the spring of 1973, when Nixon had begun to deal with the cold possibility that he might not finish his term. The President had not said to him explicitly, "I may not be around then," but there had been a recognition between them, an almost childlike expression on Nixon's face that seemed to say, "Why me? What did I do? How did we get to this horrible place?"

Price had wanted to use his own last year in the White House as a time to bring in new ideas and new talent, to harness what he saw as Nixon's better aspirations for the country and his Administration. It was not to be. Like everyone else in the White House, Price had been consumed by Watergate.

He knew there were those in the White House who regarded him as a hopeless romantic when it came to Nixon, even a worshiper. His faith persisted even now. The President was wrong, he had obstructed justice. Price conceded all this. But these things had to be understood in context. What was happening to Nixon was out of proportion. Price sat down at his typewriter to express the President's feelings. History would regard this episode as aberrant. The punishment was too heavy when weighed on the scale against the President's accomplishments and vision.

THE PRESS office was relatively quiet this day. Ziegler had spent most of it talking with the President or his lawyers. When he came in and out of his office, Ziegler appeared melancholy and anguished. There was no banter, there were no temper tantrums. His volatile personality was in check. He seemed to go out of his way to be gentle to his staff. "As if he could undo five years of shit," one of the secretaries remarked. The quiet was a clue. So were the new locks that Ziegler had installed on his desk drawers.

The White House press corps wondered where Ziegler could be. They hadn't seen him for a week. At this day's briefing they asked Warren if Ziegler had been muzzled. Warren actually had to deny it.

Ziegler was at the White House late into each evening, often with the President as they talked over the options. Over and over again. Ziegler was at sea: pulled by his loyalty to the President, pushed by the lawyers' advice, of two minds over the course he perceived Haig favored—resignation—and troubled by his own doubts. The President himself was torn. He was convinced at one moment that he could prevail in the Senate, and at the next that he would lose, that he should resign. The next moment he would rise up, ready to fight to the end, whatever the consequences. Then, again, resignation. It was a vicious cycle. Ziegler, the principal sounding board, lived the President's deep distress.

That night Judy Johnson wrote in her diary: "Quiet. Something is going to happen."

FRIDAY, AUGUST 2

FRIDAY morning was overcast and muggy. The sun was barely visible through the southern windows in Haig's office when the senior strategy group convened—Ziegler, Buzhardt, St. Clair, Timmons, Burch, Buchanan and Joulwan. Haig now wanted to bring them more fully into the picture, to give them a broad outline of the problem.

Seated on his couch, he called on Buzhardt to deliver the bad news, and everybody waited quietly as Buzhardt collected his thoughts.

"I have to tell you there's something fairly serious—"

"I can hear the assholes tightening," Haig interjected. There was nervous laughter.

Buzhardt began again. One of the tapes contained evidence that damaged the President's case. With his characteristic abstruseness, Buzhardt failed to spell out the exact nature of the problem, but he left no doubt that it tied the President to the cover-up.

"We're going to have to lay it on the leadership," Haig announced. The transcript would probably be made public on Monday.

"Al," interjected Buchanan, "give me five minutes to put on my Adidas." He had just bought new track shoes.

Haig told them that the new evidence made their task more difficult. But they were to continue to prepare the President's defense.

After the meeting, Ziegler followed Buzhardt over to his office in the EOB. Buzhardt closed the door and gave Ziegler a copy of the transcript,

331

and then went over it with him, explaining, as he had explained to St. Clair and Haig, why this and that were significant.

Ziegler sat quietly, showing no emotion as he read. Buzhardt was surprised: the President's press officer had never seemed so subdued. Ziegler put the transcript aside. He agreed with Buzhardt; it was all over. But he wanted to study it carefully.

ST. CLAIR met with the Vice-President just after eight o'clock that morning. Ford wanted a legal assessment. Without going into great detail, St. Clair informed Ford that he considered the new evidence so damaging that impeachment was certain and conviction highly probable.

Ford brought up the options Haig had presented to him the day before and asked St. Clair to comment. St. Clair offered very little advice. He emphasized that *he* was not the lawyer who had given Haig a legal opinion on the presidential pardon power.

After the meeting, St. Clair went downstairs to Buzhardt's office. He wanted to discuss legal obligations again. St. Clair was still feeling reassured by what Garment had said to him. As long as the transcript was released, he told Buzhardt, he saw no necessity to resign from the case. He could continue to defend the President. Perhaps he could even find a technical defense to win acquittal in the Senate if the President chose to fight.

Buzhardt was suffering, his tolerance worn thin. The President had lied to him for over a year—to his face. He stressed once more that he thought it was the lawyer's obligation to get his client to change his plea. The President had to resign.

St. Clair was growing weary of Buzhardt's Monday-morning moralizing. "For God's sake," he bellowed at him, "we're not the only lawyers who've had their clients lie to them." If the President released the transcript, his own ethical problem was solved, he could stay on. Every individual, even if guilty, deserved a good defense. St. Clair was willing to take it on. He was unwilling to make a recommendation on resignation, he now said. That was a political question, too monumental for a lawyer.

Buzhardt meditated on St. Clair's inconstancy. Two days earlier, he reminded him now, St. Clair had wanted to go to the President and suggest personally that he resign. Buzhardt emphasized that he too had given his professional and his personal support to the President's defense. But there was a question of the national interest. Resignation was necessary.

Next, St. Clair hurried to Haig's office to discuss how the Judiciary Committee should be informed. Haig suggested that Wiggins be told first. St. Clair was very sympathetic to this idea. He felt an obligation to Wiggins for his able and impassioned defense of the President and was anxious that Wiggins hear the news from him personally. If he could persuade Wiggins that the White House lawyers were not to blame for withholding the evidence, there would be no problem with the President's other supporters.

As HAIG and St. Clair worried over their strategy, Barry Goldwater and Hugh Scott met in Room S-230 of the Capitol to discuss the situation in the Senate. Neither of them knew about the new transcript—nor did they have any concrete hint that another tempest was brewing.

Scott had a copy of a tally sheet on which Buzhardt, the day before, had estimated the Senate vote. It showed thirty-six Senators, two more than necessary, as certain for acquittal. Scott had penciled question marks next to ten of the names Buzhardt had checked: Baker of Tennessee, Marlow W. Cook of Kentucky, Peter Dominick of Colorado, Griffin of Michigan, J. A. McClure of Idaho, William B. Roth, Jr., of Delaware, Robert A. Taft, Jr., of Ohio, Herman Talmadge of Georgia, Tower of Texas—and Scott.

Goldwater added one more name—Goldwater. He would probably vote to convict on Article Two, he said: abuse of power.

The two men agreed that by the time of a Senate vote there would be enough slippage to insure conviction. Goldwater told Scott that he was being pressured by colleagues to go down and see the President. They wanted him to tell Nixon where his duty lay and ask him to resign. But Goldwater was against the idea of having Scott, Rhodes or himself, or anyone for that matter, embark on such a mission. "Hell," he said, "he wouldn't see us." Still, Scott and he had to stay in touch should such a mission, or a joint statement, become advisable. "The President is gone," Goldwater said. "The Vice-President is the only hope for unifying the country."

At 1 P.M., Scott, Mansfield and Ford met to discuss procedure for a Senate trial. Though the Vice-President was there in his capacity as the Senate's presiding officer, he was clearly uncomfortable. Scott spoke as if conviction were a foregone conclusion, and turned to the question of the Vice-President's actions on the day of the verdict and other, still finer points of protocol. He reminded Ford that he should be in town that day, in order to assume the oath of office. "You should be easily available but not in the Senate wing of the Capitol," Scott advised. That kind of proximity would be bad form. It might indicate the sort of overanxiousness that Ford would surely want

Mansfield assured Ford that he was sensitive to his problems, and promised that he would take care to protect the President's rights zealously. There would be no railroading. Mansfield suggested that the Vice-President might stay home on the day of conviction.

No, said Scott. It would be better if the Vice-President waited on the House side of the Capitol, ready to take the oath. Somebody would have to swear him in, he reminded Ford. Whomever he picked should also be immediately available. Scott cautioned Ford again, "Avoid any contact with the Senate during the trial."

The Vice-President responded that he planned to be nowhere near the Senate during the trial. Moreover, he would stay out of the vicinity when the trial rules were debated, if things came to that. He would not exercise his tie-breaking prerogative in the Senate if such a situation arose. Ford was very uneasy discussing these hypothetical situations.

After a few other remarks concerning procedural matters, Mansfield left. Now Scott and Ford were alone, and Scott told Ford about his talk with Goldwater. The President had thirty-six votes in the Senate, Scott said, "but eleven are soft."

Ford made no comment.

Scott understood. The Vice-President had to support the President. "But continued support will make it hard later to unite the country," Scott warned. His eyes were glistening. "You're all we've got now, and I mean the country, not the party." He began sobbing.

Ford's eyes reddened. "Now, now," he said, trying to be comforting, but he too nearly broke down as he spoke of "the tragedy." Both men took a moment to compose themselves.

Ford went back to the matter of his support of the President. Within four or five days, he would make a public statement.

Scott interrupted to suggest that the occasion be used to declare neutrality. Ford could begin the address with the phrase "As the only executive officer with legislative responsibilities . . ."

Ford picked up on the idea: "Since the executive and legislative branches have now reached an adversary position, it would no longer be proper to seem to interfere in the process or to seek to affect the outcome."

But then Ford proposed to Scott that he close his remarks with a statement of confidence in the President's innocence. He would make it clear that it was his last statement on the subject. Scott decided not to argue. Ford thought that perhaps Mississippi or Louisiana would be a good place to make the speech.

Scott disagreed strongly. "A nationally important statement should be made in the nation's capital and nowhere else," he said.

Scott was probably right about that. Ford agreed to make the speech in Washington. He thanked the Minority Leader for his advice and asked him urgently to continue to consult with him and Goldwater.

Again Scott stressed the necessity of Ford's adhering to the statement they had outlined. There must be no loose ends for reporters to grab onto.

After all the months of promises to stay close to the Minority Leader, Ford still could not bring himself to tell Scott what had been going on during the last twenty-four hours.

CHARLES WIGGINS, having failed to dissuade seven of his Republican colleagues on the Judiciary Committee from voting for impeachment, had devised a new strategy—to persuade Republicans in the House to sit tight until the floor debate. If they could be prevented from being swept away in the momentum before a floor debate, Nixon might keep 180 votes. Soon after the committee hearings closed, Wiggins had taken his plan to Hutchinson and John Rhodes. They professed sympathy; you do it, they told him.

Today at about one-twenty, Wiggins found a message to call St. Clair. "Are you free to come and talk with Al Haig and me?" St. Clair asked. Wiggins was due at one of his lobbying sessions, and after that he had another appointment in his office. They settled on two-thirty. St. Clair would arrange for Wiggins to be admitted at the southwest gate.

Wiggins drove his Datsun 240-Z down to the White House through the rain. The guard at West Executive Drive did not even ask for identification. When he entered the West Wing at the basement level, the Congressman still had no idea why he had been summoned. Waiting maybe thirty seconds, Wiggins admired the large color photographs that lined the walls of the entryway: Nixon in China, Nixon mobbed by Egyptians, Nixon toasting Brezhnev, Nixon smiling broadly and giving the familiar V-for-victory signal as he stepped from Air Force One. . . .

An escort arrived to take Wiggins up to Haig's first-floor office. The general and St. Clair were seated at the big work table, and they both rose to greet him. Wiggins thought, Here's Al Haig, the guy who's running the government, and he doesn't even have a desk. Through the rain-splashed window in front of him, Wiggins gazed out at the marvelous view of the south lawn, the Ellipse beyond and the Washington Monument.

"The President and I want to thank you for what you've done," Haig said. "The President would like to thank you personally, but that would be inappropriate."

St. Clair had a half-dozen typed letter-sized pages in front of him. "During the course of preparing the tapes for Judge Sirica, we came across a tape that has a bearing on the case," he said. He identified the date of the conversation: June 23, 1972. He started to describe its background.

Wiggins, who was thoroughly familiar with the case, interrupted. "Yes, I understand the importance of that day."

St. Clair handed the sheets to Wiggins. The Congressman saw instantly that the evidence was new, that it was relevant, and that it flatly contradicted the assertions of the defense. When he finished reading, Wiggins turned back to the first page. He took five minutes to reread the transcript, and then he set it down. "What are you going to do?"

"This tape is in Sirica's possession and we'll give a copy to the House committee on Monday," said St. Clair. He said it was his "professional responsibility" to make it available before the committee submitted its report to the House.

When had Haig and St. Clair learned of this evidence? Wiggins' question was polite and calm.

St. Clair answered that they had found it in the process of transcribing the final group of tapes that were to be sent to Sirica. He began apologizing.

Haig interrupted to say that he had learned about it at the same time. He too apologized. Neither man mentioned that they had been warned urgently about this evidence nine days earlier, before the House Judiciary Committee had taken its first vote.

And the President? Wiggins wanted to know.

If he had not remembered the original conversation, Haig replied, he had learned in May, or at least he had had the opportunity to listen to the recording then. The tape had been taken to him, and when he had come out of his office he had told Haig, "I've got better things to do than listen to tapes."

One thing was certain, said Wiggins. The President could no longer sit on the evidence. There were only two options: the President could invoke the Fifth Amendment or he could disclose everything.

The decision to make the transcript public had already been made, they assured Wiggins.

"Well, then, he should put it all out and ask forgiveness," the Congressman replied. "Does he have another Checkers speech in him?"

Wiggins read the pages a third time to be sure. He looked at St. Clair. "There can be no misunderstanding this."

What was Wiggins' estimate of the probable impact on the members of Judiciary who voted against the impeachment articles? Haig asked.

The tape would be "very damaging," Wiggins replied. They would all have to reassess their positions. "Either this is gonna cost you four guys or nine guys, and I'm not even sure about me."

Wiggins was reasonably certain that the purpose of the meeting had been to get his thinking about the committee's loyalists. If he were asked about the visit, Wiggins volunteered, he would say, "No comment." He glanced down at the papers. "This is all very sad."

As he walked back to his car, Wiggins felt an immense depression. He fought not to react emotionally. He needed to be sure that he was not placing too much importance on a single transcript. But it was clear. Back in his office, he stared at the documents, the files, the lists that were piled on his desk. Nixon's defense had obsessed him for many months. Never before had he thrown himself into anything as he had into this effort to protect the President. He took the papers from his desk and tossed them into a wastepaper basket.

An aide, Patrick Roland, came into his office. "What's the good news from the White House?"

"It's not good," Wiggins replied, and he went home. It was the only way to avoid his colleagues as well as reporters.

Haig and St. Clair had hoped that Wiggins would prepare the way, spread news of devastation. But Wiggins was as good as his word. The Congressman kept his mouth shut.

HAIG RETURNED to the task of getting the Republican leadership involved. He was not having much success. Scott and Rhodes were fearful of being played off against each other and vowed they would not go down to the White House separately. When Rhodes told Scott that he was to have a meeting with Haig that afternoon, Scott recalled their pledge to stick together. Haig called Scott shortly afterward, and Scott refused to go. An hour before the general's scheduled meeting with Rhodes, Rhodes called him and canceled.

Vice-President Ford called Haig to say that he had no intention of recommending what the President should or should not do. Nothing they had talked about yesterday should be a factor in the President's decision.

Haig responded that he was in full agreement with the Vice-President's position. He hung up and considered what next to do. All he had was Wiggins' assessment, and that wouldn't begin to convince the President that it was all over. He turned to Senator Robert P. Griffin, the second-ranking Republican in the Senate and, in Haig's view, a more trustworthy man than Scott.

When Griffin picked up the phone to take Haig's call, he was preparing to leave for the weekend for his home in upstate Michigan. Haig told him he had some confidential information that he felt Griffin should know about. Jim St. Clair had listened to the tapes that had been turned over to Judge Sirica. One tape was very damaging; it was a devastating piece of evidence. It showed that the President knew of the cover-up a few days after the break-in. The President had lied to the American people. There was no satisfactory explanation, Haig said.

Griffin asked what was going to be done.

The President was going to Camp David over the weekend to consider what must and could be done, Haig replied. He himself was charged with obtaining an accurate assessment of the sentiment in the Senate. The President needed that knowledge in order to make the correct decision, a decision based on facts, not fantasy. This conversation was immensely delicate for Haig. He could not seem to be asking for more than was proper. He let Griffin know that the situation was tough; anything that would help the President come to grips with reality would be significant. In recent months it had been difficult to get through to Nixon. And momentous decisions would be made this weekend.

Griffin thanked Haig for calling and hung up. He had been a friend of Nixon's for eighteen years, since Vice-President Nixon had come to Michigan to campaign for him in his first congressional race in 1956. Griffin had won. When, in 1959, Griffin had been named one of the ten outstanding young men in the United States by the Junior Chamber of Commerce, his sponsor had been Richard Nixon.

Marjorie Griffin and Pat Nixon liked each other. As the President's Watergate problems had intensified, Nixon sometimes turned to Griffin, ten years his junior, for encouragement. "I'm innocent," Nixon had told him once after a leadership meeting. "I need your help." And Griffin had bent over backward—until his own skepticism had led him to the point of no return. By early summer, he sensed that Watergate would end in the Senate. Since then he had tried repeatedly, without success, to dampen the enthusiastic defense which his old friend and colleague from Michigan, the Vice-President, was mounting on the President's behalf. "You don't have to act like Nixon's defense lawyer," Griffin had told Ford.

But the Vice-President had been unwilling to take a step back. It might appear that he was trying to move into the presidency, Ford said.

This same afternoon, Griffin had lunched with the Vice-President and discerned no change of attitude. Ford had told him none of the things Haig was telling him now.

Griffin flew out to Michigan at about four in the afternoon. He wanted to do something to help move Nixon. He knew that the President would not do anything unless he was forced to. If there were one single thing that might make Nixon think he could skim by in a Senate trial, Griffin was sure that Nixon, a man accustomed to skimming by, would try it. The Senator thought hard about what he might do. He decided to write a letter to Nixon.

THE EFFORTS of the President's front-line defenders in the White House were getting almost nowhere. All the working groups were bogged down. There were too many hints that something was profoundly amiss. They were consumed by deep private doubt about the effort they were being asked to make. Haig, Ziegler and the others in the inner circle didn't seem to have their hearts in it. It was well known in the White House that Haig and Ford had met twice the day before.

For the first time, Jerry Warren had conceded that the President's situation in the House was grim. "You would have to put the President in the role of underdog," Warren had said at his daily press briefing. "We face an uphill struggle, but in a political struggle you have a chance to win."

McCahill and Stein worked all day under Price, developing the defense against Article One—obstruction of justice. McCahill knew from the way St. Clair was acting that something was seriously wrong, though St. Clair refused to discuss anything. Several times that day McCahill had interrupted Stein to say, "I just know we may have to change all this stuff."

Stein tried to reassure McCahill. "The tapes will show things are better than we think," he said. McCahill was dubious.

Just before six that evening, the defenders were recalled to Haig's office to review their progress. Haig seemed enormously weary and harassed. He let Joulwan do most of the talking.

Buchanan was encouraged that at last there was some structure. Joulwan's organization chart, showing all the assignments, impressed him. It looked as if a serious, coordinated defense was finally under way. He was ready for combat. "My guys will be in all weekend."

When the meeting broke up, shortly after 6:30 P.M., Haig asked Buchanan to stay behind. St. Clair and Price remained in their seats at the big table. Joulwan, as usual, sat on the couch. Ziegler arrived a few minutes later.

Haig took his usual place at the end of the table and turned to Buchanan. "We've all been living with this agony for a while," he said. "Now we want you to share it with us." The "problem tape" was deadly.

Buchanan wasn't surprised. Buzhardt had all but told him so, and Haig's and Buzhardt's remarks at the strategy meeting that morning had seemed to confirm it. "An early tape, or late?" he asked.

"Early."

"The twenty-third of June?"

"Right." Haig seemed startled.

"That was our concern all the way back," Buchanan said. His face flushed with anger and he glanced meaningfully at Price. The recollection of preparing the May 22, 1973, defense statement was painful. They had double-checked and triple-checked. They had sent Buzhardt back to see the President to make sure there was no political purpose. "CIA?" Buchanan asked knowingly.

"Yeah."

Haig told him what was on the tape. "What do you think he should do?" he asked.

Buchanan's response was quick and strong. "I think he's gotta resign."

"Basically you've come to the same conclusion everybody else has," said Haig. "The President is thinking of doing it Monday. Twice this week he came down on the side of resignation and then backed off again. Ray has been working on a resignation speech."

Buchanan asked to see a transcript of the tape. As they waited for it, they talked about what a resignation speech might say. "The President cannot state, 'I'm doing this to spare the country the agony of impeachment,'" Buchanan argued. "He has to be thoroughly consistent with the truth. Otherwise there will be more division in the country. We have to let our own people and everybody else know why it had to be done—because of what's on the tape, because he lied."

There was no discussion of whether or not the President should explicitly admit guilt in his resignation speech; the transcript would be a sufficient explanation. Haig and Buzhardt assumed that the resignation would come Monday. Even if it didn't, the transcript would be out.

"If it's not," said St. Clair, "I'm resigning." He said it matter-of-factly, and no one at the table challenged him.

Buchanan replied that the transcript must be given to the Judiciary Committee.

Haig told him Wiggins had already seen it and had concluded that it would cause many if not all of the President's defenders on the committee to switch their votes.

The transcript arrived. As Buchanan read the actual words Haldeman and the President had spoken, he gave vent to his anger by banging his fist on the table and exclaiming, "Jesus Christ."

Haig's buzzer sounded. It was the President. He wanted the transcript sent up to him immediately.

"We'd better make a copy," Joulwan said, and he grabbed the sheaf of papers from Buchanan and went out. He came back a few minutes later with a single Xerox copy and gave it to Buchanan to finish reading.

Buchanan looked up finally and said, "He has to resign."

When the forty-five-minute meeting ended, Buchanan returned to his office. His wife, Shelley, was waiting for him. "It's all over," he told her. He suggested that they head for a bar and mark the occasion with "a good old Irish reaction."

ZIEGLER HADN'T said a word during the meeting. He knew that Buchanan's judgment would carry a lot of weight with the President. Nixon regarded Buchanan almost as a son; he admired his politics and respected his views. Now Buchanan had joined Price, St. Clair, Buzhardt and Haig in judging the tape lethal. Ziegler thought they were probably right, but he was still not certain. He worried that Haig and the rest were moving too fast, creating a situation in which resignation would become inevitable whether or not it was the correct course. Buzhardt was pushing hard for resignation even before the tape came out, before anyone had a chance to gauge objectively its impact on the Senate. Confused and anguished, Ziegler took both the transcript and his doubts to Frank Gannon.

"It's not that bad," Gannon concluded. Many of the references seemed to him ambiguous. "It's an early tape showing early knowledge of White House involvement in the break-in"—but it looked to Gannon as if there was a "longer word count" in the section on legitimate CIA considerations and national security than in the brief section which referred to the political implications of the break-in. "Two weeks is not that long to hold something back. And he did tell Gray within two weeks to follow Watergate no matter where it led."

The problem, Gannon told Ziegler, was that Nixon was not really focusing on the substance of the tape in considering resignation. He was allowing himself to be swayed by the reactions of his advisers. The real damage of the tape was that it had been held back for two years. But it was not the smoking gun, he argued, unless those inside the White House chose needlessly to classify it as a murder weapon.

Gannon's argument was not unlike Nixon's explanation to Buzhardt earlier that week. To Ziegler, it was convincing. Certainly there was nothing so obvious about the tape's real meaning as to warrant locking the President into resignation at this point. Those who were pushing for resignation were those responsible for the care and keeping of the tapes, as well as for the President's defense. It was understandable. They were on the line, too. Gannon and Ziegler thought they were panicking.

Ziegler said the President might go on television Monday, probably to resign, though nothing seemed certain.

The tape failed to merit such a drastic act, Gannon argued. And if the President were eventually to step down, his reasons should not be that particular conversation.

Ziegler was persuaded.

HAIG STAYED alone in his office after Buchanan and the others left. About nine o'clock, he telephoned his younger brother Frank, a Jesuit priest and professor of nuclear physics at Loyola College in Baltimore. Although the two brothers were close, they had seen each other only once in the last four months.

Al Haig asked his brother about the health of their eighty-four-year-old mother, who suffered from angina and had recently been hospitalized. The general asked Frank to check in on her. He wouldn't be able to do it again for a while, he explained, because things were getting pretty hectic at the White House.

Frank thought his brother sounded tense, almost desperate. He knew that Al had been under severe pressure at the White House. Last month, on the phone, Frank had asked him if there were any people he could rely on to help him. Haig had mentioned Buzhardt as one of the few. But Frank knew that Buzhardt's heart attack had reduced his usefulness. Frank thought his brother might want to talk to someone outside the White House now. "It's been a long time since I saw you," Frank said. "We should get together."

There was a long pause. Then Al Haig reached for the opening. "How about tomorrow for lunch?"

They made arrangements and then talked a while longer about their mother. Frank recalled a recent conversation with her. "If only Al had had sense enough to go to law school he might have made something of himself," she had said.

What more could he be? Frank had asked. Al was already the President's chief of staff.

"He could be Senator from Pennsylvania," Mrs. Haig had replied.

SINCE LATE spring, David and Julie Eisenhower had lived nearly half the time in the White House. They had virtually moved in after the President's return from San Clemente. Their lives were built around Nixon and his defense. Though Watergate was not often discussed, it dominated life in the residence. Nixon had conveyed to them his fear that he would, in the end, lose.

Early that afternoon, David had had a long lunch with Bebe Rebozo in the third-floor solarium, a large informal room with huge picture windows and a broad view of the Washington Monument, the Jefferson Memorial and the Potomac River. They talked about the mounting Watergate difficulties for both the President and Rebozo. The Senate Watergate Committee's investigation into Rebozo's receipt of $100,000 in cash from billionaire Howard Hughes had led to a full-dress probe of his life and financial dealings. The IRS and the special prosecutor had joined those who were poring over Rebozo's records. His days were spent meeting with lawyers and investigators. But that afternoon he was more concerned with the President's problems. Rebozo was forlorn. He raised the question of resignation, the pros and cons for the President if he quit voluntarily.

Rebozo rarely discussed the situation so openly. To David, that indicated a shift, or a coming shift, in the President's attitude.

Was it worth it for Nixon to fight this thing through the Senate? Rebozo asked, and he struggled for the answer. He didn't know. He was trying to review what had happened, think through the sequence of events that had permitted Watergate to swell to such dimensions. There was very little bitterness in his voice—just bewilderment, and disgust at the lawyers. For Rebozo, they were the source of much of the difficulty. What was truly amazing, he concluded, was the President's strength, the fact that he was still around after all that had happened.

It was a thought that worried David. The President was passive, despondent. For months, David had been "waiting for Mr. Nixon to go bananas," as he sometimes phrased it. He and Julie had discussed it. David thought the President might commit suicide. Nixon's political life *was* his life—totally. And now it was going, even Mr. Nixon could see that in his clearer moments. David seemed convinced he would never leave the White House alive.

That evening, at about six-thirty, David was in his comparative-law class at George Washington University when a message came to call his wife at once. David left class and went to a phone.

"I want you home," Julie said.

David said he would be right there. "Home" meant the White House, and his wife's voice and her tenseness revealed a great deal. David rushed back to class, stuffed his books and papers into his briefcase, and walked five blocks to the White House. He concluded that the family was being called together to review another Watergate crisis, as they had been in May and December of 1973. David was used to the drill—listening, weighing options, boosting Mr. Nixon's morale, and finally resolving to fight.

When he got to the White House, he went upstairs to see Julie. She had talked with her father. "Daddy says it's all over."

David went down the hall to the Lincoln Sitting Room, where he found the President and Rebozo. As was his custom, the President had not called for anyone to come. When he wished company, he simply made himself available.

The President still had his dark-blue suit and tie on. The air conditioner was on high, and, as usual, a fire was burning in the fireplace. The President sat staring into it, his feet up on an ottoman. It was a moment before he realized that David was in the room.

"It's over," Nixon told his son-in-law. "We've got to decide by Monday night whether to get out of here." Then his voice trailed off. He continued to gaze into the fire.

"Why is it over?" David asked.

There was a new tape, the President replied. The question of whether to fight or to resign had to be decided by Monday because the transcript would be released then. "Remarks are being drafted for Monday night," he added. He didn't say what the remarks would be about.

Nixon picked up the phone and called Haig. He wanted the transcript sent up. The President turned to David. The transcript would explain the situation, he said despondently. As they waited, Nixon told him Buzhardt judged the situation hopeless. Fred had been saying it was over since the day of the Supreme Court decision, the President said.

And St. Clair?

"St. Clair is upset," the President answered without further explanation. He seemed irritated with his lawyers. They wanted to give up before he was ready.

When the transcript arrived, David took it to another room. Julie joined him. Rebozo, Tricia Cox and Mrs. Nixon moved in and out of the Lincoln Sitting Room, almost in shifts.

As he read the transcript now, David was convinced it was over, either by impeachment or by resignation. Julie did not express disagreement, though she was not ready to agree either. They went back to the Lincoln Sitting Room, and David went to the President's side.

"It's been my feeling that we're not as innocent as we said, or as guilty as they said," David said.

Nixon did not react; he kept looking into the fire. They were all familiar with his tendency to let conversations go on around him.

The President had shared his office with the family. He always included them. They were there when decisions were made. Now they were trying as a family to come to grips with impeachment or resignation. They searched for a frame of reference, some way to put into context what was happening to them. Was it like being on the losing side on election eve? Or, like Charles I, were they being beheaded? "Or are we the Romanovs?" David wondered aloud.

The secret to making a point in the Nixon family had always been to start with an accepted premise and then to offer distinctions. The premise that had been established this evening was that Watergate—whatever its significance—was an injustice, a small matter which, in fairness, should not cost Nixon the presidency. But it was the President himself who pointed out the hard realities. Impeachment was now a certainty, he said, and removal by the Senate a probability. The family had to be prepared for that. Then he lapsed into silence.

David, sitting with his back to the fireplace, could see the flames reflected in Nixon's glazed eyes. The President looked sad and broken. David had never seen him look so bad.

The phone rang and Nixon picked it up. The conversation was brief. "I wish he hadn't said that," the President said, and turned around to report that Haig had just told him Buchanan's reaction. "Pat thinks it's fatal," the President reported. "He reacted the way I expected he would." And he stared once again into the fire.

Julie was particularly concerned that her father's hand not be forced by defections. Her lines to the staff were excellent, and that afternoon she had received several calls reporting that some members were "deserting" the President.

There was no question that the staff was "dispirited," the President said. Defections had to be expected once the transcript became public.

And the Cabinet? Would they hold?

Nixon shook his head slowly. The best assessment was that six Cabinet members would resign if he tried to cling to office through a Senate fight. David was certain that his father-in-law had no basis for such a prediction, and that he was driving home the gloom as hard as possible. The drift of his conversation seemed to be that the family should prepare itself for resignation, though that was still up in the air as far as he was concerned.

Whatever happened, they would all need to summon extraordinary strength for the days ahead, he said.

About nine o'clock, Ed Cox arrived and was given the transcript to read. The tape, he said, "is not that conclusive." Cox's approach was calm and lawyerly. "Don't hurry," he advised. He sounded almost optimistic at times as the talk moved back and forth from one family member to another. They were all aware that, in his way, the President was seeking their assessments.

Julie stressed again and again her fear that her father would wake up some morning regretting it if he didn't see it through. There was no need to resign yet. Besides, the transcript hadn't even been released. Even if it meant conviction, she added, the right course might be to fight through a Senate trial.

David thought this fireside conversation was the death knell. Yet, largely out of consideration for Julie and her father, he softened his judgment, painted a brighter picture than he saw. The transcript represented only part of the story, he suggested. Mr. Nixon should not be swayed by its probable effect, only by what he thought was the right thing to do. And whatever he chose to do, David added, they would all support him. He had come up with brilliant strokes before. There was always a chance he could do it again, even now.

Rebozo offered no opinions, he simply repeated what others said. He looked stricken and tired.

Mrs. Nixon said very little. The others were extremely solicitous of her feelings, sensitive to the fact that she had never been very happy, certainly not during her time in Washington.

Whenever anyone raised the possibility that the President could survive the tape, Nixon tensed. It was over, he insisted. He seemed fearful that the others were bending backward to be considerate because they thought the tape was so damning. Their reactions seemed only to intensify his pain. No, he repeated, they all had to see that it was the end.

To David it was only a question of whether there would be a quick execution or whether they would be like the survivors in the novel *On the Beach*—waiting grimly for an end they knew must come.

Part of Nixon wanted to fight, to pull them all through, to save them. Quitting would be interpreted as a blanket admission of guilt, he said, an acknowledgment of all that his enemies had accused him of—*"all they said about us."* He wouldn't have that. The immediate question was what "they" —the Congress and the press—would do with the transcript. Perhaps there was still a way to prevail, to make "the best speech of my life." But he seemed to reject the prospect even as he mentioned it.

Normally, Nixon followed a conversation carefully with his eyes, back and forth, boring in on whoever was talking or being addressed. Not this night. David thought Mr. Nixon seemed almost tranquilized. He talked quietly, leaving sentences and thoughts unfinished, avoiding all eyes. As it grew late, his manner became more disjointed and he seemed on the verge of coming apart.

The President started reminiscing. It was the most difficult moment of all, a signal that he was capitulating. He talked about their early days in the White House—the foreign-policy initiatives, Tricia's wedding, the White House itself, its history, its comforts, the friends, the staff, the parties. One memory unlocked the next. But there was no mention of anything since June 17, 1972, not even the triumph of the reelection victory.

It was nearly midnight when the conversation finally stopped of its own weight. The question was unresolved, at least in any explicit way.

"I am deferring any decision for now," Nixon finally said. "We'll get together in the morning and decide this."

He picked up the phone by his side and called Haig. Nothing had been decided, he said. The others left and Richard Nixon was alone by the fire again.

In the Eisenhowers' bedroom, Julie called Buchanan's house.

Shelley Buchanan roused her husband, who was half asleep after a number of martinis at the Moon Palace, and told him that Julie was on the phone. Buchanan knew why she was calling. He said it could wait until the morning. Shelley told Julie that Pat was asleep.

For Julie and David, the response was answer enough. Even Buchanan was in the resignation camp.

SATURDAY, AUGUST 3

BUCHANAN arrived at his office shortly before nine-thirty on Saturday and returned Julie's call. "Come on over," she said. He took his time. Rushing right over would only contribute to the crisis atmosphere, and it was going to be a difficult enough encounter.

Buchanan, like Rebozo, was treated as a member of the family. Except for his wife, Shelley, and Woods, he had been with Nixon longer than anyone on the staff. No aide was as important psychologically to the President. The two men shared the same political instincts. Now Buchanan was about to recommend to the President's family that Richard Nixon resign from office.

After a half hour, he walked across West Executive Avenue and took the elevator upstairs to the solarium. They were drinking coffee when he arrived. Julie, David, Tricia, Ed, Rebozo.

There was no brushing over things. Quickly, Julie outlined what she called "the family position." They were against resignation, even if it meant conviction by the Senate. "Daddy's not a quitter," she reminded Buchanan. "It would be better for Daddy if he laid it all out before the country. He would have a forum to show what a trivial matter they are taking away his presidency for. He could stress his accomplishments against this smaller, less significant thing." And, she added, there was always the possibility, no matter how remote, that he could prevail in the Senate. "He wants to fight it out, Pat."

Buchanan sipped his coffee.

That morning, her father had complained that the staff was giving up before he was ready, she said. And she knew from her own phone calls that the morale of the staff was in danger of collapse.

Buchanan understood. If the President were deserted by his staff, even the dignity of fighting to the finish would be taken from him. The President could persevere only if the staff remained loyal.

Buchanan shifted uneasily. References to staff defections were disconcerting and he wanted to avoid a discussion of who might hold and who might desert. Bitterness between the family and the President's aides was the last thing anyone needed now.

"If the President decides to fight this out in the Senate, I'll be with him," Buchanan reassured them gently. "I'm not going to hit the silk. But there's no chance of winning in the Senate. If he stays, it's only a short matter of time before even his closest friends start deserting him. First the Chowder and Marching Society, then the party, then some of the staff. People are going to be demanding his resignation. The party will have a terrible defeat in November if he doesn't resign."

Buchanan was swallowing hard. "Hell, I understand why he wants to stay on. But he'd be blackened, Julie. It's a straight road downhill—for him, for the conservative cause and for the country. There comes a time when you have to say, 'It's finished, it's over.' Nothing would be served by dredging it down through the Senate—not for any of us." It wasn't easy to say, "but we're old buddies," he reminded them.

David was impressed by Buchanan's arguments. He began to refashion them in his own words, but his wife interrupted him.

"David," Julie snapped, "Pat's already been over that. We know your view."

The conversation turned once again to the White House staff. The family wanted to know why certain key members were so strong for resignation.

"Are they responding to the tape itself or other things?" Ed Cox asked.

"They're being realistic," Buchanan replied. "Look at the Wiggins thing. Judiciary's gone already." They didn't know about Wiggins. Buchanan told them about the Congressman's visit and his reaction to the transcript.

"But the tape's not that conclusive," Cox asserted. His approach was prosecutorial—not antagonistic, but probing. There was enough ambiguity about the tape, Cox insisted, to at least think about trying to redeem the situation.

Buchanan paused, searching for the right words. This was the hardest part. "The problem is not Watergate or the cover-up," he began. "It's that he hasn't been telling the truth to the American people." He paused again. "The tape makes it evident that he hasn't leveled with the country for probably eighteen months. And the President can't lead a country he has deliberately misled for a year and a half."

Rebozo broke the brief silence. He was smiling slightly. "The President thought you'd come down on the resignation side," he told Buchanan. His tone was friendly.

Pat was just being realistic and open-minded, David suggested.

Julie flashed a menacing look at David.

Rebozo resumed quickly, "Pat, this is a great man we're talking about. He's never walked away from a fight. And he's done great things for the country." He wanted to know how the tape demonstrated that the President had lied for eighteen months. It sounded to him as if the President had been saying the same thing all along. He was innocent. How could an innocent man resign the presidency of the United States?

Buchanan tried again. He explained the background of the May 22 statement. "Price and I raised the question then. We sent Fred back to ask him. At that time there was knowledge on the President's part that the tapes were there. It would have been a simple matter to check."

David was impatient. Last night's discussion, now this one, and he could see the same conversation continuing for weeks. They would all do well to consider the implications of what Pat was telling them, he said. Especially about the damage to the party, the country and Mr. Nixon if he tried to fight his way out.

Julie flared. "We've heard that from Pat already, okay, David? You don't have to tell us again."

David realized that he *was* doing a lot of repeating. He was talking as much as Buchanan. Ed appeared irritated with him, too.

Cox resumed his cross-examination. Why did there necessarily have to be a big defeat for the party in November? What were the figures? How many seats would be lost? Why did there have to be a decision on resignation right away? How many members of the staff would leave?

Buchanan was impressed with Cox—with his forcefulness, his intelligence and his insistence on dealing from facts, not emotions. He was somewhat surprised. He couldn't remember who had dubbed Ed "the Prince," but Buchanan had done his part to see that the name stuck—that and Cox's other nickname, "Fast Eddie." Buchanan was a city kid who had grown up in the streets. His perception of Cox had always been of a brat who had earned the calluses on his hand playing tennis at the country club. His opinion was changing as Cox pressed the argument: Why should the President resign before testing political and public reaction to the transcript? What harm was there in waiting until the tape hit?

Buchanan had been thinking along the same lines. He knew what the public and political reaction would be. And when the President, when even Julie, saw the reaction, they would see the wisdom of resignation—for Nixon's own sake.

"Maybe the reaction won't be as bad as you think," Julie said. "Why not give it a while—a couple of weeks?"

Buchanan was agreeable. It would be better for the President to be convinced by events than to be swayed by the judgments of his own staff.

The visit, which had lasted more than an hour, ended with both sides feeling that something had been accomplished. Buchanan recognized that the family solidarity claimed by Julie did not exist. Rebozo was confused. Cox was trying to be realistic. Tricia was silent. And obviously David thought resignation the wisest move.

ON THE way back to his office, Buchanan stopped in to see Rose Woods. Their affection for each other was profound: the White House Irish, bound by temperament, unswerving loyalty to Richard Nixon and—probably more than any of the others—an understanding of the man.

Woods was anguished; her eyes were puffy and red, her voice was tremulous.

"How's the Old Man holding up?" Buchanan asked.

She was having too much trouble holding herself together to deal with the question.

Woods had never had many illusions about Watergate, especially since the spring of 1973. She and Buchanan had discussed it more than a few times, always careful to avoid specifics. ("Rose, he's really screwing this up and you and I know it," Buchanan had said on one such occasion. "He's up to his ass in this." And Rose had nodded, an expression of helplessness on her face that said, "But what can anyone do?") There had even been fleeting moments when Woods had thought the President would be better off if he resigned. More than anyone else, she could see what it was doing to him. It would be better to escape with what honor was left him than to be crushed and humiliated in the end. But, like Buchanan, she knew that Nixon was determined to persevere, and she too believed passionately that he was a victim of his enemies.

The last nine months in the White House had been excruciating for her. Her bitterness at Garment (once a close friend), Buzhardt and Haig had intensified since the episode of the eighteen-and-a-half-minute gap. She felt ridiculed, both by the press and by the members of the staff, who found her testimony hilariously unconvincing.*

On this particular Saturday morning, Buchanan and the President's secretary did not debate the issue of resignation: each knew where the other stood. Woods was adamantly opposed; the time for resignation had long since past, the damage was done. He should go down fighting. Let everyone see what "they" were doing to a great President.

Rebozo joined Buchanan as he left Woods's office, and the two walked down the corridor to see Haig. Buchanan wanted to brief the chief of staff on his meeting with the family. But Haig had someone with him.

"Why don't we go talk to *him*?" Rebozo asked. They crossed West Executive Avenue again and entered the reception area of the President's EOB office. "Tell him we're here," Rebozo said to Manolo Sanchez. When there was still no response from the President after several minutes, Buchanan went back to his office.

Ziegler entered a few steps behind him. "The decision is to fight it through the Senate," he announced.

Buchanan exploded. This was exactly what must be avoided. The President was locking himself into a ruinous position. Ziegler, batted back and forth like a shuttlecock between the forces of fight and flight, was taking no position now. He would go along with whatever the President wanted.

After Ziegler left, Buchanan picked up the phone and had the White House operator connect him with Julie. They discussed the President's latest decision very briefly.

"We'll support Father down the line—David too," she told him. David came to the phone and confirmed Julie's statement.

"Okay," Buchanan replied. "That's the decision. Let's support him." He was less than enthusiastic about the prospect.

BUCHANAN ATE a hurried lunch in the senior staff mess and then went to Buzhardt's office. St. Clair was there.

---

* Privately Buchanan had told others, "Rose knows she erased a good part of it. She was protecting him. I've never asked her and she's never told me what happened. It's not hard to figure. After Rose had erased the first part the Old Man would say, 'Oh, my goodness, Rose, somebody left the tape on.'" And at this point in telling the story Buchanan would imitate Nixon closing his eyes and pushing the button that erased the rest of the eighteen and a half minutes. Buchanan's theory was that Nixon gave the tape to Woods because she would know what to do with it. "Either Nixon said something like 'See what you think we should do with this, Rose,' or she knew what to do without being told." When he got to the part about the President closing his eyes, Buchanan would laugh uproariously.

"The President's going to fight this thing down to the finish," St. Clair said. "We're going to show the country just what it means to impeach the President of the United States and convict him."

Buchanan was appalled. For the first time in his political life, he was the dove. He looked at Buzhardt.

Buzhardt indicated that he too was going along with the decision, although he lacked St. Clair's zeal.

"Do you know what we're getting into?" Buchanan asked him incredulously.

He repeated much the same argument he had made to the family.

Buzhardt agreed with Buchanan. He was willing to go along with the decision, he explained, because he was certain it would not be final. The "never-nevers" always seemed to change, he observed, and there was no compelling reason to think that events wouldn't force the President into another 180-degree turn.

The danger from St. Clair, Buchanan felt, was not his willingness to defend the President; it was that, in his enthusiasm to do so, he would help push the President into a public statement on Monday that they would all regret. Let Nixon defend the meaning of the tapes, Buchanan argued, but don't encourage him to swear to remain in office until every vote is counted in the Senate.

Buzhardt didn't say much. He was disgusted. He thought St. Clair was merely trying to fortify himself for arguing a hopeless case. St. Clair had been up and down on this all week, Buzhardt was thinking. Right now he was on his up cycle. He would come down again.

After fifteen minutes of fruitless argument, Buchanan returned to his office and called Haig. The two got along well. Buchanan had spent more time with Haig in fifteen months than he had with Haldeman in over four years. Haig made himself accessible. Buchanan knew he could always call him and say, "What the hell are you doing this for?" and Haig would say, "Come on over and we'll talk about it." That's what happened now.

Buchanan didn't pause for pleasantries when he entered the general's office. "Al, I don't think there's an appreciation around here of what the hell this decision means. If the President takes this to an Alamo finish, I don't think he realizes the impact on himself, the party, the country, his place in history—everything. Our job has to be to keep him from doing something like what Agnew did, something he'll regret later.* There's no reason to lock himself into a position. That tape is going to undo him. Events will do the job."

* Up until the day that Vice-President Agnew resigned his office, he insisted vehemently that he would not quit.

Haig agreed. He thought the family was pushing the President toward an irrevocable position. St. Clair's zeal worried him, too. He had long thought that St. Clair's judgments, particularly his political ones, were unrealistic.

"Some people aren't realizing the implications of what they're saying and doing," Buchanan stressed.

"You're right on that," Haig replied.

ST. CLAIR'S DEPUTY, McCahill, had not been able to track his boss down for several days. When St. Clair finally stopped by McCahill's office that after-noon, the deputy had some questions: "How's it going? What's on those tapes?"

"Some interesting things," St. Clair responded.

"How interesting?"

"Very interesting," St. Clair said, and he walked off.

ROBERT GRIFFIN hadn't slept well Friday night. He rose early on Saturday and paced back and forth in his study, weighing what he might say in a letter to Nixon. By 8:30 A.M. he was sketching notes on a yellow legal pad. As he worked, he discussed the language with his wife. He wrote and re-wrote the letter, withholding the fact that he knew about new evidence, but trying to drive home the prospect of almost certain conviction in the Senate. It took him four drafts before he was satisfied.

Late that morning, he reached the Vice-President through the White House switchboard. Ford was campaigning for House candidates in Mis-sissippi and Louisiana that day. He was omitting references to impeachment from his speeches. When pressed by the reporters who had taken note of the omission, Ford declared that he thought the President was innocent of any impeachable offense.

Ford listened as Griffin read him the text of his letter: "Dear Mr. Presi-dent, There is no doubt in my mind that, unless you choose to resign, the House of Representatives will adopt Articles of Impeachment, making necessary a trial in the Senate." The Senate would issue a subpoena for the tapes. "If you defy such a subpoena, I shall regard that as an impeachable offense and shall vote accordingly."

It was a big step for a Republican loyalist. Griffin wondered whether Ford would advise him to go ahead or would say, "No, don't do it." Ford merely said, "Thank you." Griffin told him he knew about a new and damaging tape. Ford's reply was vague, but Griffin took away the impression that the Vice-President was aware of the new evidence.

Shortly before noon, Griffin dictated the letter to his press secretary and instructed him to have it delivered to the White House right away. Griffin wanted the letter to have maximum impact. It should be released to the press, but, to avoid any suggestion of grandstanding, it would be given to the Michigan papers only. The wires would pick it up fast enough.

Griffin's letter was en route to the White House when Frank Haig arrived to pick up his brother for a late lunch. They went downstairs to the senior-staff dining room and took a corner table. Al Haig seemed greatly relieved today compared to the night before. He seemed to be in charge again, to have the situation under control. They talked first about their mother's health.

Ziegler stopped by their table to ask Haig whether they should set up a meeting that afternoon between St. Clair and the President. Haig thought it was a good idea. After dessert, Haig introduced his brother to St. Clair and his wife, who were seated at a nearby table. St. Clair was out of sorts and didn't want to chat, so the brothers went back up to the general's office.

Frank Haig sat while his brother paced around the room, describing in general terms what was going on.

To the annoyance of Muriel Hartley, Ziegler kept walking in and out, ostensibly to deliver various messages. "Why doesn't he mind his own business?" Hartley complained to Judy Johnson.

Frank Haig complimented his brother on how well he had handled the television interview with Mike Wallace the previous Sunday.

"It's an interesting problem," Haig said. "How do you play the game when you don't have any cards?"

Shortly afterward, Haig received word that the President wanted to see him. Griffin's letter had arrived. When Haig came in, Nixon was in a fury. Such threats only solidified his resolve to fight to the end. It was a cowardly letter. He raged about it at some length.

Haig did not mention his call to Griffin the day before. The general knew very well that it had triggered the letter. He listened as the President railed about weakhearted legislators. Finally Nixon calmed down.

At five-thirteen, the family followed the President up the helicopter ramp for the trip to Camp David. David thought the Griffin letter must have been a fierce jolt. The President looked awful.

To complete his cover, Haig told Buzhardt that it was probably Ford who had tipped his old friend Griffin—no one in the White House felt close enough to Griffin, Haig said.

AT DINNER with the family that evening, the President repeated his decision to stay on. At the least he would give that route a try. He wanted to keep his options open, he told them, and then he polled the family once more. Ed thought it was the right move, there was no reason to be stampeded. Julie was content with the decision. Mrs. Nixon, Tricia and David said very little, either for or against. David was pretty sure resignation was the only way. He thought the President was unconvincing. "What's your reaction?" Nixon continued to ask around the table.

The answers were vague.

"What would be your reaction if we had ten Senators?" he asked. "If so, would it be worth staying?"

David felt sad. Ten Senators? he thought to himself. They had been reduced to ten Senators? That meant ninety against. "Think of yourself," he said.

"Well, David, you're just like Al," the President responded. Haig too seemed to be saying, "Think of yourself instead of the country." If Mr. Nixon thought of the country, David knew the answer would be to fight it out; his father-in-law was utterly convinced that his country needed him. By telling him to think of himself, David was trying to soothe him, trying to say, "You can now contemplate resignation; you deserve it." It was a way to tell a proud man he could, one time at least, walk away from his opponents.

The sun was setting. Nixon gazed out the window. The swimming pool was on the right, the putting green directly in front of him, the whole valley stretched out below. He pointed to the putting green and said how much he liked it, how much he would miss it. But he was going to fight it out. Then, abruptly, he left the table, and he did not come back to join the family for the evening's movie.

JAN BARBIERI and Anne Grier had arrived in their office prepared for a hectic day. There had been a great deal of talk on Friday about preparing a defense strategy, and word had gone out that all personnel should be available to work through the weekend.

Normally on Saturdays the White House was busy by 9 A.M., with members of the staff trying to catch up on things they had put off all week. This Saturday morning was languid. There didn't appear to be any activity anywhere.

Grier and Barbieri began looking for signals to explain the calm, calling back and forth on the phone to report their findings. Aware that Gergen was researching material for the President's defense, Barbieri asked him if she should come in on Sunday.

"No," said Gergen, "and no one is looking for the materials anyway." He didn't know exactly what was going on, either, but the lights were out in many of the offices.

Then Barbieri and Grier learned that the 2 P.M. strategy-group meeting had been canceled. The whole family and Rebozo were going to Camp David. But Ray Price and his secretary, Margaret Foote, were in. That was unusual; it meant that something big was going to happen.

Sometime during the day, Grier asked Diane Sawyer, "Is the President thinking about resignation?" She expected to hear a firm no. But Sawyer said, "Wouldn't *you* be thinking about it?"

Barbieri saw Ziegler walking upstairs in the EOB. He was dragging, and it was only midday. Ziegler's energy usually increased under stress.

Later in the afternoon, Grier asked Tom DeCair if he thought Nixon would resign. He said, "I don't know, I don't know." They decided to see if Price was still there. DeCair phoned, and Foote answered. DeCair said, "Sorry, wrong number." When Grier and Barbieri left the White House at 7 P.M., Price and Foote were still in the office.

PAT BUCHANAN left the White House about five o'clock that Saturday, angry and frustrated. He had finished five beers and was starting a sixth when Price called him at home later. Price was upset, too. Haig had told him the President was going to tough it out. Now Price was writing a *non-resignation* speech which attempted to gloss over the implications of the June 23 tape. Nixon would deliver it on television Monday night.

Price thought it would be disastrous if the President announced to the nation that, in spite of evidence that confirmed two years of lying and subterfuge, he intended to fight to the finish. Price said he was concerned about the attitudes of some people he had spoken to. Particularly the lawyers. Some middle ground had to be found to keep the President from irreversible action. They decided to meet in Buchanan's office first thing in the morning.

AROUND TEN o'clock that evening, David and Julie decided to go back to Washington. Camp David had become very depressing. There was little they could do there to improve the situation. The family session the President promised hadn't really taken place. There had been no meaningful attempt to grasp the problem or discuss what must be done. And it didn't look as if it was going to happen.

David tried to get some studying done after they got back to Washington, but he found it impossible to focus on law that night. He gave up the effort just before midnight and called his friend Brooks Harrington. He needed to talk to someone.

The rest of the family was opposed to resignation, David sadly reported. Since Friday night, the President had been unable to look him in the eye. The big problem, he said, was that Mr. Nixon feared losing their respect if he resigned. So now they had to convince him they would continue to love him, whatever came.

David sounded tense and tired. Harrington searched for something to say to comfort him. The Harringtons had been to Mass that evening. "Carol and I lit a candle for you," Brooks said.

David choked and wept.

Sunday, August 4

T HE evidence that the President had chosen a disastrous course was in the speech that Price brought to Buchanan's office at nine o'clock in the morning. It confirmed Buchanan's worst fears. What had started as a speech of resignation was now a statement of defiance. The President intended to tell the nation that nothing save conviction by the Senate would cause him to leave the office to which he had been elected.

Buchanan shook his head as he read: "Though I have lost my base of political support, I will fight for the principle . . . I will appear in the Senate in person and will carry this struggle to the final conclusion." The President was committing himself to final devastation, Buchanan told Price. "He can't box himself in like that."

Price did not need convincing, he reminded Buchanan. He was only doing his job, following instructions.

They agreed that Buchanan should write a memo to Haig, and they drafted it together. It was directed to the immediate problem—keeping the President from making a public vow to fight to the finish.

The President shouldn't lock himself into a pledge to appear before the Senate—there was absolutely no gain in that, they wrote. Nor should he go on television on Monday night. If Nixon couldn't be dissuaded from appearing before the cameras, he should limit himself to a three-minute filmed statement in the press room, in which he merely laid out the contents of the June 23 tape.

Buchanan scrawled a draft of the final paragraph on a note pad: "Don't lock him into any statement going all the way. We've been unable to convince him to resign, but events will. Drop the tape and let the tape and the consequences convince him of what we can't."

Then he and Price made a few language changes and dictated the memo to Margaret Foote.

"It's for the Old Man's sake," Buchanan told Price. "For the future, it would be a terrible thing if we were to talk him into something he doesn't think he ought to do. For the rest of his life he would say, 'I was talked into it by advisers and I could have made it.' We should step back and let the thing blow; the President should feel the force of the blast himself. Let him see reality himself."

Price left to get ready to go to Camp David that afternoon. Buchanan was not scheduled to go, but now he wanted to be there. He called Haig's office to tell the general that he was available if wanted.

While he waited for Haig's call, Buchanan changed into a pair of jogging trunks. Haig's office called just as he had laced up his new blue-and-white track shoes. Buchanan would go to Camp David. He phoned Shelley and asked her to bring a jacket and tie to the office. Then he went out of the EOB through the basement, only a few feet from the office where Howard Hunt and the Plumbers had worked, and jogged down Seventeenth Street to Constitution Avenue, west to the Lincoln Memorial, east on Independence Avenue to the Jefferson Memorial. He jogged past the Washington Monument onto the Ellipse with its view of the White House South Portico. He slowed down only at the guard post on West Executive Avenue between the White House and the EOB as he went back through the iron gates.

THIS SUNDAY'S secretarial shift in Haig's office had been drawn by Diana Gwin, assistant to staff secretary Jerry Jones. Wardell, Haig's aide, had asked her to sit in the outer office and answer the phones. Gwin thought the general looked unusually strained when he and Joulwan arrived around 9:30. Haig fussed and fretted over one more problem—the weather. It was raining, making it doubtful that they could helicopter to Camp David.

Wardell made alternate plans to drive. He knew the real source of Haig's agitation. On Wednesday Haig had told him about the tape. "I'm not sure I can justify my actions," the general had said.

Gwin asked Wardell what was going on. "Just wait," he replied. "The shit is going to hit the fan. There's a damaging tape coming out tomorrow." Gwin and Wardell began calling it the "Killer Tape."

As the noon hour approached, the weather broke. The passengers were hurriedly assembled for the drive to the Pentagon helipad: Ziegler, Pat and Shelley Buchanan, Price, Joulwan, St. Clair and his wife, Haig and his wife. Climbing into the limousine, Haig looked up at the bright sky and threw a disgusted look at Wardell before shutting the door.

Ziegler and the speech writers shared the second car. Buchanan handed Ziegler a copy of the memo and said that Price was in agreement. Glumly, Ziegler nodded his assent to each of the points up to the final one, that resignation was inevitable. "I agree with the whole thing except the last paragraph," he said. Buchanan was used to Ziegler's habit of never revealing whether his words reflected his own thoughts or the President's. At least he was now on board against a public pledge to fight it out.

Inside the helicopter, Buchanan handed the memo to Haig. Haig read it quickly. The "two-step" strategy, releasing the tape and then letting events convince the President, appealed to Haig. "I agree with you," he said, passing the page back over his shoulder to Buchanan. Buchanan gave it to St. Clair, seated beside him. He hoped that the wait-and-see approach would appeal to the lawyer's natural caution and dampen some of St. Clair's recent enthusiasm for a Senate battle.

St. Clair, however, made another of his sharp turns. He rejected the recommendations and proceeded to outline his latest position: "He's got to resign tomorrow." Those who counseled otherwise were no longer serving the interests of the nation.

They all argued with him, shouting to be heard over the noise of the helicopter's engines.

When they arrived at Camp David, Haig went immediately to Aspen Cabin to join the President. Buchanan, Price, St. Clair and Ziegler went to Birch Cabin and resumed their rancorous discussion. As the argument grew more heated, Buchanan concluded that St. Clair's latest turnabout was based largely on a personal concern for his professional reputation.

Ziegler was terribly excited. Resignation the next day was out of the question. An attempt to force the President's hand would fail and might even end in disaster. The President, he said, was not convinced that the June 23 tape was fatal.

Buchanan believed that the way to Nixon was through Ziegler, and he wanted to maneuver himself into a more moderate position between St. Clair's "resignation now" and those willing to fight. To this end, he stepped up his attack on St. Clair. "Drop the tape and he'll come around in a week or ten days. And the country will be a hell of a lot better off that way." The country would need time for the tape to sink in and bring most people around to the same conclusion Nixon would have to reach. Resignation would be inevitable.

St. Clair was not convinced. "How much punishment can one person take? How much can the country take? We're not serving the President if we let him go through with this."

"But, Jim, I told him to resign three ways," Buchanan said. "Through Al, Bebe and the family."

In half an hour, Haig came back from Aspen.

"Al, did the message get through?" Buchanan asked. "Does the President know where I stand?"

"Yes," Haig replied. Buchanan turned to St. Clair with a look that said, "You see?"

St. Clair started to argue, but Haig cut him off. The President had agreed to scuttle the televised address in favor of a written statement that would be issued the next day along with the transcript.

Ziegler went to see the President, and the discussion in Birch Cabin now turned to the written statement. Price went off to work on it. It didn't take him long to figure out what to do. One section of the discarded address was an explanation of the tape. Price picked up his scissors, cut that section out, and redid it more vaguely. The statement would mention neither resignation nor any all-out, last-ditch fight.

As Price worked, Haig, St. Clair and Buchanan continued to argue. Telling the President what to do, Haig reminded St. Clair, might trigger the same reaction Griffin's letter had set off the day before, make the man more stubborn. With Haig applying pressure, St. Clair retreated.

Haig and St. Clair would brief the loyalists on the committee Monday. But that still left John Rhodes out in the open. Rhodes had scheduled a press conference for Monday, and he had assured the White House that he would direct the anti-impeachment forces in the House debate.

"You can't keep the guy out on a hook like that," Buchanan said.

Haig went to call Rhodes. "There are some developments that I can't talk to you about," he told him, "but I would advise you very strongly to cancel your press conference."

Rhodes thought he had never heard anyone so downhearted. "When will I know what this is all about?" he asked gently.

"You will know tomorrow," Haig replied. "I will have you briefed."

Rhodes thanked the general and called Jay Smith, his press aide. He told Smith to cancel the conference. "I think it might be resignation," he said.

THE ENTOURAGE came together shortly after two for lunch in Laurel Lodge. The President had insisted that some of the wives come to Camp David that

Sunday afternoon, and Patricia Haig and Billie St. Clair had spent the past few hours picking wild strawberries. There was almost a picnic atmosphere, and their husbands were determined that, during lunch at least, it stay that way. Prime minute steaks, a frequent item on the Camp David menu, were served with fresh vegetables. The conversation was purposefully light.

After the stewards had served apple pie à la mode and coffee, the men moved to the Cabinet Room in Laurel and went over Price's work. He had outlined the basic elements of the next day's statement:

1. While reviewing tapes to be turned over in compliance with the Supreme Court decision, the President discovered a serious omission in his previous statements about Watergate.

2. His review disclosed that, on June 23, 1972, he ordered the FBI's investigation to stop not only for national-security reasons but for political reasons as well.

3. Therefore, complete transcripts of the June 23 conversations were being supplied to the House Judiciary Committee which had conducted its deliberations on the basis of incomplete and erroneous information.

4. A House vote of impeachment was foregone. Therefore, the issue would go to trial in the Senate. To insure that no more relevant information was overlooked, the President would voluntarily furnish the Senate with all material that had been turned over to the special prosecutor.

5. While recognizing the damage done his case by this disclosure, the President remained convinced that the record in its entirety did not justify the extreme step of impeachment and conviction of a President. Whatever mistakes he made in his handling of Watergate, the basic truth remained that—when all the facts were brought to his attention—he insisted on a thorough investigation and prosecution of the guilty.

Price was pleased with his draft and thought it expressed his deep belief that the President's actions six days after the Watergate break-in were innocent in intent, and that nothing Nixon had done merited impeachment.

Buchanan was satisfied that the President was not committing himself to wage all-out war. Whatever words Price chose to soften the harsh facts, Buchanan thought there could be no mistaking the impact such a statement would have. It did, however, leave the President a little room.

Haig was not satisfied. It wasn't accurate, for one. It implied that Nixon hadn't listened to the tape until after the Supreme Court decision. The fact was that he had heard it sometime during May.

Price and Buchanan were confused. Why had he listened to it in May?

Haig explained. The President was, at that time, responding to Jaworski's compromise offer to settle for certain tapes in return for keeping secret

Nixon's status as an unindicted co-conspirator. Buzhardt, St. Clair and he were all involved in the May thing. The statement must make it clear that they were not aware that the President had turned down Jaworski's offer as a consequence of listening to the June 23 tape.

Buchanan and Price were outraged. They, and a lot of other people, had put their own reputations on the line defending the President and saying things that Nixon knew were false.

Ziegler defended the President. Nixon had not listened until after the Supreme Court decision. They were wrong. He rushed off to check with his boss.

Haig decided to do his own checking. He had Joulwan call Wardell and have him consult the log for May 5 to be certain that that was the day St. Clair and he had heard Jaworski outline his proposal. Joulwan returned a few minutes later: Affirmative.

Next, Haig picked up the phone to find those who could pinpoint the date the President listened to the tape: Bull, Shepard and Buzhardt. He had reached the first two and was getting ready to call Buzhardt when Ziegler returned. They fit together for Ziegler the pieces they had already found: Jaworski, Haig and St. Clair met on May 5. According to Bull and Shepard, the President listened to the tape on May 6. The next day the President instructed St. Clair to turn down the offer.

Ziegler shouted that they were wrong. "The President says he didn't listen to it then. It was late in May." They were all jumping to the wrong conclusion.

"Look, Ron," Buchanan said, his voice rising, "we've got the records. The only date they were checked out was on May 6. Here's the Jaworski thing at the same time. There's no other conclusion."

"I don't believe that," Ziegler said shrilly. "The President says it was the other way." That the tape had been checked out was simply no proof that the President had actually listened to it. And even if he had, he had not recognized its significance, Ziegler added. But he was all by himself on this one.

Haig didn't bother to dispute him. He called Buzhardt at the White House. Had the President listened to the June 23 conversation when he was reviewing tapes?

Which time? Buzhardt asked. January or May?

Either.

Buzhardt checked his own notes. They indicated that the President listened to the tape on May 6, he said.

Haig told him about the argument they were having and what Ziegler was claiming.

Buzhardt said that there was one other piece of information of crucial significance. Only twelve days ago, on July 24, as Haig might recall, the President had specifically asked Buzhardt to listen to the June 23, 1973, tape. There could be no doubt that the President had already heard the tape; otherwise he could not have singled it out as a potential problem.

That was the clincher for Buchanan, Price and St. Clair, but Ziegler persisted. He needed to be absolutely certain, to verify their thesis personally. Although Haig thought it was a waste of time, he agreed to a meeting with Bull and Buzhardt that evening at the White House. He called Bull, but he was not at the White House. It was about 6 P.M. when he was finally located. "I'm leaving Camp David shortly and I would like to see you and Jerry Jones in my office at eight," Haig told him. Jones was responsible for the record-keeping of the tapes.

As Bull got ready to go back to the White House, he received another call, this time from the President. How sure was Bull that he, Nixon, had listened to the tape on May 6?

Quite certain.

"Are you sure?" the President demanded. "I thought it was later."

Impossible, said Bull. It was in the notes.

Was it possible that Bull had cued that tape but that the President had not listened to it?

"No, Mr. President, I remember the day well." The tape counter indicated that the President had actually listened to the tape, not just that the machine had been set up. There was no question, Bull assured him.

WHEN BULL arrived at the White House, no one but Jones was there, but soon the party from Camp David returned. Buzhardt walked into Haig's office with them.

Haig asked Jones when the President had received the June 23 tape.

It had been checked out to Bull on May 6.

Haig turned to Bull. "When did he listen to it?"

As Bull was rechecking his notes Price said to him, "It's very important."

"It might be fatal," Haig added.

Bull looked at his interrogators. "My notes show that the President heard it on May 6."

"Who knows about it?" Haig asked.

Bull had told it to the grand jury when he testified on June 6. He had also turned over his notes. Bull expected Haig to be angry with him. He was not.

Haig paused. Everybody waited. "Okay, that's it," he said. "An act probably fatal." His tone was resigned. There was nothing more to discuss. Ziegler had stopped arguing.

After Bull and Jones had left, the others went back to Price's draft. Haig handed Buzhardt a copy and filled him in on how things had gone at Camp David. The President was insisting that he had not listened to the tape and that he wanted the statement to back him up. Haig's face asked, "Can you believe that?"

Buzhardt shook his head sadly. The statement could not say that the President had not listened to the tape, because the notes said the opposite and both the special prosecutor and the grand jury had the notes.

The group worked toward what they hoped would be an acceptable compromise. Price could write that the President had reviewed the tapes in May, but would not say precisely when. That might be enough. It would skirt the issue. For Haig and St. Clair, though, that was not enough. They insisted that the President say that he had not told them at that time what was on the tape. St. Clair was determined that the President also take responsibility for withholding that tape from the special prosecutor and the House Judiciary Committee.

They were talking to the President through Ziegler: the President had to stop denying facts that were already on record, and he had to clarify their situation once and for all.

Buzhardt thought Haig and St. Clair were coming close to threatening to resign. He tried to calm them; quietly he reminded them that they had all agreed not to do anything to force a resignation, that resignation had to be a willing act on the President's part, that Nixon, above all, must see it as such. Price would work something out, Buzhardt assured them.

Haig and St. Clair relented. The discussion turned to how to work out the two-step strategy. What had to be done the next day? Who would have to be briefed before the transcript hit?

Haig began making calls right after the meeting. He reached Treasury Secretary William Simon and told him, "I've got bad news—it may be fatal to the President." He described the transcript. There would also be a statement by the President offering his explanation, but that was still in the works.

Haig's frustration boiled over as he told Simon what had to be included in the statement. Buzhardt, St. Clair and he were all resigning "if the President doesn't lay it on the line."

Monday, August 5

HAIG arrived at the White House early. He had been through this
exercise many times—getting the difficult word out, letting the right
people know in the right order so that nobody was needlessly
offended. Haig made and held friends that way. He had mastered the mechanics of telling the bureaucratic and political establishments about presidential decisions slightly in advance, giving them enough time to absorb the
facts, but not enough to spread them around.

Today was delicate; this maneuver called for perfect timing. The new
transcript could not be allowed to cause a panic. But its significance must
not be lost. That was the key to the two-step plan. The President's degree
of culpability had to sink in slowly but deeply. This time, Nixon didn't have
a grand gesture in reserve to distract the country or to explain away the
obvious. No speech, as with Vietnam, the Haldeman-Ehrlichman resignations or the release of the edited transcripts. Today, Haig was on his own.

It was crucial that warning be given to the ten Republican supporters on
the House Judiciary Committee who had gone to the mat for the President;
to the Senate Republican leaders; to key Democratic friends like Eastland
and Stennis; to Jaworski; to George Bush, the Cabinet and the hard-
pressed White House staff. Haig would handle the staff personally.

Reporters would be given the statement and transcript late in the afternoon, time enough to grasp what was in them but too late to set off a stampede. On the Hill, members could ponder and consult before they went out

front or issued any statements. That way the drama would be played out over a few days.

Those who had seen the transcript were of one mind. Even so, Haig couldn't be absolutely sure of the wider response. The consensus of the President's senior staff—Ziegler, Buzhardt, St. Clair, Price, Buchanan, Burch, himself—had often been wrong. The reactions of Wiggins and Griffin might be signs that the matter was clinched. Still, he had to move carefully, preserve his position with the President, and let others draw the conclusions. He would sit tight, in the middle, and convey his feelings by simply failing to come forward with his usual, and expected, support of the President. Haig had watched the President weather hurricanes before. Nixon might just pull out of this one. There were hidden resources in the man, and immense power in the office—Haig was acutely aware of that. He doubted there was another rallying cry in Richard Nixon, but he couldn't be sure. Even now he really didn't have any confidence that he knew the President very well.

When Buzhardt arrived at Haig's office very early, George Bush was already there, briefed and somewhat relieved. Finally there was some one thing the national chairman could see clearly. The ambiguities in the evidence against the President had been tearing the party apart, Bush thought. The three men reviewed the day's plan. Buzhardt and Dean Burch would lay the situation out that afternoon for John Rhodes. That was sensitive. The press was expecting Rhodes to announce today whether he would assume leadership of the anti-impeachment forces. Haig had warned him off, but it was crucial to take Rhodes's temperature carefully.

Haig needed a consensus. The President's friends, certain trusted aides, a few politicians whose motives could not be suspect, must come succinctly to a single conclusion. Haig didn't want his ass out front alone. He didn't want his ass out front, period. There wouldn't be any attempt to strong-arm Rhodes, but Buzhardt was confident that he could help Rhodes see what was now the only solution. Bush asked to go along. It would have been impolite to refuse.

Shortly after 9:15 A.M., Burch, Timmons, Buchanan, Lichenstein, Clawson, and Richard Moore gathered in Burch's office to be briefed by Buchanan. He described the weekend at Camp David: Price, St. Clair and he stuck off in one cabin, Nixon in another, and Haig and Ziegler running back and forth with messages; the President saying that the transcript didn't mean what it said; and then the President's senior aides conducting their own "investigation" of the President, to confirm that he had listened to the tape.

Buchanan was rubbing his hands, rocking back and forth in his chair, trying to articulate what he felt after almost ten years of service to Richard Nixon. He brooded about how hard he and the others had worked on the defense, how he had persistently maintained that "the Old Man" was a victim—not without his faults, but a victim. Buchanan seemed on the verge of boiling over again. The Old Man had lied to him and everybody else. He had connived. The President had listened to the tape three months earlier, in May. He had known since then that it confirmed the worst suspicions and he had canceled the proposed compromise with Jaworski because of it. The family, Julie in particular, was pressuring the President not to resign. But Buchanan was clear in his own mind. It was over, he said.

He called down to the legal offices for a copy of the transcript. Jeff Shepard was shaking when he went off to the Xerox machine. "This is it," he told Ann Morgan, Gergen's assistant. "They found the smoking gun." Then he took the copy up to Burch's office and read it aloud.

When Shepard had finished reading, Clawson said to Lichenstein, "Unfortunately, there isn't a market for right-wing journalists."

The group had never organized strategy effectively. Now they could at least register its collapse. "Somebody get the ice," Burch said.

Someone got the Scotch.

"To the President," Timmons toasted. It was a perfectly serious moment. Hail and farewell.

Soon Timmons was on the phone. "Come on over, we're writing résumés," he said to one of his assistants.

Briefly Timmons worried about whether Haig had contacted all the key people. "Dean, does Bush know about the transcript yet?"

"Yes."

"Well, what did he do?"

"He broke out into assholes and shit himself to death," Burch replied.

IN HIS Houston law office that morning, Leon Jaworski was told that General Haig was on the line. Jaworski was in Texas to arrange his finances. Now that he was on a considerably reduced government salary of about $40,000 a year, he wanted to move some of his money around for income-tax purposes.

Haig was less than forthright. He described the new transcript, claiming that neither he nor the lawyers had known it existed until just now. "It came as a shocker," he said.

St. Clair got on the line. "It's got to be turned over. I've made contrary representations to the House Judiciary Committee."

Jaworski heard their nervousness, particularly St. Clair's. The President's attorney was not only informing the special prosecutor, he was protecting himself, getting it on the record that he had insisted on release. In seven months of dealing with St. Clair, Jaworski had concluded that the Boston lawyer was overrated. It was clear that he lacked information and was not in control of the Nixon defense. Jaworski had come to regard him as simply another component of the White House public-relations machine—another aide proclaiming presidential innocence.

The new tape was not a surprise. Jaworski had expected something like it. It sounded harmful to the President's defense, but there had already been so much. He saw no reason to rush back to Washington.

THE PRESIDENT returned from Camp David by helicopter at ten o'clock. As he was landing, Ziegler sent Connie Gerrard to Price's office to pick up an envelope, instructing her not to read what was inside. In any case, Price had taken the unusual precaution of sealing it with tape. She took the package to Stuart Stout in the usher's office in the residence and he delivered it to the President. It contained Price's eight-page, fourth draft of the afternoon's statement.

As the President was reviewing it, St. Clair called McCahill into his office. It was about 11 A.M. "The June 23 tape has some very damaging stuff on it," St. Clair said. He told him the details. McCahill agreed it was bad. "Do you think I ought to resign?" St. Clair asked.

McCahill was taken aback. The young lawyers on the team often joked about bombshells making direct hits on their bunker. "I'm getting out of here," one would say to another. Sometimes they'd joke that the special prosecutor was going to name Buzhardt as an unindicted co-conspirator. But St. Clair was deadly serious. He was telling his associate that their client had withheld evidence.

McCahill was trying to think. His first reactions to difficult disclosures had always been, Okay, how do we explain it, where is the justification, let's look at it. Oddly, St. Clair and McCahill had never discussed whether they thought the President was innocent. They were busy lawyers; they had just pushed on with a defense. McCahill used to say to St. Clair that working in the White House was like shaving in the dark. He had gone so far as to urge St. Clair to ask the President what defense he thought they should deploy, since he knew the facts and the lawyers were only speculating. But St. Clair had reminded him that the President had other matters to deal with than building a legal defense, and McCahill had accepted the rules. Now his boss was asking whether he should resign.

McCahill said no, not under the circumstances. In an ordinary case, perhaps, but St. Clair's resignation would leave the President without a lawyer. McCahill would, of course, resign too, if St. Clair did, and so probably would the rest of the legal staff. The President of the United States might not be able to get a lawyer.

St. Clair, still holding back details of the statement drafted for Nixon, mused that he might be able to get the President to say publicly that the lawyers had not been aware of this new evidence.

McCahill wondered out loud if the President was going to resign.

"As far as I know," St. Clair said, "we're going to trial in the Senate."

"Well, then," McCahill replied, "I have work to do." He wanted to attempt a full analysis of the transcript, but before that he had to go to Sirica's courtroom once again. Ben-Veniste wanted to subpoena the secretaries who had transcribed some of the tapes, to determine if there were any more gaps.

ON THE flight back to Washington that morning, Senator Robert Griffin was pondering the impact, if any, of his Saturday letter. Not enough, he decided, and he got out his yellow legal pad and a blue felt-tipped pen.

At eleven-thirty, after attending a closed Rules Committee hearing on the procedures that would govern the Senate trial, Griffin read his statement to reporters on Capitol Hill. He spoke in a low, somber voice.

"I think we've arrived at a point where both the national interest and his own interest would best be served by resigning. It's not just his enemies who feel that way. Many of his friends, and I count myself one of them, believe now that this would be the most appropriate course. Needless to say, this would be an awesome and very difficult decision for him to reach, but I believe he will see it that way, too."

The number-two Republican in the Senate had called for resignation and had predicted that the President himself would agree that it was the best course.

AT THE White House, the daily briefing was already two hours overdue when Gerald Warren entered the press room at 1 P.M. to announce that there would be another two-hour delay. Ziegler called his staff into his small office—Diane Sawyer, Jerry Warren, Judy Johnson, Connie Gerrard, Karin Nordstrom and Frank Gannon.

"I just want to tell you guys what's happened." His manner was calm, cool, sad, but not apologetic. "We are going to put out some material this afternoon that some of you will be shocked by. You'll be typing a statement by the President. Accompanying it will be three transcripts of presidential conversations." His tone was formal.

"There is a problem because while Mr. St. Clair was making certain statements, the President acknowledges he knew otherwise about what Mr. St. Clair was saying. All I can think about why this has happened this way is that the President didn't focus on the entire problem.

"Each one of you can draw your own conclusion as to what it means. I firmly believe that the President forgot he had said that and forgot that he had heard that tape."

A lot of people would be calling for the President's resignation, Ziegler said, and many in the White House would be disappointed and hurt. Ziegler himself had personally agonized over the situation, but he recognized that a President could have human frailties; a sixty-one-year-old man with a lot of responsibilities could listen to a tape and not discuss it because he did not want to focus on it or on its implications.

Judy Johnson was crying.

"We'll have no more tears," Ziegler said. "We'll be professional and do our job like we always have." He asked that they hold the information confidential until it was released.

Anne Grier had left the White House to look for a record during her lunch hour. When she came back, the press offices were empty and Ziegler's door was shut. When everybody finally emerged, Grier had trouble finding out what had happened. Diane Sawyer was saying, "My God, I can't believe all this is in here. Can you believe it?" She told Grier that Ron would see her privately in a few minutes, but Ziegler got tied up and Grier went back to Sawyer. A June 23 transcript was going to be released, Sawyer explained, and it was bad.

"What is so bad about it?"

"What is so bad about it is that the President said something on the tape and he has been letting St. Clair go out and say one thing which he knows is not so. Ron's explanation is that the President was too beat to understand what he heard and he wasn't focusing on what St. Clair was doing."

Grier thought, Well, the President is a little bit guilty, but certainly not as guilty as some people think.

But Karin Nordstrom interjected, "What bullshit. Does he really expect us to believe this?"

Soon the President's statement had been mimeographed and the transcript retyped on bond paper to be Xeroxed. Johnson, Grier and Nordstrom fanned out to the Xerox machines.

The delay in the briefing had alerted the press, and more reporters were arriving at the White House. The press room was jammed, the overflow group spilling onto the lawn in front of the West Wing entrance. Several reporters lay on the grass, which was forbidden. Tom DeCair thought the press was waiting for blood—reporters were flouting regulations and decorum because they sensed the end. Ziegler reassured him. They had had tough times before and had made it through. There was no mention of resignation.

Warren had almost stopped functioning. Ziegler told him that the problem now was to help the President survive his personal anguish.

JOHN RHODES stayed home. The cover story for delaying his press conference was that he was ill, and it would be best to play it through. Wiggins had called him at about eight-thirty that morning to describe the contents of the tape. A number of reporters visited Rhodes's house to try to get a statement. CBS correspondent Lesley Stahl rang the doorbell, and Rhodes's wife answered. She thought Stahl was the Avon Lady.

About 1:15 P.M., Buzhardt, Burch and Bush arrived at Rhodes's home. Buzhardt told the Minority Leader they had a little bomb—little but highly explosive. Rhodes's wife, Betty, served iced tea because it was too early for the Scotch Rhodes felt like having. They sat down in the living room and Rhodes read the excerpts. There was a brief silence as he laid the sheets aside.

"This is incredible."

"Yes," Buzhardt agreed. "It was to me too."

"This means that there's just no chance in the world that he's not going to be impeached," said Rhodes. "In fact, there's no chance in the world that I won't vote to impeach him."

Buzhardt sighed his relief.

"I certainly can understand that," Burch said.

"You know," Rhodes continued. "It'd be better to get this thing over to the Senate just as rapidly as possible, because there's no profit to the country, or anybody, in dragging this out in the House. If you've got any chance at all, which I doubt, it's over in the Senate."

After the beating he had taken several months earlier when he had suggested that the President resign, Rhodes was not about to mention resignation again, even in private, even to the President's closest assistants.

The three men left, satisfied. The consensus was taking hold. Rhodes later let it be known that he was offended that Bush had been briefed before he was.

AT 3 P.M., in Room H-138 of the House of Representatives, the Judiciary Committee Democrats caucused. Rodino announced that he hoped the impeachment debate on the House floor would begin in two weeks, on August 19. He proposed seventy-five hours of general debate.

At 3:30 P.M., across the street in the office of Leslie C. Arends of Illinois, the number-two House Republican, the President's defenders on the committee met at Timmons' invitation. St. Clair and Timmons were beginning their briefing when Buzhardt and Burch arrived.

This audience knew the case intimately, so the effect of the new transcript was immediate. Their reactions ranged from outrage to dismay. Their calls for "specificity" now held a terrible irony.

St. Clair defended himself to them. He had been ready to resign if the President had opposed release, he said. St. Clair failed to mention that he had learned of the new evidence on July 24—the day the Judiciary Committee debate had opened on television. The congressional defenders focused their anger on Nixon.

St. Clair, Buzhardt and Timmons moved on to Scott's office for a meeting with Senate Republican leaders—Scott, Griffin, Tower, Brock, and Norris Cotton of New Hampshire. Scott's office was decorated as a sitting room, with a desk stuck off in a corner, Oriental art on the walls, and small Chinese figurines on the mantel. A large chandelier hung from the high ceiling. The Senators sat stiffly on gold brocade couches while St. Clair told them that once again he was the bearer of bad news.

Scott interrupted. He was worried that the White House was trying again to divide the Republicans and asked if John Rhodes had been informed. He became slightly less suspicious when told that Rhodes knew.

The clock on the mantel showed just after 4 P.M. St. Clair was watching it. He said he had a new transcript that was bad, and it was being released publicly right at that moment. Copies were handed around. St. Clair said that he had insisted it be released. "I told the President that if it weren't, he'd be minus a lawyer."

No one said anything as the five Senators read.

"I've had a problem as a lawyer—whether I could continue as the President's lawyer," St. Clair said when they had finished. "But as long as he released it, he has done his part and I can continue to do my best to make a defense." He had thought he had the case won until this last tape, he said.

"Where?" Scott inquired. The other Senators, especially Tower, echoed his doubt. St. Clair didn't really answer. He had heard from Haig that senatorial skepticism about Watergate was a localized infection in and around Scott's office.

The Senators were not nearly as familiar with the case as the Republican members of the House Judiciary Committee, but the transcript's significance couldn't be missed. "This changes the picture one more time," Scott said. The meeting ended politely. Scott thought it odd that the White House representatives hadn't even tried to defend what was on the tape.

While Buzhardt, St. Clair, Timmons and Burch were on the Hill, about a hundred White House staffers assembled in a fourth-floor auditorium in the EOB. Chuck Wardell had been instructed to summon Haig when the room was filled. Every seat was taken, and people stood in the aisles. Haig was delayed because he was still notifying the Cabinet members. Housing and Urban Development Secretary James Lynn had been tracked down in the barbershop.

The staff members in the EOB were silent as Haig entered half an hour late. The blue curtains were closed behind him as he stood on a podium speaking into a microphone. There was the clipped, efficient ring of the general in his voice.

"Thank you for coming. I have the tough task of bringing you some bad news. The President has been reviewing tapes. All except one are consistent with his previous explanations. The exception is of sufficient gravity to warrant a briefing, and that is the tape of June 23, 1972."

The House committee, the special prosecutor and Judge Sirica had been informed, Haig assured them. "The tape shows that previous explanations have been incomplete and erroneous as regards CIA involvement. I know the transcript makes it difficult again for you and the President." He hoped they all would stay at their desks. "If not out of loyalty to the President, then out of loyalty to the nation. I have served with men in combat and I can say that no men and women have ever been as brave as this White House staff."

Haig then read the President's statement acknowledging that the transcript was at variance with earlier statements. Though the President had listened to the tapes in May, he had not realized the implications and hadn't bothered to inform anyone.

> This was a serious act of omission for which I take full responsibility and which I deeply regret [Haig read]. I recognize that this additional material I am now furnishing may further damage my case, especially because attention will be drawn separately to it rather than to the evidence in its entirety.

Whatever mistakes I made in the handling of Watergate, the basic truth remains that when all the facts were brought to my attention, I insisted on a full investigation and prosecution of those guilty. I am firmly convinced that the record, in its entirety, does not justify the extreme step of impeachment and removal of a President. I trust that as the Constitutional process goes forward, this perspective will prevail.

As Haig walked off the stage, the audience rose and applauded. Then suddenly, the room was silent. In the quiet, the staff had time to ponder Haig's words: "If not out of loyalty to the President, then out of loyalty to the nation."

It was hard for many of them to gauge the situation. It seemed clear that the President was determined to fight, and the President's statement ended on an upbeat note. Yet Haig's demeanor and tone were not aggressive, as they had always been in the past. The staffers filed out slowly. Many appeared unsure of what to do next. Watergate veterans were anxious to get copies of the transcript; presidential explanations had a tendency to mask the gravity of the disclosures.

This time, Haig's appeal had not touched Buzhardt's assistant Dick Hauser. He went back to his office and wrote out his resignation. "When you're a lawyer," he told Pam Dallas, "you expect your client to lie to you, but not when he is the President." He tried several versions, long and short, and spent the rest of the afternoon on the phone seeking advice from friends.

Months earlier, when Hauser had been trying to decide whether to come to work for the President, Buzhardt had told him, "I'm going to come out of this fine. I've been through worse. The President is going to come out okay. And if I come out okay, so will you." Now Hauser was convinced that he had made a mistake, and he was going to rectify it. He went to see Buzhardt. Normally, Buzhardt would have attempted to dissuade him. Today he just didn't have the time.

Ken Cole, chief domestic-affairs adviser to the President, called his staff together in his second-floor suite and said that if some of them couldn't take it, he would understand if they resigned. But if they stayed, he said, he expected them to work full time to keep the government functioning. Cole himself was in a slow burn at having been deceived.

Many among the staff were distraught. Bill Henkel took a copy of the transcript, and when he reached his office he grunted, "Fuck" and flung it across the room. Gergen and Agnes Waldron, the head of the research office, went up to McCahill and offered their sympathy. It seemed worse for the lawyers.

The usual reaction in the White House to moments of crisis was to call meetings. Joulwan gathered a group of middle-level staffers in the Roosevelt Room—among them Gergen, Jones, Powell Moore, Ken Khachigian and David Parker. The group was first given the two shorter transcripts of June 23, 1972, and for fifteen minutes they read and wondered what all the fuss was about. Then they were given the text of Nixon's initial meeting that day with Haldeman. It was thirty-four pages long.

Gergen and Parker were astounded at the contents, looking at each other as they tried to absorb one shock after another. Everyone was reading portions aloud. "Did you see this?" "Did you see that?"

There were protests. The President talking about Herb Klein: "[he] doesn't have his head screwed on right." The President not giving a shit about the lira. The arts: "The arts, you know, they're Jews, they're left wing—in other words, stay away." The coiffures of his wife and daughters: "The helicopter . . . destroys their hair and so forth." Why were these things left in? Could it be stopped? Now Joulwan realized that Haig, Ziegler and the lawyers had dropped their public-relations guard in the rush to get the material out. He ran out of the meeting and burst into the press office, insisting that the release be stopped. It was too late, more than a hundred copies had been distributed. It was unthinkable to recall them and then hand out an expurgated version.

Joulwan returned to the Roosevelt Room. The discussion had a feeling of aimlessness and gloom.

Small groups of staffers gathered all over the White House and the EOB, talking in low voices. Work had virtually ceased. Wayne Valis, an assistant to William Baroody, a political counselor to the President, got a copy of the transcript from the press office, took it back to Baroody's EOB office and read it aloud. Someone asked how many votes the President would now have on the Hill.

"There won't be any votes, don't you see?" Baroody said.

Tom Korologos took refuge in humor. Parroting Senator Howard Baker's often repeated question during the Watergate hearings the year before, Korologos asked, "What did the President know and when did he know it? We sure found out."

Bruce Herschensohn, a former United States Information Agency official who had been brought to the White House by Haldeman to write Administration propaganda, had missed the Haig briefing, but he was soon getting reports. Haig had not defended the President this time. Something had changed. Herschensohn placed a call to Haig. It was not returned. He read the June 23 transcripts and the President's statement. Something odd was going on, he concluded. He found the statement more damaging than the transcripts. He went over them again. The transcripts were defensible or, at the least, ambiguous. They could be read either way. The national-security considerations were real, even though the President had not referred to them specifically in his conversations with Haldeman. Certainly a free-wheeling investigation of Watergate the week after the break-in would have led to the Plumbers and to the important work of stopping news leaks. There was also a human factor—a President protecting his aides and friends.

Upstairs in the EOB, Lawrence Higby took a call from his former boss, H. R. Haldeman, who had heard the news. Why had so much been conceded? Haldeman asked. Higby told him that the resignation pressure was mounting and that it appeared that the President might succumb. "I think you're right," Haldeman said. "He'll do it. If he does, it's a mistake. If he does it, the problem is how he does it."

The former White House chief of staff, due to go on trial soon in the Watergate cover-up, was worried about his own papers and Nixon's tapes. What would happen to them if Nixon left?

"If he's going to pay the price and resign, he ought to end Watergate," Haldeman said. And that would include settling the issue of the tapes once and for all. Nixon ought to get control of them, and also grant pardons to everyone. He could also give pardons to the Vietnam deserters. That would make amnesty more acceptable to the anti-Nixon, antiwar crowd.

Ben Stein had listened with shock to Haig's presentation and was wandering around, expressing wonderment that Watergate had come to this. Ray Price needed time to work on the resignation address, and he needed to keep Stein busy. He assigned him to write a fight speech.

"Here's your chance to do something great," Price instructed. "Write a speech that will bring tears to the eyes of Americans and demands that the President stay in office." Stein took to his typewriter with the old enthusiasm.

Price had watched the President waver on the question of resignation, but he was sure that in the end Nixon would resign. He raised the matter with his friend Len Garment. Garment, regarded by his colleagues as the best resident analyst of the Nixon psyche, was sure the President would stick it out. They bet a dinner on it.

ON THE House floor, Barber Conable watched Wiggins and his allies on Judiciary coming in, looking very gray. It was the signal he was waiting for. John Rhodes had called at 3:45 to warn him. "You are the only member of the leadership that I care about," Rhodes had said, "and you may want to protect yourself." Now Conable walked to the TV cameras and took protective steps. "If the transcripts are as Nixon says, I will vote for impeachment on Article One. I don't approve of leaders who mislead."

Wiggins then went before the cameras with a prepared statement. His eyes were damp and the confident punch was absent from his voice. His torment was visible and moving, and his directness gave dignity to the moment of humiliation. "I have reached the painful conclusion that the President of the United States should resign," Wiggins said, struggling to speak. If the President did not resign, "I am prepared to conclude that the magnificent career of public service of Richard Nixon must be terminated involuntarily."

Of the ten defenders, only Wiggins and Iowa Congressman Wiley Mayne shifted positions publicly that afternoon. The others said they would reassess. John Anderson, the liberal third-ranking Republican, also hesitated. Since calling on the President to resign three months earlier, he had learned to move more slowly.

The Senate Republican leadership issued a one-sentence statement from Scott's office: "The President took the proper action in releasing essential additional information prior to the House vote."

RABBI KORFF reacted strongly. He wanted to see the President, but he hadn't been able to get through all day. After a long wait in the first-floor usher's office, Korff was taken to see David Eisenhower in the solarium. The rabbi's message was to fight. David told him there was a good chance that the President would resign. Then David walked to the Lincoln Sitting Room, where the President had again taken refuge, and relayed Korff's message.

The President didn't want to see Korff. He didn't seem interested in the statement that had just been released. Richard Nixon did not look at his son-in-law. He expressed sadness that his staff—Haig, St. Clair, Buzhardt and Buchanan—were not more like Korff. It would be nice to have them sticking by at this moment, the President said. But he didn't blame them.

JULIE HURRIED to the East Wing to do some organizing. The family was going out on the *Sequoia* in a little while, and she wanted to have as many female staffers as possible outside to cheer her father as he departed the White House.

At 5:15 P.M., Mrs. Nixon, David, Julie, Rose Mary Woods and the President emerged through the diplomatic entrance. Nixon was wearing a light-blue sports jacket. He looked old. About fifty secretaries were gathered along the driveway. At first Nixon seemed surprised and embarrassed. He began joking awkwardly with David about all the pretty girls. He would have liked having all these girls around when he was in the Navy, he said, and David and Julie laughed. Mrs. Nixon tried to look cheerful, smiling and kissing some good friends on the staff.

"We still love you," one of the staffers said.

The remark was repeated more than once, and there was some applause. Julie had wanted to make it a campaign send-off, and for a moment it was almost as if nothing had happened.

Fifteen minutes later, the family boarded the *Sequoia*. Lieutenant Commander Coombs decided to go downriver. He thought the President would not want to see people. As they passed the National War College, Nixon said, "Imagine George Patton riding around the courtyard." (The movie *Patton* was his favorite, and he had shown it at the White House several times.) He began reminiscing again, recalling how the family had gone to Hains Point for picnics when the girls were little. And he began talking about his presidency in the past tense. "It has been fun having use of the yacht," he said.

A FEW minutes before 7 P.M., Joulwan called an expanded group of middle-level staffers together.

Parker said the President should hold a Cabinet meeting. Speakes thought the new disclosures were insignificant and ambiguous. Khachigian and he wanted to fight on. Gergen and Jerry Jones said the only honorable thing was to resign. Most of the others were restrained, doubtful of the wisdom of expressing themselves frankly, except for Ann Morgan. "George, you're a soldier," she told Joulwan. "You can't keep sending your soldiers out without ammunition." The White House mess was closed, so arrangements were made for sandwiches to be sent in. Ziegler poked his head in nervously, but he didn't say anything.

Inside Haig's office, St. Clair and Buzhardt were giving the general a rundown on the Hill briefings. The reaction had been severe, the lawyers agreed. St. Clair said he had told the Congressmen he would have resigned had the transcripts not been released. Buzhardt thought St. Clair was grandstanding. His threat to resign had never been made to the President, and

Nixon, in any case, had never seriously considered withholding the transcripts.

Haig turned on the evening news. All three major networks devoted between thirteen and seventeen minutes to the new evidence, but the reaction seemed milder than Haig had expected, the language muted. Walter Cronkite of CBS and John Chancellor of NBC referred to "a storm in the nation's capital" and said the President had "stunned" the country, but CBS concluded that whether the tape was a smoking gun would be left to the Senate. United Press International led with the President's acknowledgment that he had "acted to slow" the FBI investigation, not necessarily to thwart it.

The House was lost, unquestionably. Probably the Senate too, though the meaning of the reaction there was difficult to gauge. Only Griffin was calling for resignation. Goldwater and Stennis had not commented. Senator Curtis did not agree that the President should resign. Senator Strom Thurmond of South Carolina stated that if the President was convinced of his innocence he should "fight it to the last." Senator Edward M. Kennedy agreed that the country would best be served by continuation of the constitutional process.

After the news, Haig turned to Buzhardt. "Maybe we were wrong," he said. Was acquittal still possible? Haig had a perplexed look on his face.

The President, waiting aboard the *Sequoia* for word of the congressional reaction, left the table just before dessert to talk with Haig by ship-to-shore phone. The general made his report as pessimistic as possible.

To hell with "those soft bastards in the House," Nixon said. He would concede the House and prevail in the Senate.

Haig said he didn't think the President could win in the Senate now.

The subject of resignation was not even up for discussion as far as the President was concerned. He was holding to his decision to fight to the finish. He hung up and went to sit alone on the covered fantail. Julie joined him a few minutes later. "I'm getting bad news," he said.

The trip was supposed to have been a pep session to fortify her father. He looked broken.

It was the President's custom to shake Lieutenant Commander Coombs's hand only as he boarded the *Sequoia*. But this evening, as the ship docked back at the Navy Yard just after seven-thirty, he paused to shake hands again with the skipper.

"It has been wonderful," he said solemnly.

Mrs. Nixon said so, too.

"It has been nice," Julie added.

AFTER REPORTING to the President, Haig went to the Roosevelt Room. Joulwan was reviewing recommendations with the strategy group. Haig announced a Cabinet meeting for the next day. "The President will not resign," he said. "That is his decision, and we have to do what he wants to do. This is not a kamikaze mission." In his stern but friendly manner, Haig discouraged any expression of contrary views.

Buzhardt could feel the power evaporating. It was urgent that they have a plan, a timetable. The Vice-President must be kept in town. Ford was scheduled for a California speaking tour at the end of the week.

Vice-President Ford had said that afternoon that he was taking himself out of the impeachment issue entirely and would not comment anymore. Then he went home. Robert Hartmann reached him there and offered to describe the transcripts. Ford said he had a general idea of what they contained. He would wait for the morning papers.

AFTER THE *Sequoia* outing, Ben Stein called Julie. "You ought to be prepared for really bad things," he said. "The end is near. You have a lot of talent and ought to be thinking about a life for yourself."

"Do you think he should resign?" she asked.

"If his health can take it," Stein replied, "he should not resign." The President's tormentors should be left with as much blood on their hands as possible, he said. Still, there was no doubt the President would be convicted in the Senate.

"It doesn't matter about his health," Julie said, "his whole life is ruined." Her voice was sad, but she did not cry. She said that her father had wanted to resign, but it was her impression that the family had succeeded in talking him out of it. It was important that he stay and fight, to make his enemies aware of what they had done. "So in future years they'll see they were wrong, and that will make them not do it again."

"Well," Stein said, "he's a great man, a great, great man."

Julie and David stayed up very late that night talking.

The President was also up late. He had Sanchez prepare an early breakfast for him before he retired around 4 A.M. Haig had taken calls most of the night, making sure that Cabinet members were informed of the meeting in the morning.

Buchanan, Richard Moore and Father McLaughlin had hung around, drinking Scotch. McLaughlin, embarrassed by the appearance of new evidence, was painting a picture of himself as the victim of a "monstrous prevarication."

In his northwest-Washington apartment that night, Goldwater was unable to sleep. Dean Burch had delivered a copy of the transcripts to him late in the afternoon. Goldwater was appalled with himself for having put up with Richard Nixon as long as he had. He knew that the President, the press and Congress all regarded him as a sort of litmus test of Nixon's chances for survival. Tomorrow he would have to figure out what to do.

THE PRESS office had been deserted since midevening. Reporters had been assured that nothing more would happen that day. Occasionally a phone would ring. The wire-service machines rattled continuously. In a fifteen-hundred-word advance, Frank Cormier of the Associated Press had written: "Once hailed as a political miracle worker, Richard M. Nixon has seen his election triumphs reduced to ashes, leaving many wondering if he really did have that sure touch for politics."

The street in front of the White House was almost deserted. Occasionally a car with an out-of-town license plate would swing over to the curb on Pennsylvania Avenue, slow to a few miles an hour as the occupants gawked, and then accelerate into the night. There was nothing to see.

Two young men with knapsacks on their backs stepped up to the guard at the gate. "Where can we get passports?" one asked.

"Right there," the guard said, pointing across Lafayette Park down several blocks to the passport office. "But they won't open until nine."

Inside, a janitor was on his rounds. In the press office he scooped up the stacks of releases and swept them into a large trash barrel.

Tuesday, August 6

B ACK at his desk on Tuesday morning, Haig called those members of the Cabinet who still had not been informed of the meeting. It was perhaps the least of his priorities. Today, Haig had to cope with the Hill and the Nixon family.

With events closing in, Haig was aware that he could easily get mousetrapped. A basic element of the scenario seemed to be failing. Each time the President heard that somebody on the Hill was calling for his resignation, he became more resolved to fight to the finish. His tirades were always the same: he would not be forced out by some legislative coup; if they wanted him out of office, let them vote to impeach and convict. Nixon was still not certain that he would lose in the Senate.

Haig and Buzhardt had discussed the problem again last night. They agreed that it was crucial that no more Republican leaders call for the President's resignation. At the same time, the leaders had to make clear to Nixon that they regarded his impeachment and conviction as a foregone conclusion. Then Nixon might begin to see that resignation was the most attractive way out. He had to come to the conclusion himself, he had to perceive it as his own decision.

Haig was perplexed about the family. He had been left with the strong impression that at least David saw the wisdom of resignation. But the President was describing the family as united behind his decision to fight on. Haig called David and asked what the hell was going on.

384

David, still confident that the President would come around, suggested that Haig stay cool. The staff was ignoring too many human factors, he said. Haig and others were focusing narrowly on the legal implications and the incriminating evidence, and not considering how the President might react to his situation. If the family were not supportive, it could make it tougher for the President to resign. "We have to show him that he doesn't have to prove anything to us," David said. Any encouragement to resign on their part would imply a devastating moral judgment. He thought that his father-in-law was resisting that moral judgment more than resignation. The family had to show the President that they still loved him no matter what.

Haig was skeptical of amateur psychologizing.

"Trust me," David said. "I know what I'm doing." Mr. Nixon could accept political defeat, but he would not allow himself to be condemned morally.

AT 9 A.M. the strategy group assembled, battered and dispirited. Most of the group—among them Buzhardt, Timmons, Buchanan, and Gergen—were ready to fold up operations. Only Clawson and Khachigian seemed anxious to fight, and they had scarcely an idea on how to proceed. This morning was different from others that had followed damaging Watergate disclosures. There was no organized propaganda campaign. There were no statements, no background briefings and few meetings.

At 10 A.M., St. Clair met with his assistants at McCahill's suggestion. St. Clair didn't particularly like meetings. He ran them tightly, never allowing the discussion to range over matters that were not immediately at hand. He reacted to his staff cagily, just as he did to outsiders. This morning there was a hint of exasperation and surliness in his voice. As he entered the room, he noticed that one of his assistants, Loren Smith, who suffered from a bronchial condition, was wearing an asthma mask.

"What's your problem?" St. Clair snapped at him.

The purpose of the meeting, St. Clair announced, was to tell everyone that the President's plan was to go to trial in the Senate. Everything was to be business as usual. As for the new evidence, "We're going to deal with it like any other problem," St. Clair said. His intention was to find a technical defense. There was no proof whatsoever, he pointed out, that the President knew of the entire cover-up.

The same distinction was being made by some of the more militant presidential defenders. There was a little cover-up: the move to slow the FBI probe by using the CIA. And there was the big cover-up: the organized clandestine payment of money to the original Watergate defendants. An argument could be made that the President was only a part of the little cover-up.

"The President wants to go to trial," St. Clair repeated. As lawyers for the President, they had work to do. The staff filed dutifully out of the office.

THE CABINET meeting, scheduled for ten o'clock that morning, had been postponed to eleven because the President was not up at ten.

On the hour, Nixon walked into the room and took his seat at the center of the oval table. There wasn't the usual applause. The President's high-backed brown leather chair was slightly taller than the others. Directly in front of him, under the lip of the table which he had donated to the White House, were two spaces for buttons. One button had summoned Haldeman. The other had been marked "Butterfield" and had activated the taping system in the Cabinet Room. Now both Haldeman and the taping system were gone.

Kissinger was on Nixon's right, Secretary of Defense Schlesinger at his left. Ford was facing the President across the table and slightly to the left. Stewards served coffee.

"I would like to discuss the most important issue confronting this nation," the President began, "and confronting us internationally too—inflation."

Cabinet members looked about in mild astonishment.

But Nixon quickly shifted to what was on everybody's mind. "I want the facts out," he said. He described Watergate as "one of the most asinine things that was ever done. I'll take whatever lumps are involved." He had consulted expert lawyers and they had told him that there was no obstruction of justice and no impeachable offense.

"If there were," he said, "I wouldn't stay in this office one minute. I simply was not tending the store on the domestic side. Because the CIA and the FBI were at loggerheads, I sought to act . . . You all know I was concerned almost exclusively with national-security interests . . . but I did mention certain political interests.

"The Cabinet has been splendid in standing up. I have been very moved by it. Some, including some good friends, believe it would be best to resign and not go through the ordeal of a Senate trial. Not go through this step which would relieve me of great personal pressure and change the Constitution, that would allow other Presidents to be forced out of office. I've considered that, as a matter of fact. It should be considered, but I have had to make a decision.

"A President is really not in the position of an ordinary citizen on this kind of matter. My view is that I should not take the step that changes the Constitution and sets a precedent for the future. It would be the parliamentary system with all of its weaknesses and none of its strengths, from my own standpoint and that of my family, something which I have had to consider.

"I will accept whatever verdict the Senate hands down, recognizing the possibility that the outcome may not be favorable."

The President didn't look at anyone as he spoke.

HUD Secretary Lynn was watching for a flicker of the eye or nervousness in the hands, some sign that the President was bluffing. He concluded that Nixon was going to fight. Or else he was playing the best poker Lynn had ever seen.

"I've analyzed the best I can," the President went on, "the best memory I can, buttressed by miles and miles of tape, and I have not found an impeachable offense, and therefore resignation is not an acceptable course.

"I don't ask any of you to do anything that would be embarrassing to you, your personal interest. All I ask is that you run this government well.

"I've vetoed thirty-five billion dollars in appropriations during Watergate. I intend to fight this inflation battle with all the tools we can. It's not been a very easy year or week. I want to do the right thing for the country. For me too, but the other matter comes first.

"I have a very loyal, competent Cabinet. If I resign, it would change the Constitution. Some of you may disagree, and I respect that. But I've made my decision. You don't have to talk about Watergate. I suggest that you talk about the good things the Administration has done. Watergate will be brought to an end by the constitutional process."

He would make all evidence available to the House. "Although I could delay for a month, nothing will be withheld. I don't ask you to get involved in my problems, but it is time to do a bit extra in running the government.

"If I knew there was an impeachable offense, I would not make the Senate go through the agony of trying to prove it. I've got a hell of a good Cabinet. I will go through this with my head high—right up to the end, if it comes."

Treasury Secretary Simon, sitting across from the President, to Ford's right, felt that the President was beseeching his Cabinet to stand up and cheer. But it wasn't going to happen. The silence, Simon thought, was telling the President what he already knew. There would be no clamor that he stay on the job.

The President turned to Ford and waited.

"I'm in a difficult position," Ford said. "I share your view that the whole episode is a real tragedy. Nobody has more admiration and affection for you. I made a decision yesterday that because of commitments to Congress and the public, I will have no further comments on the issue, because I am a party in interest.

"Sure, there will be impeachment," Ford said, perhaps too frankly. "I can't predict the Senate outcome. I will make no comment concerning this. You have given us the finest foreign policy this country has ever had, a super job, and the people appreciate it. I support without hesitation your policies on inflation."

"I think your position is exactly correct," the President responded, looking across the table at the Vice-President.

To Ford, the meeting and the President's speech seemed off-key. He thought Nixon was handling the moment badly.

"If you have to run for office again," the President said to Ford, "you're going to have to run your own campaign. I had very decent people, but it doesn't excuse their actions."

Turning to the budget, the President repeated that there would be no sacred cows on cuts in spending. That discussion went on for about a half hour. Then the President turned to a forthcoming summit meeting on the economy.

Attorney General Saxbe, directly across from the President, interrupted. "Mr. President, I don't think we ought to have a summit conference. We ought to be sure you have the ability to govern."

The President replied quietly and condescendingly, as if he were lecturing a schoolboy, "Bill, I have the ability, just as I have had for the last five years."

George Bush, sitting at the end of the table to the President's right, said he agreed with Saxbe. The President's ability to govern was impaired.

The President began to lecture him, but Kissinger intervened. He wanted to avoid any open disagreement. "It is a difficult period for the country. We must show that it is a going concern. It is essential that we show it is not safe for any country to take a run at us, so we can vindicate the structure for peace."

The President adjourned the meeting at 12:30 P.M.

Large crowds were gathering outside the White House gates, and more than the usual number of reporters were waiting for the departing Cabinet members. Simon was surrounded. "The President sincerely believes he has not committed any impeachable offense," he said. "He intends to stay."

From outside the gates voices shouted, "Tell us what happened. Tell us what happened."

Kissinger stayed behind when the meeting broke up, and spoke briefly to the President. Then the Secretary walked back to his office in the West Wing. "There was precious little support for the President," he told General Scowcroft. "Weak-livered" was the way he characterized Attorney General Saxbe. Saxbe and George Bush had been petty and insensitive, Kissinger said. He compared the situation to a seventeenth-century royal court with the courtiers scurrying about, concerned with themselves rather than their country. The Cabinet meeting had depressed him; there was always the possibility that some foreign power would do something foolish.

BARRY GOLDWATER had driven to his office early. After having spent a brooding evening, he was angry. He blamed himself in part for the current nightmare. He should have pushed Nixon harder to be open and frank. His concern had been the office and the party, not Nixon, but he had been overly protective nonetheless. It had taken him too long to apply his stern, no-nonsense judgment. Christ, Goldwater was thinking, he had never really had a conversation with Nixon, he had never gotten through to him. He would come in to discuss one thing, and damned if the President didn't act as if he hadn't heard it. Now Goldwater realized that he didn't even like the man. Nixon had an obsession with the outward signs of power—trumpets, dressing up the White House guards, ceremonies. To Goldwater, this was, in one of his favorite expressions, "a bucket of shit."

Goldwater thought Nixon was not a man's man, someone with whom he could drink or joke or have a frank heart-to-heart discussion. He was thinking of the contrast with John F. Kennedy. At a particularly tense moment during the Bay of Pigs invasion period, President Kennedy had said to him, "So you want this fucking job."

Goldwater now concluded that Nixon was off his head and had been for quite a while, and that he had probably known about the Watergate break-in in advance.

Shortly after Goldwater arrived at his office, Bush called to tell him that an emergency Cabinet meeting was scheduled. The Senator was snappish. "I don't think the President can get fifteen votes in the Senate," he told Bush, "and I'm not going to protect him anymore."

Bush wasn't sure what to do next. Apparently Nixon was ready to bring even further ruin on himself and the party. "How can we impress upon the President the seriousness of this?" he asked Goldwater.

The Senator didn't have any answers, but he promised to stay in touch.

Before the Cabinet meeting, Bush spread the word of Goldwater's gloomy assessment to others, including Dean Burch.

Goldwater was at a Senate Space Committee hearing on the Hill when he received a message to call Haig or Burch. Interrupting a witness to whom he had addressed a question, he apologized and went out to return the call. He reached Burch. "Between thirteen and seventeen Senate votes," Goldwater told him, refining his earlier estimate of fifteen. "And that is all. I have talked to enough people on the floor to know that he has lost." He asked Burch to pass the information on to Haig.

Burch informed Haig at the end of the Cabinet meeting. This was what Haig had needed. He planned to use it to help tip the scales, and it would not have to come out of his own mouth.

THE VICE-PRESIDENT had canceled a morning speech to attend the Cabinet meeting. At 1:15 P.M. he headed for the Senate GOP policy luncheon.

Senator Tower immediately asked him to report on the Cabinet meeting. Ford tried to brush it over, saying that he had told the Cabinet he would make no more comments and that the President had agreed. "The balance of the Cabinet meeting dealt with the economy," Ford said.

The usually placid lunch erupted. The Senators wanted more detail on the earlier part of the Cabinet meeting.

"The President said that he was not guilty of an impeachable offense," Ford replied. "He conceded that the House battle was lost, and that the Senate would make the final decision. The Cabinet members did not speak much. George Bush did speak out and noted that the situation in the House was serious."

"What else did George say?" Goldwater asked, wondering to himself if Bush was peddling a different line to the Cabinet than he had peddled to Goldwater that morning.

"He just generally spoke of the deteriorating situation in the House," Ford answered.

"Well, that bothers us a great deal," Goldwater said. He exploded. "The House Judiciary Republicans and John Rhodes realize that the situation is hopeless. Maybe the President is right, in that the Senate will determine the final outcome, but he is only right legally and technically. We can't support this any longer. We can be lied to only so many times. The best thing that he can do for the country is to get the hell out of the White House and get out this afternoon." Goldwater's well-tanned face was red.

"We have all been waiting to hear from Barry on this," said Senator Jacob K. Javits of New York. "He made a moving statement. Everybody would be better off if the President resigned today."

Goldwater was called out of the room to take a call from Haig. When he picked up the line, the operator said that General Haig was calling from the Oval Office. Goldwater heard a click on the line and guessed that the President was listening on an extension.

"Barry," Haig said, "what is your gut feeling about what the Senate will do?" Haig knew from Burch that Goldwater was in a message-sending mood.

Goldwater was now convinced that the President was listening. This was his chance to get his message across forcefully.

"Al," Goldwater said angrily, "the President has only twelve votes in the Senate. He has lied to me for the last time and lied to my colleagues for the last time."

Back inside at the Republican policy lunch, the Vice-President was trying to cool off the group. "Henry Kissinger made a fervent plea to hold firm because of foreign-policy problems," Ford said. "Regardless of Watergate, the Cabinet as a whole, he said, should be undivided on foreign policy. He was not making a casual comment on this. He said this would be a very adverse time to show a lack of support for U.S. foreign policy or its implementation." Ford seemed almost shy about discussing what had happened.

"It is a frightening experience that all of this concern by Republicans is not having any impact at all on the White House," Senator Brock said.

Seventy-four-year-old conservative Senator Norris Cotton offered the first concrete proposal. He was sitting one seat from Ford, and he turned to him. "I have suffered through this along with everybody else," he said. "We are all in an impossible position. We are potential jurors, and our positions are hardening even though we have not heard the evidence. For the welfare of this nation, however, all of this talking to each other is foolish. We should talk to the President and convey to him the danger of his position if the Senate holds a trial. We should send a special Senate delegation to see him— an uncommitted delegation. I sympathize with Barry. We sit here very quietly, and the President is going along in his own way and at his own pace. We can't sit quietly any longer."

When Norris Cotton started talking about not sitting quietly, things were serious.

"Gentlemen," said Ford, "in light of this discussion, I really must leave the room. I can't stay any longer. It wouldn't be proper for me to remain." He left at one-forty to a standing ovation.

The Senators continued their discussion.

Wallace Bennett of Utah: "In my opinion, his resignation is more damaging than a conviction."

Dominick of Colorado: "Does the President know how we feel? The list of potential charges against him is incredible. His case is insupportable. He ought to get out now and not be forced out by the Congress."

Tower of Texas: "We have not yet gone to the White House with any of this because right now there is too much filtering of information. We can't get through."

Clifford P. Hansen of Wyoming: "We must send a delegation to the White House. I suggest that Barry Goldwater, Jack Javits and Bob Griffin transmit our personal thoughts to the President."

Brock of Tennessee: "The White House is currently doing a 'damage evaluation.' Let Tom Korologos or Bill Timmons know your feelings."

Roth of Delaware: "We ought to move today."

Charles H. Percy of Illinois: "I think we ought to ask ourselves if the country is moving as fast as this city is. Peoria says slow down a bit. Don't jump the gun."

Milton R. Young of North Dakota: "If the Senate holds a trial, then the Republican Party goes down with it."

Griffin of Michigan: "I hope that what we are saying here today does not find its way into the *Washington Post* tomorrow morning. Bill Brock is right, the White House information is good, and head counts have been taken. I spoke to Al Haig and to Tom Korologos."

Edward W. Brooke of Massachusetts: "We must be realistic. The country and the party have been hurt. . . . The two-party system is important. A Senate trial, which St. Clair says could take six months, would kill all important legislation now pending in Congress. This would be detrimental to the country. . . . As for the President, what can he gain by going to trial in the Senate? If he chooses to go through the impeachment process, he will lose decisively. . . . A delegation must be sent to see him and explain the options. If he doesn't resign now, serious harm will come to the country and the party."

William L. Scott of Virginia: "We are all shocked by recent events, but will we feel this way next week? I support the delegation idea. But we really ought to think about this for a few days."

McClure of Idaho: "I agree with Bob Griffin on the problem of leaks today. If you're going to talk to reporters, don't include me in any assessment of our mood. Don't curry favor with the press by revealing our comments to them. The White House must get an accurate account of this meeting. The leadership can go down there, but Barry Goldwater is the one blunt enough to do the job."

Charles M. Mathias, Jr., of Maryland: "Norris Cotton's suggestion is good in terms of what the White House should know. We must convey our feelings directly to the President. The question is how?. . . . It must be an impressive demonstration."

Cotton of New Hampshire: "If the country gets the idea that we are pre-judging this thing, we are in trouble. We must keep an open mind."

Mathias: "I agree. The House has not yet voted."

Peter V. Domenici of New Mexico: "Our leadership should go to the White House."

JERRY WARREN was confused. In spite of the President's firm declaration to the Cabinet that he would not resign, Ziegler had taken Warren aside be-fore the press briefing and instructed him to back off slightly. Don't close the door as tightly as Simon, Ziegler advised.

"I think resignation is inevitable, Ron," Warren volunteered. He was rarely this outspoken with his boss, who he was sure had enough problems dealing with the President. Ziegler just looked at Warren and allowed the observation to pass.

Ziegler wasn't saying much for more than the usual reasons. Earlier, Ray Price's secretary had called Judy Johnson.

"It's ready," Margaret Foote said.

Johnson had no idea what was ready, but relayed the message to Ziegler.

Ziegler himself had walked to Price's office in the EOB to pick up the folder. He brought it back to his office and locked it up. It contained Price's draft of a resignation speech. Ziegler didn't want Warren to know. For eighteen months, Warren had been the Administration's front man. He was always the last to know, deliberately kept in the dark so that he would not have to tell outright lies. The President, and Haig and Ziegler as well, tried never to feed patently false information through Warren. His credibility, such as it was, had to be preserved.

Warren had learned the role the hard way and had accepted it. Now he had expressed his opinion. Ziegler's silence was a signal, perhaps, or maybe Ziegler was just too tired and worn out to argue.

Ziegler recognized that the reason the President had insisted to the Cab-inet that he would stay was to keep his options open for a little while longer. To have even hinted that he might not hold firm would be tantamount to announcing his departure. It might even be a provocation. The desertions would steamroll. The last contingent of loyalists would then have their rea-son to abandon the cause. Also, there was the possibility that the President might still resist. Or there might be a foreign crisis that would preclude resignation.

Ziegler told Warren to say that the President intended to pursue the constitutional process. That would be construed as a less rigid position than Simon had described. During his thirty-minute press briefing, Warren used the phrase "constitutional process" a dozen times. It was a rough session, even by prevailing standards, and Warren's mission was to cut around the edges, to shift position slightly. He could not contradict Simon. That would mean contradicting the President.

Question: "Can you say today that the President will not resign?"

Warren: ". . . The President's intention is to follow the constitutional process."

Question: "Jerry, you are dodging the question."

Warren: "I am not dodging the question. I am putting it in perspective."

Question: "Can you repeat for us today, Jerry—this is important. Yesterday you said he will not resign. Can you say that today?"

Warren: "The issue is not—if I may be so bold—whether or not the President will resign. The President intends—and he told the Cabinet this today—the President intends to pursue the constitutional process. That means, ladies and gentlemen, he does not intend to resign."

But by the time Warren's briefing was over, all ten of the President's supporters on the House Judiciary Committee had announced that they would vote to impeach. So had Rhodes, though he had carefully refused to join the call for resignation.

The House and the Senate were very tense. Members hung around the cloakrooms, they hung around the wire machines, they wrung their hands. They were unsure who was really running the White House. Al Haig was not a sufficient symbol of sovereignty. Most were looking for a way to accelerate the process of Richard Nixon's abdication.

GRIFFIN WAS worried. His call for resignation, a difficult thing for him to do, had fizzled. In his office that afternoon, he was notified that Ed Cox was on the phone. He had met Cox only casually. He picked up the phone and found a very disturbed young man on the other end of the line. Cox didn't know where to turn. He wanted to speak with someone in a leadership position in the Senate. The conversation was to be strictly confidential.

As the President's son-in-law, Cox felt some responsibility for what was happening. As a member of the family he had access to some disturbing information. It had to happen, the President had to resign. David Eisenhower agreed, Cox said, but they had not been able to persuade their wives. The President's daughters had closed their minds on the subject, and they had tremendous influence on their father. Cox couldn't even talk to his wife about it.

On the *Sequoia* trip the night before, Cox said, the President had made it clear he was not going to quit. Cox asked what was happening in the Senate.

At least one of the members, Griffin told him, was going to go down and tell the President how desperate the situation had become.

That was good, Cox said, but he repeated his belief that the President was going to hang on. Cox sounded distraught. He was worried about the President's mental health. The President was not sleeping, and he had been drinking. The man couldn't take it much longer, Cox said. The President had been acting irrationally.

Griffin interrupted to say that he had been to meetings with the President recently, and Nixon had been rational.

That was the problem, Cox replied. The President went up and down. He came back from meetings and was not rational, though he had been fine at the meeting.

"The President . . ." Cox began. His voice rose momentarily. "The President was up walking the halls last night, talking to pictures of former Presidents—giving speeches and talking to the pictures on the wall."

Griffin braced himself.

Cox was worried about Mrs. Nixon too. She was the only one near the President late at night, and her strength was gone, her depression too deep to cope with anything that might happen. Cox tried to explain. He hated to raise it, but he was worried about what the President might do to himself. *"The President might take his own life."*

Griffin asked about the Secret Service. They could help Mrs. Nixon.

Yes, Cox said, that was a good idea. He would see about getting the Secret Service to stay in the family quarters.

Then Cox and Griffin agreed that it was amazing that the President had been able to stand up at all under this pressure. Griffin wanted to calm Cox, who was rambling and sounding slightly unstable himself.

"I can't talk to my wife," Cox said. "She is determined that her father shall not resign."

Griffin was most concerned about Mrs. Nixon. Who were her close friends?

Mamie Eisenhower, but she was not that close, Cox said.

How about the Reverend Billy Graham?

Cox agreed that that was a good idea, and Griffin promised to contact Graham to see if he would talk to the Nixons.

Griffin called Graham in Chicago and left a message. He was shaken. Ed Cox, a young lawyer, was not given to hysterics. Griffin had rarely heard an adult so disturbed. The possibilities of catastrophe seemed endless. Macabre visions flashed. There was no way to let this slide by. Griffin walked over to Ford's office in the Senate and told his worries to the Vice-President.

Ford was not upset or worried, though he expressed sympathy for the Nixon family. He seemed to have a plan all laid out. He had talked with Haig again today. Things were going smoothly. The President had not done a good job at the Cabinet meeting that morning, Ford said; it was all very sad. Griffin wasn't sure exactly what Ford was talking about.

President Nixon was expected to resign, Ford said, and he was going to become President. That was to be kept very quiet. Ford seemed matter-of-fact and somewhat removed.

Griffin left rather perplexed. He had done all he could as a Republican leader. He had written an extraordinary letter saying he would vote to convict the President if all the tapes were not turned over, and then had gone so far as to call upon the President to resign. Those were bold steps for a normally cautious man. Now it seemed that the President was going in one direction, Haig and Ford in another, Ed Cox, perhaps, in still another.

When Griffin finally talked to Graham, he told him that the Nixon family needed help. The President was terribly depressed, and it would be helpful if Dr. Graham could get to him and reach him spiritually. As an old friend, he was one of the few who could help. It was serious.

Graham didn't want to seem to be forcing himself on Richard Nixon, certainly not at this moment. He called the White House and left word that he was available. Then he flew to New York so that he would be in the East. If he went to Washington, it might be interpreted as another signal. Once in New York, he called the White House again and left his phone number. He was nearby and could get a plane to Washington on a moment's notice.

THE PRESIDENT was not fully persuaded by Goldwater's assessment. Goldwater was excitable. The President was sure he still had friends in the Senate. The week before, Bill Timmons had passed word through Haig that the President had thirty-five votes and that there were another eight to ten that might go either way. Now the President called Timmons to his office alone.

The President's hard core was down to twenty votes, Timmons said, and he saw no hope of getting the thirty-four votes for acquittal. But he was not an attorney, Timmons added cautiously, and if the attorneys felt that the case could be won on its legal merits, some of the lost ground might be recovered. Nixon was interested in specifics. He gave Timmons the names of five Senators to call.

Timmons reported back that all five, Nixon loyalists, had said they would not vote to convict, but that they all said the situation was hopeless.

At 4:30 p.m., eight members of the Senate GOP leadership met to decide who should carry a message to the White House. Senators Javits and Goldwater were present as representatives of the party's left and right. They joined Hugh Scott, Griffin, Brock, Tower, Bennett and Cotton.

John Stennis was suggested, but Scott insisted that it was a Republican mess and that Republicans should handle it.

Goldwater was finally chosen to go alone.

At five-nineteen, Goldwater placed a call to Bill Timmons. He didn't get through. On his way back to his office, Goldwater stopped by to see Stennis and ask if he wanted to go with him to the White House the next day. "I'd go," Stennis said, "but I'd prefer the constitutional process." Goldwater was sure that Stennis could be persuaded, but he didn't try.

Next Goldwater reached Dean Burch by phone at the White House. "I know what you want," Burch said. He suggested that Goldwater come to lunch at his house the next day before he saw the President. Goldwater agreed.

White House staff members were watching for signals. Price was being observed very closely to see if he was working. If the President was going to resign, he'd have to announce it; he'd need a speech. Price was the logical man to write it.

There were reports that Vice-President Ford was about to cancel his speaking trip to the West Coast that was to begin on Thursday.

Rabbi Korff saw the President in the afternoon. "Is there anything I can do for you?" the President asked.

"I don't want you to resign."

"Foreign affairs might suffer irreparable harm," the President said. "If I am busy in the Senate with a trial, televised before the nation, the nation would be polarized."

For half an hour Nixon reviewed his thinking. He didn't say what he was going to do, but Korff got the impression that the President was going to step down. Nixon vacillated, now lashing out at his enemies, proclaiming the massive injustice of it all, and then drifting back to the damage a Senate trial might do the country.

Korff requested an autographed photograph and left. He had scheduled a press conference after the meeting, but he canceled it and went out a side exit. One reporter caught up with him. Korff was visibly discouraged, but he would continue to support the President. "Richard Nixon will go down in history as the greatest President of the century."

WASHINGTON WAS rife with rumors. Some of the Senators who had been at the GOP policy lunch told reporters that there was a wave of anti-Nixon sentiment, and that Goldwater felt that the President should resign. One report had it that Goldwater had said the President *would* resign. This made it onto television. So did an equally incorrect report that Goldwater had tried to gain entrance to the White House that afternoon but was refused.

Just before 7 P.M., Goldwater called Scott to complain that a member of the Minority Leader's staff had leaked the plan for Goldwater to go to the White House. Next Goldwater called one of the TV reporters and gave him hell for the false story. The more Goldwater thought about it, the angrier he got. Finally he stormed onto the Senate floor and asked for unanimous consent to speak for thirty seconds. It was granted and Goldwater denied the reports. Then he looked up at the press gallery, which was rapidly filling, raised his fist and said loudly, "You are a rotten bunch."

There was applause from the visitors' gallery and from some members of the Senate.

Burch had told Goldwater that the President was heading toward resignation, but he had emphasized that it was important that no one else publicly join Griffin.

That evening Goldwater discussed the situation with his wife. Wednesday he would call for resignation, and that would be a political disaster in Arizona, where he was running for reelection. He wondered if he should withdraw from the race. "No," his wife said.

UNTIL MID-TUESDAY the President had acted almost smug about the reaction to the June 23 transcripts. Once again, Haig worried about his own credibility with the President. He had to get the President to appreciate that the staff was telling him the truth. The sour news from the Hill removed that problem but raised another. Haig was concerned about a meeting between the President and Goldwater. It must not be initiated by Goldwater.

Also, Goldwater was apt to fly off the handle. A confrontation would be disastrous and could serve only to buttress the President's resistance. The President couldn't resign because of congressional pressure any more than because of pressure from his own staff. First he had to be convinced that he had the option to stay. Haig sat in his office considering the next move. "The next few days will be full of tragedy," he told his staff, and he repeated the remark he was becoming famous for among his associates: "You just can't believe what these last weeks have been like."

Haig had been through enough Nixon decisions to sense that the President had just about decided to quit. Nixon's statements on the matter had by no means been consistent, but they pointed that way. That was the best he could expect at that moment. Nixon's support had crumbled or had at least been neutralized. The news from the Hill—Goldwater, Rhodes, the Judiciary loyalists, Nixon's favorite Southern Democrats—was all negative. Ford wasn't knocking on any doors to urge a fight. The Cabinet had been muted.

Haig was working for a resignation announcement on Thursday night. There was a problem. The President had said he would *consider* a Thursday-night resignation announcement. Consider it. The decision was far from final. So Haig had to take some steps. He told Kissinger and Ford that Thursday would be the day.

HAIG HAD a call from Haldeman on that Tuesday. Haldeman wanted a pardon. Haig was noncommittal, unencouraging, and worried. This was something he didn't need, especially now. He called Jaworski in Houston.

"Leon, you'd better come back. I think you ought to be here."

Jaworski promised to return at once.

THAT NIGHT, Philip Buchen took a cab to Gerald Ford's home in Alexandria for dinner. Mrs. Ford had called Buchen the week before and reminded him that he hadn't been out to the house for some time. At first, dinner was set for Friday, August 2, but then it was moved to Tuesday so that Buchen could return to Michigan for a dental appointment and his annual physical.

The taxi arrived at Ford's house about seven o'clock. Betty Ford greeted Buchen at the door and the two went into the den to watch the evening news and await Ford. Buchen had a martini on the rocks. "The GOP gave up today on Richard Nixon," led the CBS news. There was an obituary tone to all references to the President.

NBC correspondent Ronald Nessen was shown asking Ford if President Nixon was keeping him informed. Ford's smiling response: "No comment. See you later. Nice try, Ron."

The Vice-President arrived and dashed upstairs to change into his swimming trunks. As a mess steward completed preparations for dinner, Ford swam some laps in the back-yard pool. The dinner conversation conveyed no sense of urgency. They talked about Steve Ford's plans. The Vice-President's eighteen-year-old son had a summer job mowing grass on the George Washington Memorial Parkway. He had been accepted at Duke University for the fall term, but he was considering taking a year off.

After supper, Ford, Mrs. Ford and Buchen sat in the living room. Ford looked almost serene.

Buchen couldn't stand it any longer. "Look," he said, "you'd better tell me what's going on."

"It will all be over in seventy-two hours," Ford replied calmly. He had received word from Haig earlier in the day.

Dammit, Buchen thought, wondering if he ought to dash out that moment and get down to serious organizing. Ford's demeanor only made Buchen more agitated. He was distressed at Ford's slowness. He understood that his friend had been unwilling to make any move that might look as if he were elbowing his way into the presidency, but now there was no longer time for appearances. Buchen's friend of thirty-five years was about to take over the government.

Buchen told Ford what he and Whitehead had been doing. Pitifully inadequate work with the transition seventy-two hours away. "Now, look," Buchen said, "tell me who I can call on immediately." The transition team would have to be expanded. Buchen, Whitehead, Jonathan Moore, Brian Lamb and Larry Lynn were not equipped for this. Maybe no one was. People with more stature and experience would have to be included. Ford suggested Senator Griffin, former Congressman John W. Byrnes of Wisconsin, Secretary of the Interior Morton, U. S. Steel vice-president William G. Whyte, and Bryce Harlow, who had left the White House several months earlier.

Buchen wanted someone from outside Washington and suggested former Pennsylvania Governor William W. Scranton. Ford agreed.

Buchen said he would contact them that night. Betty Ford got her address book and gave Buchen the phone numbers of the men who would be added to the transition team.

"We'll get them together as quickly as possible," Buchen said. Ford explained that it was essential that no information get out.

Buchen, more than Ford, seemed struck by all that had to be accomplished—the swearing in, immediate appointments, briefings, an inaugural speech, and all those matters that a new President normally had months to consider. Buchen was eager to leave and get to a phone.

As they went to the door, he kissed Betty Ford and put his arm around the next President. He mumbled a few words of encouragement. Everyone would rise to the occasion, he felt. He had been through a lot with his friend. "It's happening," he said. Events were about to thrust into the presidency a man who had stood for election only in Ionia and Kent Counties in one of Michigan's nineteen congressional districts. "I'm proud of you," Buchen said.

The cab arrived to take him downtown to the University Club, where he was staying. On the way, Buchen reflected on his long friendship with Ford. In the summer of 1940 Buchen had clerked for a New York City law firm and almost joined it, but instead he had gone into partnership with Ford. The New York law firm was the one Richard Nixon joined in the early 1960s. Buchen wondered, if he had stayed in New York, might he have been one of the law partners Nixon brought to Washington? What would he have done during Watergate?

The first call Buchen made when he got back to his club was to his wife. Next he called Whitehead. "I've just talked to Jerry," Buchen said with deep concern in his voice, "and he said that Haig has told him, 'You'll be President in seventy-two hours.'" They agreed to gather the old and new transition teams.

Buchen was less precise to Bill Whyte. "The Vice-President wants a group of his close advisers to meet," he said. Whyte offered his house.

Buchen had to introduce himself to Bryce Harlow over the phone. Announcing that he spoke on the Vice-President's behalf, Buchen asked Harlow to attend an important meeting the next night. Harlow wondered who the hell Buchen was and why it was so important to meet him, but he put his reservations aside when he heard that the gathering was at Bill Whyte's. Harlow knew that Whyte wouldn't be involved in any skullduggery.

IN THE East Wing—where the staff members most involved in the First Family's personal life worked—Susan Dolibois, a former aide to Charles Colson and a hard-core loyalist, said the new transcript was a slap in the face. Chief usher Rex Scouten, who had been on the Nixon Secret Service detail during the vice-presidential days, was forgiving. His main concern was the family. Terry Ivey, assistant press aide to Mrs. Nixon, was torn and unhappy, shattered by the fact that the President had let his daughter Julie go around the country defending him and had not told her the truth. The President had told his daughter not to do it, Ivey knew, but he had never explained why she should not. Ivey, like many others, was beginning to realize that she might not have a job much longer.

Haig got a few hours' sleep that night. He was more determined than ever to deal toughly with Congress. Republican leaders must not be allowed to descend on the White House and try to force a resignation. To Haig, that was more menacing than a military coup. It would alter the American political system forever.

Haig was sinking into bitterness, or as much bitterness as he would ever allow himself. Nixon was a product of the political system, not an aberration, and he didn't see things getting better with Ford. He believed that someone like himself could never make it in politics.

Wednesday, August 7

O N this morning Alexander Haig felt the burden of government acutely. His job was to prevent a rout. Haig wanted to smooth the way—for the country, for the President and for himself. He could see, hear and feel the erosion. Everything was crumbling at once. This was the last dismal stage of the battle, a defeat of dimensions such as he had never experienced. He had read about defeat; this was what it was—noise, irrationality, collapse on all sides. The completeness seemed so unexpected. Then, in calmer moments, it seemed clear and inevitable. The Hill, the press, traditional Nixon supporters, members of the White House staff, even old friends—Haig was sure he could deal with them. He was not sure he could deal with Nixon. He was afraid the President might kill himself.

Over the past months, there had been certain references to death and suicide. At first they were oblique and often expressed in Nixon's impatient manner; the President was thinking out loud, probably. This week, Nixon had finally approached the subject head on. The two men had been alone.

"You fellows, in your business," the President began, meaning the Army, which he always seemed to consider Haig's real business, "you have a way of handling problems like this. Somebody leaves a pistol in the drawer." Haig waited.

"I don't have a pistol," the President said sadly, as if it were one more deprivation in a long history of underprivilege. As if he were half asking to be given one. It was the same tone he used when he talked about his parents not having had any money.

Afterward, Haig called the President's doctors. He ordered that all pills be denied the President, and that the sleeping pills and tranquilizers he already had be taken away.

Haig also discussed the matter with Buzhardt. At first Haig was vague. He mentioned pills. It was not necessarily a question of suicide; pills might interfere with decisions the President had to make and follow through on. Pills must not be available to act as a shield against reality.

Then Haig told Buzhardt he was taking every possible precaution to make sure that Watergate did not end in a presidential suicide. The President might see it as the only way to spare himself and the country the pain of more recrimination. So Haig had taken steps to make sure the President did not have the means to kill himself.

The President wasn't the type, Buzhardt responded. Nixon had weathered adversities. The tougher things got, the tougher he seemed to get. And Buzhardt was convinced that Nixon was a very religious man deep down. Religious men don't kill themselves.

Haig said the President was a battered man, strained to his limit. He compared Nixon's behavior to that of Captain Queeg, the erratic naval officer in *The Caine Mutiny*. Queeg had been relieved of duty by his second in command because he was unable to function as his ship swirled out of control in a typhoon. Buzhardt thought the analogy argued against a suicide. Queeg was a fighter. He had fought to the end.

Haig and Buzhardt talked about their experiences with Nixon. Haig was concerned that he didn't really know the President and had never felt close to him. Nixon was so private. Haig wondered sometimes what Nixon did when he was alone, because he spent so many hours that way. Buzhardt said he felt the same overwhelming distance, but he thought he had been given a glimpse of the man that no other person had.

Haig knew what Buzhardt was referring to. After the secret taping system had been revealed, and they had to contend with the two missing tapes and the missing Dictabelt of April 15, Nixon had delivered some other Dictabelts to Buzhardt—recordings of his daily reflections. Perhaps they would allay his lawyers' suspicions, Nixon implied. When he'd heard them, Buzhardt recognized that they were clearly not meant for anyone else's ears. Nixon hadn't even let Rose Woods transcribe them. Some of them were under subpoena, but Buzhardt had argued to Judge Sirica that they were too personal to be released. Sirica had listened to one, had agreed and had told the special prosecutor that they were not relevant to any investigation.

From those recordings—sometimes they were small cassettes—Buzhardt believed he had heard Nixon with his defenses peeled away. It was rare for a man in such a public position to keep so truthful a diary, Buzhardt told Haig. Normally the diaries of public men serve to provide a cover story for history. The Nixon dictations were a stark contrast. Buzhardt said that his own most emotional moments in all of Watergate had come as he listened to the President reveal his emotions. The tapes provided a dark, almost Dostoevskian journey into Nixon's fears, obsessions, hostilities, passions, and inadequacies.

Buzhardt, who had spent years consulting doctors about his mother's mental illness, felt that the dictating sessions were genuine therapy for Nixon. The lawyer would not reveal any details, even to Haig. He would say only that Nixon had talked out of his real feelings and, oddly, he would discourse on everyday occurrences—the weather, the flowers in the White House garden, birds.

One thing was clear, Buzhardt said: the President thought he had to submerge his true feelings at any cost. At a young age he had decided that he would have to keep his real emotions suppressed and expose only calculated emotions. He was convinced that was what others wanted.

Sadly enough, Nixon's instincts were often finer than his calculations. The President had a secret life of sorts—material for a psychological novel, Buzhardt said. He had compassion. He had talked about John Dean: Dean should not be judged harshly, because he was a young man who was in over his head, Nixon had said.

The President was an introvert by nature. He had talked into his machine about his reactions to meeting people and campaigning: he hated it all, but he did it anyway and thrust forward an outer shell. No one could get through. Close relationships were impossible. His relationship with his wife was totally formalized. Even with his daughter Julie he had rarely revealed his emotions. He played the strong, consoling father when what he really wanted was to reach out and be consoled. But Buzhardt was certain that the exterior was still solid, and that it would hold.

Haig was not inclined to linger over such analyses. He turned impatiently to the operational problems before him. He had to continue laying the foundation for resignation as quietly as possible.

Most immediately, there was Goldwater's request to see the President with a message from the Republican leadership. The message was resignation. He had to head that off at all costs, and he had to do it himself. He had to see Goldwater personally, but not at the White House. There was too much rumor already. The Hill was also impossible. Haig talked to Burch, who told him Goldwater had already accepted an invitation to lunch at his home. It was decided that Haig should join them.

Goldwater spent the morning in his large apartment on Cathedral Avenue, surrounded with his ham-radio equipment and model cars. Burch called to set the time—twelve-thirty—and tell him that Haig would be there.

"Are you going to wear a suit?" Burch asked. Goldwater generally showed up at his house in Levis and cowboy boots.

"Shit, what do you expect me to wear?" Goldwater responded; it was a serious occasion. Then Burch told him that the President would see him that afternoon about four o'clock.

Meanwhile, Haig went to see the President and discussed the upcoming meeting in terms of giving Goldwater an opportunity to tell the President about his chances in the Senate. The President said he wanted a broader picture and decided that Rhodes and Scott should come along as well. Haig left. It was too late to meet personally with Scott and Rhodes. He asked Timmons to invite them to the four-o'clock meeting and to brief them.

Timmons too thought congressional pressure might push Nixon backward. If the leaders were simply to tell the President that the situation was hopeless, they could all live comfortably with themselves. No one, Timmons believed, including himself, should take responsibility for any more. Nixon would do what he wanted to in spite of everyone. That was what he had always done.

At one-fifteen Timmons arrived at Scott's office. The Senator was eating lunch. Timmons told him the President had asked personally to see the two Minority Leaders as well as Goldwater. Scott was flattered; he thought it appropriate. "The President has been up and down on resignation," Timmons explained. "The family wants him to stay on. We just don't know exactly what will happen. It looks like he'll resign. But while I'm talking he could change his mind." He said bluntly that a demand for resignation would increase the President's resistance, and Scott promised to tread lightly.

Timmons was less frank with Rhodes. "The President wants to talk to you and to Hugh Scott and Barry Goldwater," he began.

"Well, what about?" Rhodes asked.

"He's thinking about making a decision and wants to know exactly what his situation on the floor of the House and the Senate is before he makes it."

"Well, Bill, does this decision encompass the possibility of resignation?" Rhodes asked.

"Yes, it does," Timmons said. He told Rhodes the meeting was set for four o'clock at the White House.

Haig wanted to underscore the strategy to Scott. He put his grievances aside for the moment and called him. "Hugh," he said, "he has almost been persuaded several times. The problem now is the family. If you demand his resignation, he'll probably harden up again. Would you just tell him the situation? He knows it. But he needs to hear it from you. He needs to know there are no alternatives. Nothing else."

Scott agreed.

BOB HALDEMAN stepped briskly along the pavement a few blocks from the White House. He went into the Bowen Building at 815 Fifteenth Street, NW, and took the elevator to the sixth floor. He was worried and wanted to review the situation with one of his attorneys, Frank Strickler. Haldeman had reached the President by phone the day before, but the question of pardons, though implicit, had not been directly discussed. Strickler came to the point. If Haldeman wanted a pardon, he had better get a specific request to the President quickly. A direct personal appeal might be the only way.

For ten days both Haldeman and Strickler had known that a new crisis was building. Haig had called Haldeman soon after the Supreme Court decision to ask him what he recalled of the three conversations he had had with the President on June 23, 1972. Haig had been very concerned and had asked a lot of questions. What was the context of the conversations? What went on before and after each discussion?

Haldeman wouldn't help. He couldn't remember much, had blocked most of it out of his mind, and on Strickler's advice didn't bother to recall any more. When Haldeman hung up, he was sure that Haig had been saying that the President might not be able to remain in office once the tapes were disclosed.

Now, Haldeman told Strickler, he was sure the end was imminent. Haig and the lawyers were panicking. The importance of those transcripts was being vastly overplayed. The President had revealed worse and had withstood it. Nixon was the victim of a putsch in his own White House, Haldeman thought.

Strickler suggested that Haldeman get his justification for a pardon down on paper. Haldeman agreed. He needed to collect his own thoughts, and he knew that the President preferred to deal with formal proposals.

> On a personal basis [he began writing], better to close the chapter now than to have to sit by helplessly for the next several years and watch trials and appeals.
>
> Historically—would be far better to grant the pardon and close the door to such process than to let it run and have the trials become a surro-

gate impeachment. Also, history will look kindly on loyalty and compassion to subordinates caught in the web.

Solves problem of potential prosecutor access to files and tapes by eliminating basis for further prosecution—also solves problem of defense forcing access to files.

The only way to wipe the slate clean is to shut down the prosecution totally. As long as it is there, there is a possibility of other new things.

To avoid trauma of country, injustice to defendants, personal problems to RN, adverse historical effects—all point to necessity of overall pardon.

Haldeman tried to get through by phone to Nixon, failed and finally reached Haig. He quickly stated his request and outlined his reasons.

Haig was appalled. He knew a threat when he heard one. Haldeman was talking about "loyalty," about avoiding a "trauma," "personal problems" for the President, and "adverse historical effects." To Haig, it sounded as if Haldeman was warning that he would send Nixon to jail if he didn't get a pardon.

Haig suppressed his anger and was again merely unencouraging. He didn't want to think about it, and he didn't want the President to have to think about it. The timetable for resignation was at least tentatively set, and this sort of thing could upset it. Nonetheless, Haig promised Haldeman that the request would get full consideration.

The general was sensitive about Watergate conspirators asking for executive clemency. A crucial element in the first Watergate cover-up had been Howard Hunt's demands for clemency in exchange for silence. Now someone was trying to blackmail the White House again. Nightmare visions of new cover-ups and obstructions of justice presented themselves, and he saw himself getting tangled up in them this time. But before he could ask for advice from the lawyers, Haig had to leave for Burch's house to meet Goldwater.

The Senator was already there when he arrived. Goldwater was shocked at Haig's appearance. The general's face was drawn and pale. He looked older, thinner, beaten physically and mentally. "You look like death warmed over," Goldwater told him. "You should get out into the country." He offered his place as a retreat.

Haig said he'd been up for four straight days and nights.

Goldwater figured that there was only one person who could keep Haig up four nights. That meant that the President had been sleepless—no condition in which to make decisions. He asked how the President was holding up physically and mentally.

"Fine," Haig said. Burch nodded.

Bullshit, Goldwater thought, but he decided to stick to business.

The three men sat down to a lunch of fruit and mixed seafood. Goldwater reported what many of the Senate Republicans had said at the GOP policy lunch the day before.

"No chance in the Senate," he summarized, adding that he himself was prepared to vote to convict on Article Two, the abuse-of-power charge.

"You know he'll tell you to shove it up your ass," Burch said of any attempt Goldwater might make to explain his position to the President.

"We don't need any more pushing him," Haig said. "We've had enough of that." He went through his standard drill. Some of the family were the major obstacles. They had been fiercely opposed to resignation.

It was going to be dreadful when the family realized he had lied to them, Goldwater said. That would be hard on them and on him.

Haig suggested that some members of the family were no longer resisting resignation. The two sons-in-law seemed to understand what had happened and what was happening now. The President was weighing his options: whether to stand trial and face certain defeat in the Senate or to resign in the best interests of himself and the country. It was ninety percent certain that the President would resign, Haig said. But a sudden, rapid spasm of the old Nixon will could change that. And the President would not permit Congress or the Republican leaders to dictate his decision. To even appear to be trying to force his hand could prove fatal, Haig explained. The problem was to keep Nixon on track.

Goldwater saw the link between Griffin's inflammatory call for resignation on Monday and this lunch. Haig was quelling the fires.

The general laid out the scenario. Goldwater would not be going alone, Scott and Rhodes would join him. The idea was to show the President how hopeless his situation was—nothing more, nothing less.

"Don't even mention the word 'resignation,' " Haig insisted.

Goldwater agreed.

There was an additional problem. Haldeman wanted pardons for everyone, Haig explained. There was a lot of pressure on the President to issue pardons before resigning—pressure in the form of old loyalties. A simple signature on a piece of paper for old friends who had served so well. What would Goldwater advise?

"I don't think that would be wise," Goldwater said. "But he has the power and if that is the cost, so be it."

Goldwater was willing to pay almost anything to get Richard Nixon out of office.

IT WAS about 2 P.M. when Haig arrived back at the White House. He went straight to the EOB office and briefed the President about Haldeman's request and his reasons, and Goldwater's reaction to it. Nixon wanted more time to think about it and asked Haig to consult the lawyers.

As Haig left, he ran into Garment. "Len, walk along with me," he said. Garment fell into step.

"I'm going to see Fred or Jim," Haig said, and asked if Garment knew where they were.

Buzhardt was at the dentist and St. Clair was in his favorite courtroom, explaining that nine of the sixty-four subpoenaed tapes didn't exist or couldn't be found, Garment said.

Haig motioned Garment into St. Clair's empty office. The two men sat down. Garment thought Haig looked emaciated. The general was clutching his lighter and cigarettes nervously in one hand.

Things had to be brought to a conclusion, Haig said. The President was probably going to resign and it was best that he go on his own steam. One final snag had developed. Haldeman was urging the President to grant pardons for everyone involved in Watergate. The pressure was tremendous, Haig said. He had briefed the President. He had promised him he would check it out with the lawyers. What was the legal judgment? Could the President do it?

"Totally out of the question," Garment said. "It would be grotesque. Up to this point, he has, oddly enough, worked within the system, even though it is undoing him. Pardons would be outside the system. It would be saying to hell with the system, with justice. It would bring the roof down." Garment felt the heat increase in his body, his face. "It would be the single most devastating thing that could be contemplated," he said.

Goldwater found pardons tolerable, Haig said, if that was the price of resignation. The President wanted to know why, if Goldwater could stomach it, some of the staff couldn't.

"Is it conceivable?" Haig asked again. "Can it be done?"

Sure, Garment said, a President has the legal authority to grant pardons. But what would Watergate pardons include? Where did Watergate begin and other crimes stop? What do you do—empty the prisons?

"Why can't it be done?" Haig insisted.

Garment couldn't get the arguments out fast enough. The President might have the technical power, but he didn't have enough political strength to exercise it for old friends and aides. The President had to go out of office in presidential fashion. Imagine, Garment said, Nixon's last act being pardons for all his old cronies. That would insure that Watergate could never be put into perspective.

Haig said that the President felt that pardons would allow him to assume the entire burden of Watergate. He felt responsible for the plight of his old friends.

All the guilt and responsibility and the public outrage falling on Nixon: Garment knew how that would appeal to him. They just couldn't let him do it, Garment told Haig. But as Haig got up and went across the hall to the washroom, Garment worried that he hadn't mustered all his arguments.

Buzhardt and then St. Clair returned. Haig and Garment met them in Buzhardt's office. Buzhardt was also opposed. He had already taken steps to block any pardon requests that might come through the Justice Department—the normal route.

Haig told them that he had been negative on the subject with the President and that he was supposed to be checking with the lawyers. Haldeman was really pushing and had tried to get through directly to the President, but Haig had intercepted the call. He was afraid that Haldeman would find a way to get through to Nixon.

Haig's conversion now seemed complete. "That criminal has asked for a pardon," he said. He expressed disbelief; the arrogance was incredible, it was blackmail, it had to be stopped.

Buzhardt calmly offered to call Haldeman's chief attorney, John Wilson, and explain that pardons would be impossible.

"Well," said St. Clair at last, "maybe pardons should be considered." It was worthwhile to explore the possibility before leaping to conclusions.

Haig and Garment pounced on him.

"If the President grants this pardon," Garment said, "he will be insuring his own trial. He will be forcing it. The public has to have a head, and if the President takes the heads away the public will have his. And that would be the Monkey Trial of all time. The President has to take his chances."

St. Clair was soon persuaded that they should urge the President to reject the request.

HAIG HAD word that David Eisenhower and Ed Cox wanted to see him. He called Buchanan and asked him to go talk to the President's sons-in-law. Although there were signs that the family was relenting, Haig said, they were still the last stumbling block to resignation.

Bruce Herschensohn, Haig said, was talking to Julie, reinforcing her opinion that her father should never resign. Herschensohn wanted the President to go down in history as a fighter, and he was telling her that winning or losing in the Senate was not the important thing—that standing up for the office would assure the President his proper role in history. Buchanan said he would be glad to take on the task.

David and Ed arrived in Buchanan's office shortly afterward. "We've come to see you about the President," Cox said. They were trying to get both sides, and they wanted to hear the arguments in favor of resignation again.

For an hour Buchanan calmly plowed back through the ground covered Saturday, insisting still that resignation was the only solution.

David was impressed that Buchanan, the ultimate Nixon man, had overcome his conditioning. He had the character to arrive at his own conclusion and hold to it in the face of the President's resistance. This gave David confidence that he too would be able to hold his ground against his wife and his father-in-law.

Cox did most of the talking and questioning. He weighed both sides carefully, as if he were going to make a presentation and wanted to be able to state each side of the case fully and fairly.

David and Ed thanked Buchanan. Then they picked up Tricia and walked over to the President's EOB office. Because the discussion was to be a lawyerly review, Tricia did not go inside. The President was sitting alone. David was glad they were in the EOB office. He felt that this room, unlike the Oval Office with its ceremonial trappings, invited conversation on a human scale.

David divided conversations with his father-in-law into two categories. Either Nixon dominated and did most of the talking or he was withdrawn and allowed conversations to simply go on around him. This time it was different. They had information to exchange.

Ed explained that he and David had been canvassing people to get recommendations. There were arguments for and against staying. If he stayed and didn't resign, Cox said, the Administration still had vast resources to make a defense in a Senate trial. It would be heroic, and a vigorous defense might narrow the charges. Whatever the result, the full airing would lend perspective to Watergate and show that it was a small matter.

Borrowing from Buchanan, David and Ed then outlined the arguments for resignation. A Senate trial could take months, disrupt the government, hurt the economy and complicate foreign relations. The country needed a leader, David said.

The President shot a glance at him. David thought he might have gone too far, but the President seemed, for once, willing to discuss Watergate matter-of-factly.

"Unless something happens," Nixon said, "my friends in the Senate are saying I should resign." He looked away from David and Ed. Those friends included Senators Stennis, Long, Bennett, and James B. Allen of Alabama, Nixon said.

"I haven't decided anything for sure," he said abruptly, but David sensed that he had. The President was calm about the subject, one of the few times David had seen him so. He was dealing rationally with arguments on both sides.

His visitors nodded understandingly. They were not pushing.

"Do you think they're going to give us a hard time on our papers and tapes?" Nixon asked.

That too seemed to indicate he was planning to leave office, David thought.

They both said he should certainly be entitled to keep his papers, tapes and files—as other Presidents had.

Nixon took another step. He wondered about transporting his files to California. If he resigned, that was where he would go. He wanted to own the papers so that he could work on his book. He would write his memoirs. If he didn't get his papers, people would be rummaging through them for years.

The President posed other questions about his future. It was a future out of office, in California.

"I want to take some time off to travel."

That would be a good idea.

"What about the climate of retribution?" he asked. He answered his own question, slowly. If he resigned, people would become apathetic about him. And, of course, resignation would silence him politically for a long time.

David knew that the great unspoken item of business was a pardon for his father-in-law. But the President didn't broach it.

Nixon seemed to lose interest in the conversation. Normally, he would have dismissed his visitors at that point. But Nixon seemed to cling to them, letting the talk wander back and forth. Clearly he didn't want them to leave, so they stayed. David thought it was as if Mr. Nixon didn't have anything to do.

Finally the President picked up the phone and called Steve Bull. "When the fellows come in, put them in the office, and I'll be over in a few minutes."

David and Ed left.

BULL DIDN'T make it to the Oval Office with the President's visitors—Scott, Goldwater and Rhodes. As they came in at the West Wing basement, Timmons had them intercepted and brought to his office. Haig, Burch and Timmons once again reviewed the necessity of keeping the meeting cool.

"He's been up and down," Haig said. "It's about ninety percent set with him now. Please don't raise the question of resignation. He knows what you're going to tell him about the situation. He needs to hear it from you."

"He'll get the truth," Goldwater said. "That's what he wants?" Goldwater was disbelieving; Nixon rarely wanted that.

"Yes," Haig said.

Haig meant to turn the meeting into a ritual in which the Senators could imagine they were asserting their authority, and the President could preserve the illusion that he was acting independently.

The three leaders left Timmons' office and walked down the hall and into the Oval Office. It was about 5 P.M.

The President entered seconds later. He shook hands with all three. "How's that boy of yours?" he asked Rhodes.

"He's fine," the Minority Leader answered, astounded. But Nixon always remembered personal details. "He's working in the trust department of the Valley National Bank," Rhodes said.

"That's great," the President said. "That's a great bank."

The President turned and sat down behind the large desk. Rhodes took the chair to the President's left, Scott the one to his right. Goldwater was directly in front. Scott realized it was probably the first time he had talked to the President without one of the White House aides in attendance. He had had private conversations with Presidents Kennedy and Johnson, but never with Nixon.

The President seemed at ease, almost serene, as he leaned back in his swivel chair and began chatting. Goldwater thought he looked as though he had just shot a hole in one.

Disappointment was audible in his voice, however. The President referred briefly to men he had campaigned for who had turned against him. He knew their names.

Rhodes was thinking that there was no sense of wrongdoing in the President's attitude. Nixon was talking politics and votes as if it were another bill on which he wanted a head count. Then, abruptly, Nixon cut the small talk. "Well, we are all aware of why you are here. We might as well get down to it."

He turned to Rhodes. "I guess I've got maybe ten votes on the floor of the House?" he asked, with a faint hint of sarcasm.

Before Rhodes could answer—he was going to say that the President had more, maybe fifty or sixty—Nixon turned to the others. "Who wants to open up?"

"We've asked Barry to be our spokesman," Scott replied.

"Go ahead, Barry," the President said, staring straight ahead at Goldwater.

"Mr. President, this isn't pleasant, but you want to know the situation and it isn't good."

Goldwater was certain the President had heard his estimate on the phone to Haig the day before. But lots of numbers had been flying around for several days. Twelve, fifteen, less than twenty, Goldwater was thinking—what had he told Haig?

"Pretty bad, huh?"

"Yes, sir," Goldwater answered, still trying to recall the exact number he had quoted.

"How many would you say would be with me—a half dozen?" the President asked. Was there sarcasm in his voice?

"More than that," Goldwater said, "maybe sixteen to eighteen."

"Hugh," the President said, turning to his right, "do you agree with that?"

"I'd say maybe fifteen," Scott said. "But it's grim," he added, "and they're not very firm."

"Damn grim," the President shot back.

Goldwater said, "We've discussed the thing a lot and just about all of the guys have spoken up and there aren't many who would support you if it comes to that." Goldwater decided to ram it home. "I took kind of a nose count today, and I couldn't find more than four very firm votes, and those would be from older Southerners. Some are very worried about what's been going on, and are undecided, and I'm one of them."

That final kick had delivered, Goldwater hoped.

The President turned to Rhodes. "John, I know how you feel, what you've said, I respect it, but what's your estimate?"

Rhodes was thinking there would still be some support for the President in the House, but he wanted the message to be stern. "About the same, Mr. President," he said.

"Well, that's about the way I thought it was. I've got a very difficult decision to make, but I want you to know I'm going to make it for the best interests of the country."

There were nods around three sides of the desk.

"I'm not interested in pensions," the President continued. "I'm not interested in pardons or amnesty. I'm going to make this decision for the best interests of the country."

Goldwater could feel tears in his eyes. He could see that the others were emotional, too.

"Mr. President," Scott said, "we are all very saddened, but we have to tell you the facts."

"Never mind," the President replied, almost jerking out the words, watching the eyes of his visitors. "There'll be no tears. I haven't cried since Eisenhower died. My family has been fine. I'm going to be all right."

He talked about how much he had loved President Eisenhower. It had been a long time in politics, the President said. Goldwater and he had been campaigning for about twenty years. He started to muse again about things he had done for some of the people who now wanted him out of office, then stopped himself short. "But this is water over the dam," he said, "it's beside the point."

He leaned toward Rhodes. "Do I have any other options?"

"Mr. President," Rhodes answered, "when I leave this room I want to tell the people who are waiting outside that we never discussed any options."

"Oh, I do, too," the President said hastily. "I didn't mean that." He paused. "I'm going to make the decision," he said flatly.

All the points in the script had been covered. The President stood up from behind his desk. "Well, thank you very much," he said.

"Thank you," Rhodes replied, "you're a great friend."

The President didn't reply. He shook their hands, but he seemed locked in thought as they walked out.

Haig and Burch were waiting for the three leaders in Timmons' office. Goldwater summarized the session.

Haig wanted to be certain. "Did the President make any statement beyond what you've said?" he asked intently.

No.

No.

No.

There had been no slipups, no demands, no deals for resignation.

Goldwater said that they were going to meet with reporters but would not get into any details.

Haig assented.

As they walked out of Timmons' office, Goldwater asked Rhodes, "Is there any doubt in your mind what he's going to do?"

"No. Any doubt in yours?"

"No. It's sort of amazing: Here's the first time that this has ever happened, and who was sitting there with the President? Two guys from one of the smallest states."

The meeting had not taken long. It was 5:42 when they walked to the cameras. "Whatever decision he makes, it will be in the best interest of our country," Goldwater said. "There has been no decision made."

The reporters pressed.

Goldwater lied. "I have no way of knowing, and we have no way of making nose counts," he said. "I myself have not made up my mind. And I think I can speak for most of the Senators that they haven't made up their minds."

Scott backed him up.

"We have not discussed or taken any counts ourselves as far as I know."

WHILE THE congressional leaders were with the President, Haig had called Buzhardt, St. Clair and Garment into his office. He wanted them all there as witnesses in case any improper suggestions were made. Then he phoned Haldeman. St. Clair listened to the conversation on an extension.

"Bob, the matter has been seriously considered," Haig said. "It just can't be done. We've talked about it here thoroughly."

Haldeman asked for an opportunity to put his request and his thoughts in writing. It was already being worked on, he said.

"Sure, make the presentation," Haig said, glad for another opportunity to stall.

GOLDWATER DROVE back to the Senate with Scott and spent more than an hour on the phone with Arizona reporters. Content that resignation was set, he then escorted his daughter-in-law to a dinner at the Iranian Embassy.

Senator Scott returned to his office and gave his staff the President's schedule for the next two days, which Timmons had given him. Scott warned that it was not to leak to the press.

Thursday: 5:30 P.M. President meets with the Bipartisan congressional leadership.
6:30 P.M. President meets with his old congressional friends.
9:00 P.M. Television address to the nation announcing resignation.
Friday: Noon Resignation effective and Ford sworn in. Small ceremony in Oval Office.

Haig stayed in his office, trying to keep the story of the President's expected resignation under wraps. For one thing, the President could change his mind. For another, there must be no interregnum; the transition, when it came, had to be quick and smooth. But Nixon was still President and he had to be in a strong enough position to handle a crisis.

Haig had to sustain the appearance that the President was still active and in charge. There were lies that had to be told to staff, to friends, to the press. Bill Baroody had scheduled a meeting of twenty-three housing and construction leaders in the Cabinet Room for the following day. Haig didn't tell him the President couldn't make it. The tea-leaf readers all over the White House were looking for clues. The secretarial group in the counsels' office heard that Steve Bull was at the Exchange, a local bar, drinking one Scotch after the other. They took that as an indication that it was all over. Actually, Bull didn't know what was happening, either. He was at another bar, the Class Reunion, arguing with a friend that resignation was ill-advised. Haig was confident that the lid was on tight. Rose Mary Woods was circulating among staff members in the East Wing, saying that the President would not resign.

IT WAS common knowledge that more than one speech was in the works. At lunch that afternoon in the White House mess, Price had lied flatly to his chief assistant, Gergen, and to Ann Morgan: he was not working on a resignation speech. Gergen and Morgan were unconvinced.

After lunch Gergen went back to his office and began an "eyes only" memo to Price. "Overall, Ray," Gergen typed on his electric typewriter, "I'm suggesting a brief, dignified, generous, almost upbeat speech. It's absolutely essential that he be neither vindictive nor mawkish. This could be one of his shining hours, and the way he departs will have a tremendous impact on the country's future."

By the time Price read the memo, he already had a draft of a resignation speech. The President had to resign, but there was nothing upbeat about the moment to Price, and there never could be.

Then Ben Stein came around with his nonresignation speech in which the President was contrite, admitted his complicity, and talked about the country's great people and their capacity for forgiveness.

"Nixon would never give it," Price said. "He'll never say, 'I'm sorry.' "

THE PRESS was searching frantically for information. Terry Ivey had confirmed to UPI correspondent Helen Thomas that Ed and Tricia Cox had arrived from New York. The story went over the wire and Manolo Sanchez angrily called Ivey to complain, saying that nothing was to be given to the press.

Ivey argued back to one of Julie's best friends on the staff, Patricia Matson, that it was foolish not to answer routine press inquiries. Refusing to answer only bred more rumors and heightened the tension. "Remember who you work for," Matson shouted at Ivey. "These people's hearts are breaking. How can you want to help the press? You've got to figure out your priorities."

Ivey refused all press calls for the rest of the day.

The commotion and the incessant search for the slightest detail were getting on the nerves of the press-office staff. Finally Ziegler couldn't handle it any longer. He summoned Warren. "Goddammit, Jerry, cool them off."

There was no way.

The confusion was shared by the group that Buchen and Whitehead assembled at Whyte's house around 5 P.M. Ford wouldn't let anyone contact the Secret Service to obtain more office space for the transition effort. The Vice-President had told the *New York Times* that neither he nor his staff had made any plans.

Earlier that day, at a regular weekly prayer meeting with Rhodes and Laird, Ford had shunned any discussion of his possible succession. But he had quietly directed his top aide, Robert Hartmann, to draft a speech—"just in case."

Buchen and Whitehead took the precaution of going to Whyte's house in separate cars. Former Congressman Byrnes was already there. Griffin and Bryce Harlow arrived soon after. Whyte's son, Roger, was assigned to monitor the television set and answer the phone. Peggy Whyte cooked some steaks.

As the group worked on an eleven-item agenda prepared by Whitehead and Buchen, a call came for Griffin. The Senator stepped out of the living room and picked up the phone. It was Ed Cox.

Cox said he wasn't at all sure the President was going to resign. David and he had just met with Nixon and had received no assurances. There were hints, but nothing firm. The President had talked about being out of office and going back to California. It seemed to Cox that he was thinking about being impeached and convicted. That would take months. More alarming, Cox said, his mother-in-law had told him, "Dick is not talking about resigning!"

Griffin tried to calm Cox down. He again sounded distraught and mixed up. Cox told him once more that the family was deeply worried about the President's mental condition, the lack of sleep, the pressure.

As Griffin rejoined the group, he was confused. He told the others that apparently the President was not talking about resigning. Buchen was overwhelmed. They were moving on something that might not happen. In a week or a year, this meeting might be a great personal embarrassment to them all and most of all to the Vice-President. It could be made to look like a Beer Hall Putsch.

Griffin went over his conversation with Cox. The uncertainty was terrible. Could it be a hoax or a setup? several asked.

Buchen comforted himself that the Vice-President would not proceed unless he was positive. Ford always played on the side of caution. Anyway, it was more sensible to deal with the logistics of transition than with the possibility that Nixon would not resign. The President could only delay his departure. He could no longer avoid it.

"We can't sit here and speculate whether it will happen or not," Buchen finally said. "We have to assume it will and proceed." He had a copy of the agenda in his hand, and he read the first item: " 'Assumption of Office, the swearing in.' "

Griffin was concerned about the tone of the swearing in. It must be low-key, before a small audience. To hold the ceremony in the Oval Office might seem presumptuous. It was not Ford's office until he took the oath. There was disagreement on whether Nixon should be invited or whether Ford should mention Nixon in his remarks afterward. Byrnes said it was essential to avoid the kind of ceremony that took place when Ford was nominated to replace Agnew—the tasteless strolling strings and the pomp suggesting an occasion of national pride.

Griffin urged that Nixon's staff be cleared out of the White House as soon as possible. It was assumed that the staff and the Cabinet would resign. Everyone agreed that full disengagement from the Nixon White House was essential. But it would not happen overnight. Ford would have to meet with the White House staff at once and solicit their help in the transition.

"The number-one priority is to get rid of Ziegler," Buchen said. OMB Director Ash and his deputy, Malek, had to go immediately, others suggested. They were Nixon symbols. Buchen recognized that everyone was expressing his particular frustrations. Griffin wanted Congress to play more of a role.

"We can't decide that now," Buchen said. Working his way down the list, he focused on smaller problems. Should Ford attend church the first Sunday of his administration?

About nine o'clock, as they sat down to dinner, Scranton arrived. They went on until midnight. When the meeting broke up, Buchen thanked Whyte's wife. "You might lose your dining-room table to the Smithsonian someday," he told her.

THE PRESIDENT stayed awhile in the Oval Office after his meeting with Goldwater, Scott and Rhodes. Then he had his picture taken in the Rose Garden, and then went to the solarium.

The family had gathered there. Rose Mary Woods had come in a few minutes before his arrival. "Your father has decided to resign," she said, looking at the President's two daughters.

David had been telling Julie for days it would all be over soon. Now she heard it, stunned, relieved, and consumed with sadness and a sense of unfairness.

The President stepped into the room. "We're going back to California," he said, and indicated that there would be no discussion.

His daughters broke down. Mrs. Nixon did not cry.

There was a knock on the door, and photographer Ollie Atkins came in. Ziegler had instructed him that morning to photograph absolutely everything.

"Ollie," Mrs. Nixon said, "we're always glad to see you, but I don't think we need any pictures now."

"Oh, come on, Ollie," the President said, "take a few shots."

The President directed everyone to stand between a bookcase and the yellow-print drapes. He was wearing a coat and tie. His wife and daughters had on print dresses. Ed wore a tie, but his coat was off. David was tieless, his sleeves rolled up.

The daughters were weeping and Atkins had to take shot after shot to get a picture with everyone smiling. The family stood in a line, their arms about each other or holding hands. Atkins finally thought he had some shots with no one crying. But as he backed out the doorway, still snapping, Julie and the President fell weeping into each other's arms. Standing next to them, Tricia broke down, her face contorted, arms dangling.

The weight lifted only slightly during dinner. The President talked about life in California. He hoped the girls and their husbands would be able to visit often. Dinner lasted about forty-five minutes. Then the President left, saying he was going down to work on his speech.

At 7 P.M. he was in the Oval Office. He had a message from Haig. The general was waiting in his office with the lawyers when the President telephoned back.

Haldeman had been told that pardons could not be granted, Haig reported. The President seemed to indicate that he had overcome the biggest barrier, his family. They had been informed. They didn't like the decision, the President said, but he could handle them. Nixon asked Haig if he had lingering doubts.

"It is absolutely the right course," Haig replied.

THE PRESIDENT left the Oval Office at about eight o'clock and went upstairs to the Lincoln Sitting Room, in the southeast corner of the mansion. It was his favorite room, the smallest in the White House, only about sixteen by thirteen feet, designed and arranged for one person. All the furniture—Victorian chairs, a deep, low couch with high sleigh arms—was uncomfortable except for Nixon's overstuffed brown leather chair and ottoman in the corner. The room was his retreat. He had his music—a stereo and two five-foot shelves of records were within reach. Nineteenth-century prints were arranged over the gray marble fireplace. One was of President Lincoln's last reception. There was another of Lincoln and his son, another of Lincoln and his wife, and still another of Lincoln and his family.

Now Nixon summoned Kissinger.

Kissinger was expecting resignation, and had had his assistants, Eagleburger and Scowcroft, devise a fourteen-step plan to deal with the transition. It included a statement by Ford at the time of swearing in concerning the continuity of foreign policy, specific presidential messages to thirty-seven countries, and calls by Kissinger himself to fourteen key ambassadors.

For the first time in five and a half years, Kissinger would not be reviewing his plans with Nixon. He was, in fact, supremely relieved that Nixon was finally going. For months, the Secretary of State had been worrying that the world might blow up. But as he walked over and took the elevator to the second floor, he was also angry. Watergate had wrecked his foreign-affairs strategy. The domestic impact was tiny compared to the repercussions abroad. If someone had suggested ten years before to Harvard Professor Henry Kissinger that a superpower could be paralyzed in the nuclear age by a domestic scandal, he would have answered, "Never. Preposterous."

He walked into the alcove. There was the President in his chair, as he had seen him so often. Kissinger really didn't like the President. Nixon had made him the most admired man in the country, yet the Secretary couldn't bring himself to feel affection for his patron. They sat for a time and reminisced about events, travels, shared decisions. The President was drinking. He said he was resigning. It would be better for everyone. They talked quietly—history, the resignation decision, foreign affairs.

Then Nixon said that he wasn't sure he would be able to resign. Could he be the first President to quit office?

Kissinger responded by listing the President's contributions, especially in diplomacy.

"Will history treat me more kindly than my contemporaries?" Nixon asked, tears flooding to his eyes.

Certainly, definitely, Kissinger said. When this was all over, the President would be remembered for the peace he had achieved.

The President broke down and sobbed.

Kissinger didn't know what to do. He felt cast in a fatherly role. He talked on, he picked up on the themes he had heard so many times from the President. He remembered lines about enemies, the need to stand up to adversity, to face criticism forthrightly.

Between sobs, Nixon was plaintive. What had he done to the country and its people? He needed some explanation. How had it come to this? How had a simple burglary, a breaking and entering, done all this?

Kissinger kept talking, trying to turn the conversation back to all the good things, all the accomplishments. Nixon wouldn't hear of it. He was hysterical. "Henry," he said, "you are not a very orthodox Jew, and I am not an orthodox Quaker, but we need to pray."

Nixon got down on his knees. Kissinger felt he had no alternative but to kneel down, too. The President prayed out loud, asking for help, rest, peace and love. How could a President and a country be torn apart by such small things?

Kissinger thought he had finished. But the President did not rise. He was weeping. And then, still sobbing, Nixon leaned over and struck his fist on the carpet, crying, "What have I done? What has happened?"

Kissinger touched the President, and then held him, tried to console him, to bring rest and peace to the man who was curled on the carpet like a child. The President of the United States. Kissinger tried again to reassure him, reciting Nixon's accomplishments.

Finally the President struggled to his feet. He sat back down in his chair. The storm had passed. He had another drink.

Kissinger lingered. He talked on, building a case, pouring his academic talents into a lecture on why Richard Nixon would go down in history as one of the great peacemakers of all time. "You made the tough decisions," he said.

The two men had another drink. Their conversation drifted around to personalities and to the role Nixon might be able to play once he was out of office. He might be an adviser, or a special ambassador. Nixon wondered again if he would be exonerated by history. Kissinger was encouraging; he was willing to say anything. But he was certain that Nixon would never escape the verdict of Watergate.

At last Kissinger got up to leave. Nixon had never really asked as much of him as he had that night. Vietnam, Cambodia, Russia, China—they all seemed easier. Weak in the knees, his clothes damp from perspiration, Kissinger escaped. Though he was the President's only top adviser to survive Watergate, he had never really been consulted about resignation.

As he walked through the West Wing corridor to his office, Kissinger thought he had never felt as close to or as far from Richard Nixon. Never as close to or as far from anyone he had ever known.

Eagleburger and Scowcroft were waiting. It was almost eleven. Kissinger looked somber and drained. He did not shout orders, ask for messages, make phone calls or demand reports. He was clearly upset. To get control over his own tensions, Kissinger began talking about the encounter. The President was definitely resigning, he said.

"It was the most wrenching thing I have ever gone through in my life—hand holding," Kissinger added. The President was a broken man. What a traumatic experience it had been, what a profound shock to see a man at the end of his rope. He was convinced that historians would at least treat Nixon better than his contemporaries had, but it might take some time before that particular revisionist history would be written.

Scowcroft mentioned that he thought it significant that the President had turned to Kissinger for sustenance in his most awful moment. Not to Haig, not to any of the others.

"Henry," Eagleburger said, "at times I've thought you're not human. But I was wrong. I've never seen you so moved."

The phone rang. It was the President.

Eagleburger picked up an extension to listen. That was the custom—Kissinger rarely took a call alone. Eagleburger was shocked. The President was slurring his words. He was drunk. He was out of control.

"It was good of you to come up and talk, Henry," the President said. "I've made the decision, but you must stay. You must stay on for the good of the country."

Eagleburger could barely make out what the President was saying. He was almost incoherent. It was pathetic. Eagleburger felt ill and hung up.

The President had one last request: "Henry, please don't ever tell anyone that I cried and that I was not strong."

WHILE THE President was talking to Kissinger, Mrs. Nixon was making plans to leave. She called chief usher Rex Scouten and told him that the President had decided to resign and that the family would be going to California on Friday. That didn't leave much time. She asked Scouten to make sure the packing was completed by then. He was to do whatever was required, bring in extra help and make sure there were enough boxes and cartons.

David and Julie went back to their apartment at the Columbia Plaza. Julie called some old friends on the staff, including Lieutenant Colonel

Brennan. The White House switchboard phoned to say that John Ehrlichman was on the line. She told David.

"I'll get on the extension," he said. "Don't make any promises." He knew
about Haldeman's pardon request and he wanted Julie to stay clear of
such matters.

Ehrlichman bantered briefly. "You know," he finally said, "I was thinking one solution to the problems would be pardons. It would save a lot of
embarrassment to the President."

Julie put him off politely.

David was infuriated. It was blackmail. How appropriate, he thought,
that it came from the man Hunt had been blackmailing in the Watergate
cover-up. Ehrlichman sounded like Hunt. No wonder the President had gotten into so much trouble.

David took a call from Buchanan. Buchanan remained convinced that the
President had to resign, but some questions could be raised about the timing.
As David listened he was thinking that the pressure was unbearable, that
neither the President nor Julie could take any more. He hoped Buchanan
wasn't shifting ground.

"Let the death watch go away first," Buchanan advised. Wait a few days
so that the President could leave office more under his own control. Why
hurry him?

David said he'd exchange a little dignity for a little relief.

At midnight, the President was still working on his resignation speech.
He phoned Ziegler twice before 2 A.M. and again at 3:58.

Between 4:15 and 5:07 the President talked with Price four times to
offer suggestions and additions to the speech. His last call to Ziegler was at
5:14 in the morning.

Thursday, August 8

HAIG was at his office before eight, figuring out how to get the President through the day and to the resignation speech at nine that night. Today Haig would have to sound out Jaworski. Clearly it was the intention of the Watergate grand jury to prosecute Nixon, but ultimately the decision would be Jaworski's. Haig felt strongly that Nixon should not be prosecuted, that neither the country nor the President could bear it. Nixon was pathetic—the victim of a tragedy, Haig sometimes said. He knew Nixon was frightened about what lay in store for him, even though the President rarely mentioned it. Haig wanted badly to help, to bring home some guarantee against prosecution. It would be a fine thing to do—the right thing for Nixon and for the family.

There was also the matter of pardons. Haig had to make Jaworski aware that Haldeman and Ehrlichman had made demands, and damn fast, before he heard it from someone else. That could make them all look bad, it might look as if the White House was once again plotting. Haig was uneasy that the matter had even been discussed. Had he compromised himself already? The White House lawyers said no, but Haig thought he had always gotten better legal advice from Jaworski than from anyone else. Haig wanted to be as open and aboveboard with Jaworski as possible, to notify him of the resignation in advance and lay out the whole picture. He wanted to convey his feelings and get some kind of reading on how Prosecutor Jaworski intended to deal with Citizen Nixon.

Haig had already scheduled a tentative meeting with the prosecutor, but it couldn't take place at the White House or at Jaworski's office. If word got out that the two were meeting, there would be cries of plea-bargaining. Haig got back to Jaworski. "You can't come over here," he said. "Every single entrance is covered by the press." He suggested that they meet at his home, a stone house the general rented in the wooded Wesley Heights section of northwest Washington. The meeting was set for eleven-thirty.

THE PRESIDENT was up by eight-thirty, after three hours of sleep. He had his regular breakfast—cold cereal, orange juice and milk—and just after nine he walked from the residence through the Rose Garden to the Oval Office. He took no phone calls. Even a call from Billy Graham was taken by Woods.

Two minutes after the President arrived in the office, Haig presented himself. Nixon told him he wanted to see Vice-President Ford, and that he would spend the rest of the day working on his speech. After Haig left, the President spent twenty minutes alone, and then Ziegler came to get permission to call the television networks and reserve air time.

Ziegler returned to his office and called CBS. Then he took a file from his drawer and opened to the first page:

> Fifth Draft
> August 8, 1974
> Words 1,835
> This is the_____time I have spoken to you from this office, where so many decisions have been made that shaped the history of this nation.

Ziegler asked Johnson and Grier to find out the number of Oval Office speeches. Then he sent Warren out to tell the press that there would be a Nixon-Ford meeting. For two hours reporters had been milling around the small briefing room. At 10:55 Warren appeared in his pin-striped suit and blue button-down shirt. He moved through the crowd acknowledging acquaintances. "How are you?" he asked, smiling. "Haven't seen you in a while." He was so cordial that one reporter thought she was going to be offered a midmorning drink.

"We will be posting some routine information," Warren began. "Bill actions, and appointments and nominations, messages to the Congress. . . ."

The reporters weren't interested in that kind of news, and they stirred restlessly.

"The President will be meeting at eleven with Vice-President Ford. . . ."

That started a stampede down the narrow hallway that led to the press cubicles and telephones.

"Can we get pictures of Ford and Nixon, Jerry?" a photographer shouted. "No."

"There's nothing going on," screamed a reporter from the middle of the crunch. "God, these people are hysterical. It's like a goddam zoo."

In the First Lady's press office in the East Wing it was quiet. After three days of unanswered calls, reporters had given up.

St. CLAIR GATHERED some of his assistants together. He was still looking for a legal defense on the June 23 transcripts. Jack McCahill, for one, was astonished. Was St. Clair putting on a good show or was he crazy?

St. Clair had been informed that Nixon was going to resign, but he still wasn't absolutely convinced it would happen. Watching the President make decisions was like watching sausages being made, he had once observed. When you saw what went into them, you lost your appetite. He no longer believed anything he was told. He'd do his job, stick to the case, and hope to be safe at home in Boston soon.

MILTON PITTS, the President's barber, was at home at 10 A.M. when Steve Bull called. "Milt, the President wants to see you about ten-fifteen," Bull said.

Pitts drove to the White House and headed for a small office on the ground floor of the West Wing. He had been serving the President since 1970, when he had gotten a call from Alexander Butterfield. Butterfield and Pitts had met privately in a small back room in Georgetown, and Butterfield had asked Pitts to keep their conversation strictly confidential. He told him the FBI would run a full investigation on him.

A week later Pitts had cut the President's hair for the first time. The second time, Pitts made a suggestion: "I can improve your hair very much by shampooing first, then blending the hair with a razor and using a hot-air drier on it. That will give your hair a softer, more natural look and straighten it some." The President's steel-gray hair was a bit oily and curly and had a shiny look even though it was healthy and free of dandruff. The President told Pitts to go ahead. Within two weeks *Time* magazine had sent a reporter to find out why Nixon's hair looked so much better. The press office said that it was because the President had changed barbers. Pitts felt honored.

THE FINAL DAYS : 429

In the White House that Thursday morning, Pitts prepared the set of tools he used only on the President. Promptly at ten-fifteen, a Secret Service agent opened the door to the one-chair barbershop, and the President strolled in. The door was shut. Nixon and his barber were alone.

As the President approached the chair, he flashed a smile. "Hello, Mr. Pitts, how are you?"

Pitts replied that he was fine, and the President handed him his blue-gray suit jacket for the barber to hang up. He then settled in the chair.

"The same as usual," Nixon said. "I hope you're not too upset over all the news."

Pitts wasn't sure what the President was referring to, but he assumed it was to the tape.

"No, sir," he said.

"Well," the President said, "we've made some mistakes and we've done a lot of things right, too, and I'd like to thank you for your good service over the years."

Pitts thought that meant for sure that it was over. As Pitts finished, Nixon told him he was going on television that night. "But I'll see you again," he said. "I'll probably come over to your shop in the Carlton sometime and get a haircut from you. I'll call you for an appointment, just like anyone else. I won't just drop in on you."

"Mr. President," Pitts said, "it's been a pleasure working for you, sir. I still have great confidence in you and I think you've been a great President. If I can ever be of any service to you in the future, it will always be my pleasure."

"You've been very kind," the President said, rising and putting his arms out for his jacket, which Pitts was holding. Nixon buttoned the jacket and then held out his hand. "Goodbye," he said and then turned toward the door. He held the doorknob for a moment and turned to Pitts. "Say goodbye to Mrs. Pitts."

Pitts felt sad. The President had always remembered his wife, had sent her a letter after she had had a cancer operation, and had invited the Pittses to several White House receptions.

Pitts stood there for a few moments and then readied the shop for his next customer, Henry Kissinger.

THE PRESIDENT's haircut had taken twenty-two minutes. At 10:42, Nixon was back in the Oval Office to receive Price for a quick review of the speech before Ford arrived.

That morning, at a ceremony at Blair House, just across Pennsylvania Avenue from the White House, the Vice-President had presented Medals of Honor to the families of seven American servicemen killed in Vietnam. Ford had been applauded by the crowds on the street, and his presence had caused a traffic jam. When he returned to his office in the EOB, Hartmann told him the President wanted to see him.

It was just before eleven when the Vice-President walked across the private drive between the EOB and the White House. Haig greeted him in the hall, taking him aside.

"We still don't know which way he's going." Haig made a back-and-forth motion with his hand. "He has wavered."

Haig had already told Ford that he was going to be President. Now he was taking a step backward. Straddling both sides with the man who was likely to be his Commander in Chief might not make Haig a prophet, but it would demonstrate that he prepared carefully for any contingency.

When Bull escorted Ford into the Oval Office at 11:01, Nixon was seated at his desk. Except for his double pen set, the phone, a binder and several blank writing tablets, the top was clean, its surface gleaming. Ford took the chair to the right.

Atkins came in to record the scene. He clicked off several frames. The President, as usual, was looking down at the floor, hunched forward as he talked. Atkins interrupted. "Mr. President, this is such an important picture, I'm going to ask you to move a little closer and talk directly to the Vice-President."

Nixon straightened up. Atkins took his picture. Then they were alone.

Nixon talked slowly, demonstrating his control and calm.

"Jerry, you'll do a good job," the President said. He offered him advice, especially in the area of foreign affairs. He praised Kissinger to the Vice-President, and thanked Ford for his support. His tone was not apologetic. Both men knew that the only reason Ford was sitting across from the President now, listening to these words, was that Nixon had lifted him out of the comparative obscurity of the House.

Ford had always been a loyal party man, and his relationship with Nixon had never been more personal than that. Both men had been in politics for decades, and both were accustomed to the formality that smooths over ups and downs, political shifts, changes of fortune. Both were used to falling back, in moments of potential embarrassment, on rhetoric. There was no talk of past mistakes, no attempt to express honest emotions. Instead, they expressed high hopes for the future. They shared a conservative philosophy, were products of the Cold War and the politics of post–World War II

America—hard-working lawyers from small towns who went to Congress in the late 1940s.

Nixon explained the mechanics of the transition to Ford. It required merely that the President write a letter of resignation to the Secretary of State. When Kissinger received the letter, Nixon would cease to be President. Then Ford could take the oath of office.

As NIXON and Ford talked, Haig told Joulwan to take Pat McKee's car and pick up Jaworski at the Jefferson Hotel. A White House sedan called for Haig at the Seventeenth Street entrance of the EOB. Haig arrived home a few moments before Jaworski.

Pat Haig, the daughter of one Army general and the wife of another, brought the two men coffee in the living room. Jaworski declined; he never drank coffee. Haig placed a teaspoon of sugar in his cup and lit a cigarette.

"Alec, you have to understand that we're to have no understanding," Jaworski said. He wanted to close the door to a deal before Haig had a chance to open it.

A moment passed before Haig spoke. "Well, the President is going to announce his resignation tonight," he said—and waited.

Jaworski thought Haig seemed beat but was showing little emotion. "It's a tragedy," the prosecutor said, but he was relieved that it would soon be over.

Haig looked at him. "Leon," he said, "I'm very much worried about the President."

Jaworski was silent.

Haig alluded to the pressure on Nixon and how agonizing his decision to quit had been.

Jaworski expressed sympathy.

Also, Haig said, he had another item for Jaworski's immediate attention. Haldeman and Ehrlichman had requested pardons, and pardons would not be granted.

That was good, Jaworski indicated. He was not concerned about the general matter of pardons, as long as they were being turned down.

Again Haig tried to approach the question of Nixon's future. He mentioned Nixon's intense depression and suggested that, by resigning, the President was saving the country a great deal of anguish. Jaworski said nothing. If necessary, Haig said, the President would invoke his rights under the Fifth Amendment and refuse to testify at any trial or legal proceeding, on the grounds that it might incriminate him.

Jaworski changed the subject. "Do you think you'll stay on?" he asked.

"I think I will, at least for a while," Haig said.

The meeting ended with some small talk.

AT NOON, the signature machine in the correspondence section of the White House was shut down. There would be no more letters from 1600 Pennsylvania Avenue signed "Richard M. Nixon." The news spread rapidly through the White House.

Ken Clawson went down to Ziegler's office. He had heard that Ziegler was going to make an announcement and seemed dazed when told that the President was going to speak that night.

In the press room, the reporters began to mass around the podium. A briefing, this time by Ziegler, was rumored. The bright television lights were turned on and a stenographer appeared. It was 12:19.

"He's probably going to announce the new ambassador to Iceland," someone said. Those in the room broke into laughter, but it was cut off as Ziegler walked in and went to the microphone. He looked stricken.

Ziegler's secretaries fell into a hush and listened over the voice box piped back to their offices. Ziegler was sweating and his hands shook as he placed a sheaf of papers on the podium. His statement was being covered live by radio and television.

"I am aware of the intense interest of the American people and of you in this room concerning developments today and over the last few days. This has, of course, been a difficult time."

His voice cracked. He tried to clear his throat, and his voice cracked again. The muscles in his cheek twitched. "The President of the United States will meet various members of the bipartisan leadership of Congress here at the White House early this evening," he said, gaining his composure. "Tonight, at nine o'clock Eastern Daylight Time, the President of the United States will address the nation on radio and television from his Oval Office."

With that, Ziegler walked quickly out. His secretaries went back to work. Anne Grier was trying to finish Ziegler's thank-you notes from the Mideast and Russian trips. She went out to the press room to get a Pepsi and was stopped by CBS reporter Robert Pierpoint.

"What are the chances of seeing Ron?" he asked.

"Not very good."

"I have to ask this question," Pierpoint said in an apologetic tone. "Can you ask it for me? When Ron said 'the President of the United States,' did he mean President Ford or President Nixon?"

Ziegler had very deliberately said, "The President of the United States" and had not used a name.

Grier went back and saw Ziegler. He was now in his shirtsleeves. "Ron, Pierpoint's got this question . . ."

"President Nixon," he said, laughing and shaking his head.

ZIEGLER WAS in the process of selecting the members of the staff who would be going to San Clemente for the transition. He called Anne Grier to his office. "How are you?" he asked her. The question had taken on a special meaning. Staff members were asking each other how they were adjusting to the shock.

"Oh, fine," Grier responded a little uncertainly.

"The President is going to San Clemente tomorrow," Ziegler said. "Please don't say anything to anyone about this. I'm going out there with him, and Diane and Frank are going. Would you like to go?"

Ziegler was silent for a moment as she considered her reply.

"You don't *have* to go," he added, but his tone said he expected her to say yes.

"I wouldn't want to be anywhere else," she finally answered. "Of course I'll go."

"Fine," Ziegler said, "talk to Diane and work it out. It will be for between thirty and sixty days. We'll be working on transition things."

Grier turned to leave.

"Now, remember," Ziegler repeated, "don't say anything to anyone."

The packing in Ziegler's office began. A couple of foot lockers were brought in, and tennis balls, eyedrops, Marlboro cigarettes and a large brown jar of Titralac stomach medicine were thrown in with other things.

Grier and Johnson stood at a window, looking at the crowd of several hundred people outside the gates. Ziegler strolled by and asked them what they were doing.

"We're looking at the people," Grier said.

"What are they looking at?" Ziegler asked. He checked himself. "They're looking at us!"

ST. CLAIR CALLED John Wilson. "Have you a paper for me?" St. Clair asked delicately.

The last draft of Haldeman's suggestions on the pardons and two drafts of speeches were just going through the typewriter.

"Have we got two hours?"

"Yes," said St. Clair.

Two separate drafts—one of which included pardons for draft evaders—were rushed over to St. Clair.

AFTER HIS meeting with Ford, the President went to his EOB office and summoned Buzhardt. Buzhardt got there one minute after Ziegler had begun his announcement. The lawyer had not spoken with Nixon for more than a week, since they had disagreed about the June 23 tapes.

The President was in his armchair. He greeted Buzhardt shyly, explaining that he had not asked him to Camp David the previous weekend because he was concerned about Buzhardt's health. The weekend had been the toughest time of all, the President said, it would have been a terrible strain on him. Nixon didn't look at him.

Buzhardt understood. He knew Nixon had still been angry with him. The business about Buzhardt's health was one more cover story.

There seemed now to be no particular item on the agenda. Then the President inquired about his own future. Would he be prosecuted?

Buzhardt said he wasn't sure what would happen.

"If they want to put me in jail, let them," Nixon said. "The best writing done by politicians has been done from jail." He mentioned Gandhi.

Brave talk notwithstanding, the President seemed deeply worried. He wanted to sound Buzhardt out on the legal situation. Again he likened himself to Gandhi. If he went to jail, he would be a sort of political prisoner, he implied. Really, he had been persecuted.

Buzhardt agreed. If any other President had been investigated so thoroughly, he said, similar or even worse abuses would have been uncovered. If the Republicans had had a majority in the Congress, the investigations could have been stopped; the Senate Watergate Committee would never have been established and the House Judiciary Committee would never have begun impeachment hearings. The normal restraint of the press had been relaxed in Nixon's case, because the publishers and editors didn't like him.

Nixon concurred. It was terribly difficult not to take the issue down to the line. He deplored not fighting it all the way. He regretted leaving the world in so precarious a situation.

Buzhardt thought that Nixon had been pursued so relentlessly because he lacked the personality and charisma of an Eisenhower or a Kennedy, but he didn't say so. Nixon still didn't grasp the meaning of the June 23 tape; his reactions were reactions to his staff's conclusions. He had never figured it out for himself. Buzhardt felt pity and empathy. Probably Nixon had not held back the tapes with any criminal intention.

After fifteen minutes Ziegler came in, and immediately afterward Haig, who had just returned from his meeting with Jaworski. Jaworski was glad it was over, Haig said. The special prosecutor had expressed sympathy and understanding. There was no firm commitment that he would not prosecute. However, based on eight months of dealing with Jaworski, Haig had the distinct impression that Jaworski would not prosecute. He might be wrong. But certainly Jaworski wasn't out for the President's blood.

The President's face was expressionless as he listened to Haig's account. Jail wouldn't be that bad, he said again after Haig had left. That was not what worried him. He hated quitting. He had never quit. At Whittier High School he had made the football team by being the eleventh man to turn out for the squad. He wasn't very good, but he hadn't quit. In track, too. There was a foot race and he had been sure he couldn't finish, but he pushed himself, and though he hadn't won, he hadn't come in last either.

"All these people have come in here crying," Nixon said. "I ought to be the one crying. I don't want anyone crying." Praying was okay. "Last night, the Secretary of State and the President of the United States got down on their knees and prayed for the country," he said.

He was proud of his family. They wanted him to fight all the way. His attitude conveyed no sense that there had been wrongdoing. Well, that wasn't necessary, Buzhardt thought. Neither he nor Haig nor Ziegler had ever suggested that the President had acted improperly, not until they were in danger themselves. But Buzhardt did wonder who had come in crying. The only unusual visitor that day had been the Vice-President.

The President got back to business: Buzhardt was to call John Wilson right after the speech that evening and tell him that no pardons would be granted. Buzhardt left the office. The hour-long discussion had been the most personal discussion he'd had with the President in all the fifteen months he'd served in the White House.

ED COX, in charge of coordinating many of the arrangements for the trip to California, checked with Rex Scouten, who was packing on the second floor of the residence. There wasn't much time to separate state gifts, which belonged to the government, from the Nixons' personal belongings, and Scouten had to decide what should go directly to the San Clemente estate and what should be put in storage until the Nixon library was built. David and Julie would be staying behind to help him.

Steve Bull called Cox. Bull was handling preparations for the President's farewell to the staff, which would take place the next morning. Would television coverage be permitted? he asked. Would the family want to stand with the President on the elevated platform? "Can they handle it?"

Cox wasn't sure. But a short while later he told Bull that the whole family would like to be standing right behind the President during the farewell. It could be televised.

At about 2 P.M. David got a call from Haig, who had finally found time to see him. The day before, Buchanan had told him and Eddie what they needed to know, but David decided to walk down to see Haig anyhow.

Now David learned to what extent the President had misrepresented the family's position. It was the President who had acted as go-between, and he had given Haig false reports of a unified family position unalterably opposed to resignation. Nixon had used his family; David and Haig agreed on that.

"This is all politics, however," Haig said. "I'm proud of your father-in-law and you should be, too."

David thought Haig's remark was gratuitous, that the general was only trying to cheer him up. He was about to say that it was unnecessary, but he didn't. Haig had enough problems and, in any case, things were going smoothly. David gazed outside at the overcast sky. It had been raining on and off. Haig said that the President seemed to be holding up now, and that he would make it. Yes, David agreed, but it had been tough. In fact, David said, he had thought sometimes that the President might commit suicide. But then he had realized that his father-in-law had become more passive in despondency—catatonic, reposed and apathetic.

Haig said that pressure was part of the job. In spite of everyone's doubts, the President seemed to be coming through all right.

David was thinking that it wasn't over yet. He was exhausted and he wanted to get some sleep in case the night was another long one. He walked back to the residence and up to the third-floor bedroom, where he fell on the bed and slept.

THOSE WHITE House Staff members who had something to do stumbled through their tasks. Diana Gwin, who worked for staff secretary Jerry Jones and was the former keeper of Haldeman's files, was determined to push through some of the business that had been piling up over the last two weeks. Some of it had been kicking around longer. One item had to do with the funding of the Federal Property Council, which was supposed to decide what to do with government property when military bases closed down. She couldn't get any action. But she gathered up as many routine items of business and nominations as she could.

"These are for the President's signature," she said, walking into Bull's office with a stack of documents.

Bull looked up at her. He was tired. The last thing he cared about at this moment was the Federal Property Council or anything like it. He wasn't going to bother the President with anything nonessential.

"To hell with it," he said, dismissing her with a frustrated wave of his hand. "Let Ford do it."

SHORTLY AFTER two o'clock, Ford called Senate Minority Leader Scott. "As you know, Hugh, things have come to pass," Ford said. He explained that he had just been with the President. The Vice-President had tentatively arranged for the swearing in to take place at noon the next day. "We don't want any big show." It would be in the Oval Office. The ceremony would be small and solemn. Leaders from Congress, the family, a few special friends.

"You may remember, Jerry," Scott said, "that months ago I spoke to you about constant and close communication if this sort of thing happened."

"Our relationship has been excellent," Ford replied, "and I expect it to continue as it has been between friends. Accessibility and openness will be a hallmark of my Administration. No filtering of leadership views through others. No, sir!"

Buchen came in to discuss transition details. Ford was at his desk, and Hartmann was with him. They needed a new press secretary. Buchen recommended Jerald F. terHorst, the fifty-two-year-old Washington Bureau chief of the *Detroit News,* a reporter whom Ford had initially known in Grand Rapids, when he had first been elected to Congress. Ford approved the choice. Buchen called terHorst and offered him the job. "Jerry, can you give us an answer in half an hour?" Buchen asked terHorst.

TerHorst wanted to check with his wife and his newspaper. He called back soon and accepted.

Buchen told Ford that he was having a tough time convincing Chief Justice Burger to come back from Europe for the swearing in, because Burger just couldn't believe it was happening. Ford got Burger on the phone and said it was indeed happening and it would please him very much if Burger could come. A military plane was dispatched for the Chief Justice.

Ford was concerned about his first impression as President. Should he address Congress? No, Buchen said. Keep everything simple and short. But the guest list for the ceremony was swelling, and it was decided to move the swearing in to the East Room.

Ford mentioned his meeting with the President that morning. He was shocked by the way Nixon had looked. In the forty-eight hours since the Cabinet meeting, Ford said, the President's appearance had changed dramatically. He was a broken man.

After Buchen had left, Ford spent two hours with Kissinger reviewing the world situation.

Near Ford's house on Crown View Drive in Alexandria, Virginia, the city police, by request of the Secret Service, had barricaded the street and tied yellow plastic rope along the opposite sidewalk.

FOR MANY staffers there wasn't much to do besides wait. Ann Morgan went out to get some six-packs of beer for the speech writers' offices. Buchanan had a few assistants in for drinks in midafternoon. In the lawyers' wing, the drinking started at about the same time. Jack McCahill bought some Scotch. People were milling around in the corridors all afternoon. McCahill thought it was like the last day of college, or an Irish wake. There was emotion, a feeling of closeness. People were shaking hands and hugging each other. At times, they tried to act lighthearted. In the White House mess, staffers sat around eating tacos. It was Thursday, Mexican-lunch day.

Rabbi Korff sat heartbroken in the West Wing lobby, waiting to see Ziegler. He couldn't get an appointment with the President. "Is he really going to do this?" he asked as Bull passed through the lobby. "Is he really going to do this?"

"Yes," replied Bull. The trip to San Clemente was already planned.

Korff expressed surprise that the President would go immediately to California.

Ziegler wouldn't receive Korff, either, so Korff was to be taken to see Bruce Herschensohn in the EOB.

As he rose to leave, Korff turned to Bull. "There are many of us who will keep fighting," he said. "You haven't heard the last from us yet."

In the military office in the East Wing the liquor was flowing. There were bottles and buckets of ice on the desks. Lieutenant Colonel Brennan came in even though it was his day off. Everyone had a lot to drink.

Bull and DeCair went from office to office and party to party, announcing that the President's speech would be on the economy; the delay was deliberately designed to generate suspense, they suggested.

Tom Korologos demurred. "You know why we're going on TV?" he said. "We're vetoing a bill. We'll fool everybody."

During one of Timmons' earlier staff meetings that summer, there had been a discussion of leaks from the House Judiciary Committee. "We've got to put a stop to these leaks," Korologos had said. "Let's form a group called the Carpenters." When bad news dominated Timmons' meetings, Korologos would walk in energetically clapping his hands, saying, "We're out of the woods now. We've finally turned the corner." Thursday was no exception. After he had extended invitations to the Senators who would meet with the President that evening, he had popped his hands together enthusiastically and said, "We've really got Congress on the run now."

Manolo Sanchez was despondent. He too had been drinking. As he wandered over to the EOB, he met Wayne Valis in the corridor. "The President can't sleep at night so he sleeps in the afternoon," Sanchez told him. There were things the President hadn't known about Watergate. "The President is innocent." There were tears in his eyes. "Those fuckers crucified him."

AFTER HIS talk with Buzhardt, the President took a forty-minute nap and made a call to Price. He left his lunch—cold salad and cottage cheese—untouched. He spoke again to Price and Ziegler, and then Rose Mary Woods came in to visit for half an hour. Afterward the President had a quick visit with Dr. Tkach, and then he summoned Ziegler to the EOB office.

There were a number of business details to complete—some large and some small. Nixon picked up a two-by-three-foot photo of himself and wrote: "To Rabbi Korff—for whose friendship, support and wise counsel I shall always be grateful. Richard Nixon, August 8, 1974."

He divided the rest of the afternoon among Haig, Ziegler, Kissinger and Woods. At 4:18 another call from Haldeman was refused. The President vetoed an appropriations bill for the Department of Agriculture and the Environmental Protection Agency as inflationary. It was $540 million over his recommendation.

At 6:51 Nixon returned to the residence. The cameras on the lawn were turned on him, in violation of press-office regulations. In his quarters, the President took a shower, changed clothes, and instructed Haig that he wanted to be able to walk alone without encountering anyone, especially cameramen, when he went back to the EOB to talk to the congressional leaders.

Joulwan ordered the Executive Protective Service to make sure no one was on the grounds after seven o'clock. They overreacted. Staff members were told they couldn't leave their offices between 6:30 and 7:30 P.M. Reporters were locked, without explanation, in the press room. The drivers of the White House fleet, parked on West Executive Avenue, were told to get down on the floors of their cars.

When the President finally emerged from the residence at 7:25, he was alone and his head was bowed. The crowd outside the gates waved American flags and some among them sang "America." A few staffers went to the windows to watch Nixon, but their colleagues shouted at them to get back from the windows.

TerHorst, Ford's new press secretary, was among those trapped in the EOB and was late for a meeting with Ziegler. After a brief discussion, Ziegler called his entire staff to his office. Sitting at his desk, his office packed with people, Ziegler was at his most controlled and unemotional.

"I don't think I have to tell you all what the President is going to say tonight," he began. He gestured toward Warren. "Jerry will be the transition officer for the Administration. Anne, Diane and Frank are going to San Clemente. I just had a meeting with Jerry terHorst. He knows all of you, and that you're all professionals. None of you are to worry about your jobs. Someday, not right now, I will tell each of you what I think of each of you."

Most of them were shaken as they filed out of Ziegler's office to go back to answering the phones. Johnson broke down again, and Ziegler called her back into his office.

"Don't worry," he said, "you'll be taken care of. Pack up and do your job. Jerry will be here and will help you and oversee the transition. He'll get you an office in the EOB."

Ben Stein went to Price. "Ray, why'd you have me write this speech?" he asked. "It was to distract me so I wouldn't distract you, wasn't it?"

"Yes."

Price had planned to go to dinner at the Sans Souci restaurant with Garment, Buzhardt and William Safire for one last get-together, but he had to stand by for any last-minute changes the President might want to make in his resignation address.

Over dinner, the others talked politics. Whom would Ford select as his Vice-President? Garment guessed George Bush. Buzhardt was sure Ford would select someone from the Hill and definitely not a governor or former governor. Garment noted that the President was now meeting with the congressional leaders. A smart idea, he said. He'd probably break down and get it out of his system, so he wouldn't do it on national television.

BEFORE THEY went over to see the President in the EOB, the five congressional leaders—Senators Mansfield, Scott and Eastland, and Representatives Albert and Rhodes—had a drink with Timmons in his office. These men were the most powerful in a Congress which the President had alternately battled, scorned and ignored for five and a half years.

There was no scorn this evening.

"I've asked you to come here to hear my decision," the President began. "Tomorrow I will submit my letter of resignation to Henry Kissinger, to be effective at noon. At ten o'clock, Mrs. Nixon and I expect to leave. And the Vice-President will be sworn in at noon. There is one more speech I have to deliver.

"The whole Watergate thing has been hard on all of you for the last year and a half. I understand what you had to say. I feel no resentment. It's been hard on me too."

No one interrupted him.

"My own inclination is to fight," Nixon continued. "I have a wonderful family and a pretty good wife."

Several of the leaders exchanged glances at the reference to Mrs. Nixon.

"All of them want me to fight it through," he added with conviction. But he was obliged to look at the impact the fight would have. A Senate trial would take four to eight months and would tear the country apart. Even if it lasted only four months, that would be bad enough. Foreign affairs and inflation could not be dealt with as they must.

"It would not be fair to the country. I would be a part-time President. You would be a part-time Congress.

"You are all my good friends. Give the new President your full support. . . . God bless you."

He told them that he would probably never return to Washington again. He would miss his leadership breakfasts with Mansfield and Speaker Albert, the give-and-take with the loyal opposition. He thanked them for their support, particularly on foreign policy.

"Well, Mr. President," Albert said, "you've always been great to me."

"To me you'll always be a great President," said Senator Eastland, who knew he could never have voted to convict Nixon in a Senate trial.

Nixon stood up without replying. He said that he had lost weight and wondered about the fit of his dark-blue suit. "I guess there's nothing more to be said. I guess this is it." The pain showed on his face. "God bless you," he repeated.

The President took each man's hand. Rhodes was the last.

"Stay in touch," Rhodes said, and he put his other hand on Nixon's shoulder. He felt a slight shudder go through the President's body, and Nixon turned sharply away. Rhodes slipped quietly out of the room.

Within fifteen minutes, Nixon was ready to go to the Cabinet Room, where more than forty of his old friends from the Hill had gathered. He seemed in better spirits as he walked back, swinging his arms loosely at his sides. Bull walked beside him.

"Do you think I'm doing the right thing?" he asked Bull.

"No, sir."

Nixon halted. He appeared flustered. "Do you support me?" he asked.

"Yes, sir. But you should hang in there."

"Well, I've made up my mind," Nixon said, walking on rapidly.

Dean Burch stood waiting behind the President's chair in the Cabinet Room. All those invited were there except Senator Russell Long, who was in Louisiana.

At 8:05 the President came into the room, smiling. There was applause as everyone rose. A few were crying.

The President took his seat and looked around. There was silence. Nixon hesitated a long time before he began.

"Let me start with my family," he said finally, pulling himself up in his chair. Through all this trouble, the family had been constant in urging him to see the constitutional process through. " 'We don't care what the consequences are,' " he quoted them. "As you know, I'm not a quitter." He told them the story of the football team at Whittier High School, and the track race. It might sound far afield, he said, but it emphasized his will to fight. "I will take what's coming to me. My decision to resign is based on the premise that the presidency is bigger than any man. Yes, even bigger than your personal loyalty."

His judgment was that a House vote to impeach was inevitable. And arithmetic was one of his better subjects. He didn't have enough votes in the Senate. "Timmons is a pretty good vote counter, but I'm better, and I checked this one myself."

The President's thoughts drifted: foreign affairs, the energy crisis, inflation and the tough calls coming up. The Middle East might blow up any day. One of his greatest regrets was that a Middle East settlement had eluded him. He had wanted it to be one of the three great things for which the Administration would be remembered. He did not say what the other two were. "As I am winging my way back to California," he said, "I will still have the little black box aboard the plane up to the moment of transition."

Some in the room were not clear whether this was meant to reassure them or remind them of his power.

"Jerry Ford is a good man, but no matter how good a man, how clever, he needs your support, your affection and your prayers."

He paused, struggling to keep his composure. His head was bent down, and he gripped the table with both hands. After a few moments he looked up again. "This is my last meeting in this room. I will not be back here. But without you, believe me, boys—gentlemen—I couldn't have made these tough calls without you. I particularly appreciate your calls of comfort. Mrs. Stennis called Pat the other evening."

His voice softened and the words came haltingly. "I want to say most of all I appreciate your friendship more than ever, and I just hope—I just hope you won't feel I have let you down."

Now only a wheezing sound came from his throat. His eyes welled over. He pushed his chair to the side and back and tried to rise. His face was streaming with tears. The room was crowded and he was momentarily hemmed in.

Almost everyone was weeping.

The President finally managed to get to his feet and started forward. He stumbled slightly and seemed confused, as if he were not sure where the door was. A Secret Service agent took his arm gently and guided him through the door and into Bull's office. Nixon tried to choke back the tears.

"I've got a little bit of a cold, the sniffles or something," he told Bull, who was waiting there. It was 8:27, just half an hour before air time.

Some of the Congressmen had followed the President into Bull's office, so Secret Service agents took Nixon into the Oval Office and shut the door. He stood there for a few moments, composing himself. Then he crossed to a little sitting room on the other side of the Oval Office. The makeup woman started working on him. But he began weeping again, and she was asked to leave for several minutes while the President calmed himself.

When he had been lightly made up, the President went back to the Oval Office, where the technicians were waiting to test his voice and the lighting. As usual, much of the furniture had been moved out into the hall. He sat down behind his desk at 8:55. Bull, Ollie Atkins and Secret Service agent Dick Keiser were also in the room. One of the technicians took a light reading.

"Blondes, they say, photograph better than brunettes," Nixon said. His voice sounded as if he were about to break down again.

No one responded.

"That true or not?" he asked one of the television crew. "You are blond, aren't you?"

"No, sir."

"Redhead?" the President asked.

He was introduced to the CBS crew, which was handling the pool broadcast for all three networks.

"Have you got an extra camera in case the lights go out?" Nixon asked.

"This is the primary camera and this is the backup camera," a technician explained.

The President pointed to the backup camera. "That's an NBC camera, I presume?"

"No, they're both CBS cameras."

"Standard joke," the President said and laughed nervously. He cleared his throat loudly.

"Let me see, did you get these lights properly?" They were shining in his eyes. He squinted. "My eyes always have . . . you'll find they get past sixty . . ." his voice trailed off.

"That's enough," he directed the technician who was adjusting the lights. Atkins took a picture.

"My friend Ollie always wants to take a lot of pictures of me," Nixon said and laughed self-consciously. "I'm afraid he'll catch me picking my nose."

Very mild laughter.

"He wouldn't print that, would you, though, Oddie"—he corrected himself—"ah, Ollie?"

"No, sir."

"You can take a long shot," Nixon said, "but that's enough right now." His voice was still quavering. He looked down at the pages of his speech. "I guess I can see it."

The technicians asked him to test the microphone.

"Oh, you want a level, don't you? Yes, yes," he said. He picked up the pages. Abruptly, his tone shifted—solid, sincere, presidential. "Good evening, this is the thirty-seventh time I have spoken to you from this office where so many decisions have been made that shaped the history of our nation."

He set the pages down. "Need any more?" he asked.

Yes.

He went back to the presidential voice. "Each time I have done so to discuss with you . . ."

Enough.

"Okay," he said with relief. Then he snapped to Atkins, "Ollie, only the CBS crew now is to be in this room during this, only the crew."

Atkins wanted to stay and take pictures.

"No, no, there will be no picture. Didn't you take one just now? That's it." Nixon was almost shouting.

"Yes, sir."

Then he ordered Atkins to take another—to be used as the official after-broadcast picture. "Just take it right now. This is right after the broadcast. You got it. Come on. Okay."

Atkins took several more shots while the President obliged a technician's request to look into the TV camera.

"Okay . . . all right . . . fine . . . fine. I'm not going to make the other photographers mad by giving you too many. Now that's enough. Okay."

Atkins stopped clicking.

"Now," Nixon continued, "all Secret Service . . . are there any Secret Service in the room?"

"Yes," said Bull. "Just one agent."

"OUT!"

Agent Keiser didn't move.

"You don't have to stay, do you?"

"Yes, sir."

"You're required to?"

Keiser indicated that he was.

"I was just kidding you," Nixon said. "Didn't we usually have more than one?"

"Not when you speak in here."

"I see. Fine. But it's better for the crew—as few strangers around as possible. Sometimes . . . I have talked to some of my Hollywood friends, and it drives them nuts to have people around them."

"One and a half minutes to air," a technician said.

Nixon cleared his throat. "I'd better get in position."

Bull went through his standard procedure, reminding the President to place the sheets of paper to one side as he finished with them so that they would not hit the microphone and make a loud noise.

"Well, if I can . . . I mean I'll try to. You mean move them like this?" He shifted the pages one by one. "Would that help you?"

"Yes."

"Am I, am I straight in the back?" the President asked. "Would you mind checking my collar? Is it . . . it's not ruffled up?"

It wasn't. He cleared his throat and coughed.

Bull went out through the Cabinet Room, where Burch and Timmons were still sitting. They were sobbing.

The family had gathered in the third-floor solarium. They had thought of going down to wait outside the Oval Office, but they worried that the President would find out they were there. Their presence would surely make him nervous during the speech.

Nixon looked into the camera. "Good evening," he began. It was exactly forty-five seconds after 9 P.M.

A pause and a half-smile.

"This is the thirty-seventh time I have spoken to you from this office . . ."

And much of the world listened for sixteen minutes.

IN HIS office, Room 2462 of the Rayburn House Office Building, Peter Rodino sat in a leather chair in front of his television set. He held his chin with his right hand. There was a blank, solemn expression on his face.

"I no longer have a strong enough political base in Congress . . ."

Rodino shook his head in disgust, repeating sardonically, "I have lost my political base."

In the solarium, David Eisenhower watched, praying that Mr. Nixon would make it through, that emotion would not overtake him, that the ritual of reading page after page would carry him to the end, that he would not hear what he was saying and be overcome with self-pity.

"I would have preferred to carry through to the finish, whatever the personal agony it would have involved, and my family unanimously urged me to do so."

Not true, David thought to himself, but he would not protest. It was part of the Nixon personality, almost like a formula. His father-in-law couldn't do anything unless it was against a unanimous recommendation—of the Congress, of his advisers, of the military, of the experts, even of his family. Every act had to be in defiance.

At their law offices, Haldeman's attorneys sat watching.

"By taking this action, I hope that I will have hastened the start of healing . . ." The reference to "healing" was from the draft of Haldeman's recommendation for pardons.

"Here it comes," cried Wilson.

It didn't.

Steve Bull wolfed down several sandwiches in the East Room theater as he watched the speech. Just let him get through, he thought to himself.

"Therefore, I shall resign the presidency effective at noon tomorrow."

A hundred reporters were gathered around a large color television set in the press room. Someone tried a joke. There was no laughter.

"To have served in this office is to have felt a very personal kinship with each and every American. In leaving it, I do so with this prayer: May God's grace be with you in all the days ahead."

As THE lights in the Oval Office dimmed, Nixon's face seemed to sag. He thanked the television technicians and then greeted Kissinger, who had walked into the office. Kissinger told him the speech had great dignity. They left together, and Nixon put his arm around Kissinger's shoulder.

Bull went back to the Oval Office. He felt on the verge of tears as he watched the technicians packing their equipment. "Do you all have souvenirs?" he asked. No one answered. He reached into the drawer in the President's desk. "What's the difference?" he asked no one in particular. Then he gave out all the cufflinks, tie bars, pins for wives, pens, paperweights and golf balls. All bore the inscription "Richard M. Nixon, President of the United States."

After he had emptied the drawer, Bull walked over to the press office. No one there was answering any questions. Bull felt that was wrong, so he walked out of the White House and across Pennsylvania Avenue to Lafayette Park, and gave interviews to all three television networks.

Many of those in the White House could find no other way to release their emotions than by giving away to tears. Ben Stein was crying uncontrollably, and when Ray Price's secretary, Margaret Foote, saw him, she went over and hugged him. "Don't give them the satisfaction of seeing you cry," she told him. "When you walk out, hold your head up high."

The West Wing and the residence had been almost entirely cleared. Staff, doormen, ushers, kitchen help, even some of the Secret Service, had been sent home.

The President left Kissinger in the West Wing and walked alone back to the mansion. Normally, there would have been ten or fifteen people around him, and another four or five in a train. The family was waiting at the end of about thirty yards of red carpet that led into the main floor. They were silent as he walked toward them. Then they all embraced, and everyone congratulated him. They were proud, he had made it through.

They walked the rest of the way together and went up to the solarium. Now that the speech was safely delivered the tension had been cut somewhat. They talked about the future and expressed their relief. Everyone was exhausted. The President sat down. Vicki, the family poodle, who had been at the vet's, was brought up, and her arrival seemed to raise Nixon's spirits.

The President stayed with his family until after ten o'clock. He took no phone calls. Once again, Haldeman was unable to get through. Even a call from Haig, who had watched the speech in his office with his wife, was put off. Woods told him that the President would talk to him in a few minutes. Then Nixon went to the Lincoln Sitting Room and called Ziegler to find out what the reactions to the speech had been.

In Ziegler's office it was almost business as usual. The networks were being monitored for postspeech commentary and reaction. Grier and Gerrard reported that the reaction was gentle, with the exception of Roger Mudd of CBS, who had said that the President had evaded the issue and had not admitted his complicity in the cover-up.

Vice-President Ford watched the President's speech at his home in Alexandria. Afterward he stepped out into his front yard to speak to reporters. He wore the same light pin-striped suit and bold print tie that he had worn during the earlier part of the day. It was raining lightly as he walked to the cluster of microphones. "I think that this is one of the most difficult and very saddest periods and one of the very saddest incidents that I have ever witnessed," he said.

He announced that he wanted Kissinger to stay on as Secretary of State and that Kissinger had agreed. Saying he didn't have an enemy in Congress, Ford promised a new spirit of cooperation with the Hill. He declined to answer questions and walked back into his house.

Haig was trying to complete the final arrangements for the transition when he realized that a resignation letter had not been drafted. He gave the task to Joulwan, who called Gergen, telling him to keep it brief. Gergen was not sure what was required and called Buzhardt at home.

"Shit," Buzhardt said, "I can't believe it's not done." He had done the legal research and passed the information to Haig's office.

Gergen checked the Agnew letter of resignation and had three versions drafted for Nixon and sent back to Joulwan. Each was one sentence long.

Ziegler was in his office, thinking about how to say farewell to the White House press in a last briefing. He arrived at the briefing room at 11:02 P.M., forty-five minutes late. He looked pallid. His collar was too big, a result of his diet; his tightly knotted tie almost brought the collar ends together.

"I don't have a great deal of additional information at this time to provide you," he began. He outlined the President's day sketchily. He praised Nixon. The President's courage and strength had sustained the staff.

"But I just would like to take a minute myself to say goodbye." He was proud and honored to have served Nixon for five and a half years.

His manner reflected the tone of the President's speech—Ziegler was conciliatory, almost apologetic. "I have tried to be professional, as all of you are professionals, and I hope I have never underestimated the difficulty of your jobs or the energy and intelligence you bring to them." There had been many historic and many difficult times, he said. "I will remember the good ones and I hope you will, too. I think I take away from this job a deep sense of respect for the diversity and strength of our country's freedom of expression and for our free press."

He went back to his office. There was one more task. The President wanted one last news summary before he went to California. Ziegler relayed the request to Sawyer, who eventually got John Hoornstra about 2:30 A.M. at home. He came back and spent hours viewing videotapes of the network news and going over the early editions of the newspapers. He managed to come up with fifteen single-spaced pages of summary by morning.

AFTER HIS interlude with his family, Nixon had gone to the Lincoln Sitting Room to meet Haig. The two sat quietly in the dimly lit room. David Eisenhower dropped by to say good night, as was his custom. Nixon was talking about foreign affairs and Kissinger. He reminisced about their times together, the decisions, the trips. Since Kissinger had become Secretary of State the year before, Nixon said, he had felt a little distance between himself and his chief foreign-affairs adviser. He regretted that. In that very room the night before, Nixon told Haig, he had said his farewell to Kissinger. "It was the toughest goodbye. Very emotional. But Henry is still a comrade. You and he are the ones who were here from the beginning, the entire five and a half years."

At about 10:45 Mrs. Nixon and Tricia had gone down to the state floor to walk around the rooms for one final look. The weather was odd for August—cloudy, rainy and cool. The chapel at the Washington Cathedral was kept open late, in expectation that many people might wish to come and pray. Only two people arrived.

Just before midnight, the President started making his calls. At 11:59 to Les Arends. Then Stennis, Price and Eastland. At 12:20 A.M., the President asked the switchboard to get Len Garment at home. Garment had half expected a call and was thinking of sending the President a note when the phone rang in his bedroom.

"I know how you and Ray are feeling," Nixon began. He knew that Garment and Price felt let down. He had let them down. The President's tone indicated relief, not remorse. Garment was glad that Nixon seemed to be taking the experience philosophically. He complimented the President on his speech, trying to give such comfort as he could, to be philosophical himself. The tone of the speech had been just right, he said. Nixon was concerned about the future. What did Garment think would happen next? The speech was not likely to satisfy those who were demanding his head. Garment could not tell what might happen. It could go either way.

"There are worse things than jail," Nixon said almost offhandedly. "There is no telephone there. There is, instead, peace. A hard table to write on. The best political writing in this century has been done from jail." He mentioned Lenin and Gandhi.

Whatever happened, Garment said, the speech had helped. Garment reached for more comforting words.

Well, Nixon said, we accepted certain risks and committed ourselves to great endeavors, and in a political situation any mistakes—and we made them—are fatal.

Garment tried to get Nixon's mind off the subject. The bitterness of the last several years would surely pass, he said; people were tired of it. They talked about California.

"Give my love to Grace and the children," Nixon said. There was no whimpering. And for one of the few times Garment could recall, Nixon did not castigate anyone. Only himself. And maybe that was healthy.

The President made twelve more calls to his congressional supporters. At 1:34 A.M. the phone rang in the bedroom of Congressman Glenn Davis of Wisconsin. "It must be some drunk or a newspaperman," Davis mumbled to his wife. He rolled over and went back to sleep.

The President's last call, at 1:46 A.M., was to Representative Samuel L. Devine of Ohio. "I hope I haven't let you down," Nixon said.

Friday, August 9

THE President did not sleep well or long. By 7 A.M. he was standing in the doorway of the second-floor kitchen, barefoot, in blue pajamas. The White House chef, Henry Haller, was already at work, preparing breakfast.

"Chef," Nixon said, "you know, I've eaten all over the world, but yours is the best."

Haller thanked him. Working by Haller's side was his assistant, Johnnie Johnson.

Looking at Johnson, the President raised his arm slightly. "Tell Mr. Ford to hang in there and fight," he said.

Haller said that he thought the President's address the night before had been a fine speech.

"Forget it," Nixon said, dismissing the compliment with a wave of his hand as he padded out of the kitchen. He returned to his bedroom to dress and have his breakfast—a half grapefruit, milk and wheat germ.

Nixon called Haig to check and make sure everything was set before he went down to the Lincoln Sitting Room. Haig arrived there soon with one last piece of business—the one-sentence letter to Kissinger:

> DEAR MR. SECRETARY,
> I hereby resign the Office of President of the United States.

The President took his pen and scrawled "Richard Nixon" at the bottom.

VICE-PRESIDENT FORD was up early. Buchen and Byrnes arrived and had coffee at Ford's house. Then the three got into Ford's limousine for the ride into Washington. Byrnes handed his old friend a four-page memo. It specified the first decisions that the new President would have to make.

"We share your view that there should be no chief of staff, especially at the outset," Ford read. "However, there should be someone who could rapidly and efficiently organize the new staff, but who will not be perceived or be eager to be chief of staff."

The transition team recommended that former HEW Secretary Frank Carlucci be named. Deputy Defense Secretary William P. Clements, Jr., and NATO Ambassador Donald H. Rumsfeld were listed as alternates.

There was a blank space for Ford to write in his choice.

As the car moved over the bridge from Virginia, Ford wrote "Rumsfeld."

Under the section titled "Old White House Staff," Ford read:

> You must walk a delicate line between compassion and consideration for the former President's staff and the rapid assertion of your personal control over the executive branch. The old White House staff will submit their resignation, but they should be asked to stay on for a time to help with the transition. It will be clear that most of the political types will be expected to leave within a reasonable time. The one exception we recommend is Al Haig. Al has done yeoman service for his country. You should meet with him personally as soon as possible and prevail upon him to help you and your transition team, thus completing the holding-together he has done for so long. . . . However, he should not be expected, asked, or be given the option to become *your* chief of staff.

Ford wrote "OK" after this.

BY 9 A.M., the second-floor staff in the East Wing, including butlers, maids and kitchen staff, had been called together. They stood in the West Hall. The President and Mrs. Nixon appeared to say goodbye.

Nixon thanked them for their service, their smiles and encouragement during the five and one-half years. "I'm sorry to leave. You made it comfortable in hard times. In foreign countries maybe they had more help."

He explained that other world leaders had bigger houses, more rooms, finer houses with expensive decorations and art. "But this is the best house. This house has a great heart which comes from you who serve. There is only one White House. And I will never forget . . ." He walked down the line, shaking hands.

The family rode down in the elevator with the President so that they could walk into the East Room together. When they emerged, Bull was waiting to escort them. The President hesitated. The sound of the Marine band could be heard. It was a tune from *Oklahoma!*

"Are we ready?" the President asked Bull.

"We've got plenty of time," Bull said. "We'll wait all day and collect ourselves if necessary."

The women had been crying. Julie and Tricia's eyes were still red. Nixon was composed.

The East Room was overflowing. Bull began to brief the President on the location of the three television cameras.

"Television?" Mrs. Nixon asked with a start. "Who authorized television?" She looked around in wonderment. The band had shifted to another show tune.

"I did," the President said sharply. There was no need to wait, he said. "No, we'll go out there and do it."

He marched forward. The others followed.

Lieutenant Colonel Brennan stepped to the microphone. He wore his dress uniform and medals.

"Ladies and gentlemen," Brennan said, "the President of the United States of America." He almost shouted the last two words.

The band struck up "Hail to the Chief." The Cabinet and the staff were packed in. They rose and broke into applause.

Mrs. Nixon followed her husband. She wore a white dress and pearl earrings. It was the first time she had appeared in public during the Nixon presidency without her hair done. Also for the first time, she wore heavy pancake makeup. It took out some of the redness, but her face, this morning, seemed to convey her whole life.

The family placed themselves on the small platform behind the President. Small pieces of tape designated where each was to stand. Mrs. Nixon was on the President's left, slightly closer to him than Julie, who was on his right. David and Ed stood by their wives. Ed was carrying a book. The applause did not stop for four minutes.

Nixon stepped up to the podium and leaned down to the three microphones set together. Then he lifted his head. "Members of the Cabinet, members of the White House staff, all of our friends here.

"I think the record should show that this is one of those spontaneous things that we always arrange whenever the President comes to speak, and it will be so reported in the press, and we don't mind because they have to call it as they see it."

He sucked in his breath and gave a three-quarter smile.

"But on our part, believe me, it is spontaneous."

Speaking without notes, the President repeated his comments to the personal staff upstairs about the grandeur and special spirit of the White House. As the emotion seemed to overcome him, his voice grew more defiant. He pushed hard on the podium. His shoulders rose and his head sank slightly.

"We can be proud of it—five and a half years."

He started poking his finger toward those in the first row. Herb Stein was there, sobbing.

"No man or no woman came into this Administration and left it with more of this world's goods than when he came in. No man or no woman ever profited at the public expense or the public till." His head wagged from side to side. "That tells something about you.

"Mistakes, yes. But for personal gain, never. You did what you believed in. Sometimes right, sometimes wrong. And I only wish that I *were* a wealthy man—at the present time I have got to find a way to pay my taxes."

There was laughter. Nixon furrowed his brow. His cheeks seemed puffy.

"And if I were, I would like to recompense you for the sacrifices that all of you have made to serve in government."

Manolo Sanchez was weeping.

Nixon made three more references to money. "I remember my old man," he said without transition. "You know what he was? He was a streetcar motorman first, and then he was a farmer, and then he had a lemon ranch. It was the poorest lemon ranch in California, I can assure you. He sold it before they found oil on it."

Mild laughter.

"And then he was a grocer . . ."

Nixon turned, and his eyes had a vacant stare. "Nobody will ever write a book, probably, about my mother," he said with his head a quarter of the way down. "Well, I guess all of you would say this about your mother."

He shook his head. Perspiration streamed down his face and tears came to his eyes. "My mother was a saint. And I think of her, two boys dying of tuberculosis, nursing four others in order that she could take care of my older brother for three years in Arizona, and seeing each of them die, and when they died, it was like one of her own. Yes, she will have no books written about her. But she was a saint."

The President was shaking.

Garment thought, Oh, my God, he's beginning to break down. A binge of free association. Money, father, mother, brothers, death. The man is unraveling right before us. He will be the first person to go over the edge on live television.

David Eisenhower felt his legs stiffen. The morning had been full of excitement, almost gay. Everyone had been busy, and laughing as they had coffee. There had been a feeling that the family, all of them, even the President, had come to their good senses—that throwing off the office was right and realistic, and would free them all from the burden and tensions. Now the President was pressing his luck. It was almost wild. David feared his father-in-law would crack right there in front of him.

"Now, however," Nixon said, pulling himself back to the moment, "we look to the future. I had a little quote in the speech last night from T. R. As you know, I kind of like to read books. I am not educated, but I do read books."

There was laughter, the sound of relief, David felt. Move, get this over with, he urged silently.

Ed Cox handed him the book. Nixon put on his eyeglasses, which he had never worn in public before. He opened the book and read from Roosevelt's diary about the death of his first wife: "And when my heart's dearest died, the light went from my life forever."

He closed the book. The room was full of the sound of weeping, of muffled sobbing. Some people held handkerchiefs to their faces, others clutched their arms, a few held hands. Many were stunned and immobile.

"That was T. R. in his twenties," Nixon said. "He thought the light had gone from his life forever—but he went on. And he not only became President, but as ex-President he served his country always in the arena, tempestuous, strong, sometimes wrong, sometimes right, but he was a man."

He talked about other, similar disappointments—failure to pass the bar exam, the death of someone close, the loss of an election. "We think, as T. R. said, that the light had left his life forever. Not true. It is only a beginning always."

He had one additional counsel. "Always remember, others may hate you—but those who hate you don't win unless you hate them, and then you destroy yourself.

"And so, we leave with high hopes, in good spirits and with deep humility, and with very much gratefulness in our hearts. . . ."

And he was gone.

Bruce Herschensohn, one of the last who opposed resignation, turned and said to no one in particular, "That's probably the real Nixon. It's a shame he couldn't have been like that more often."

That was the Nixon Buzhardt had heard on the Dictabelts. He looked around the roomful of people—sad, torn, in tears. They had lost their place in the sun because of what one man had done. And the bitterness would probably take many forms, he thought.

Nixon and his family moved downstairs to the Diplomatic Reception Room. The women were weeping.

Ford and his wife were waiting.

"Good luck, Mr. President," Nixon said to Ford, staring him down. They shook hands.

Nixon walked down to the South Portico.

Mrs. Nixon did not say anything. Her eyes closed momentarily. She grasped the hands of several of her close staff members.

Nixon, Mrs. Nixon, Ed and Tricia then walked out to the waiting helicopter. Nixon was the last to board. He turned, smiled, and gave the thumbs-up sign to his daughter Julie, who stood back with her arm around David. She returned the thumbs-up sign and forced a smile. As the helicopter rose, Julie put her head on David's shoulder and closed her eyes.

GERALD FORD lingered for a minute, and then turned. He grasped his wife's arm with both his hands and the two walked back to the White House.

CHRONOLOGY

NOVEMBER 5, 1968—Richard Nixon elected President with 43.4 percent of the popular vote.

JANUARY 20, 1969—Nixon inaugurated as 37th President.

MAY 12, 1969—The first of 17 "national security" wiretaps on White House aides and newsmen is installed, following newspaper disclosure of the secret bombing of Cambodia.

JULY 23, 1970—The President approves the Huston plan for expansion of domestic intelligence-gathering activities. It is apparently rescinded five days later.

JUNE 13, 1971—The *New York Times* begins publishing the Pentagon Papers.

SEPTEMBER 3–4, 1971—White House aides E. Howard Hunt, Jr., and G. Gordon Liddy supervise burglary of the office of Daniel Ellsberg's psychiatrist.

JUNE 17, 1972—Five men are arrested in the Democrats' headquarters at the Watergate.

JUNE 20, 1972—In a phone call, the President and his campaign manager, John N. Mitchell, discuss the arrests; according to the White House, this conversation was not recorded on the President's automatic taping system. Also on this day, the President and H. R. Haldeman meet to discuss the arrests. The tape of this conversation was obliterated by an 18½-minute gap.

JUNE 23, 1972—The President and Haldeman formulate a plan to have the CIA impede the FBI's investigation into the Watergate break-in.

SEPTEMBER 15, 1972—Hunt, Liddy and the five Watergate burglars are indicted on federal charges. The President meets with John Dean and congratulates him on his handling of the problem to date.

NOVEMBER 7, 1972—President Nixon and Vice-President Agnew are re-elected, winning 60.8 percent of the popular vote and 97 percent of the electoral vote.

JANUARY 8–30, 1973—Trial of the seven men indicted for the Watergate burglary. Guilty pleas entered by all except Liddy and James W. Mc-Cord, both of whom are convicted by the jury.

FEBRUARY 7, 1973—The Senate votes, 70–0, to establish a select committee to investigate Watergate.

FEBRUARY 27, 1973—Dean's first meeting with the President since September 15, 1972—the first of a series of meetings in which the two discuss the cover-up.

MARCH 21, 1973—The crucial meeting between Dean and the President. Discussion focuses on ways to insure the continued silence of the burglars and those involved in the cover-up. "Hush money" and offers of executive clemency discussed. Later that day, Howard Hunt's lawyer receives $75,000.

MARCH 23, 1973—Judge John J. Sirica reads a letter from McCord charging that he and the other burglars were under "political pressure" to plead guilty and remain silent, that perjury was committed at the trial, and that the break-in was approved by higher-ups.

APRIL 15, 1973—At an evening meeting, according to Dean, the President asked "leading questions, which made me think that the conversation was being taped." It was in this conversation that Dean told the President that he had been meeting with federal prosecutors. According to the White House, the recorder in the President's EOB office ran out of tape and thus there were no recordings made on this day. The President also said that he could not locate a Dictabelt containing his recollections of this day.

APRIL 30, 1973—The President announces the resignations of Haldeman, John D. Ehrlichman, and Attorney General Richard Kleindienst, and Dean's dismissal. Leonard Garment is named to succeed Dean as White House counsel and Elliot Richardson is appointed as Kleindienst's successor.

MAY 4, 1973—The White House announces the appointment of Gen. Alexander M. Haig, Jr., as interim chief of staff.

MAY 4, 1973—Dean discloses that, before leaving the White House, he removed certain documents and placed them in a safe-deposit box. He turns the key to the box over to Judge Sirica.

MAY 10, 1973—The White House announces the appointment of J. Fred Buzhardt as special counsel to the President for Watergate.

MAY 17, 1973—The Senate Watergate Committee begins its nationally televised hearings.

MAY 18, 1973—Archibald Cox is named Special Prosecutor.

MAY 22, 1973—In a 4,000-word statement, the President again denies knowledge of the Watergate burglary or cover-up. He acknowledges ordering an initial restriction on the Watergate investigation, citing reasons of national security. He also acknowledges approval of the Huston plan and of the wiretapping of reporters and Administration aides— also on grounds of national security.

JUNE 3, 1973—The *New York Times* and the *Washington Post* run stories indicating that Dean's testimony to the Senate Watergate Committee will accuse the President of participation in the cover-up. That evening the President begins listening to his tapes.

JUNE 4, 1973—The President reviews more tapes. In discussions with Haig and Ronald Ziegler, he explains how information from the tapes will be used to undercut Dean's testimony.

JUNE 25–29, 1973—Dean testifies before the Watergate Committee and accuses the President.

JULY 13, 1973—In an interview with the staff of the Senate Committee, Alexander Butterfield reveals the existence of the White House taping system.

JULY 16, 1973—Butterfield testifies publicly about the taping system. Nixon tells his lawyers they may not listen to any of his tapes.

JULY 18, 1973—The President's taping system is disconnected.

JULY 23, 1973—Cox subpoenas the recordings of nine presidential conversations and meetings.

JULY 25, 1973—The President, citing executive privilege, refuses to turn over the subpoenaed tapes.

AUGUST 29, 1973—Judge Sirica rules that the President must turn over the subpoenaed tapes. The White House announces it will appeal.

SEPTEMBER 29, 1973—Rose Mary Woods begins transcribing some of the President's tapes.

OCTOBER 10, 1973—Vice-President Agnew resigns.

OCTOBER 12, 1973—The U.S. Court of Appeals upholds Judge Sirica's order that the tapes must be surrendered.

OCTOBER 12, 1973—The President nominates Representative Gerald L. Ford as Vice-President.

OCTOBER 20, 1973—The Saturday Night Massacre: Cox fired; Richardson and Deputy Attorney General William Ruckelshaus resign.

OCTOBER 23, 1973—On this and the following day, 44 Watergate-related bills are introduced in the Congress, including 22 that call for an impeachment investigation.

OCTOBER 23, 1973—Charles Alan Wright announces in Sirica's courtroom that the subpoenaed tapes will be turned over.

NOVEMBER 1, 1973—Leon Jaworski is named Special Prosecutor, succeeding Cox.

NOVEMBER 3, 1973—White House lawyers Buzhardt and Garment fly to Key Biscayne to recommend that the President resign.

NOVEMBER 9 and 12, 1973—Buzhardt testifies in Judge Sirica's courtroom about the missing tapes.

NOVEMBER 21, 1973—White House attorneys disclose the 18½-minute gap to Judge Sirica, who makes the matter public the same day.

DECEMBER 20, 1973—John Doar is appointed as chief counsel to the House Judiciary Committee.

JANUARY 4, 1974—The White House announces the appointment of James St. Clair as chief Nixon counsel for the Watergate defense.

MARCH 1, 1974—The grand jury indicts Haldeman, Ehrlichman, Mitchell, Robert Mardian, Charles W. Colson, Gordon Strachan and Kenneth W. Parkinson in the cover-up. Richard Nixon is named an unindicted co-conspirator by the grand jury, although this information is held secret.

APRIL 11, 1974—The Judiciary Committee subpoenas 42 tapes.

APRIL 18, 1974—After weeks of unsuccessful negotiations, Jaworski subpoenas 64 additional taped presidential conversations.

APRIL 28, 1974—Mitchell and Maurice Stans are acquitted in the Vesco conspiracy case.

APRIL 29, 1974—Appearing on national television, the President announces he will supply the Judiciary Committee with edited transcripts of the subpoenaed conversations and make the transcripts public.

APRIL 30, 1974—The transcripts—1,254 pages of them—are released. St. Clair says the President will refuse to surrender tapes and documents sought by the Special Prosecutor.

MAY 5, 1974—Jaworski offers not to reveal Nixon's status as an unindicted co-conspirator, in exchange for a reduced number of tapes.

MAY 5–6, 1974—The President begins listening to tapes again, including conversations of June 23, 1972, between himself and Haldeman. He later rejects Jaworski's offer.

MAY 20, 1974—Sirica refuses a White House motion to quash the Special Prosecutor's subpoena.

MAY 24, 1974—Jaworski appeals directly to the Supreme Court for a ruling on his subpoena for 64 recorded presidential conversations.

JUNE 10–19, 1974—The President visits the Middle East.

JUNE 25–JULY 3, 1974—The President is in Russia for a summit meeting.

JULY 24, 1974—The Supreme Court rules 8–0 that the President must turn over the 64 tapes sought by Jaworski.

JULY 24, 1974—Nixon instructs Buzhardt to listen to the tape of June 23, 1972.

JULY 27, 1974—The House Judiciary Committee passes first article of impeachment, 27–11, charging the President with obstruction of justice in attempting to cover up Watergate.

JULY 29, 1974—Second article of impeachment passes.

JULY 30, 1974—Third and final article of impeachment passes.

AUGUST 5, 1974—The White House releases transcripts of the three conversations of June 23, 1972.

AUGUST 8, 1974—In a televised address, the President announces his resignation.

AUGUST 9, 1974—President Nixon resigns. Gerald L. Ford becomes President.

INDEX

463